Business
Plans
Handbook

Business Plans

A COMPILATION OF BUSINESS PLANS DEVELOPED BY INDIVIDUALS THROUGHOUT NORTH AMERICA

Handbook

VOLUME

21

**Lynn M. Pearce,
Project Editor**

GALE
CENGAGE Learning

Detroit • New York • San Francisco • New Haven, Conn • Waterville, Maine • London

GALE
CENGAGE Learning™

Business Plans Handbook, Volume 21

Project Editor: Lynn M. Pearce

Editor: Paul Schummer

Product Manager: Jenai Drouillard

Product Design: Jennifer Wahi

Composition and Electronic Prepress: Evi Seoud

Manufacturing: Rita Wimberley

For product information and technology assistance, contact us at
Gale Customer Support, 1-800-877-4253.
For permission to use material from this text or product,
submit all requests online at **www.cengage.com/permissions.**
Further permissions questions can be emailed to
permissionrequest@cengage.com

Gale, a part of Cengage Learning
27500 Drake Rd.
Farmington Hills, MI 48331-3535

ISBN-13: 978-1-4144-6833-4
ISBN-10: 1-4144-6833-4
1084-4473

.b1887798
.o 1043389
60114391

Printed in Mexico
1 2 3 4 5 6 7 13 12 11

Contents

Highlights vii
Introduction ix

BUSINESS PLANS

AV Equipment Rental Business
Galaxy Equipment Works Inc. 1

Business Consulting Firm
Blake & Associates 9

Day Spa
Temple Creek Day Spa. 19

DJ Service
Mid-Mo Music 29

Food Truck
Eddie's Edibles Mobile Food 35

Go Kart Track
Supersonic Racing. 51

Gold Mining
Davis Gold Mining 67

Junk Removal Business
Harry's Haul-Away Service Inc. 83

Media Duplication & Transferring Business
DupliPro Inc. 89

Mobile App Development Business
AppStax LLC 97

Music Lessons Business
MelodyWorx Inc. 103

Plant Nursery
Village Garden Center 109

Printing Business
Big Picture Press Inc. 125

Personal Organizing Consultant
All In Place Inc.. 133

Professional Organizing Consultant
Marilyn Ruby Inc. 139

Sharpening Service
The Razor's Edge LLC 145

Soap Making Business
Felson's Homemade Soaps Inc.. 153

Specialty Bakery
Kate's Cupcakery 161

CONTENTS

Transcription Business
Speedy Transcription Services LLC 167
Used Records & Collectibles Business
Rudy's Record Shop 173
Waste Management
Waste Removal Serivces, Inc. 179

APPENDIXES

Appendix A
Business Plan Template 195
Fictional Plan 1 - Food Distributor 199
Fictional Plan 2 - Hardware Store 203
Appendix B
Associations... 207
Consultants 209
SBA Regional Offices.. 224
Small Business Development Centers 225
Service Corps of Retired Executives Offices 229
Venture Capital & Financing Companies 254
Appendix C
Glossary of Small Business Terms.................................. 285
Appendix D
Cumulative Index.. 309

Highlights

Business Plans Handbook, Volume 21 (*BPH-21*) is a collection of business plans compiled by entrepreneurs seeking funding for small businesses throughout North America. For those looking for examples of how to approach, structure, and compose their own business plans, *BPH-21* presents 21 sample plans, including plans for the following businesses:

- AV Equipment Rental Business
- Business Consulting Firm
- Day Spa
- DJ Service
- Food Truck
- Go Kart Track
- Gold Mining
- Junk Removal Business
- Media Duplication & Transferring Business
- Mobile App Development Business
- Music Lessons Business
- Plant Nursery
- Printing Business
- Personal Organizing Consultant
- Professional Organizing Consultant
- Sharpening Service
- Soap Making Business
- Specialty Bakery
- Transcription Business
- Used Records & Collectibles Business
- Waste Management

FEATURES AND BENEFITS

BPH-21 offers many features not provided by other business planning references including:

- Twenty-one business plans, each of which represent an attempt at clarifying (for themselves and others) the reasons that the business should exist or expand and why a lender should fund the enterprise.
- Two fictional plans that are used by business counselors at a prominent small business development organization as examples for their clients. (You will find these in the Business Plan Template Appendix.)

- A directory section that includes: listings for venture capital and finance companies, which specialize in funding start-up and second-stage small business ventures, and a comprehensive listing of Service Corps of Retired Executives (SCORE) offices. In addition, the Appendix also contains updated listings of all Small Business Development Centers (SBDCs); associations of interest to entrepreneurs; Small Business Administration (SBA) Regional Offices; and consultants specializing in small business planning and advice. It is strongly advised that you consult supporting organizations while planning your business, as they can provide a wealth of useful information.
- A Small Business Term Glossary to help you decipher the sometimes confusing terminology used by lenders and others in the financial and small business communities.
- A cumulative index, outlining each plan profiled in the complete *Business Plans Handbook* series.
- A Business Plan Template which serves as a model to help you construct your own business plan. This generic outline lists all the essential elements of a complete business plan and their components, including the Summary, Business History and Industry Outlook, Market Examination, Competition, Marketing, Administration and Management, Financial Information, and other key sections. Use this guide as a starting point for compiling your plan.
- Extensive financial documentation required to solicit funding from small business lenders. You will find examples of: Cash Flows, Balance Sheets, Income Projections, and other financial information included with the textual portions of the plan.

Introduction

Perhaps the most important aspect of business planning is simply doing it. More and more business owners are beginning to compile business plans even if they don't need a bank loan. Others discover the value of planning when they must provide a business plan for the bank. The sheer act of putting thoughts on paper seems to clarify priorities and provide focus. Sometimes business owners completely change strategies when compiling their plan, deciding on a different product mix or advertising scheme after finding that their assumptions were incorrect. This kind of healthy thinking and re-thinking via business planning is becoming the norm. The editors of *Business Plans Handbook, Volume 21* (*BPH-21*) sincerely hope that this latest addition to the series is a helpful tool in the successful completion of your business plan, no matter what the reason for creating it.

This twenty-first volume, like each volume in the series, offers business plans used and created by real people. *BPH-21* provides 21 business plans. The business and personal names and addresses and general locations have been changed to protect the privacy of the plan authors.

NEW BUSINESS OPPORTUNITIES

As in other volumes in the series, *BPH-21* finds entrepreneurs engaged in a wide variety of creative endeavors. Examples include a proposal for an AV Equipment Rental Business, a DJ Service, and a Gold Mine. In addition, several other plans are provided, including a Day Spa, a Mobile App Development Business, and Organizing Consultants, among others.

Comprehensive financial documentation has become increasingly important as today's entrepreneurs compete for the finite resources of business lenders. Our plans illustrate the financial data generally required of loan applicants, including Income Statements, Financial Projections, Cash Flows, and Balance Sheets.

ENHANCED APPENDIXES

In an effort to provide the most relevant and valuable information for our readers, we have updated the coverage of small business resources. For instance, you will find: a directory section, which includes listings of all of the Service Corps of Retired Executives (SCORE) offices; an informative glossary, which includes small business terms; and a cumulative index, outlining each plan profiled in the complete *Business Plans Handbook* series. In addition we have updated the list of Small Business Development Centers (SBDCs); Small Business Administration Regional Offices; venture capital and finance companies, which specialize in funding start-up and second-stage small business enterprises; associations of interest to entrepreneurs; and consultants, specializing in small business advice and planning. For your reference, we have also reprinted the business plan template, which provides a comprehensive overview of the essential components of a business plan and two fictional plans used by small business counselors.

SERIES INFORMATION

If you already have the first twenty volumes of *BPH*, with this twenty-first volume, you will now have a collection of over 434 business plans (not including the updated plans); contact information for hundreds of organizations and agencies offering business expertise; a helpful business plan template; more than 1,500 citations to valuable small business development material; and a comprehensive glossary of terms to help the business planner navigate the sometimes confusing language of entrepreneurship.

ACKNOWLEDGEMENTS

The Editors wish to sincerely thank the contributors to *BPH-21*, including:

*   BizPlanDB.com
*   Paul Greenland
*   Kari Lucke

COMMENTS WELCOME

Your comments on *Business Plans Handbook* are appreciated. Please direct all correspondence, suggestions for future volumes of *BPH*, and other recommendations to the following:

Managing Editor, Business Product
Business Plans Handbook
Gale, a part of Cengage Learning
27500 Drake Rd.
Farmington Hills, MI 48331-3535
Phone: (248)699-4253
Fax: (248)699-8052
Toll-Free: 800-347-GALE
E-mail: BusinessProducts@gale.com

AV Equipment Rental Business

Galaxy Equipment Works Inc.

2117 Smith Ave.
Worchester, WI 53512

Paul Greenland

Galaxy Equipment Works Inc. rents audiovisual equipment to organizations in the Denton-Worchester, Wisconsin market.

EXECUTIVE SUMMARY

Business Overview

Galaxy Equipment Works Inc. rents audiovisual equipment to organizations in the Denton-Worchester, Wisconsin market. Owners Jeff Peterson (a native of Denton) and Miles Kimball (a native of Worchester) have a considerable amount of experience in the audiovisual communications industry. Both have 15 years of experience working as technicians, and Jeff also has five years of managerial experience. The partners, who met while working for AV Star Enterprises in Milwaukee, have decided to establish their own business because (1) the Denton-Worchester market is underserved and (2) they wish to return to their home communities.

Galaxy Equipment Works' partners have been planning the establishment of their own business for five years. Throughout this time period they have made a number of strategic equipment purchases when presented with opportunities to acquire items at highly competitive prices. In addition, they have personally saved money that will be used for startup purposes.

Jeff and Miles could begin operations by utilizing their existing inventory of equipment and renting/marking up the equipment that they do not currently own. However, the owners have been presented with a unique opportunity to acquire most of the equipment needed for operations from a large Milwaukee-area corporation that is liquidating its audiovisual equipment and other related assets. The owners are seeking financing to purchase this inventory and begin operations next quarter.

Examples of the equipment that Galaxy Equipment Works will offer include:

- Amplifiers and Speakers
- Camcorders
- Cameras
- DVD Players
- Film Projectors
- Laptop Computers

- LCD Projectors
- Lecterns
- Microphones
- Projection Screens
- Slide Projectors
- TV/DVD/VCR Carts
- Wireless Microphones

MARKET ANALYSIS

Overview

Galaxy Equipment Works is located in a geographic area comprised of two communities: Denton and Worchester, Wisconsin. Although the market for AV equipment providers is saturated in larger markets, such as Madison and Milwaukee, an analysis of the Denton and Worchester markets reveals significant opportunity. The majority of prospective customers in these communities provide AV services in-house, or occasionally outsource to providers from other cities for special needs and/or large events and conferences.

Utilizing IBM SPSS Statistics 19, a statistical analysis software package, the owners of Galaxy Equipment Works conducted a basic survey of prospective customers in the markets of Denton and Worchester. Requests to answer the five-minute survey were sent by direct mail, and respondents answered questions online. A complete report is available upon request. However, a key finding of the research was that nearly 40 percent of respondents indicated they would consider outsourcing their AV services to the right vendor. In addition, 15 percent of respondents (key prospects) indicated that they were ready to outsource AV services immediately.

Primary Markets

The community of Denton was home to 1,051 establishments in 2011, and Worchester was home to 2,634 establishments. Within each town, we have classified prospective customers as follows:

Denton

Advertising Agencies (4)

Churches (42)

Conference & Convention Centers (2)

Health & Medical Service Providers (36)

Hospitals (7)

Hotels & Lodging (7)

Legal Services (11)

Membership Organizations (80)

Museums & Zoos (5)

Professional Services (22)

Worchester

Advertising Agencies (6)

Churches (108)

Conference & Convention Centers (3)

Health & Medical Service Providers (79)

Hospitals (9)

Hotels & Lodging (14)

Legal Services (48)

Membership Organizations (99)

Museums & Zoos (3)

Professional Services (50)

Competition

The majority of organizations in these communities that outsource their AV needs have done so to companies from Madison. Galaxy Equipment Works will provide them with an opportunity to work with a local service provider that is a vested member of the regional community. Presently, there is no other local AV communications service provider.

INDUSTRY

As of 2011, AV communications was a multibillion-dollar industry. Many industry participants were represented by the nonprofit trade association InfoComm, which was established in 1939. According to InfoComm, the association "offers industry expertise and market research serving press and others seeking information about the industry. Through activities that include tradeshows, education, certification, government relations, outreach and information services, InfoComm promotes the industry and enhances members' ability to conduct business successfully and competently."

PERSONNEL

Owners Jeff Peterson (a native of Denton) and Miles Kimball (a native of Worchester) have a considerable amount of experience in the audiovisual communications industry. Both have 10 years of experience working as technicians, and Jeff also has five years of managerial experience. The partners, who met while working for AV Star Enterprises in Milwaukee, have decided to establish their own business because (1) the Denton-Worchester market is underserved and (2) they wish to return to their home communities.

During the first years of the new business, Jeff and Miles will focus on sales and service, personally completing jobs for new customers and developing relationships with them. When needed, they will rely upon a reliable crew of freelance technicians from the Milwaukee market (e.g., for the completion of especially large jobs) with whom they already have established relationships. Over time, they will develop a crew of reliable freelance talent from the local/regional market local. The addition of a third employee with a sales and customer service focus will be considered during the second year of operations (see Growth Strategy).

Professional & Advisory Support

Galaxy Equipment Works has established a business banking account with Worchester Bank, as well as a merchant account for accepting credit card payments. Accounting and tax advisory services will be provided by Denton Accounting Services. The owners have utilized an online legal document service to prepare the paperwork necessary for incorporating their new business.

GROWTH STRATEGY

Galaxy Equipment Works is fortunate to begin operations with one service contract, the Denton-Worchester Hotel & Conference Center. Building upon this initial contract, which will provide us with a regular stream of income, we will adhere to the following five-year growth strategy:

Year One: Establish a base of core, repeat customers. Expand pool of local/regional freelance crew members to accommodate larger jobs.

Years Two-Four: Gradually expand customer base via the addition of a third employee (part-time sales, part-time customer service). Adhere to a conservative inventory strategy focused on replacement of existing equipment and the acquisition of the most in-demand equipment.

Year Five: Complete payback of financing. Begin expanding equipment inventory at a more aggressive pace.

PRODUCTS & SERVICES

Galaxy Equipment Works offers a wide range of audiovisual communications equipment for organizations. Our business offers everything needed for meetings, conferences, presentations, and special events. For customers with highly specialized needs, or very large orders, we are able to rent the equipment that is not part of our regular inventory (supplier lists available upon request). Services include delivery, setup, tear-down, and on-site technicians when needed.

Equipment Examples

- Amplifiers and Speakers
- Audiocassette Tape Player
- Boom Mic Stands
- Camcorders
- Cameras
- DVD Players
- Film Projectors
- Laptop Computers
- LCD Projectors
- Lecterns
- Microphone Mixers
- Microphones
- Projection Screens
- Recorders
- Scan Converters
- Slide Projectors
- Smart Carts
- Smart Consoles
- Table-top Mic Stands

- TV/DVD/VCR Carts

- Video Cassette Recorders

- Videoconferencing carts

- Wireless Microphones

MARKETING & SALES

Galaxy Equipment Works has developed a marketing plan that concentrates on the following primary tactics:

1. A glossy, four-color sales sheet that can be included in direct mailings, presented during sales calls, and distributed at local and regional events attended by business owners and decision-makers.

2. A sustained (quarterly) direct-mail campaign to key prospects in the Denton-Worchester market. Arrangements have been made to obtain a mailing list from a reputable list broker, and we have identified a local mail house that can assist us.

3. Sales calls to prospective customers, especially those that, in the aforementioned survey, indicated a desire to outsource their AV needs immediately.

4. A Web site with complete details about our capabilities and services.

5. A customer incentive program that provides a 15 percent discount off of a customer's first order.

6. Magnetic signage that can be affixed to our vehicle in order to promote the business.

7. Magnetic business cards that will double as advertising specialties.

8. Active membership in the local Chamber of Commerce.

9. Trade show marketing at the Annual Regional Business Expo and Denton-Worchester Economic Development Council quarterly breakfast meetings.

OPERATIONS

Facility & Location

Galaxy Equipment Works has made arrangements to lease a 2,500-square-foot section of a warehouse in Worchester. Due to economic conditions, we were able to negotiate very competitive terms. The warehouse owner has agreed to lease the space to us at a steep discount for the first year ($5,000), and $7,125 annually ($2.85 per square foot) thereafter. Benefiting us is the fact that the facility is equipped with storage racks that are suitable for our purposes, and it has garage door access for easy loading/unloading. There is a small office space in the corner of the warehouse area that is suitable for filing and completing paperwork. A detailed floor plan of our warehouse is available upon request.

Vehicle

Our business has negotiated for the purchase of a used, 17-foot diesel box truck (105,233 miles) from a local U-Haul dealer for $4,296. Complete maintenance records are available for the vehicle, and it has been well maintained. In the event of an unusually large job, we will rent a 26-foot U-Haul from the same dealer.

Hours of Operation

Due to the nature of its business, Galaxy Equipment Works will maintain irregular business hours. Customers will often require the business to set up equipment the evening before a conference or event, or provide service for dinners and functions that happen during the evening hours. In order to maximize accessibility, the partners will have a dedicated telephone number where customers can opt to leave them a voicemail message, or be transferred to one of their mobile phones (in event of an urgent request). They will attempt to return all routine inquiries within one business day.

Pricing

Projectors

35MM slide projector (with wired remote control)	$ 25
35MM slide projector (with wireless remote control)	$ 55
Overhead projector	$ 25
LCD video projector (1,000 lumens, VCR, mixer & cart)	$225
LCD video projector (2,000 lumens, VCR, mixer & cart)	$275
Computer projector (800 × 600 resolution, 1,000 lm)	$225
Computer projector (1,024 × 768 resolution)	$225
1,000 lm	$275
1,500 lm	$300
2,000 lm	$325
3,000 lm	$375

Screens

Movie screen 5' × 5'	$15
Movie screen 6' × 6'	$20
Movie screen 7' × 7'	$25
Movie screen 8' × 8'	$30
Movie screen 7½' × 10' (front or rear)	$70
Movie screen 9' × 12'—fast fold (front or rear)	$75
Movie screen 10' × 10'—fast fold (front only)	$80
Movie screen dress kit (blue or black)	$50

Monitors

17" S-VGA data monitor	$ 75
29" XGA data monitor	$175
27" color monitor, VCR and cart	$100
27" color monitor with stand	$ 60
32" color monitor, VCR and cart	$120
32" color monitor with stand	$ 80
42" plasma monitor & floor stand	$325
60" plasma monitor & stand	$600
Pick-up and delivery charge for plasma monitors	$ 75

Players & recorders

VHS player/recorder with remote	$50
S-VHS player/recorder with remote	$50
DVD player with remote	$75
Cassette tape player	$25
Dual cassette player	$35
Cassette recorder/player	$25
CD (single) player	$25
Combination CD & cassette player	$45
5-disc player	$40

Video cameras

AV cart	$15
VHS-C format or 8MM camcorder	$65
VHS camcorder & tripod	$75

Telecommunications

Speaker phone system (small rooms)	$30
Speaker phone system (large rooms)	$55

Sound equipment

Microphone	$15
4 channel audio mixer	$25
Amplified speaker system (small rooms)	$45
Portable sound system (amplifier & two speakers on stands)	$75
Lavaliere microphone (wired)	$40
Hand-held or lavaliere microphone (wireless)	$75

Podiums & lecterns

Tabletop podium	$15
Floor podium	$25
Floor podium (built-in sound system)	$35
Tabletop podium (built-in sound system)	$35

Flip charts & whiteboards

Whiteboard	$15
Flipchart size	$15
3' × 5'	
4' × 6'	
Flipchart stand (with paper, markers & tape)	$15
Additional pads of paper	$10
Flipchart stand or easel (stand only)	$10

Labor

Audio visual attendant (per hour)	$30
Audio visual technician in room (per hour)	$40

Office/productivity equipment

Speaker phone system (small rooms)	$30
Speaker phone system (large rooms)	$55
Fax machine	$40
Tabletop copier	$50
Laser printer	$50

Miscellaneous

Laser pointer	$ 15
Laptop computer with PowerPoint	$100
Wireless remote & laser pointer	$ 20
Computer/video scaler	$225
Spotlight	$ 50

Insurance

Galaxy Equipment Works has secured appropriate business and liability insurance coverage through Thompson Insurance Associates.

FINANCIAL ANALYSIS

Financial Projections

Based on our knowledge of the AV communications equipment rental business, as well as local market conditions, we estimate that Galaxy Equipment Works will generate gross sales of $95,000 during its first year of operations. Assuming our growth strategy is successful, we anticipate annual growth of 15-20 percent during our second and third years. Detailed projections, as well as a projected balance sheet that has been developed in partnership with our accounting firm, are available on request.

Startup Expenses

Galaxy Equipment Works will incur start-up costs of $65,000, in order to procure the remaining equipment needed for operations. The owners plan to provide $30,000 from their personal savings to partially cover these startup costs and are seeking a business loan in the amount of $50,000 to cover the remainder, as well as funds needed for continuing operations and general business purposes.

Evaluation & Adjustment

This plan will be evaluated on a quarterly basis during our first and second years of operation, and semi-annually thereafter.

Business Consulting Firm
Blake & Associates

5456 Universal Ave.
Cleveland, OH 76891

Blake & Associates offers numerous consulting and advisory services (primarily to smaller businesses). It will specialize in advice on business planning. Because this is an example of a document which our consulting firm hopes others will ask our advice, it should serve to effectively highlight the general approach.

This plan originally appeared in Business Plans Handbook, Volume 1; it has been updated for this volume.

EXECUTIVE SUMMARY

Blake & Associates provides several consulting and advisory services to the business community, with particular emphasis on small businesses of 25 to 175 employees. These services include: seminars and work-shops on writing business plans, as well as complete business plan development and writing; financial analysis and balance sheet restructuring; business valuations for purchase, sale or buy/sell agreements; cash flow analysis; computer technology analysis and training; and workshops on a variety of topics. One overarching theme is helping businesses to succeed in a challenging economic climate.

The company currently is a sole proprietorship with a small staff of specialized individuals who are well suited to providing our services to small and medium-sized companies and, in some instances, to the general public. In addition to the above mentioned services, we are creating DVDs and online videos on subjects such as business plan writing and computer technology. The videos will be sold online, through direct mail, e-mail, magazine advertisements, and at our company-sponsored workshops.

Blake & Associates has an opportunity to fill a need in the business community and become profitable in its first year. A loan of $85,000 will be a sufficient operating account to start the business, along with approximately $17,000 in existing capital assets and grants.

The first year should see total revenues of just over $288,000 and a net after tax loss of ($6,143), or -2.13%. The second year, we anticipate revenues of just over $970,000 with profits of nearly $110,000. The third year, we estimate revenues will be nearly $1,950,000, with a profit of over $260,000. The high profit margin in the third year reflects the results of building the organization in the first two years and developing a demand for higher attendance at our seminars and workshops, as well as greater demand for our books, videos, and audio recordings.

Objectives
In the first year we will achieve revenues of approximately $290,000 while returning a net, after tax loss of ($6,143), or a -2.13% profit margin.

We are targeting growth of more than 100% in the second year, based on the development of our strategic alliances and our access to the public and small businesses through our seminars and workshops. By focusing on the seminars and workshops, books (print and e-books), videos (DVDs and streaming media), and audio recordings (CDs and downloadable MP3s), we can increase revenues to more than $1,900,000 by the third year and show a net after-tax profit of 13.7%, or $266,183, on growth of nearly 30%.

The key to growth and profitability is to develop the marketing of seminars, workshops, and tools (i.e., videos, audio recordings, and booklets). We expect these services to provide as much as 50% of our total revenues in the first year and approximately 70% by the third year. Using the workshops and seminars as a marketing vehicle for our services, we will see an increase in our consulting revenues and our seminar and workshop revenues.

Mission

To improve the performance and efficiency of small businesses and their chances of survival in highly competitive, expanding, and unpredictable political and economic business environments.

COMPANY

Blake & Associates is a sole proprietorship, with a small staff of specialized individuals who are well suited to providing our services to small- and medium-sized companies and, in some instances, to the general public. Our services include: analysis and development of business plans; business valuations; cash flow analysis; demographic research for marketing plans; computer hardware and software analysis, installation, and training; and consultation and workshops on sales management and sales staff motivation. In addition, we are creating videos on such subjects as business plan writing, fundraising during challenging economic times, and using social media as a marketing tool.

Company Ownership

Blake & Associates is a sole proprietorship owned by Brad Dunn. In the future, the company will be incorporated—most likely as an "S" corporation and, at that time, there will be other stockholders. Further, it is expected that, should any future funding for this venture come from an investor, the investor will require (and be entitled to) a percentage of ownership.

Company History

Blake & Associates is a start-up company, beginning its operation on September 1, 2010; however, most of the time during the first few months was spent developing the feasibility research. Some services were offered in the fall of 2010, and although clients were billed for services, no revenues were generated. These projects did help in the research process and much of that research will be evident in the body of this plan.

Services & Products

We will provide numerous services to businesses, including: assistance in writing effective and concise business plans and financial analysis; conducting demographic market research; and providing business valuations. We also will provide consulting services and conduct a variety of workshops and seminars.

Company Location & Facilities

The company has not made final arrangements for its office location. Brad Dunn is conducting business from his home at the present time, but the conditions are unsuitable for business operations. To obtain the most effective amount of space at the lowest possible price, we have concluded that our best choice would be shared office facilities. These facilities provide private offices, secretarial support, copiers, faxes, wireless Internet access, Internet-based telephone service, reception, and so on. The prices range from approximately $1,000-$1,500 per month for each room, plus a cost for phones and furniture.

The least expensive facility we have found is Troy Commons. Two offices with two telephone lines would cost a total of $1,822 per month. This facility provides minimal space for meetings (eight people, maximum), no storage space, no audio/visual support and no training space. The most feasible location, for the first few months, would provide conference facilities for 10 to 12, Internet connectivity, Web conferencing technology, audio/video, and an extensive array of additional services, including color copying. Although we would be using the shared office concept for the first year to 18 months, the business plan reflects the cost of a private facility from the first day of the second year of operation. Our concern with the shared office concept is the exceedingly high cost of ancillary services and the lack of conference, training, and storage space.

When we are ready for our own offices, our facilities will require six specific areas including a conference/training room, reception area, storage and equipment room, marketing office, operations office and administrative offices. The total space requirement would be between 2,000 and 2,500 square feet and we would enter into a lease of five years, negotiating for lower lease payments in the first three to six months of the lease. A chart of the office options available can be provided.

PRODUCTS & SERVICES

Blake & Associates provide a number of necessary services and products to the business community and to the public. Although the products and services seem complex, they can be summed up in two areas—business finance services and business computer services. Our business finance services include business plan workshops, consulting and writing, financial and cash flow analysis, planning and restructuring, business valuation for purchases or sales, or for the structuring of a buy/sell agreement, demographic market studies, computer hardware and software analysis, and computer/network installation and training. In addition, we conduct seminars and workshops on such topics as sales and sales management, motivation, starting a business, developing vision in the staff and so on. Our business computer services include workshops on computer networking and technology. Many of the topics we cover would be of interest to the general public. We also provide consulting services to businesses on their hardware and software needs.

Our business planning services include: assisting companies with the research and structuring of comprehensive, written business plans; conducting workshops and seminars on business plan writing; and providing a written business plan package, which delivers a complete, detailed business plan to the client, specifically designed to meet their needs (i.e., venture capital search, bank loans, SBA loans, restructuring, new product development, expansion market, and so on). In many cases, businesses of 25 to 175 employees consider next year's budget an acceptable business plan. Any investor or banker will disagree and insist on much more information prior to making a financial decision regarding funding a business. We want to provide the opportunity for businesses that have potential to receive the funding that would help them become solid employers and corporate taxpayers in their communities. Other services included in Business Planning are:

- Business valuations for the purpose of establishing a value on a business that is being bought or sold, as well as establishing a value for buy/sell agreements for partnerships and other business entities who wish to insure against the premature death of a principal in the business.

- Cash flow analysis that allows a company to anticipate lulls in production or sales, due to seasonal, political, or economic market adjustments that would cause unanticipated drains on "cash on hand" and the cash surplus. It is our observation that a company can borrow monies to cover an anticipated depression in cash flow much easier than trying to borrow monies to get out of a negative situation.

- Demographic information that can help a company identify the best location for expansion or product introduction, based on retail sales, per capita income, competition, real estate values and lease rates, union vs. nonunion labor, population, and so on. Many times a company sees an opportunity for growth or the introduction of a new product through "rose colored glasses." We help them realize the realities of the endeavor and provide guidance that would allow them to find a better location, reconsider their timing, or any other alternative that might exist.

Information Systems consulting provides much needed assistance to the smaller companies who must be careful of every dollar spent on potentially "unnecessary" computer technology. Hundreds of software packages are sold every day to unsuspecting buyers who think the software will perform a specific task for them, only to find that it won't. Furthermore, businesses and individuals alike spend thousands of dollars to buy computers and peripheral components to improve their efficiency and work environment only to find out that the system they got was too much, too little, or the totally wrong kind. We will help these individuals and businesses to make the proper decision on software and hardware. We will evaluate dozens of software packages (including hosted applications) for ease of operation, extent of benefits, learning time, and levels and cost. We will then be able to properly advise our clients as to what software package will do their task at the least cost and with the least amount of start-up time. As for hardware we can analyze the system needs of the client and advise them of upgrades which might be available for their current system or network, without going to the expense of replacing an entire computer. On the other hand, we can advise the client on just how much upgrading might need to be done.

Important Features & Comparison

Although there are a number of attorneys and accountants who profess to writing, or assisting in the writing of, business plans, the reality is that these professionals provide invaluable services in the areas in which they are best, but lack the imagination to write a comprehensive and effective business plan. The attorneys tend to dwell on the legal aspects and contractual arrangements while accountants sweat over the balance sheet, cash flow statements, product costs and income statements. Additionally, these vitally necessary professionals cannot afford to spend the many hours necessary to work on a business plan when they could be earning a high hourly rate concentrating on their particular field of expertise.

Our expertise lies in the ability to listen to a business owner and perceive their vision for their company over the next few years. We can envision what the business person is looking for in the future and then put it in writing—and at a cost they can live with.

As for computer consulting, there literally are hundreds of companies and individuals who provide "consulting" services to businesses. However, as in the case of the business plan writing area, most of them are too wrapped up in "their" ideas and opinions to hear what the client really needs. Further, many of these "consultants" are re-sellers of software and are less objective than they otherwise might be. We want the needs of the client to be the most important thing to us, so we will not be a re-seller of software or hardware.

We will continually research the market so we can advise the clients as to where they can find the software and hardware they need at the most reasonable prices. Finally, we are offering workshops and seminars where the knowledge we have gained can be shared with the smallest of businesses without costing them hundreds of dollars. The average business planning seminar will have a ticket price of $75 and the workshop, where participants will actually be able to write a business plan with the tools and information provided, will have a price of $125. Our computer technology evaluation seminars will have an average ticket price of $75 and the attendee will be able to make decisions as to what software or hardware might be best for their situation. Even the smallest of businesses can afford these prices, as can the individual seeking this information. However, the greatest of seminars and workshops cannot give anyone ALL necessary information. Ultimately, our seminars and workshops become one of our most effective marketing tools, causing the attendees to come to us for further information (at our hourly rate of $75 to $135) or to have us write the plan, do the evaluation, perform network configurations or technology upgrades, etc.

Promotional Tactics

Blake & Associates has developed an extensive Web site outlining the services we provide. The site includes profiles of our staff, a blog, as well as a free library of white papers and expert articles. In addition, we offer an intake form that potential clients can use to contact us and request a complimentary consultation. We also have enabled sharing functionality throughout our site, so that users can redistribute our information through various social media channels, including Facebook, LinkedIn, and Twitter.

Traditional print literature is being designed by Graphics Inc. Our literature will consist of a pocket folder, which will allow us to custom design the type of package needed for each client, an 8 1/2 x 11, bi-fold "mailable" brochure, which is designed to sell the need for service (rather than explain the services offered) and inserts for the folder that will detail the various services offered by the firm. The copy is being written by Laurie Metcalf. She has an equally impressive list of clients and has written countless business and technical pieces for *The Post Dispatch, The St. Louis Business Journal* and several national publications. She has also co-authored several technical manuals and textbooks. Her expertise is in taking the most complicated ideas and making them simple to understand.

MARKET ANALYSIS

According to an article in the September 23, 2010, issue of *The Huffington Post*, the United States is home to approximately 27 million small businesses. As major industry continues to "downsize," and unemployment rates increase, more and more talented, educated, and experienced people are finding themselves going into business. Many of these people will work from home, while others will open offices, hire staff and begin producing products and providing services. Each and every one of these individuals will need some sort of support we are providing. However, it is a mixed bag and the common thread we have found which would provide us with access to these new (as well as the existing) businesses is their need for an attorney, an accountant, and a banker. Therefore, we will concentrate our marketing efforts on these professionals, relying on them, and later our clients, for referrals.

Industry Analysis

According to the U.S. Department of Labor's *Career Guide to Industries, 2010-11 Edition*, the management, scientific, and technical consulting services industry employed approximately 1 million wage and salary workers during the late 2000s. Although the consulting industry is dominated by a number of large players with thousands of employees, the majority of industry establishments are small firms, most of which have less than five employees.

Nearly 40 percent of industry establishments provide administrative management and general management consulting, and nearly 19 percent of establishments focus on scientific and technical consulting. Wage and salary workers in the overall management, scientific, and technical consulting services field are projected to experience growth of 82.8 percent from 2008 to 2018, according to the U.S. Department of Labor. Despite these lofty growth projections, competition for work will remain highly competitive. The primary professional organizations within our field are the Association of Management Consulting Firms and the Institute of Management Consultants.

Market Segmentation

Our target market covers companies of 25 to 175 employees. The most likely types of businesses to require our services include:

- New businesses seeking investment or start-up capital

- Existing companies who are expanding or introducing a new product or service

- New and existing companies who need to upgrade their computer network, hardware or software

- Individuals and businesses who want to learn more about technology

- Employers looking for fresh approaches to goal setting and technique

- Governmental agencies assisting displaced or disabled individuals to find employment

As mentioned, our target market is businesses of 25 to 175 employees, but we will be providing services to many entities of greater or lesser numbers. In doing the research for this plan, 390 businesses were contacted that met our target size. Of those, only 55 have current business plans. More importantly, 310 of them said their banker or investor group wanted an updated business plan. Of the 310, a total of 160 said they would be willing to attend, or send a representative, to a workshop on business planning, and over 200 were interested in seminars and workshops on computer technology. Additionally, 285 said they were "less than satisfied" with either the hardware or software they were currently using, or their network performance.

Competitive Forces & Buying Patterns

The most important factor in this market is the quality of the service. Most of the companies we spoke with said the price they paid for services was not as important as the quality and availability. The majority of the companies said they were not satisfied with the current condition of their planning efforts, because their accountant was unfamiliar with the fundamentals of their business and they were less satisfied with the quality of the "experts" they had hired to improve their productivity. Hence, quality service will command a fair price.

Main Competitors

There are 122 companies operating in the metropolitan area who classify themselves as "business consultants." There are some companies that provide services similar to those offered by us. This healthy competition should keep us awake and appreciative. There are seven companies who seem to closely parallel our services. Each of these companies offers business plan writing. Some offer technology consulting services, with an emphasis on serving small and start-up businesses. However, most of our top competitors are one- or two-person businesses.

Keys to Success

We never want to forget the fact that we are a small business and the mainstay of our business comes from small businesses. We want to provide our services to our clients as though we were friends. We want to always be available when a client needs our help or has a question and we always want to make certain that we are giving our clients advice that will help them operate efficiently and effectively. We offer a background in consulting with the Small Business Development Center and our management and speaking expertise services, writing business plans and conducting seminars and workshops. One cofounder has operated his own Web development business for five years and has been writing computer programs for software development companies even longer. His friendly demeanor and extensive knowledge of technology give him a distinct advantage and workshops will give us access to people we might otherwise lose because they feel that they already have "advisors" in their attorneys or accountants.

BUSINESS STRATEGY & IMPLEMENTATION

We do not want to compete with attorneys and CPAs. We want them as allies. We intend to show them how we can be of value to them by freeing their time up and still being paid for services through our firm. We also want to work with the commercial and business loan officers at numerous banks throughout neighboring areas and states, showing them how we can assist their clients and applicants with SBA loan packages, direct bank loans and other services, making the loan officer's job easier and more effective. By developing relationships with these professionals, we can develop a referral system which could keep us supplied with enough business to be profitable. In addition, our seminars and workshops will create business and provide one avenue for the sale of books, videos, and audio recordings on the topics we are presenting.

Marketing Strategy

Our strategy calls for the development of relationships with attorneys, accountants, and bankers to support our business with referrals. Interviews with commercial loan officers have indicated that there is a serious need for a firm like ours to help their clients develop comprehensive, concise business plans. We have already received permission from one financial institution to place our literature in their commercial loan lobby and they have agreed to mail several of the pieces to recent business applicants who don't have business plans. This same type of referral can come from the attorneys and accountants with whom we have developed relationships. Our consulting work and advertising will generate business for our technology services section, including service contracts with some of the law and accounting firms from whom we receive referrals.

Target Markets & Market Segments

Our target market is small businesses of 25 to 175 employees. The industry they are involved in has little relevance. We are able to work equally well with operations focused on manufacturing, assembly, sales, or service. All types of businesses need to know where they are headed, and there is hardly any business in operation today that does not use computer technology. Furthermore, there are many 1- to 4-person shops, like our business in the initial stages, who still need help in identifying where they want to go and how they want to get there. For these types of "micro companies," our seminars and workshops are ideal. The workshops will cause them to think the process through and develop their own plans of action.

Pricing Strategy

For our hourly services we must make ourselves profitable but be competitive. For business consulting we will charge an hourly rate of $135. Our hourly fee for computer consulting is $75 to $115, depending on the task. If it simply involves research and advice on software, the $75 would apply. However, if the client wishes us to evaluate, upgrade and service a network of computers, the rate would be $115. Finally, our seminars will have an average fee of $75 and our workshops will average $125 per attendee. All of these rates are highly competitive, and in some cases, are far less.

Marketing Programs & Strategies

We will be instituting a regular schedule of e-mail and direct mail solicitations to our target market. Every month, a communication will be sent to a section of our market, with follow-up calls made to confirm that the information arrived. Then, those leads will be followed up on over the next few weeks by the Research or Technology Associates. There will be frequent visits to our strategic alliances, including lawyers, accountants, and bankers. These will be face to face discussions of our services and upcoming seminars and workshops. Graphic Design is developing a comprehensive package of materials we can use to promote the company, including small brochures of a mailable size and a larger folder, which will allow us to build a "customized" package containing information pertinent to a particular customer. In addition, an HTML template also is being developed for customized e-mail solicitations.

Sales Forecast

Charts and tables representing our forecast of sales for the first twelve months of operation, by product, have been prepared.

Strategic Alliances

Our strategic alliances are also part of our marketing strategy. As outlined earlier, our existing and anticipated relationships with legal and accounting firms, as well as bank lending officers, will provide us with the strong referral base we will need. In most cases, it will not be easy to win these groups over. Some will resist because they are offering some abbreviated form of one or more of our services now. However, if we can show them how we can do the work and still provide them a fee opportunity, it should appeal to them. We have already developed relationships with a local bank and law firm. They will provide us with much of the credibility we will need to access other professional and financial organizations.

ORGANIZATION

An Organizational Chart is available upon request.

Organization Structure

The company, simply because of its small size, will function more as a partnership than a corporate organization, in the early stages. With such a small group, it will be simple to communicate with and support one another. As the company grows, there will be more structure to the organization, with new hires being assigned a supervisor or subordinates. When the company is at its full staff potential, it will operate as any closely held corporation, but maintain the personal interest in each employee's personal and family welfare and their contributions to the business.

Management Team

A complete resume for each of the management staff is available upon request.

Management Team Gaps

There are three positions that we will need to fill in the first six months of operation. Although two of the roles are not considered a part of the management team, they are integral to the fulfillment of the plan. The first vacancy to be filled is a Business Planning Associate to assist the owner in the writing of business plans and the presentation of seminars and workshops. This person could allow the company to nearly double the volume of business plans written by conducting the preliminary client interviews and performing research on competition and market.

The second person needed is a Marketing Director. This person will be responsible for keeping us on target with our seminars and workshops, as well as defining the specific marketing objectives of clients who hire us to write their business plans. Further, this person would work with our outside consultants on public relations, publicity and advertising, and in some cases, conduct seminars and workshops on marketing plans and studies. Until this person is hired, these responsibilities will be handled by the owner with the help of the rest of the staff. We anticipate hiring this person near the end of the first year.

The third person needed is a Technology Associate, who would perform similar tasks to the Business Planning Associate. That is, to assist in conducting research into client needs, analyze software products for usability and learning curve, interview clients to obtain information on the daily usage of computers and software to evaluate needed upgrades or replacement, and assist in conducting technology seminars and workshops.

Personnel Plan

We do not intend to be a large corporation or "top heavy." We want the company to stay lean and flexible so that we can respond to a client's needs quickly. To do this, we will use outside consultants whose fees, in most cases, will be passed on to the client, indirectly, through our fees. A personnel forecast by both month and year has been prepared.

FINANCIAL ANALYSIS

Blake & Associates has an opportunity to fill a need in the business community and become profitable in the first year. $85,000 will be a sufficient operating account to see the business through the start-up phase and beyond break-even. In addition to the $85,000 loan, the company comes to the table with approximately $15,000 in assets, including $10,000 in computer technology.

The first year should see total revenues of just over $288,000 and a net, after tax loss of ($6,143). The second year, we anticipate revenues of just over $970,000 with profits of nearly $110,000. The third year, we estimate revenues will be nearly $1,950,000, with a profit of over $265,000. The high profit margin in the third year reflects the results of building the organization in the first two years and developing a demand for, and therefore higher attendance at, the seminars and workshops, as well as greater demand for the books and audio and videos. In other words, the third year will allow us to do twice the business with virtually the same number of people and a small increase in expenses.

Financial Plan

To put the operation into full swing, we require $85,000 of operating capital, which will cover payroll, rent, Internet access, telephones and other general expenses for at least six months, assuming no revenues were received during that same period. It is expected that there will be no more funds needed after this initial infusion of capital. It is our intent to repay the loan in the first three years of operation, with principle and interest payments beginning in the third month. The company has no plans to "go public." It is our intent to keep the organization small, efficient and closely held. However, it is possible that the company, or a portion, could be sold to another consulting firm, attorney, CPA, or the like. If such an offer is made, the decision to sell will be made at that time.

First Twelve Months: Pro Forma Income Statement

The Income Statement reflects three larger expenditures in the first 90 days. These expenses include:

$8,500 for video, audio, and book production

$14,000 for advertising and promotion

$5,250 for legal and accounting

The first of these items is the cost to produce the audio recordings and videos we will sell at seminars and through advertisements. $4,590 is for video production, including equipment, filming, editing and so on. The audio recordings can be produced from the sound track on the video except for a few special recordings we want to include. The remaining $3,910 is for the initial production of the business plan writing guideline, which accompanies the audio recordings and videos, and the packaging of the audio recordings and videos, as well as the layout of the books, which can be produced using digital, print-on-demand technology, and also distributed in an e-book format. After this initial investment, we have calculated a monthly expenditure that will cover the replacement of those products that were sold.

The second major expense item is advertising and promotion. Included in this $14,000 is the cost of newspaper and magazine advertising to announce the opening of the company for business. We have calculated a monthly advertising budget that will allow us to keep our name before the public and advertise our seminars and workshops. With these budgeted amounts, we will be able to buy our advertising in advance and receive as much as a 50% discount from standard rates in local publications. The advertising budget grows to $84,000 in the second year and $140,000 in the third, with the expansion of the company to a larger geographic service area.

The third large item is the expense for legal and accounting. The $5,250 is sufficient to cover the cost of incorporation, contracts and agreements and setting up the general journal and general ledger.

In the first year, we expect gross sales of $288,640 and cost of sales to be $106,707, for a gross margin of $181,843 or 63%. Profit before taxes and interest expense are projected to be ($6,143). With interest expense of $5,623 and taxes of ($1,733), the company will show a net loss, in the first year of ($6,143). This is an acceptable result, considering the start-up time and expenses incurred during the first year.

The second and third years, FY11 and FY12, show gross sales of $972,228 and $1,941,285, respectively. Unit cost of sales are $307,676 for FY11 and $575,874 for FY12. The second year net, after-tax profit is projected to be $ 109,758. The third year net, after-tax profit is estimated at $266,183.

Financial Ratios & Break-Even Analysis

Ratio analyses, including profitability ratios, activity ratios, debt ratios, liquidity ratios, and others have been forecasted through 2015 and are available upon request.

It is our opinion that we can exceed the "usual and customary" ratios through the combination of services we are offering. Nearly half of the revenues, in the third year, will come from the sale of books, videos and audio recordings. These products require little staffing and overhead and generate excellent profits once the initial cost of production is absorbed.

Charts representing the sales revenues, personnel needs, expenses, and profit for the next three years have been prepared. Each chart reflects genuine estimates of the company's capabilities, and the achievement of these results is totally dependent upon the $85,000 loan.

Spreadsheets to accompany financial projections, as well as examples of advertising layouts and marketing materials, are available upon request. These include: general assumptions; sales forecasts; personnel plan; the Pro Forma Income Statement, Cash Flow Statement, and Balance Sheet; ratio analyses; and advertising.

Spa
Temple Creek Day Spa

450 South Jasmine St.
New Town, Missouri 63301

Kari Lucke

Linda Wallace, Owner. Temple Creek is a day spa that offers a variety of services for a reasonable price for local residents of New Town, Missouri, and the surrounding communities.

1.0. INTRODUCTION

1.1. Executive Summary
Temple Creek is a day spa that offers a variety of services for a reasonable price for local residents of New Town, Missouri, and the surrounding communities.

1.2. Business Philosophy
Owner Linda Wallace is a member of the International Spa Association (ISPA) and follows the Code of Conduct put forth by the organization. Members are expected to follow the guidelines in the Code, which is divided into 12 sections dealing with the following issues:

- Freedom of Expression

- Privacy and Confidentiality

- Consumer Protection and Provision of Information to Consumers

- Standard Terms and Conditions

- Unsolicited Communications

- Cyber Crime

- Protection of Minors

- Lawful Conduct

- Unlawful Conduct and Activity

- Internet Standards

- Compliance with the Code of Conduct

- Alterations

In the day spa industry, consumers have both rights and responsibilities. Based on guidelines endorsed by the ISPA and the Resort Hotel Association, consumers' rights include the right (a) to a safe and sanitary environment; (b) to stop a treatment at any time for any reason; (c) to be treated with respect; (d) to confidentiality; (e) to treatment by well-trained staff members; (f) to ask questions at any time; and (g) to access information about staff training, licensing, and certification. At the same time, spa guests are expected to (a) clearly communicate their preferences, expectations, and concerns; (b) provide complete and accurate health information; (c) treat staff with respect and courtesy; (d) follow guidelines set by the individual spa; and (e) submit acceptable payment for services.

Spa operators also have rights and responsibilities; the most important of the latter include: (a) to provide a safe and clean environment for customers; (b) to offer quality services for at a reasonable cost; (c) to provide written materials that are accurate and clear regarding prices, expectations, hours, and so on; (d) to keep customers' personal information strictly confidential; (e) to respond quickly and courteously to all questions and/or complaints from spa guests or clients; (f) to not discriminate against clients based on ethnicity, gender, etc.; (g) to provide access to services by disabled individuals; and (h) to follow all federal, state, and local laws governing the spa industry. Overall, operators are to be guided in all activities by "truth, accuracy, fairness, and integrity, " according to the ISPA.

1.3. Goals and Objectives

*   Establish a reputation as a quality day spa in the area

*   Realize a profit the first year of business

*   Protect the environment and follow sustainable practices in all services

2.0. INDUSTRY AND MARKET

2.1. Industry Analysis

According to *Spa Magazine*, "Spas are places devoted to overall well-being through a variety of professional services that encourage the renewal of mind, body, and spirit." These services have come into higher demand in the United States, with the number of spas rising an average of 20 percent annually during the first decade of the twenty-first century. By 2010 there were about 21,000 spas in the United States, according to the ISPA, with about 79 percent of these operating as day spas. Other types of spas include medical spas, cruise ship and resort spas, cosmetic spas, and destination spas. Day spas focus on services that can be experienced "in a day."

Other figures from the ISPA show that U.S. spas represent a $11 billion industry that employs more than 330,000 full-time, part-time, and contract employees. About 78 percent of revenues come from four main categories of services: massage and bodywork, skin care, hair, and nails. One in four Americans have visited a spa, and as of 2010 there were approximately 32 million consumers who visited a spa on a regular basis.

Some of the factors that are expected to have an impact on the day spa industry include the increase in demand for anti-aging products and treatments, including sun care and self-tanning products; a move toward more technologically-enhanced services; an increase in the role of social networking; and a move toward specialization. Temple Creek Day Spa, as a brand-new facility with the latest in products, services, and equipment, will be poised to take advantage of these influences. Factors that will represent challenges for the industry include more government regulation, an increase in certification/education requirements for staff members, and a rise in the number of at-home products that are available. One of the strategies for dealing with these challenges is to remain constantly updated on the state of the industry and to strive to meet whatever requirements arise. Other important factors will be providing a level of personal service that consumers cannot find elsewhere.

2.2 Market Analysis

Anna Lempereur-Moine of *Skin Inc.* magazine divided day spa customers into four personas. Lempereur-Moine's method is helpful for assessing the status of the local market. According to her, day spa customers consist of:

- those focused on lifestyles of health and sustainability (LOHAS)

- trend followers

- family consumers

- value seekers

The first category of consumers (LOHAS) is especially interested in organic products and sustainable and environmentally responsible services, and they view spa-going as a "wellness activity" that is vital for their continued mental and physical health. Trend followers (what Lempereur-Moine calls "UberMEs") are more interested in the newest treatment and hotteset trends. This group is very into technology and has no problem spending significant amounts to pay for it. For them, spa-going may be the "in" thing to do. Family consumers, on the other hand, visit spas for a respite from their busy lives. This consumer has many responsibilities, including family, work, community, and other commitments, and values speed and convenience. Last, value seekers are cost-conscious and often experience spas through gift certificates or the result of other promotional or discounted marketing.

One of the ways Wallace intends to increase business at Temple Creek is to literally take note of the type of customers that visit the spa, categorizing them as detailed above. Over a period of time, this will give her a better idea of who her customers are and what type of service will be the most appealing and the most profitable in the future.

2.3. Competition

There are three other day spas in the New Town area that constitute the main competition for Temple Creek: Windsong Spa & Salon, All About You, and the Amanda Rose Treatment Center. Several other, more specific services are also available, such as salons that provide hair and nail services and businesses that focus on massage. However, the previously mentioned three are the ones that provide the same services as Temple Creek (hair and nail services, massage, and skin care) and thus constitute the main competition. All About You is the only other spa located in the same general part of town as Temple Creek; Windsong and Amanda Rose are both located in the southwest.

However, because the day spa industry as well as the population of New Town is growing, there is room for another spa in the northern part of the city. Temple Creek intends to draw customers from All About You with better customer service, a larger variety of products and services, including organic, and the appeal of a new facility. Temple Creek will also attract those who have not previously been spa-goers with special discounts and promotions.

3.0. PERSONNEL

3.1. Management

Linda Wallace is the sole owner and proprietor of Temple Creek Day Spa. Wallace's credentials include a bachelor's degree in business management and ISPA certification as a Spa Supervisor. In addition, she operated a successful hair salon in Colorado Springs, Colorado, for eight years prior to her move to Missouri, so she has the background, skills, and experience needed to manage this type of business. Wallace will manage the day-to-day operations of the business, including hiring, scheduling, and training employees; promoting the business; determining prices and services; and managing inventory.

3.2. Staffing

Initially, there will be eight staff members besides Wallace, with two of each of the following positions: receptionist/secretary, nail technician/hair stylist, massage therapist, and skin care consultant. These employees will be hired based on their experience in the field, educational qualifications, past employment history, and other related factors. Certification and/or licensure will be required of all employees except the receptionists, although experience in the field in some capacity will be beneficial for these staff members as well.

If the demand for certain services surpasses Temple Creek's capacity, Wallace will hire additional independent contractors (ICs) to make up the difference. These ICs will be employed on a short-term or project basis and will sign contracts that stipulate conditions and payment agreements.

All employees except the receptionists will be paid 50 percent of income from services they perform. Employees will be scheduled to work according to appointment times. The two receptionists will split the 60 hours per week that the spa is open and will receive an hourly wage of $11.

All staff will be entitled to the following, as recommended by the ISPA:

- a staff handbook, updated annually.

- up-to-date publications related to the spa industry and its individual specializations, including the ISPA Spa Operations Manual.

- a detailed job description that includes expectations, benchmarks, supervision structure, and other job details.

- job training in relation to the specific operations of Temple Creek Day Spa.

- monthly or as-requested meetings with Wallace to discuss questions, concerns, etc.

3.3. Professional and Advisory Support

Wallace is a member of two trade associations: the Day Spa Association (DSA) and the International Spa Association (ISPA). The DSA provides an online quarterly report (*In Touch Day Spa Industry eNews*) and the annual Evolution and Future of the Day Spa Industry, as well as other publications both online and in hard copy. Membership in DSA allows opportunities for certification, a free listing in the Day Spa Directory, and entrance into national trade shows, expos, and conferences. Membership in the DSA is $199 a year.

Founded in 1991, the ISPA has been the international voice of the spa industry for 20 years. It makes available to its members a plethora of resources, including conferences, certification courses, publications (including the magazines *Pulse* and *Live Spa*), expert advice and assistance, online networking opportunities, and many other benefits. The organization offers a "Spa Under Development" membership for up to one year for $550, after which members are transferred to a regular spa membership program, which runs $620 a year. Although the membership fees are high, the resources available through ISPA are invaluable and the investment well worth it; according to the association's website, ISPA member spas earn twice the revenue of nonmembers and experience double the spa visits of nonmembers.

Other support for Temple Creek will be provided by George Smith, attorney; Dennis Naught, insurance agent; Tina Caldwell, personal banker; and Sheila Johnston, accountant.

4.0. STRATEGIES

4.1. Business Strategy

At Temple Creek, the focus is on the client: providing what he or she wants/needs and making him or her want to return. Retention of clients is key. According to Maribeth Kuzmeski, author of *And the Clients Went Wild! How Savvy Professionals Win All the Business They Want* (Wiley, 2010), "You have to create strong emotional connections with your clients that won't quickly be cancelled out when they find a better deal somewhere else." There are several ways Temple Creek will achieve this goal during its day-to-day business. For example, staff are expected to know their regular clients by name, as well as know any background information about family, job, medical problems, etc., that the client has shared with them. This helps staff provide more personal service and helps the client feel welcome and comfortable. In addition to exemplary customer service, the emotional connection a client has with staff members at a spa becomes the driving reason they keep returning. Other ways Temple Creek seeks to impress and connect with customers is to provide them with extras at no charge, make special exceptions and personalized accommodations whenever possible, mail out appropriate cards at certain points in the customer's life (e.g., a sympathy card if someone in the family has passed away), and present them with personalized services that are tailored specifically to their situation or need.

4.2 Growth Strategy

The day spa industry is growing in many directions, and the trends that Temple Creek capitalizes on will depend on the local implications of these. For example, more older people are visiting spas, partly due to the growing population of aging baby boomers, so increasing services that cater toward them may be one avenue for growth. Another growing market in the spa industry is male clients. Although in the past a majority of customers have been female, more men are paying attention to the health of their skin as well as striving for a condition of overall wellness that can be enhanced by spa visits. According to "The State of Cosmetics in 2011," the market for men's skin care products increased more than five-fold between 1997 and 2009. This figure demonstrates the possibility that men visiting spas may become less of an anomaly in the future.

Other trends in the spa industry that will be embraced by Temple Creek include the increaesd demand for "mini" spa treatments, such as those lasting 15 to 30 minutes. These may be pared-down versions of the regular services the spa offers, or they may be full service but involve simultaneous treatments. For example, a client may receive a pedicure and a facial at the same time by two different specialists.

Temple Creek is prepared to explore any or all of these avenues in the future in order to generate more business. Such moves may require hiring more staff, expanding the facility, or a number of other changes.

5.0. PRODUCTS AND SERVICES

5.1. Description

Temple Creek offers the following services, either individually or in combination with other services, in a relaxed and screne environment:

- massage
- facials
- make-up application
- pedicures
- manicures
- hair cutting, coloring, styling
- waxing
- other services as requested

The spa also sells the products used in the spa, including Jane Iredale mineral make-up, Dr. Mark Lees' skin care products, and Redken hair products.

5.2 Unique Features

One of the special features of Temple Creek Day Spa is the level of personal service clients receive. Staff will be trained to always do certain things that help guests feel valued. Some of these tasks include greeting customers warmly, or if the client is new, shaking hands and introducing oneself and providing a tour of the spa and a brochure about services. Others include always escorting guests to the door and thanking them when they leave.

The most important special feature of Temple Creek is its staff, which will consistently display a cheerful and friendly manner. No employee at Temple Creek is allowed to break this convenant due to "just having a bad day." This is such an important aspect of business at Temple Creek that anyone who does not feel he or she can fulfill these requirements will not be hired as a staff member, and anyone who states they can meet these requirements and then later, on the job, shows that they actually cannot, will be released from their duties. It does take a special kind of person to work in a business that requires such consistent positive behavior—just as it takes a special kind of person to be a teacher, or a nurse, or an air traffic controller—and Temple Creek will be diligent and unmoving in its philosophy of hiring only the most positive and uplifting people. Indeed, a big part of the reason many people visit a spa is to feel special, pampered, and relaxed; these goals are not achievable with a cranky receptionist or an impatient hair stylist.

5.3. Pricing

Fees will be based on the menu of services that can be combined in various ways. Although there are several types of the following services (for example, Swedish massage vs. deep tissue massage), the following represents standard base fees for the services at Temple Creek:

	1/2 hour	1 hour
Massage	$40	$75
Facial	$30	$50
Make-up	$25	$40
Pedicure	$30	$50
Manicure	$25	$40
Haircuts/style/color	$30	$75

Clients may also purchase package deals, such as the following:

Packages

Ultimate package

4 hours: massage, facial, pedicure and manicure, make-up application, shampoo and cut/style	$200

Gold package

3 hours: massage, facial or make-up application, pedicure and manicure	$150

Silver package

2 hours: massage and facial	$100

Other special packages include those for couples, friends, pregnant women, and bridal parties and other special-occasion groups. Service packages will be revised and/or expanded based on demand during the first year of business.

Retail items such as shampoo and other hair products, make-up, skin care items, and so on will be priced based on wholesale plus the standard 50 percent.

6.0. MARKETING AND SALES

6.1. Advertising and Promotion

Advertising for Temple Creek will consist of the following: business cards, a professionally printed brochure, and a 2-inch by 3-inch display ad in the local telephone company's Yellow Pages. In addition, because Americans are spending increasing amounts of time online, Temple Creek will also make use of a professionally designed and easy-to-navigate web site and social media sites such as Facebook. The web site will include a basic price list, information about the staff and the facility (including photos), updated news on new treatments and products, guidelines for what guests can expect, and other important information. In addition, guests can make appointments online.

Word of mouth and referrals are especially important forms of advertising in the spa industry, as potential clients tend to trust their friends' and family's recommendations. Temple Creek will also offer discount coupons and special promotions throughout the year.

6.2. Cost

Total cost of start-up advertising is estimated at $800: $300 for the Yellow Pages ad, $400 for design and printing of the brochures, and $100 for business cards.

7.0. OPERATIONS

7.1. Customers

Customers of Temple Creek will be residents of New Town, Missouri, and the surrounding communities. New Town is a small city with a population of about 150,000, with an additional 50,000 people from smaller surrounding "sleeper towns." Most spa customers are women (although a growing number of men are visiting spas for services such as skin care and hair treatments), and a majority of customers come from an income bracket above $100,000 a year. Factoring in the surrounding communities, about 53 percent of the population of the New Town area is female and, of those, 20 percent have an annual household income above $100,000. New Town has a high percentage of upper-income residents due partly to the existence of four major hospitals and dozens of related clinics, which employ an average of one doctor per 100 residents.

7.2 Suppliers and Equipment

Products and equipment needed for the spa will be purchased from online wholesalers such as PureSpa Direct.com.

7.3. Hours

Temple Creek will be open seven days a week from 9:00 A.M. to 6:00 P.M. Monday through Friday, 8:00 A.M. to 6:00 P.M. on Saturday, and noon to 5:00 P.M. on Sunday. Walk-ins are accepted during these hours if they do not conflict with scheduled appointments, but most guests will schedule appointments ahead of time. The spa will be closed on major Christian holidays including Christmas and Easter.

7.4. Facility and Location

Temple Creek Day Spa will be located at 450 South Jasmine Street in northern New Town. Free parking is available in a paved lot adjacent to the building. The spa will feature a reception area in the front with a receptionist's desk and comfortable couches and chairs in a waiting area; a shelved retail area to the right of the front door where customers can try out and purchase products; a hair services area with three chairs; three private treatment rooms; a changing room/restroom; a larger open area with a counter and chairs where manicures, pedicures, and facials/make-up are done; an office; a unisex restroom; and a staff break room. Décor will follow a traditional style that incorporates soft colors, overstuffed furniture, unobtrusive artwork, and other features such as fresh flowers and tabletop fountains.

7.5. Legal Environment

In addition to a City of New Town business license, Temple Creek will be licensed by the state of Missouri.

Because sanitation is a major issue in the spa industry, Temple Creek will designate constant cleaning, disinfection, and sterilization of equipment, tools, and supplies as a vital and necessary part of the daily function of the spa. The spa will put into place written procedures based on legislation and guidelines from such agencies as the United States Environmental Protection Agency (EPA) and the Centers for Disease Control (CDC), as well as state agencies such as the Missouri State Board of Cosmetology. Temple Creek will not only meet these standards but will go above and beyond the requirements to ensure customers' safety and health.

8.0. FINANCIAL ANALYSIS

The most significant investment for Temple Creek Day Spa will be the initial remodeling of the space. Wallace intends to secure a business loan to cover start-up expenses.

	Start-up costs
Remodel	$20,000
Equipment	$ 5,000
Furniture and décor	$ 5,000
Retail inventory	$ 500
Advertising	$ 800
Memberships and dues	$ 750
Insurance	$ 200
Supplies	$ 500
Total	**$33,250**

Monthly expenses are estimated based on typical costs in the New Town area.

	Estimated monthly expenses, year 1
Spa supplies	$ 200
Office supplies	$ 100
Laundry/linens	$ 200
Insurance	$ 200
Utilities/phone	$ 300
Loan payment	$ 500
Receptionist salaries	$2,860
Rent	$2,500
Advertising	$ 200
Other miscellaneous	$ 500
Total average monthly expenses	**$7,560**

Income will depend on number of clients and services performed, which will be tracked meticulously. In the first year, Temple Creek expects to perform the equivalency of 10 one-hour services a day at an average cost of $50 an hour.

	Estimated annual income, year 2
Services	$181,500
Minus 50% commission to technicians	$ 90,750
Gross income from services	**$ 90,750**
Retail sales	$ 10,000
Minus 50% wholesale price	$ 5,000
Gross income from retail	**$ 5,000**
Total income from services & retail	**$ 95,750**
Minus expenses	$ 90,720
Total gross profit	**$ 5,030**

As Temple Creek grows it client base and establishes a reputation in the area, sales are expected to increase. In Year 2, Temple Creek estimated the client base will have grown to represent about 12 one-hour services per day and, by Year 3, 15. Both retail sales and expenses are estimated to grow about 10 percent per year.

	Estimated annual income, year 2
Services	$217,800
Minus 50% commission to technicians	$108,900
Gross income from services	**$108,900**
Retail sales	$ 11,000
Minus 50% wholesale price	$ 5,500
Gross income from retail	**$ 5,500**
Total income from services & retail	**$114,400**
Minus expenses	$ 99,792
Total gross profit	**$ 14,608**

	Estimated annual income, year 3
Services	$272,250
Minus 50% commission to technicians	$136,125
Gross income from services	**$136,125**
Retail sales	$ 12,100
Minus 50% wholesale price	$ 6,050
Gross income from retail	**$ 6,050**
Total income from services & retail	**$142,175**
Minus expenses	$109,771
Total gross profit	**$ 32,404**

DJ Service

Mid-Mo Music

3010 Fox Tail Lane
Columbia, MO 65201

Kari Lucke

Mid-Mo Music is a mobile DJ Service available for a variety of events and venues.

1.0. INTRODUCTION

1.1. Executive Summary

Mid-Mo Music is a mobile DJ and emcee service that strives to provide quality entertainment at special group events such as wedding receptions, dances, and other formal and informal parties.

1.2. Business Philosophy

As a member of the American Disc Jockey Association, owner Paul Johnson follows the organization's Code of Professional Conduct:

I commit myself to business excellence and will:

- Operate my business in an ethically sound manner while maintaining the highest standards of professional conduct.

- Abide by all laws and regulations governing my professional activities.

- Use legal forms of music and performance materials in the conduct of my entertainment services.

- Be honest and realistic conveying talent, abilities, and level of services to my clients.

- Deliver products and services to my clients, as promised, to the best of my abilities.

- Use a written contract clearly stating all charges, services, products, performance expectations and other essential information.

- Provide a safe work environment with adequate protection for my clients and their guests.

- Maintain adequate and appropriate insurance coverage for all business activities.

1.3. Goals and Objectives

The main objective of Mid-Mo Music is to create a customer base that will (a) use the service on a regular basis for annual or semiannual events (e.g., prom or other school dances) and (b) spread the word to other people about the quality and affordability of the service so that further business is generated.

1.4. Company History

Mid-Mo Music is a new company that has its roots in a small firm created by Paul Johnson in 2000. From 2000 to 2009, Paul operated Denver DJs LLC in a suburb of Denver, Colorado. Because Paul held a regular full-time job as well, the company was a part-time endeavor. Paul provided music and emcee services for approximately 15 weddings a year. In 2009, Paul moved to Columbia and now proposes to begin a full-time DJ service that targets both the wedding sector and other markets in the mid-Missouri area.

2.0. INDUSTRY AND MARKET

2.1. Industry Analysis

In the past few years, using a DJ service has become the standard procedure for many special events in the Midwest as well as around the country. Whereas one used to expect to see a live band when walking into the average high school prom or wedding reception, now it is much more common to see a DJ booth and accompanying equipment and lighting. One reason DJ services are more common is because they are often more economical. Live bands can charge up to several thousand dollars, whereas the average price for a DJ for one evening is around $500. In addition, live bands do not provide the variety of music and options that DJ services do.

In the wedding reception sector especially, the entertainment is a vital part of the experience for both the wedding party as well as the guests. According to research gathered by Redbeard Sound Company of Moberly, Missouri, the priority of choosing wedding reception entertainment tends to be trumped by such factors as attire, caterer, and reception site. However, one week after the wedding, 78 percent of brides surveyed said they would have made the entertainment their highest priority, and 72 percent said they would have spent more time choosing their reception entertainment. In addition, 81 percent of wedding guests said the thing they remember most about a wedding is the entertainment. These figures show that the entertainment provided by a DJ service is indeed very important. In other words, a good DJ service can "make" an event, whereas a bad one can ruin it.

2.2 Market Analysis

The market for Mid-Mo Music includes the following:

- brides and grooms planning a wedding reception and dance.

- junior highs, high schools, and colleges.

- to a lesser extent, others planning special events such as graduation, anniversary, retirement, or other kinds of parties.

Columbia, Missouri, is home to three junior highs, two high schools, two private colleges, and one major state university. The school market is harder to break into, as schools tend to use the same service once they have found one they are happy with. However, the people who plan dances and other events can change, and businesses come and go. Mid-Mo Music intends to maintain a presence in the school market in order to capitalize on any changes that provide an opportunity to gain an audience in this sector.

The wedding market is the sector with the most possibilities for bookings in the Columbia area. Columbia has a relatively young population, so there is an ongoing market for DJ services for wedding receptions. The market for other parties, such as graduation parties, is also seen as a strong growth area. Although fewer people invest in DJ services for such parties, there are still many families that spring for the all-out package when hosting such special events. Most of these customers are in a higher income and higher education bracket. According to the U.S. Census Bureau, more than half of Columbia residents have bachelor's degrees and more than a quarter hold master's degrees, making it the thirteenth most highly educated city in the United States. In addition, about 20 percent of the population reports a household income of more than $100,000.

2.3. Competition

There are approximately 10 other businesses in Columbia that provide the same services as Mid-Mo Music. Some of these include Music Express, Main Event Productions, and HB Sounds. None of the other DJ services in the area, however, match the level of professionalism exhibited by Mid-Mo Music. Several of the services have web sites, but many are amateur looking and/or hard to navigate and contain poorly written text and incomplete information. The web site for Mid-Mo Music, on the other hand, is professionally designed and written, reflecting the quality of service potential clients will expect. Mid-Mo Music's web site also provides a booking engine that tells customers immediately whether the service is available on the date of their event. Last, customers have the option to email Paul for a free consultation. With the vast increase in Internet use for researching such services, the importance of a professional-looking, complete, and easy-to-use web site is unquestionable and will provide Mid-Mo Music a competitive edge over other companies.

3.0. PERSONNEL

3.1. Management

Paul Johnson is the sole owner and operator of Mid-Mo Music. He brings 10 years of experience in the business from his previous endeavor in Denver. In addition, Paul is very outgoing, charismatic, and entertaining—all important characteristics of a DJ—and has a deep knowledge of and interest in all types of music. Paul is also very aware of social conventions and protocols, which is vital for providing entertainment that is both appropriate and in tune with the audience. Paul has the ability to read a crowd and play music that will produce the results his clients are looking for. At wedding receptions, he operates by a DJ creed that is important but sometimes overlooked: "never compete with the couple for popularity." In other words, Paul knows that the wedding reception is about the bride and groom, not about the DJ, and in accordance provides the background and environment to best showcase the couple. Some DJs make the mistake of thinking this is their "show"—and although it may look to the DJ like everything is going great if he or she has the full attention of the crowd, the bride and groom may not agree. Paul knows that the objective is not to get the crowd to laugh at his jokes or to applaud him for his music choice but rather to help everyone have a good time and make the bride and groom happy with their choice of entertainment.

3.2. Professional and Advisory Support

Paul belongs to the American DJ Association (ADJA) and benefits from such perks as a subscription to *Mobile Beat*, the only magazine dedicated to "the specialized interests of working mobile entertainers," which keeps him up-to-date on all aspects of the business; 25 free "Get-A-DJ-Fast" full-color postcards, used when customers have an immediate need for a DJ due to a no-show or other plan failure; a listing on the Association of Bridal Consultants web site as a vendor; discounts on insurance, advertising materials, and Visa/Mastercard merchant accounts; as well as a wide variety of other services including networking opportunities, legal advice, sales tips, and other related information.

4.0. STRATEGIES

4.1. Business Strategy

Mid-Mo Music's business strategy is simple: Provide professional-level, dependable, quality entertainment based on customers' needs and desires.

Professionalism is one of Paul's priorities, both when meeting with clients and when conducting the event. Clients are provided with a free consultation, during which Paul goes over the contract, obtains specifics about the event, and finds out what tone/atmosphere as well as what kind of music the customer would like at the event (e.g., for a wedding reception, couples can provide a list of songs or leave it up to Paul to create a list based on their preferences). One of Paul's lines to emphasize his professional approach is: "No rubber chickens! "—or clown costumes, or awkward, worn-out jokes, or any of the other faux pas that some may have witnessed at DJ "performances." Professionalism will also be apparent in Paul's attire, which will always be at least a suit or tie, depending on the event.

Mid-Mo Music also strives to be dependable. The true goal of the DJ at a wedding or any event is to provide entertainment and a relaxed atmosphere for the host as well as the guests. Clients do not want to worry about whether the DJ's equipment might break down—or even whether the DJ will show up at all. Paul arrives two hours before the start of the reception to set up and has backup items for every component of the service, from music files to lighting and microphones. In addition, at wedding receptions Paul coordinates with the other service providers, such as the caterer, photographer, and others, to ensure that the event proceeds without a hitch.

Mid-Mo Music also provides quality service. Part of this is related to the dependability factor, but it also encompasses the vital component of giving clients what they want. If a wedding couple wants all country music played at their reception, then that is what they get—no classic rock is thrown in because the DJ thinks it will liven things up. If a junior school principal requests only "clean" versions of the latest hits at a dance, then he does not have to worry about a slip-up resulting in several four-letter words being blared from the speakers into the crowd of young teenagers. If a bride makes a point of telling the DJ that her father is not present at the wedding due to family conflict, then she does not have to worry that the DJ will call for the father/daughter dance halfway into the reception. Other variable factors that are decided on ahead of time and followed by Paul include volume of music and level of audience participation.

Some of these details seem small but actually are the cornerstone of building a reliable and successful DJ service. Realizing that, and holding to the principles established in this business plan, are what make Mid-Mo Music a prime candidate for success.

4.2 Growth Strategy

The best way to grow a business such as a DJ service is to complete a successful event that makes clients happy—and then another, and then another, and so on. In this sense, growth comes from customers spreading the word that Mid-Mo Music can be counted on to provide great music, upbeat and entertaining emceeing, and all the details needed for a special event, like professional lighting and high-tech equipment. As Mid-Mo Music expands its list of satisfied customers, it will use testimonials, published on the web site, as a free and effective means of advertising.

5.0. PRODUCTS AND SERVICES

5.1. Description

Mid-Mo Music provides music and emcee services for any special event. A typical package includes a planning consultation, music list customization, at least four hours of music play time as well as any requested commentary or coordination, all the equipment needed, including lights and sound system, and set up and tear down. Mid-Mo Music also provides free services on its web site such as a checklist of "things to do" when planning a reception or dance, surveys that help customers determine what they want done as well as when and how, links to sites that list popular and traditional songs, and other helpful information.

Paul's music library consists of almost 5,000 songs from every genre, and requests not included in his database will be added with two weeks advance notice. Lighting options include everything from simple colored floodlights to more elaborate special-effects lighting.

5.2. Unique Features/Niche

DJ services may be known for a variety of features. One may be known for providing the best top 40 dance music for the high school crowd; another might be seen as a good "traditional" wedding DJ that provides everything from the Hokey Pokey and the Chicken Dance to the announcement of the bride and groom's entrance, the bouquet toss, and the first dance. Mid-Mo Music strives to fill two niches that can apply to every venue and event: It provides the highest level of professionalism and the latest in technology. As discussed previously, Mid-Mo Music aims to become known as the most professional DJ service in the area. In addition, the business will use the best technology to deliver music and entertainment to its audiences. This includes such features as the ability to download and play requested music instantly, and to play music from guests' iPods or cell phones; the use of wireless microphones and other high-tech equipment; and the ability to double-check every song for quality of sound and accuracy before playing. Music technology is one of Paul's passions, and keeping up-to-date with the latest available options is one of his priorities. This dedication will show in the quality and high level of service provided by Mid-Mo Music.

5.3. Pricing

The standard package is $500 and includes four hours of music and emceeing, all necessary equipment, and set up and tear down. Customers wanting more than four hours of entertainment pay an additional $50 an hour. Transportation is included up to 40 miles round-trip. Any further services are negotiated on an as-needed basis and are included in the contract.

6.0. MARKETING AND SALES

6.1. Advertising and Promotion

The two main forms of advertising will be a web site and a quarter-page ad in the Yellow Pages. In addition, Mid-Mo Music will be listed on DiscJockeys.com and several other web sites, including the Association of Bridal Consultants. Word of mouth will be an important, free form of advertising by the second six months of business. In the wedding segment, Paul will develop relationships with other businesses such as caterers, photographers, and reception-site providers in order to make connections with people who are in the business and can offer referrals.

6.2. Cost

The bulk of advertising costs will come from the Yellow Pages ad, which runs approximately $300 twice a year.

7.0. OPERATIONS

7.1. Customers

The main clientele for Mid-Mo Music will be Columbia-area residents. Columbia is a growing city, with a population that increased from 69,000 in 1990 to approximately 94,000 in 2009. The median household income of Columbia residents is $42,163, with a race distribution of 83 percent White, 9 percent Black, and 8 percent other.

Customers include brides and grooms planning a wedding, school event coordinators, and other people who are planning a special event that includes music. These could include anniversary parties, bar/bat mitzvahs, graduating parties, birthday parties, or other events.

7.2. Equipment

Equipment will be state-of-the-art and include the following:

- BOSE Professional Amplification System

- American DJ lighting system

- Apple Macbook computers

- Shure wireless microphones

- Numark mixers

7.3. Hours

Mid-Mo Music will operate on an appointment basis only, although the business phone line (Paul's cell phone) will be answered 24 hours a day. The busiest months are expected to be March through September, with December bringing in holiday business. A majority of bookings will occur on the weekends.

7.4. Facility and Location

Paul will operate Mid-Mo Music out of his home at 3010 Fox Tail Lane, Columbia, Missouri.

7.5. Legal Environment

Insurance is a vital aspect of protecting the business, thus Mid-Mo Music will hold a minimum of $1 million in liability insurance, in addition to insurance on the equipment and business vehicle.

All specifications of services provided, fees, expectations, and other details will be provided in a contract, which is signed by Paul and the customer after the initial consultation. A nonrefundable fee of $200 is required from the client on signing the contract, with the balance due on the day of the event.

8.0. FINANCIAL ANALYSIS

The projected earnings of Mid-Mo Music are conservative and based on average sales that Paul recorded as owner of Denver DJs LLC. Equipment costs include upgrading the systems Paul brings from Denver DJs LLC.

	Year 1	Year 2	Year 3
Sales	$30,000	$40,000	$50,000
Expenses			
Advertising	600	700	800
Vehicle/travel	700	850	1,000
Insurance	1,000	1,200	1,400
Equipment	800	1,000	1,200
Pro. fees	300	350	400
Misc.	500	750	1,000
Total	$ 3,900	$ 4,850	$ 5,800
Gross profit	$26,100	$35,150	$44,200

Food Truck

Eddie's Edibles Mobile Food

99 Broadway
New York, NY 10010

BizPlanDB.com

Eddie's Edibles Mobile Food will provide mobile sales of food to customers in the New York Metropolitan area.

1.0 EXECUTIVE SUMMARY

The purpose of this business plan is to raise $50,000 for the development of a food truck while showcasing the expected financials and operations over the next three years. Eddie's Edibles Mobile Food, Inc. ("the Company") is a New York based corporation that will provide mobile sales of food to customers in its targeted market. The Company was founded by Eddie Ostrander.

1.1 The Services

The primary revenue center for the business will come from the sale and distribution of food served from the food truck that will operate throughout the New York metropolitan area. The business will specialize in serving general food including:

- Hamburgers

- Hot Dogs

- Fries

- Beverage

- Ethnic Specialties

The third section of the business plan will further describe the services offered by Eddie's Edibles Mobile Food.

1.2 Financing

Mr. Ostrander is seeking to raise $50,000 as a bank loan. The interest rate and loan agreement are to be further discussed during negotiation. This business plan assumes that the business will receive a 10 year loan with a 9% fixed interest rate. The financing will be used for the following:

- Financing for the first six months of operation

- Capital to purchase a company vehicle and customize it to our needs

Mr. Ostrander will contribute $10,000 to the venture.

1.3 Mission Statement

Management's mission is to provide the New York metropolitan area (and other areas where the Company expands) with quality food served on a mobile basis.

1.4 Management Team

The Company was founded by Eddie Ostrander. Mr. Ostrander has more than 10 years of experience in the food and beverage industry. Through his expertise, he will be able to bring the operations of the business to profitability within its first year of operations.

1.5 Sales Forecasts

Mr. Ostrander expects a strong rate of growth at the start of operations. Below are the expected financials over the next three years.

Proforma profit and loss (yearly)

Year	1	2	3
Sales	$407,778	$440,400	$475,632
Operating costs	$236,809	$266,492	$297,851
EBITDA	$ 68,871	$ 63,642	$ 58,694
Taxes, interest, and depreciation	$ 33,754	$ 29,919	$ 27,833
Net profit	$ 35,117	$ 33,723	$ 30,861

Sales, operating costs, and profit forecast

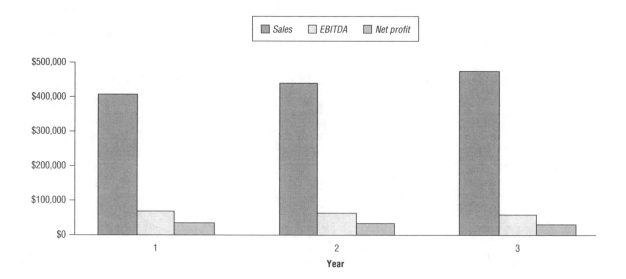

1.6 Expansion Plan

As time progresses, the Company will continually expand its presence throughout New York City by attending music concerts, trade shows, sporting events, and other venues that feature a large number of people. Additionally, over time, the business will generate a strong repeat customer base from the continual servicing of the routes planned by Management. In the fourth year of operation, Mr. Ostrander intends to acquire a second truck that will operate within selected sections of New York. It should also be noted, after the fifth year of operation, Management may acquire several additional mobile food service trucks in order to greatly expand the revenues of the business.

2.0 COMPANY AND FINANCING SUMMARY

2.1 Registered Name and Corporate Structure
The Company is registered as a corporation in the State of New York.

2.2 Required Funds
At this time, Eddie's Edibles Mobile Food requires $50,000 of debt funds. Below is a breakdown of how these funds will be used:

Projected startup costs

Initial lease payments and deposits	$10,000
Working capital	$15,000
FF&E	$ 5,000
Leasehold improvements	$ 1,500
Security deposits	$ 5,000
Insurance	$ 2,500
Food truck	$15,000
Marketing budget	$ 2,500
Miscellaneous and unforeseen costs	$ 3,500
Total startup costs	**$60,000**

Use of funds

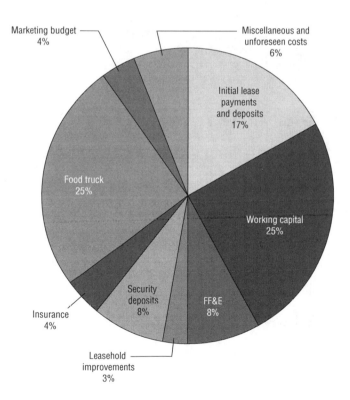

2.3 Investor Equity
Mr. Ostrander is not seeking an investment from a third party at this time.

2.4 Management Equity

Eddie Ostrander owns 100% of Eddie's Edibles Mobile Food, Inc.

2.5 Exit Strategy

If the business is very successful, Mr. Ostrander may seek to sell the business to a third party for a significant earnings multiple. Most likely, the Company will hire a qualified business broker to sell the business on behalf of Mr. Ostrander. Based on historical numbers, the business could fetch a sales premium of up to 4 times earnings.

3.0 PRODUCTS AND SERVICES

As stated in the executive summary, the primary focus of the Company's operations will be to provide freshly cooked food and beverages to the general public of the New York metropolitan area. The business will operate solely in a mobile capacity through its food truck. In the fourth year of operations, the Company intends to acquire a second truck that will operate through selected sections of New York City.

The business also intends to do a significant amount of sales via catering, delivery of pastries, and by having the truck positioned near popular events (such as concerts and sporting events) during the weekends. Approximately 1/3 of all food and beverage sale revenues will come from this aspect of Eddie's Edibles Mobile Food's operations.

During days of inclement weather, the Company intends to provide delivery services of food and beverages to third party restaurants, cafes, and other food serving venues so that the business can not only generate additional revenues but also reduce inventory spoilage.

4.0 STRATEGIC AND MARKET ANALYSIS

4.1 Economic Outlook

This section of the analysis will detail the economic climate, the food truck industry, the customer profile, and the competition that the business will face as it progresses through its business operations.

Currently, the economic market condition in the United States is in a recession recovery. However, Eddie's Edibles Mobile Food will be able to remain profitable and maintain a positive cash flow as the business produces very strong gross margins from the sale of its fare. Additionally, the business is mobile, and can be readily moved to areas where substantial sales can be made.

A primary concern for the Company is its ability to price its services affordably during times of economic recession or spikes of oil prices. This volatility in oil prices has caused the general public's discretionary income to decrease significantly over the last three months and will impact the cost of running our operations.

4.2 Industry Analysis

The coffee and non-alcoholic retail industry (including mobile food service businesses) has experienced a healthy level of growth over the past decade. The U.S. Economic Census estimates that there are over 190,000 individual cafes, mobile food service businesses, and specialty food restaurants in the United States. This number is expected to increase at a rate of 5% per annum. While the growth rate of the number of establishments has increased 5% per year, the revenues generated per establishment have increased at a rate of 10% per year.

As the country is currently in recession, the industry's revenues are expected to remain flat until the economic recovery period begins.

4.3 Customer Profile

As the business intends to operate among several sections of New York, it is hard to categorize the "average" customer of Eddie's Edibles Mobile Food. Management expects a broad range of customers including employees within office buildings in New York City, tourists, and residents that simply want a quick meal as they go through their day.

Based on the size on New York City, there are more than 2 million people living and working within the New York metropolitan area that could become potential customers of Eddie's Edibles Mobile Food. As everyone needs to eat, especially during lunch time hours, it is hard to categorize the competition that the business will face as it progresses through its operations.

4.4 Competition

There are a number of food truck vendors operating throughout the greater New York metropolitan area. As stated above, there are more than 2 million people living in working directly within Manhattan. Based on estimates from the US Economic Census, there are more than 10,000 food trucks and street vendors operating within this market. However, Eddie's Edibles Mobile Food will differentiate itself by providing specialized foods including organic entrees.

5.0 MARKETING PLAN

Eddie's Edibles Mobile Food intends to maintain an extensive marketing campaign that will ensure maximum visibility for the business in its targeted market. Below is an overview of the marketing strategies and objectives of Eddie's Edibles Mobile Food.

5.1 Marketing Objectives

- Establish a strong presence in the New York metropolitan area via prominent signage on the mobile food truck.
- Heavily advertise the Company's large selection of food and beverages.
- Establish connections with local suppliers and vendors.

5.2 Marketing Strategies

The primary method of marketing to be used by the Company will be the highly visible signage affixed to the mobile truck. This signage will focus on the affordable nature of the Company's wide selection of food and beverages.

In regards to the catering aspect of the business, the Company intends to send packets of information to event planners throughout New York City that will call on the business for catering needs. As the business serves a broad variety of food and beverages, the mobile food truck will be able to effectively provide catering services for a broad spectrum of casual events.

Additionally, the business will develop relationships with venue managers that will allow Eddie's Edibles Mobile Food to place the truck outside of these locations so that sales can be made. These venues will include sports stadiums, concerts, and other large-scale entertainment events.

The business will also maintain a website that showcases the mobile food service truck, the menu, information about catering, and other relevant contact information. This website will be listed on major search engines such as Google, Yahoo, and MSN Live.

5.3 Pricing

Management anticipates that the average order will generate $5 to $10 for the business, which includes the purchase of an entrée and a beverage. Gross margins from each sale will be approximately 75%.

6.0 ORGANIZATIONAL PLAN AND PERSONNEL SUMMARY

6.1 Corporate Organization

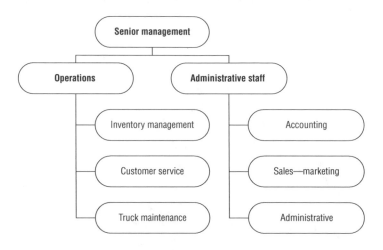

6.2 Organizational Budget

Personnel plan—yearly

Year	1	2	3
Owner	$ 35,000	$ 36,050	$ 37,132
Manager	$ 27,500	$ 28,325	$ 29,175
Owner's assistant	$ 22,500	$ 23,175	$ 23,870
Drivers	$ 52,500	$ 72,100	$ 92,829
Accounting (P/T)	$ 25,000	$ 25,750	$ 26,523
Total	**$162,500**	**$185,400**	**$209,528**

Numbers of personnel

Owner	1	1	1
Manager	1	1	1
Owner's assistant	1	1	1
Drivers	3	4	5
Accounting (P/T)	2	2	2
Totals	**8**	**9**	**10**

Personnel expense breakdown

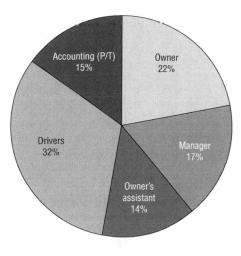

Owner 22%

Manager 17%

Owner's assistant 14%

Drivers 32%

Accounting (P/T) 15%

7.0 FINANCIAL PLAN

7.1 Underlying Assumptions

The Company has based its proforma financial statements on the following:

- Eddie's Edibles Mobile Food will have an annual revenue growth rate of 16% per year.

- The Owner will acquire $50,000 of debt funds to develop the business.

- The loan will have a 10 year term with a 9% interest rate.

7.2 Sensitivity Analysis

The Company's revenues are somewhat sensitive to the overall conditions of the economy. As the US is currently outgoing a recession, the Company may have a decrease in its top line revenues as people will demand fewer café beverages/food products from mobile food locations. However, the Company's revenues provide high levels of operating income for the business, and Eddie's Edibles Mobile Food would need to have a significant decrease in its top line income before the Company becomes unprofitable. Additionally, the business is not bound by location, and the Company can relocate at any time to more populous areas to secure sales.

7.3 Source of Funds

Financing

Equity contributions	
Management investment	$ 10,000.00
Total equity financing	**$ 10,000.00**
Banks and lenders	
Banks and lenders	$ 100,000.00
Total debt financing	**$100,000.00**
Total financing	**$110,000.00**

7.4 General Assumptions

General assumptions

Year	1	2	3
Short term interest rate	9.5%	9.5%	9.5%
Long term interest rate	10.0%	10.0%	10.0%
Federal tax rate	33.0%	33.0%	33.0%
State tax rate	5.0%	5.0%	5.0%
Personnel taxes	15.0%	15.0%	15.0%

7.5 Profit and Loss Statements

Proforma profit and loss (yearly)

Year	1	2	3
Sales	**$407,778**	**$440,400**	**$475,632**
Cost of goods sold	$102,098	$110,266	$119,087
Gross margin	74.96%	74.96%	74.96%
Operating income	**$305,680**	**$330,135**	**$356,545**
Expenses			
Payroll	$162,500	$185,400	$209,528
General and administrative	$ 13,200	$ 13,728	$ 14,277
Marketing expenses	$ 2,039	$ 2,202	$ 2,378
Professional fees and licensure	$ 5,219	$ 5,376	$ 5,537
Insurance costs	$ 1,987	$ 2,086	$ 2,191
Travel and vehicle costs	$ 17,596	$ 19,356	$ 21,291
Rent and utilities	$ 5,000	$ 5,250	$ 5,513
Miscellaneous costs	$ 4,893	$ 5,285	$ 5,708
Payroll taxes	$ 24,375	$ 27,810	$ 31,429
Total operating costs	**$236,809**	**$266,492**	**$297,851**
EBITDA	**$ 68,871**	**$ 63,642**	**$ 58,694**
Federal income tax	$ 22,727	$ 19,660	$ 18,137
State income tax	$ 3,444	$ 2,979	$ 2,748
Interest expense	$ 4,369	$ 4,066	$ 3,734
Depreciation expenses	$ 3,214	$ 3,214	$ 3,214
Net profit	**$ 35,117**	**$ 33,723**	**$ 30,861**
Profit margin	**8.61%**	**7.66%**	**6.49%**

Sales, operating costs, and profit forecast

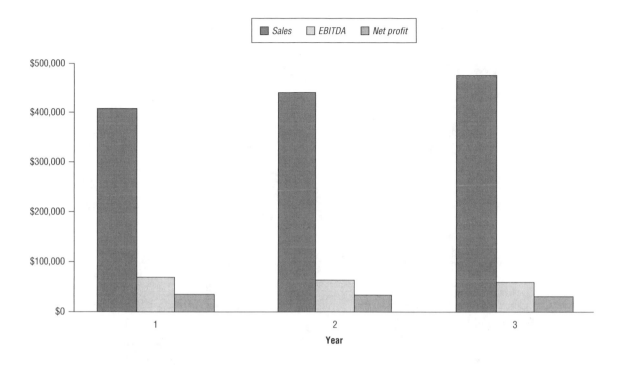

7.6 Cash Flow Analysis

Proforma cash flow analysis—yearly

Year	1	2	3
Cash from operations	$ 38,331	$36,937	$34,075
Cash from receivables	$ 0	$ 0	$ 0
Operating cash inflow	**$ 38,331**	**$36,937**	**$34,075**
Other cash inflows			
Equity investment	$ 10,000	$ 0	$ 0
Increased borrowings	$ 50,000	$ 0	$ 0
Sales of business assets	$ 0	$ 0	$ 0
A/P increases	$ 37,902	$43,587	$50,125
Total other cash inflows	**$ 97,902**	**$43,587**	**$50,125**
Total cash inflow	**$136,233**	**$80,525**	**$84,201**
Cash outflows			
Repayment of principal	$ 3,232	$ 3,535	$ 3,866
A/P decreases	$ 24,897	$29,876	$35,852
A/R increases	$ 0	$ 0	$ 0
Asset purchases	$ 45,000	$ 5,541	$ 5,111
Dividends	$ 30,665	$29,550	$27,260
Total cash outflows	**$103,794**	**$68,502**	**$72,090**
Net cash flow	**$ 32,440**	**$12,023**	**$12,111**
Cash balance	**$ 32,440**	**$44,462**	**$56,573**

Proforma cash flow (yearly)

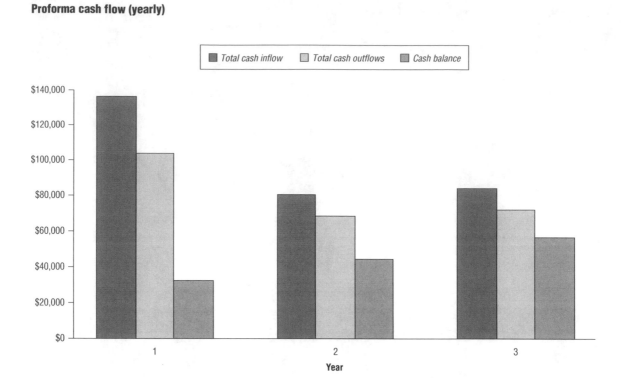

7.7 Balance Sheet

Proforma balance sheet—yearly

Year	1	2	3
Assets			
Cash	$32,440	$44,462	$ 56,573
Amortized development/expansion costs	$25,000	$25,554	$ 26,065
Food truck	$15,000	$19,155	$ 22,989
FF&E	$ 5,000	$ 5,831	$ 6,598
Accumulated depreciation	($ 3,214)	($ 6,429)	($ 9,643)
Total assets	**$74,225**	**$88,575**	**$102,583**
Liabilities and equity			
Accounts payable	$13,005	$26,716	$ 40,990
Long term liabilities	$46,768	$43,233	$ 39,699
Other liabilities	$ 0	$ 0	$ 0
Total liabilities	**$59,773**	**$69,949**	**$ 80,688**
Net worth	**$14,452**	**$18,625**	**$ 21,894**
Total liabilities and equity	**$74,225**	**$88,575**	**$102,583**

Proforma balance sheet

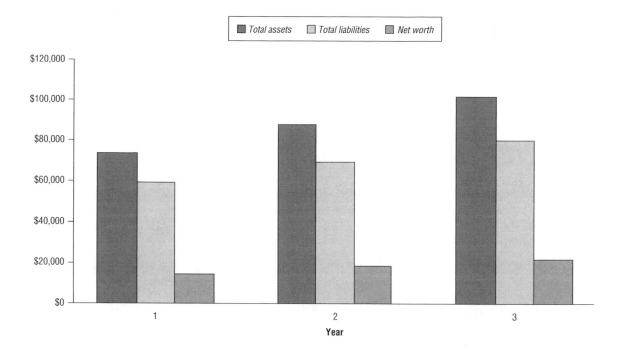

7.8 Breakeven Analysis

Monthly break even analysis

Year	1	2	3
Monthly revenue	$ 26,325	$ 29,625	$ 33,111
Yearly revenue	$315,904	$355,501	$397,334

Break even analysis

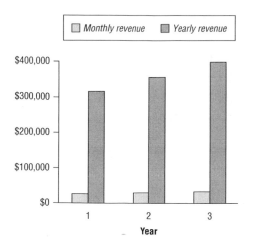

7.9 Business Ratios

Business ratios—yearly

Year	1	2	3
Sales			
Sales growth	0.0%	8.0%	8.0%
Gross margin	75.0%	75.0%	75.0%
Financials			
Profit margin	8.61%	7.66%	6.49%
Assets to liabilities	1.24	1.27	1.27
Equity to liabilities	0.24	0.27	0.27
Assets to equity	5.14	4.76	4.69
Liquidity			
Acid test	0.54	0.64	0.70
Cash to assets	0.44	0.50	0.55

7.10 Three Year Profit and Loss Statement

Profit and loss statement (first year)

Months	1	2	3	4	5	6	7
Sales	**$33,250**	**$33,383**	**$33,516**	**$33,649**	**$33,782**	**$33,915**	**$34,048**
Cost of goods sold	$ 8,325	$ 8,358	$ 8,392	$ 8,425	$ 8,458	$ 8,492	$ 8,525
Gross margin	75.0%	75.0%	75.0%	75.0%	75.0%	75.0%	75.0%
Operating income	**$24,925**	**$25,025**	**$25,124**	**$25,224**	**$25,324**	**$25,424**	**$25,523**
Expenses							
Payroll	$13,542	$13,542	$13,542	$13,542	$13,542	$13,542	$13,542
General and administrative	$ 1,100	$ 1,100	$ 1,100	$ 1,100	$ 1,100	$ 1,100	$ 1,100
Marketing expenses	$ 170	$ 170	$ 170	$ 170	$ 170	$ 170	$ 170
Professional fees and licensure	$ 435	$ 435	$ 435	$ 435	$ 435	$ 435	$ 435
Insurance costs	$ 166	$ 166	$ 166	$ 166	$ 166	$ 166	$ 166
Travel and vehicle costs	$ 1,466	$ 1,466	$ 1,466	$ 1,466	$ 1,466	$ 1,466	$ 1,466
Rent and utilities	$ 417	$ 417	$ 417	$ 417	$ 417	$ 417	$ 417
Miscellaneous costs	$ 408	$ 408	$ 408	$ 408	$ 408	$ 408	$ 408
Payroll taxes	$ 2,031	$ 2,031	$ 2,031	$ 2,031	$ 2,031	$ 2,031	$ 2,031
Total operating costs	**$19,734**	**$19,734**	**$19,734**	**$19,734**	**$19,734**	**$19,734**	**$19,734**
EBITDA	**$ 5,191**	**$ 5,291**	**$ 5,390**	**$ 5,490**	**$ 5,590**	**$ 5,689**	**$ 5,789**
Federal income tax	$ 1,853	$ 1,861	$ 1,868	$ 1,875	$ 1,883	$ 1,890	$ 1,898
State income tax	$ 281	$ 282	$ 283	$ 284	$ 285	$ 286	$ 288
Interest expense	$ 375	$ 373	$ 371	$ 369	$ 367	$ 365	$ 363
Depreciation expense	$ 268	$ 268	$ 268	$ 268	$ 268	$ 268	$ 268
Net profit	**$ 2,414**	**$ 2,507**	**$ 2,600**	**$ 2,693**	**$ 2,787**	**$ 2,880**	**$ 2,973**

Profit and loss statement (first year cont.)

Months	8	9	10	11	12	1
Sales	$34,181	$34,314	$34,447	$34,580	$34,713	$407,778
Cost of goods sold	$ 8,558	$ 8,591	$ 8,625	$ 8,658	$ 8,691	$102,098
Gross margin	75.0%	75.0%	75.0%	75.0%	75.0%	75.0%
Operating income	$25,623	$25,723	$25,822	$25,922	$26,022	$305,680
Expenses						
Payroll	$13,542	$13,542	$13,542	$13,542	$13,542	$162,500
General and administrative	$ 1,100	$ 1,100	$ 1,100	$ 1,100	$ 1,100	$ 13,200
Marketing expenses	$ 170	$ 170	$ 170	$ 170	$ 170	$ 2,039
Professional fees and licensure	$ 435	$ 435	$ 435	$ 435	$ 435	$ 5,219
Insurance costs	$ 166	$ 166	$ 166	$ 166	$ 166	$ 1,987
Travel and vehicle costs	$ 1,466	$ 1,466	$ 1,466	$ 1,466	$ 1,466	$ 17,596
Rent and utilities	$ 417	$ 417	$ 417	$ 417	$ 417	$ 5,000
Miscellaneous costs	$ 408	$ 408	$ 408	$ 408	$ 408	$ 4,893
Payroll taxes	$ 2,031	$ 2,031	$ 2,031	$ 2,031	$ 2,031	$ 24,375
Total operating costs	$19,734	$19,734	$19,734	$19,734	$19,734	$236,809
EBITDA	$ 5,889	$ 5,988	$ 6,088	$ 6,188	$ 6,288	$ 68,871
Federal income tax	$ 1,905	$ 1,912	$ 1,920	$ 1,927	$ 1,935	$ 22,727
State income tax	$ 289	$ 290	$ 291	$ 292	$ 293	$ 3,444
Interest expense	$ 361	$ 359	$ 357	$ 355	$ 353	$ 4,369
Depreciation expense	$ 268	$ 268	$ 268	$ 268	$ 268	$ 3,214
Net profit	$ 3,066	$ 3,159	$ 3,253	$ 3,346	$ 3,439	$ 35,117

Profit and loss statement (second year)

Quarter	Q1	2 Q2	Q3	Q4	2
Sales	$88,080	$110,100	$118,908	$123,312	$440,400
Cost of goods sold	$22,053	$ 27,566	$ 29,772	$ 30,874	$110,266
Gross margin	75.0%	75.0%	75.0%	75.0%	75.0%
Operating income	$66,027	$ 82,534	$ 89,136	$ 92,438	$330,135
Expenses					
Payroll	$37,080	$ 46,350	$ 50,058	$ 51,912	$185,400
General and administrative	$ 2,746	$ 3,432	$ 3,707	$ 3,844	$ 13,728
Marketing expenses	$ 440	$ 551	$ 595	$ 617	$ 2,202
Professional fees and licensure	$ 1,075	$ 1,344	$ 1,451	$ 1,505	$ 5,376
Insurance costs	$ 417	$ 522	$ 563	$ 584	$ 2,086
Travel and vehicle costs	$ 3,871	$ 4,839	$ 5,226	$ 5,420	$ 19,356
Rent and utilities	$ 1,050	$ 1,313	$ 1,418	$ 1,470	$ 5,250
Miscellaneous costs	$ 1,057	$ 1,321	$ 1,427	$ 1,480	$ 5,285
Payroll taxes	$ 5,562	$ 6,953	$ 7,509	$ 7,787	$ 27,810
Total operating costs	$53,298	$ 66,623	$ 71,953	$ 74,618	$266,492
EBITDA	$12,728	$ 15,911	$ 17,183	$ 17,820	$ 63,642
Federal income tax	$ 3,932	$ 4,915	$ 5,308	$ 5,505	$ 19,660
State income tax	$ 596	$ 745	$ 804	$ 834	$ 2,979
Interest expense	$ 1,046	$ 1,027	$ 1,007	$ 986	$ 4,066
Depreciation expense	$ 804	$ 804	$ 804	$ 804	$ 3,214
Net profit	$ 6,351	$ 8,421	$ 9,261	$ 9,691	$ 33,723

Profit and loss statement (third year)

Quarter	Q1	3 Q2	Q3	Q4	3
Sales	$95,126	$118,908	$128,421	$133,177	$475,632
Cost of goods sold	$23,817	$ 29,772	$ 32,153	$ 33,344	$119,087
Gross margin	75.0%	75.0%	75.0%	75.0%	75.0%
Operating income	$71,309	$ 89,136	$ 96,267	$ 99,833	$356,545
Expenses					
Payroll	$41,906	$ 52,382	$ 56,572	$ 58,668	$209,528
General and administrative	$ 2,855	$ 3,569	$ 3,855	$ 3,998	$ 14,277
Marketing expenses	$ 476	$ 595	$ 642	$ 666	$ 2,378
Professional fees and licensure	$ 1,107	$ 1,384	$ 1,495	$ 1,550	$ 5,537
Insurance costs	$ 438	$ 548	$ 591	$ 613	$ 2,191
Travel and vehicle costs	$ 4,258	$ 5,323	$ 5,749	$ 5,962	$ 21,291
Rent and utilities	$ 1,103	$ 1,378	$ 1,488	$ 1,544	$ 5,513
Miscellaneous costs	$ 1,142	$ 1,427	$ 1,541	$ 1,598	$ 5,708
Payroll taxes	$ 6,286	$ 7,857	$ 8,486	$ 8,800	$ 31,429
Total operating costs	$59,570	$ 74,463	$ 80,420	$ 83,398	$297,851
EBITDA	$11,739	$ 14,674	$ 15,847	$ 16,434	$ 58,694
Federal income tax	$ 3,627	$ 4,534	$ 4,897	$ 5,078	$ 18,137
State income tax	$ 550	$ 687	$ 742	$ 769	$ 2,748
Interest expense	$ 966	$ 945	$ 923	$ 901	$ 3,734
Depreciation expense	$ 804	$ 804	$ 804	$ 804	$ 3,214
Net profit	$ 5,793	$ 7,704	$ 8,482	$ 8,882	$ 30,861

7.11 Three Year Cash Flow Analysis

Cash flow analysis (first year)

Month	1	2	3	4	5	6	7	8
Cash from operations	$ 2,682	$ 2,775	$ 2,868	$ 2,961	$ 3,054	$ 3,148	$ 3,241	$ 3,334
Cash from receivables	$ 0	$ 0	$ 0	$ 0	$ 0	$ 0	$ 0	$ 0
Operating cash inflow	$ 2,682	$ 2,775	$ 2,868	$ 2,961	$ 3,054	$ 3,148	$ 3,241	$ 3,334
Other cash inflows								
Equity investment	$10,000	$ 0	$ 0	$ 0	$ 0	$ 0	$ 0	$ 0
Increased borrowings	$50,000	$ 0	$ 0	$ 0	$ 0	$ 0	$ 0	$ 0
Sales of business assets	$ 0	$ 0	$ 0	$ 0	$ 0	$ 0	$ 0	$ 0
A/P increases	$ 3,159	$ 3,159	$ 3,159	$ 3,159	$ 3,159	$ 3,159	$ 3,159	$ 3,159
Total other cash inflows	$63,159	$ 3,159	$ 3,159	$ 3,159	$ 3,159	$ 3,159	$ 3,159	$ 3,159
Total cash inflow	$65,840	$ 5,934	$ 6,027	$ 6,120	$ 6,213	$ 6,306	$ 6,399	$ 6,492
Cash outflows								
Repayment of principal	$ 258	$ 260	$ 262	$ 264	$ 266	$ 268	$ 270	$ 272
A/P decreases	$ 2,075	$ 2,075	$ 2,075	$ 2,075	$ 2,075	$ 2,075	$ 2,075	$ 2,075
A/R increases	$ 0	$ 0	$ 0	$ 0	$ 0	$ 0	$ 0	$ 0
Asset purchases	$45,000	$ 0	$ 0	$ 0	$ 0	$ 0	$ 0	$ 0
Dividends	$ 0	$ 0	$ 0	$ 0	$ 0	$ 0	$ 0	$ 0
Total cash outflows	$47,333	$ 2,335	$ 2,337	$ 2,339	$ 2,341	$ 2,343	$ 2,345	$ 2,347
Net cash flow	$18,507	$ 3,598	$ 3,690	$ 3,781	$ 3,872	$ 3,963	$ 4,054	$ 4,145
Cash balance	$18,507	$22,106	$25,795	$29,576	$33,448	$37,411	$41,466	$45,611

Cash flow analysis (first year cont.)

Month	9	10	11	12	1
Cash from operations	$ 3,427	$ 3,520	$ 3,614	$ 3,707	$ 38,331
Cash from receivables	$ 0	$ 0	$ 0	$ 0	$ 0
Operating cash inflow	**$ 3,427**	**$ 3,520**	**$ 3,614**	**$ 3,707**	**$ 38,331**
Other cash inflows					
Equity investment	$ 0	$ 0	$ 0	$ 0	$ 10,000
Increased borrowings	$ 0	$ 0	$ 0	$ 0	$ 50,000
Sales of business assets	$ 0	$ 0	$ 0	$ 0	$ 0
A/P increases	$ 3,159	$ 3,159	$ 3,159	$ 3,159	$ 37,902
Total other cash inflows	**$ 3,159**	**$ 3,159**	**$ 3,159**	**$ 3,159**	**$ 97,902**
Total cash inflow	**$ 6,586**	**$ 6,679**	**$ 6,772**	**$ 6,865**	**$136,233**
Cash outflows					
Repayment of principal	$ 273	$ 276	$ 278	$ 281	$ 3,232
A/P decreases	$ 2,075	$ 2,075	$ 2,075	$ 2,075	$ 24,897
A/R increases	$ 0	$ 0	$ 0	$ 0	$ 0
Asset purchases	$ 0	$ 0	$ 0	$ 0	$ 45,000
Dividends	$ 0	$ 0	$ 0	$30,665	$ 30,665
Total cash outflows	**$ 2,348**	**$ 2,351**	**$ 2,353**	**$33,020**	**$103,794**
Net cash flow	**$ 4,238**	**$ 4,328**	**$ 4,419**	**−$26,155**	**$ 32,440**
Cash balance	**$49,849**	**$54,176**	**$58,595**	**$32,440**	**$ 32,440**

Cash flow analysis (second year)

Quarter	Q1	2 Q2	Q3	Q4	2
Cash from operations	$ 7,387	$ 9,234	$ 9,973	$10,342	$36,937
Cash from receivables	$ 0	$ 0	$ 0	$ 0	$ 0
Operating cash inflow	**$ 7,387**	**$ 9,234**	**$ 9,973**	**$10,342**	**$36,937**
Other cash inflows					
Equity investment	$ 0	$ 0	$ 0	$ 0	$ 0
Increased borrowings	$ 0	$ 0	$ 0	$ 0	$ 0
Sales of business assets	$ 0	$ 0	$ 0	$ 0	$ 0
A/P increases	$ 8,717	$10,897	$11,769	$12,204	$43,587
Total other cash inflows	**$ 8,717**	**$10,897**	**$11,769**	**$12,204**	**$43,587**
Total cash inflow	**$16,105**	**$20,131**	**$21,742**	**$22,547**	**$80,525**
Cash outflows					
Repayment of principal	$ 854	$ 874	$ 893	$ 914	$ 3,535
A/P decreases	$ 5,975	$ 7,469	$ 8,067	$ 8,365	$29,876
A/R increases	$ 0	$ 0	$ 0	$ 0	$ 0
Asset purchases	$ 1,108	$ 1,385	$ 1,496	$ 1,551	$ 5,541
Dividends	$ 5,910	$ 7,387	$ 7,978	$ 8,274	$29,550
Total cash outflows	**$13,848**	**$17,115**	**$18,434**	**$19,104**	**$68,502**
Net cash flow	**$ 2,257**	**$ 3,016**	**$ 3,307**	**$ 3,443**	**$12,023**
Cash balance	**$34,697**	**$37,713**	**$41,020**	**$44,462**	**$44,462**

Cash flow analysis (third year)

Quarter	Q1	3 Q2	Q3	Q4	3
Cash from operations	$ 6,815	$ 8,519	$ 9,200	$ 9,541	$34,075
Cash from receivables	$ 0	$ 0	$ 0	$ 0	$ 0
Operating cash inflow	**$ 6,815**	**$ 8,519**	**$ 9,200**	**$ 9,541**	**$34,075**
Other cash inflows					
Equity investment	$ 0	$ 0	$ 0	$ 0	$ 0
Increased borrowings	$ 0	$ 0	$ 0	$ 0	$ 0
Sales of business assets	$ 0	$ 0	$ 0	$ 0	$ 0
A/P increases	$10,025	$12,531	$13,534	$14,035	$50,125
Total other cash inflows	**$10,025**	**$12,531**	**$13,534**	**$14,035**	**$50,125**
Total cash inflow	**$16,840**	**$21,050**	**$22,734**	**$23,576**	**$84,201**
Cash outflows					
Repayment of principal	$ 934	$ 956	$ 977	$ 999	$ 3,866
A/P decreases	$ 7,170	$ 8,963	$ 9,680	$10,038	$35,852
A/R increases	$ 0	$ 0	$ 0	$ 0	$ 0
Asset purchases	$ 1,022	$ 1,278	$ 1,380	$ 1,431	$ 5,111
Dividends	$ 5,452	$ 6,815	$ 7,360	$ 7,633	$27,260
Total cash outflows	**$14,579**	**$18,011**	**$19,397**	**$20,102**	**$72,090**
Net cash flow	**$ 2,261**	**$ 3,039**	**$ 3,337**	**$ 3,474**	**$12,111**
Cash balance	**$46,724**	**$49,762**	**$53,099**	**$56,573**	**$56,573**

Go Kart Track
Supersonic Racing

17239 Menahan St.
Flushing, NY 11385

BizPlanDB.com

The purpose of this business plan is to raise $350,000 for the development of a go kart track while showcasing the expected financials and operations over the next three years. Supersonic Racing, Inc. ("the Company") is a New York based corporation that will provide usage of go karts, food/concessions, and event hosting to customers in its targeted market. The Company was founded by Mitch Applegate.

1.0 EXECUTIVE SUMMARY

The purpose of this business plan is to raise $350,000 for the development of a go kart track while showcasing the expected financials and operations over the next three years. Supersonic Racing, Inc. ("the Company") is a New York based corporation that will provide usage of go karts, food/concessions, and event hosting to customers in its targeted market. The Company was founded by Mitch Applegate.

1.1 The Services

The primary revenue stream for the business will come from the ongoing usage of the Company's go karts within the business' state-of-the-art facility. The Company will have approximately 30 go karts in its inventory. All go karts owned by the business will have proper safety controls to ensure maximum speed limits.

The secondary streams of revenue for the business will come from the sale of food, concessions, and event hosting services.

The third section of the business plan will further describe the services offered by Supersonic Racing.

1.2 Financing

Mr. Applegate is seeking to raise $350,000 from a bank loan. The interest rate and loan agreement are to be further discussed during negotiation. This business plan assumes that the business will receive a 10 year loan with a 9% fixed interest rate. The financing will be used for the following:

- Development of the facility.

- Financing for the first six months of operation.

- Capital to purchase go karts.

- Financing for the Company's marketing budget.

Mr. Applegate will contribute $50,000 to the venture.

51

1.3 Mission Statement

Supersonic Racing, Inc.'s mission is to become the recognized leader in its targeted market for providing safe and fun go kart usage to the general public.

1.4 Management Team

The Company was founded by Mitch Applegate. Mr. Applegate has more than 10 years of experience in the retail management industry. Through his expertise, he will be able to bring the operations of the business to profitability within its first year of operations.

1.5 Sales Forecasts

Mr. Applegate expects a strong rate of growth at the start of operations. Below are the expected financials over the next three years.

Proforma profit and loss (yearly)

Year	1	2	3
Sales	$784,890	$863,379	$949,717
Operating costs	$472,495	$490,604	$509,603
EBITDA	$164,138	$209,692	$260,723
Taxes, Interest, and depreciation	$117,419	$121,792	$139,745
Net profit	$ 46,719	$ 87,900	$120,978

Sales, operating costs, and profit forecast

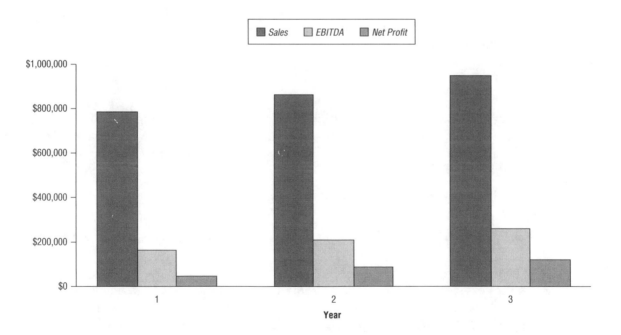

1.6 Expansion Plan

Mr. Applegate expects that the business will aggressively expand during the first three years of operation. He intends to implement marketing campaigns that will effectively target individuals within the target market.

2.0 COMPANY AND FINANCING SUMMARY

2.1 Registered Name and Corporate Structure

The Company is registered as a corporation in the State of New York.

2.2 Required Funds

At this time, Supersonic Racing requires $350,000 of debt funds. Below is a breakdown of how these funds will be used:

Projected startup costs

Land acquisition and track development	$125,000
Working capital	$ 40,000
FF&E	$ 50,000
Land improvements	$ 25,000
Security deposits	$ 15,000
Insurance	$ 25,000
Go Karts	$100,000
Marketing budget	$ 17,500
Miscellaneous and unforeseen costs	$ 2,500
Total startup costs	**$400,000**

Use of funds

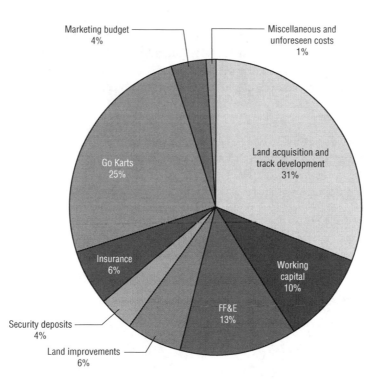

2.3 Investor Equity

Mr. Applegate is not seeking an investment from a third party at this time.

2.4 Management Equity

Mitch Applegate owns 100% of Supersonic Racing, Inc.

2.5 Exit Strategy

If the business is very successful, Mr. Applegate may seek to sell the business to a third party for a significant earnings multiple. Most likely, the Company will hire a qualified business broker to sell the business on behalf of Supersonic Racing. Based on historical numbers, the business could fetch a sales premium of up to six to nine times earnings.

3.0 PRODUCTS AND SERVICES

Below is a description of the services offered by Supersonic Racing.

3.1 Usage of Go Karts

The primary revenue stream for the Company will come from the ongoing usage of the business' go kart track. As stated in the executive summary, the Company's outdoor track will be able to accommodate up to 30 go karts. At all times, the Company will require users to wear helmets and to abide by several rules that will be posted throughout the facility. Individuals that break these rules will be barred from using Supersonic Racing. Additionally, the minimum age for a go kart user will be 12 years old. A minimum height requirement of 48 inches will also be required.

Usage of the Company's go karts will generate substantial gross margins for the Company.

3.2 Sales of Food and Concessions

The business will also maintain an area of the retail facility that will provide limited food and beverage service. This revenue center is extremely important for the business because it will provide an additional stream of income for the business will providing parents of children using the facility with an incentive to stay for a longer period of time. This business model is akin to Barnes and Noble's installation of cafes in most of their bookstores. This part of the business will serve small sandwiches, coffee/tea, and fountain drinks.

3.3 Event Hosting

The final revenue center for the business will be the hosting of birthday parties and other events at the facility. These parties are anticipated to generate approximately $300 to $400 from each event (with approximately 8 to 10 people).

The Company will also provide food and beverages for each event. The average party is expected to last two hours.

4.0 STRATEGIC AND MARKET ANALYSIS

4.1 Economic Outlook

This section of the analysis will detail the economic climate, the retail entertainment industry, the customer profile, and the competition that the business will face as it progresses through its business operations.

Currently, the economic market condition in the United States is in recession. Many economists expect that this recession will continue for a prolonged period of time, at which point the economy will begin a prolonged recovery period. However, due to the low pricing point of the services offered by the Supersonic Racing, the business will be able to remain profitable and cash flow positive despite deleterious changes in the economy. This is primarily due to the fact that people will seek lower cost forms of entertainment for their families during times of difficult economic climates.

4.2 Industry Analysis

The entertainment (retail) industry generates approximately $1.5 billion dollars a year among 2,700 companies that operate retail entertainment (including go kart tracks) establishments. These revenue numbers do not include amusement parks, casinos, or resorts that provide go kart tracks as a value added benefit to patrons. The industry employs more than 30,000 people and provides aggregate annual payrolls of $350 million dollars.

As stated earlier, the industry is mature. The expected continued growth of these businesses is expected to mirror the general population growth plus the rate of inflation. As time progresses, Mr. Applegate may add other forms of entertainment in order to further promote the entertainment nature of the business. This may include a limited arcade that will be featured on site.

4.3 Customer Profile

Mr. Applegate has developed the following demographic profile of the average customer:

- Ages 10+

- Male or female

- Annual family income of $50,000+

- Is seeking a facility that provides entertainment for both parent and child

Within the greater New York metropolitan area there are more than 500,000 families that fall into the demographic profile above. As such, the business will be able to attract families with children that are seeking lower cost forms of entertainment given the current economic climate.

4.4 Competition

In the five boroughs of New York City, there are only two other go kart tracks that operate. As such, the competition within this industry is very limited. The business will maintain a distinct competitive advantage in that the business has few competitors and the development costs for Supersonic Racing is relatively high. As such, once established, the business will be able to immediately generate an extensive amount of business.

5.0 MARKETING PLAN

Supersonic Racing intends to maintain an extensive marketing campaign that will ensure maximum visibility for the business in its targeted market. Below is an overview of the marketing strategies and objectives of the Company.

5.1 Marketing Objectives

- Develop an online presence including a company website and placing the Company's name and contact information with online directories.

- Implement a local campaign with the Company's targeted market via the use of flyers, local newspaper advertisements, and word-of-mouth advertising.

5.2 Marketing Strategies

Management intends on using a number of advertising and marketing channels to promote traffic to Supersonic Racing. The Company primarily intends to use a broad-based advertising campaign that will raise the awareness of the retail location among the targeted young adolescent and adult demographic.

To that end, Management will place a number of advertisements in locally-based newspapers and advertisements from the onset of operations which may include discount coupons or coupons for discounted admission. Management expects that this strategy will create an immediate draw to the Company's initial location.

Management also expects that the business will generate significant word-of-mouth advertising as the Company hosts events for birthday parties. As more and more people (children 10 or older) are invited to Company-hosted birthday parties, these youngsters may have their parents host their next birthday party at the facility. The Company anticipates that this type of advertising will take three to six months to become effective.

5.3 Pricing

Management anticipates that each use of Supersonic Racing's facilities will generate $5 of income. Additionally, consumers are expected to purchase approximately $15 to $20 of concessions per visit to the Company's facilities.

6.0 ORGANIZATIONAL PLAN AND PERSONNEL SUMMARY

6.1 Corporate Organization

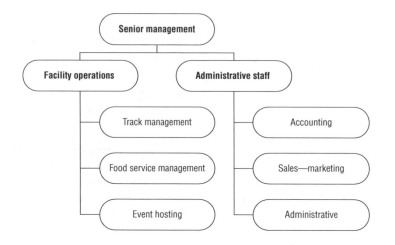

6.2 Organizational Budget

Personnel plan—yearly

Year	1	2	3
Owner	$ 50,000	$ 51,500	$ 53,045
Facility manager	$ 90,000	$ 92,700	$ 95,481
Track employees and staff	$114,000	$117,420	$120,943
Bookkeeper (P/T)	$ 12,500	$ 12,875	$ 13,261
Administrative	$ 50,000	$ 51,500	$ 53,045
Total	**$316,500**	**$325,995**	**$335,775**

Numbers of personnel

Owner	1	1	1
Facility manager	2	2	2
Track employees and staff	6	6	6
Bookkeeper (P/T)	1	1	1
Administrative	2	2	2
Totals	**12**	**12**	**12**

Personnel expense breakdown

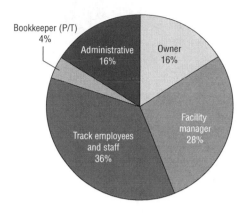

7.0 FINANCIAL PLAN

7.1 Underlying Assumptions

The Company has based its proforma financial statements on the following:

- Supersonic Racing, Inc. will have an annual revenue growth rate of 10% per year.

- The Owner will acquire $350,000 of debt funds to develop the business.

- The loan will have a 10 year term with a 9% interest rate.

7.2 Sensitivity Analysis

The Company's revenues are somewhat vulnerable to changes in the general economy. The Company is providing entertainment to customers, which is not a necessity. However, the pricing point for Supersonic Racing's services is extremely low, and the general economy would need a serious recession before a revenue decline. The high margin revenue generated by the business will allow the Company to operate profitably despite negative economic climates.

7.3 Source of Funds

Financing

Equity contributions	
Management investment	$ 50,000.00
Total equity financing	**$ 50,000.00**
Banks and lenders	
Banks and lenders	$ 350,000.00
Total debt financing	**$350,000.00**
Total financing	**$400,000.00**

7.4 General Assumptions

General assumptions

Year	1	2	3
Short term interest rate	9.5%	9.5%	9.5%
Long term interest rate	10.0%	10.0%	10.0%
Federal tax rate	33.0%	33.0%	33.0%
State tax rate	5.0%	5.0%	5.0%
Personnel taxes	15.0%	15.0%	15.0%

7.5 Profit and Loss Statements

Proforma profit and loss (yearly)

Year	1	2	3
Sales	**$784,890**	**$863,379**	**$949,717**
Cost of goods sold	$148,257	$163,083	$179,391
Gross margin	81.11%	81.11%	81.11%
Operating income	**$636,633**	**$700,296**	**$770,326**
Expenses			
Payroll	$316,500	$325,995	$335,775
General and administrative	$ 25,200	$ 26,208	$ 27,256
Marketing expenses	$ 31,396	$ 34,535	$ 37,989
Professional fees and licensure	$ 7,500	$ 7,725	$ 7,957
Insurance costs	$ 15,000	$ 15,750	$ 16,538
Travel and vehicle costs	$ 8,000	$ 8,800	$ 9,680
Utility expenses	$ 17,500	$ 18,375	$ 19,294
Miscellaneous costs	$ 3,924	$ 4,317	$ 4,749
Payroll taxes	$ 47,475	$ 48,899	$ 50,366
Total operating costs	**$472,495**	**$490,604**	**$509,603**
EBITDA	**$164,138**	**$209,692**	**$260,723**
Federal income tax	$ 54,166	$ 59,807	$ 77,413
State income tax	$ 8,207	$ 9,062	$ 11,729
Interest expense	$ 30,582	$ 28,460	$ 26,139
Depreciation expenses	$ 24,464	$ 24,464	$ 24,464
Net profit	**$ 46,719**	**$ 87,900**	**$120,978**
Profit margin	**5.95%**	**10.18%**	**12.74%**

Sales, operating costs, and profit forecast

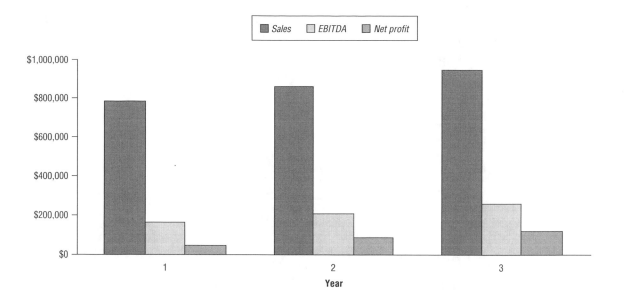

7.6 Cash Flow Analysis

Proforma cash flow analysis—yearly

Year	1	2	3
Cash from operations	$ 71,184	$112,364	$145,442
Cash from receivables	$ 0	$ 0	$ 0
Operating cash inflow	**$ 71,184**	**$112,364**	**$145,442**
Other cash inflows			
Equity investment	$ 50,000	$ 0	$ 0
Increased borrowings	$350,000	$ 0	$ 0
Sales of business assets	$ 0	$ 0	$ 0
A/P increases	$ 37,902	$ 43,587	$ 50,125
Total other cash inflows	**$437,902**	**$ 43,587**	**$ 50,125**
Total cash inflow	**$509,086**	**$155,951**	**$195,568**
Cash outflows			
Repayment of principal	$ 22,622	$ 24,744	$ 27,065
A/P decreases	$ 24,897	$ 29,876	$ 35,852
A/R increases	$ 0	$ 0	$ 0
Asset purchases	$342,500	$ 28,091	$ 36,361
Dividends	$ 49,829	$ 67,418	$ 87,265
Total cash outflows	**$439,847**	**$150,130**	**$186,543**
Net cash flow	**$ 69,238**	**$ 5,822**	**$ 9,025**
Cash balance	**$ 69,238**	**$ 75,060**	**$ 84,085**

Proforma cash flow (yearly)

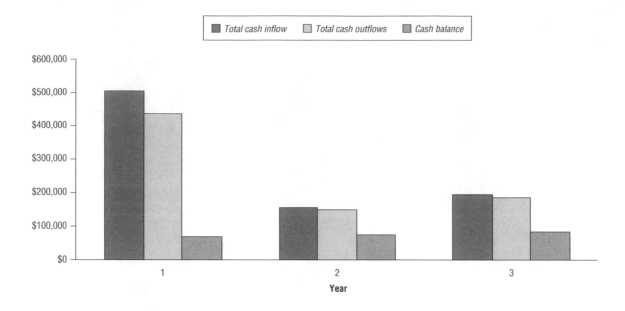

7.7 Balance Sheet

Proforma balance sheet—yearly

Year	1	2	3
Assets			
Cash	$ 69,238	$ 75,060	$ 84,085
Amortized development/expansion costs	$192,500	$195,309	$198,945
Go Kart inventory	$100,000	$114,045	$132,226
FF&E	$ 50,000	$ 61,236	$ 75,781
Accumulated depreciation	($ 24,464)	($ 48,929)	($ 73,393)
Total assets	**$387,274**	**$396,722**	**$417,643**
Liabilities and equity			
Accounts payable	$ 13,005	$ 26,716	$ 40,990
Long term liabilities	$327,378	$302,634	$277,890
Other liabilities	$ 0	$ 0	$ 0
Total liabilities	**$340,383**	**$329,350**	**$318,880**
Net worth	**$ 46,891**	**$ 67,372**	**$ 98,764**
Total liabilities and equity	**$387,274**	**$396,722**	**$417,643**

Proforma balance sheet

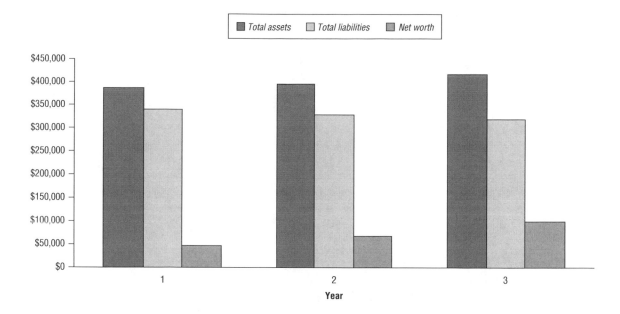

7.8 Breakeven Analysis

Monthly break even analysis

Year	1	2	3
Monthly revenue	$ 48,544	$ 50,405	$ 52,356
Yearly revenue	$582,528	$604,855	$628,277

Break even analysis

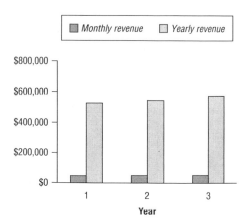

7.9 Business Ratios

Business ratios—yearly

Year	1	2	3
Sales			
Sales growth	0.0%	10.0%	10.0%
Gross margin	81.1%	81.1%	81.1%
Financials			
Profit margin	5.95%	10.18%	12.74%
Assets to liabilities	1.14	1.20	1.31
Equity to liabilities	0.14	0.20	0.31
Assets to equity	8.26	5.89	4.23
Liquidity			
Acid test	0.20	0.23	0.26
Cash to assets	0.18	0.19	0.20

7.10 Three Year Profit and Loss Statement

Profit and loss statement (first year)

Months	1	2	3	4	5	6	7
Sales	**$61,200**	**$61,965**	**$62,730**	**$63,495**	**$64,260**	**$65,025**	**$65,790**
Cost of goods sold	$11,560	$11,705	$11,849	$11,994	$12,138	$12,283	$12,427
Gross margin	81.1%	81.1%	81.1%	81.1%	81.1%	81.1%	81.1%
Operating income	**$49,640**	**$50,261**	**$50,881**	**$51,502**	**$52,122**	**$52,743**	**$53,363**
Expenses							
Payroll	$26,375	$26,375	$26,375	$26,375	$26,375	$26,375	$26,375
General and administrative	$ 2,100	$ 2,100	$ 2,100	$ 2,100	$ 2,100	$ 2,100	$ 2,100
Marketing expenses	$ 2,616	$ 2,616	$ 2,616	$ 2,616	$ 2,616	$ 2,616	$ 2,616
Professional fees and licensure	$ 625	$ 625	$ 625	$ 625	$ 625	$ 625	$ 625
Insurance costs	$ 1,250	$ 1,250	$ 1,250	$ 1,250	$ 1,250	$ 1,250	$ 1,250
Travel and vehicle costs	$ 667	$ 667	$ 667	$ 667	$ 667	$ 667	$ 667
Utility expenses	$ 1,458	$ 1,458	$ 1,458	$ 1,458	$ 1,458	$ 1,458	$ 1,458
Miscellaneous costs	$ 327	$ 327	$ 327	$ 327	$ 327	$ 327	$ 327
Payroll taxes	$ 3,956	$ 3,956	$ 3,956	$ 3,956	$ 3,956	$ 3,956	$ 3,956
Total operating costs	**$39,375**	**$39,375**	**$39,375**	**$39,375**	**$39,375**	**$39,375**	**$39,375**
EBITDA	**$10,265**	**$10,886**	**$11,506**	**$12,127**	**$12,747**	**$13,368**	**$13,988**
Federal income tax	$ 4,223	$ 4,276	$ 4,329	$ 4,382	$ 4,435	$ 4,487	$ 4,540
State income tax	$ 640	$ 648	$ 656	$ 664	$ 672	$ 680	$ 688
Interest expense	$ 2,625	$ 2,611	$ 2,598	$ 2,584	$ 2,570	$ 2,556	$ 2,542
Depreciation expense	$ 2,039	$ 2,039	$ 2,039	$ 2,039	$ 2,039	$ 2,039	$ 2,039
Net profit	**$ 738**	**$ 1,312**	**$ 1,885**	**$ 2,459**	**$ 3,032**	**$ 3,606**	**$ 4,180**

Profit and loss statement (first year cont.)

Month	8	9	10	11	12	1
Sales	$66,555	$67,320	$68,085	$68,850	$69,615	$784,890
Cost of goods sold	$12,572	$12,716	$12,861	$13,005	$13,150	$148,257
Gross margin	81.1%	81.1%	81.1%	81.1%	81.1%	81.1%
Operating income	$53,984	$54,604	$55,225	$55,845	$56,466	$636,633
Expenses						
Payroll	$26,375	$26,375	$26,375	$26,375	$26,375	$316,500
General and administrative	$ 2,100	$ 2,100	$ 2,100	$ 2,100	$ 2,100	$ 25,200
Marketing expenses	$ 2,616	$ 2,616	$ 2,616	$ 2,616	$ 2,616	$ 31,396
Professional fees and licensure	$ 625	$ 625	$ 625	$ 625	$ 625	$ 7,500
Insurance costs	$ 1,250	$ 1,250	$ 1,250	$ 1,250	$ 1,250	$ 15,000
Travel and vehicle costs	$ 667	$ 667	$ 667	$ 667	$ 667	$ 8,000
Utility expenses	$ 1,458	$ 1,458	$ 1,458	$ 1,458	$ 1,458	$ 17,500
Miscellaneous costs	$ 327	$ 327	$ 327	$ 327	$ 327	$ 3,924
Payroll taxes	$ 3,956	$ 3,956	$ 3,956	$ 3,956	$ 3,956	$ 47,475
Total operating costs	$39,375	$39,375	$39,375	$39,375	$39,375	$472,495
EBITDA	$14,609	$15,229	$15,850	$16,470	$17,091	$164,138
Federal income tax	$ 4,593	$ 4,646	$ 4,699	$ 4,751	$ 4,804	$ 54,166
State income tax	$ 696	$ 704	$ 712	$ 720	$ 728	$ 8,207
Interest expense	$ 2,528	$ 2,514	$ 2,499	$ 2,485	$ 2,470	$ 30,582
Depreciation expense	$ 2,039	$ 2,039	$ 2,039	$ 2,039	$ 2,039	$ 24,464
Net profit	$ 4,753	$ 5,327	$ 5,902	$ 6,476	$ 7,050	$ 46,719

Profit and loss statement (second year)

Quarter	Q1	Q2	Q3	Q4	2
Sales	$172,676	$215,845	$233,112	$241,746	$863,379
Cost of goods sold	$ 32,617	$ 40,771	$ 44,032	$ 45,663	$163,083
Gross margin	81.1%	81.1%	81.1%	81.1%	81.1%
Operating income	$140,059	$175,074	$189,080	$196,083	$700,296
Expenses					
Payroll	$ 65,199	$ 81,499	$ 88,019	$ 91,279	$325,995
General and administrative	$ 5,242	$ 6,552	$ 7,076	$ 7,338	$ 26,208
Marketing expenses	$ 6,907	$ 8,634	$ 9,324	$ 9,670	$ 34,535
Professional fees and licensure	$ 1,545	$ 1,931	$ 2,086	$ 2,163	$ 7,725
Insurance costs	$ 3,150	$ 3,938	$ 4,253	$ 4,410	$ 15,750
Travel and vehicle costs	$ 1,760	$ 2,200	$ 2,376	$ 2,464	$ 8,800
Utility expenses	$ 3,675	$ 4,594	$ 4,961	$ 5,145	$ 18,375
Miscellaneous costs	$ 863	$ 1,079	$ 1,166	$ 1,209	$ 4,317
Payroll taxes	$ 9,780	$ 12,225	$ 13,203	$ 13,692	$ 48,899
Total operating costs	$ 98,121	$122,651	$132,463	$137,369	$490,604
EBITDA	$ 41,938	$ 52,423	$ 56,617	$ 58,714	$209,692
Federal income tax	$ 11,961	$ 14,952	$ 16,148	$ 16,746	$ 59,807
State income tax	$ 1,812	$ 2,265	$ 2,447	$ 2,537	$ 9,062
Interest expense	$ 7,321	$ 7,186	$ 7,047	$ 6,905	$ 28,460
Depreciation expense	$ 6,116	$ 6,116	$ 6,116	$ 6,116	$ 24,464
Net profit	$ 14,727	$ 21,904	$ 24,859	$ 26,409	$ 87,900

Profit and loss statement (third year)

Quarter	Q1	3 Q2	Q3	Q4	3
Sales	$189,943	$237,429	$256,424	$265,921	$949,717
Cost of goods sold	$ 35,878	$ 44,848	$ 48,436	$ 50,229	$179,391
Gross margin	81.1%	81.1%	81.1%	81.1%	81.1%
Operating income	$154,065	$192,581	$207,988	$215,691	$770,326
Expenses					
Payroll	$ 67,155	$ 83,944	$ 90,659	$ 94,017	$335,775
General and administrative	$ 5,451	$ 6,814	$ 7,359	$ 7,632	$ 27,256
Marketing expenses	$ 7,598	$ 9,497	$ 10,257	$ 10,637	$ 37,989
Professional fees and licensure	$ 1,591	$ 1,989	$ 2,148	$ 2,228	$ 7,957
Insurance costs	$ 3,308	$ 4,134	$ 4,465	$ 4,631	$ 16,538
Travel and vehicle costs	$ 1,936	$ 2,420	$ 2,614	$ 2,710	$ 9,680
Utility expenses	$ 3,859	$ 4,823	$ 5,209	$ 5,402	$ 19,294
Miscellaneous costs	$ 950	$ 1,187	$ 1,282	$ 1,330	$ 4,749
Payroll taxes	$ 10,073	$ 12,592	$ 13,599	$ 14,103	$ 50,366
Total operating costs	$101,921	$127,401	$137,593	$142,689	$509,603
EBITDA	$ 52,145	$ 65,181	$ 70,395	$ 73,003	$260,723
Federal income tax	$ 15,483	$ 19,353	$ 20,901	$ 21,676	$ 77,413
State income tax	$ 2,346	$ 2,932	$ 3,167	$ 3,284	$ 11,729
Interest expense	$ 6,760	$ 6,612	$ 6,461	$ 6,305	$ 26,139
Depreciation expense	$ 6,116	$ 6,116	$ 6,116	$ 6,116	$ 24,464
Net profit	$ 21,440	$ 30,167	$ 33,750	$ 35,621	$120,978

7.11 Three Year Cash Flow Analysis

Cash flow analysis (first year)

Month	1	2	3	4	5	6	7	8
Cash from operations	$ 2,777	$ 3,350	$ 3,924	$ 4,497	$ 5,071	$ 5,644	$ 6,218	$ 6,792
Cash from receivables	$ 0	$ 0	$ 0	$ 0	$ 0	$ 0	$ 0	$ 0
Operating cash inflow	$ 2,777	$ 3,350	$ 3,924	$ 4,497	$ 5,071	$ 5,644	$ 6,218	$ 6,792
Other cash inflows								
Equity investment	$ 50,000	$ 0	$ 0	$ 0	$ 0	$ 0	$ 0	$ 0
Increased borrowings	$350,000	$ 0	$ 0	$ 0	$ 0	$ 0	$ 0	$ 0
Sales of business assets	$ 0	$ 0	$ 0	$ 0	$ 0	$ 0	$ 0	$ 0
A/P increases	$ 3,159	$ 3,159	$ 3,159	$ 3,159	$ 3,159	$ 3,159	$ 3,159	$ 3,159
Total other cash inflows	$403,159	$ 3,159	$ 3,159	$ 3,159	$ 3,159	$ 3,159	$ 3,159	$ 3,159
Total cash inflow	$405,936	$ 6,509	$ 7,082	$ 7,656	$ 8,229	$ 8,803	$ 9,377	$ 9,951
Cash outflows								
Repayment of principal	$ 1,809	$ 1,822	$ 1,836	$ 1,850	$ 1,864	$ 1,878	$ 1,892	$ 1,906
A/P decreases	$ 2,075	$ 2,075	$ 2,075	$ 2,075	$ 2,075	$ 2,075	$ 2,075	$ 2,075
A/R increases	$ 0	$ 0	$ 0	$ 0	$ 0	$ 0	$ 0	$ 0
Asset purchases	$342,500	$ 0	$ 0	$ 0	$ 0	$ 0	$ 0	$ 0
Dividends	$ 0	$ 0	$ 0	$ 0	$ 0	$ 0	$ 0	$ 0
Total cash outflows	$346,383	$ 3,897	$ 3,911	$ 3,924	$ 3,938	$ 3,952	$ 3,966	$ 3,981
Net cash flow	$ 59,552	$ 2,612	$ 3,172	$ 3,731	$ 4,291	$ 4,851	$ 5,410	$ 5,970
Cash balance	$ 59,552	$62,164	$65,336	$69,067	$73,358	$78,209	$83,619	$89,589

Cash flow analysis (first year cont.)

Month	9	10	11	12	1
Cash from operations	$ 7,366	$ 7,940	$ 8,514	$ 9,089	$ 71,184
Cash from receivables	$ 0	$ 0	$ 0	$ 0	$ 0
Operating cash inflow	**$ 7,366**	**$ 7,940**	**$ 8,514**	**$ 9,089**	**$ 71,184**
Other cash inflows					
Equity investment	$ 0	$ 0	$ 0	$ 0	$ 50,000
Increased borrowings	$ 0	$ 0	$ 0	$ 0	$350,000
Sales of business assets	$ 0	$ 0	$ 0	$ 0	$ 0
A/P increases	$ 3,159	$ 3,159	$ 3,159	$ 3,159	$ 37,902
Total other cash inflows	**$ 3,159**	**$ 3,159**	**$ 3,159**	**$ 3,159**	**$437,902**
Total cash inflow	**$10,525**	**$ 11,099**	**$ 11,673**	**$12,247**	**$509,086**
Cash outflows					
Repayment of principal	$ 1,920	$ 1,934	$ 1,949	$ 1,964	$ 22,622
A/P decreases	$ 2,075	$ 2,075	$ 2,075	$ 2,075	$ 24,897
A/R increases	$ 0	$ 0	$ 0	$ 0	$ 0
Asset purchases	$ 0	$ 0	$ 0	$ 0	$342,500
Dividends	$ 0	$ 0	$ 0	$49,829	$ 49,829
Total cash outflows	**$ 3,995**	**$ 4,009**	**$ 4,024**	**$53,867**	**$439,847**
Net cash flow	**$ 6,530**	**$ 7,090**	**$ 7,649**	**−$41,620**	**$ 69,238**
Cash balance	**$96,119**	**$103,209**	**$110,858**	**$69,238**	**$ 69,238**

Cash flow analysis (second year)

Quarter	Q1	2 Q2	Q3	Q4	2
Cash from operations	$22,473	$28,091	$30,338	$31,462	$112,364
Cash from receivables	$ 0	$ 0	$ 0	$ 0	$ 0
Operating cash inflow	**$22,473**	**$28,091**	**$30,338**	**$31,462**	**$112,364**
Other cash inflows					
Equity investment	$ 0	$ 0	$ 0	$ 0	$ 0
Increased borrowings	$ 0	$ 0	$ 0	$ 0	$ 0
Sales of business assets	$ 0	$ 0	$ 0	$ 0	$ 0
A/P increases	$ 8,717	$10,897	$11,769	$12,204	$ 43,587
Total other cash inflows	**$ 8,717**	**$10,897**	**$11,769**	**$12,204**	**$ 43,587**
Total cash inflow	**$31,190**	**$38,988**	**$42,107**	**$43,666**	**$155,951**
Cash outflows					
Repayment of principal	$ 5,980	$ 6,115	$ 6,254	$ 6,396	$ 24,744
A/P decreases	$ 5,975	$ 7,469	$ 8,067	$ 8,365	$ 29,876
A/R increases	$ 0	$ 0	$ 0	$ 0	$ 0
Asset purchases	$ 5,618	$ 7,023	$ 7,585	$ 7,865	$ 28,091
Dividends	$13,484	$16,855	$18,203	$18,877	$ 67,418
Total cash outflows	**$31,057**	**$37,462**	**$40,108**	**$41,504**	**$150,130**
Net cash flow	**$ 134**	**$ 1,526**	**$ 1,999**	**$ 2,163**	**$ 5,822**
Cash balance	**$69,372**	**$70,898**	**$72,897**	**$75,060**	**$ 75,060**

Cash flow analysis (third year)

Quarter	Q1	3 Q2	Q3	Q4	3
Cash from operations	$29,088	$36,361	$39,269	$40,724	$145,442
Cash from receivables	$ 0	$ 0	$ 0	$ 0	$ 0
Operating cash inflow	**$29,088**	**$36,361**	**$39,269**	**$40,724**	**$145,442**
Other cash inflows					
Equity investment	$ 0	$ 0	$ 0	$ 0	$ 0
Increased borrowings	$ 0	$ 0	$ 0	$ 0	$ 0
Sales of business assets	$ 0	$ 0	$ 0	$ 0	$ 0
A/P increases	$10,025	$12,531	$13,534	$14,035	$ 50,125
Total other cash inflows	**$10,025**	**$12,531**	**$13,534**	**$14,035**	**$ 50,125**
Total cash inflow	**$39,114**	**$48,892**	**$52,803**	**$54,759**	**$195,568**
Cash outflows					
Repayment of principal	$ 6,540	$ 6,689	$ 6,840	$ 6,995	$ 27,065
A/P decreases	$ 7,170	$ 8,963	$ 9,680	$10,038	$ 35,852
A/R increases	$ 0	$ 0	$ 0	$ 0	$ 0
Asset purchases	$ 7,272	$ 9,090	$ 9,817	$10,181	$ 36,361
Dividends	$17,453	$21,816	$23,562	$24,434	$ 87,265
Total cash outflows	**$38,436**	**$46,558**	**$49,899**	**$51,649**	**$186,543**
Net cash flow	**$ 678**	**$ 2,334**	**$ 2,904**	**$ 3,110**	**$ 9,025**
Cash balance	**$75,737**	**$78,071**	**$80,975**	**$84,085**	**$ 84,085**

Gold Mining

Davis Gold Mining

9876 Nome-Council Rd.
Nome, Alaska 99762

BizPlanD B.com

The purpose of this business plan is to raise $600,000 for the development of a private gold mining business. Davis Gold Mining ("the Company") is a Alaskan-based corporation that will excavate gold from leased mines within United States. The Company was founded by Mike Hamilton.

1.0 EXECUTIVE SUMMARY

The purpose of this business plan is to raise $600,000 for the development of a private gold mining business while showcasing the expected financials and operations over the next three years. Davis Gold Mining ("the Company") is a Alaskan-based corporation that will excavate gold from leased mines within United States. The Company was founded by Mike Hamilton.

1.1 The Services

As stated above, the Company intends to acquire land leases on properties known to have gold deposits. The business will then develop gold mines on these properties with the intent to extract, smelt, and package the gold into bars for sale in the open market. The initial capital sought in this business plan will allow the business to acquire its first land lease while concurrently sourcing the equipment needed to operate a moderate-sized gold mining operation.

It should be noted that, at all times, the business will comply with all applicable federal, state, and local laws (including OSHA) in order to ensure the safety of all employees working at the gold mine site.

The third section of the business plan will further describe the gold mining operations conducted by Davis Gold Mining.

1.2 Financing

At this time, Mr. Hamilton is seeking $600,000 of private funds for the development of the Company's gold mining operations. Tentatively, Management is seeking to sell a 40% interest in the business in exchange for the capital sought in this business plan. The financing will be used for the following:

- Development of the Company's location.

- Financing for the first six months of operation.

- Capital to purchase equipment for mining.

67

1.3 Mission Statement

The mission of Davis Gold Mining is to cost-effectively extract gold from known precious metal deposits with the intent to sell the refined precious metal to the open market.

1.4 Management Team

The Company was founded by Mike Hamilton. Mr. Hamilton has more than 10 years of gold mining experience. Through his expertise, he will be able to bring the operations of the business to profitability within its first year of operations.

1.5 Sales Forecasts

Mr. Hamilton expects a strong rate of growth at the start of operations. Below are the expected financials over the next three years.

Proforma profit and loss (yearly)

Year	1	2	3
Sales	$2,406,600	$2,887,920	$3,378,866
Operating costs	$ 846,767	$ 920,329	$ 997,280
EBITDA	$ 476,863	$ 668,027	$ 861,096
Taxes, interest, and depreciation	$ 219,422	$ 292,065	$ 365,431
Net profit	$ 257,441	$ 375,962	$ 495,665

Sales, operating costs, and profit forecast

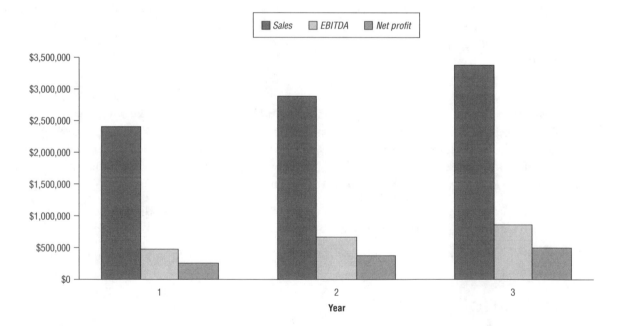

1.6 Expansion Plan

The Founder expects that the business will aggressively expand during the first three years of operation. As the business becomes profitable it will make substantial reinvestments into the Company's gold mining infrastructure. Additionally, the Company may seek to acquire additional land leases on proven grounds for gold mining.

2.0 COMPANY AND FINANCING SUMMARY

2.1 Registered Name and Corporate Structure

Davis Gold Mining is registered as a for-profit corporation in the State of Alaska.

2.2 Required Funds

At this time, the Company requires $600,000 of equity funds. Below is a breakdown of how these funds will be used:

Projected startup costs

Initial land lease	$ 50,000
Working capital	$ 65,000
FF&E	$250,000
Leasehold improvements	$ 75,000
Security deposits	$ 25,000
Insurance	$ 15,000
Lease deposits on vehicles	$ 50,000
Initial distribution budget	$ 50,000
Miscellaneous and unforeseen costs	$ 20,000
Total startup costs	**$600,000**

2.3 Investor Equity

At this time, Mr. Hamilton is seeking to sell a 40% interest in the business in exchange for the capital sought in this business plan. The investor(s) will receive a seat on the board of directors and a regular stream of dividends starting in the first year of operations.

2.4 Management Equity

After the requisite capital is raised, Mr. Hamilton will retain a 60% ownership interest in the business.

2.5 Exit Strategy

The Management has discussed and planned for three possible exit strategies. The first strategy would be to sell the Company to a larger entity at a significant premium. Since the precious metals mining industry maintains a moderately low risk profile once the business is established, the Management feels that the Company could be sold for ten to fifteen times earnings.

The second exit scenario would entail selling a portion of the Company via an initial public offering (or "IPO"). After a detailed analysis, it was found that comparable companies sell for ten to fifteen times earnings on the open market. However, taking a company public involves significant legal red tape. Davis Gold Mining would be bound by the significant legal framework of the Sarbanes-Oxley Act in addition to the legal requirements set forth in form S1 of the Securities and Exchange Commission. The Company would also have to comply with the Securities Act of 1933 and the Exchange Act of 1934.

The last exit scenario would involve the use of a private placement memorandum to raise additional capital from private sources. This is also a significantly expensive process that requires the assistance of both an experienced securities law firm and an investment bank. Funds would be raised from private equity and merchant banking sources in exchange for a percentage of the Company's stock.

2.6 Investor Divestiture

This will be discussed during negotiations.

3.0 GOLD MINING OPERATIONS

As stated in the executive summary, the Company intends to operate in a gold mining capacity. Prior to the onset of operations, Mr. Hamilton will have acquired a land lease on a property that is known to have gold deposits. At this time, it is unclear as to the method that the Company will use in order to extract gold. The most profitable method of exacting gold would be to lease an existing gold mine facility with the intent to pan gold deposits from the underlying soil. This manual method of gold acquisition would provide the greatest return on investment for the business. The Company, depending on its land lease, may engage in sluicing/dredging if the land is known to have a significant amount of gold that is buried deep within the ground.

Mr. Hamilton is also sourcing the necessary equipment so that the business can immediately begin its operations once the land lease has been acquired. The gold mining facility will also have all of the necessary chemical treatment and smelting equipment to allow the business to shape its collected gold into 1 kilogram bars for resale to the open market.

4.0 STRATEGIC AND MARKET ANALYSIS

4.1 Economic Outlook

This section of the analysis will detail the economic climate, the gold mining industry, the customer profile, and the competition that the business will face as it progresses through its business operations.

Currently, the economic market condition in the United States is recessed. The meltdown of the sub prime mortgage market coupled with increasing gas prices has led many people to believe that the US is on the cusp of a double dip economic recession. This slowdown in the economy has also greatly impacted real estate sales, which has halted to historical lows. However, gold mines operate with great economic stability as it is a product that is in continued demand. This is especially true in today's economic environment as inflation has pushed the per ounce price of gold up substantially over the last 12 months. As long as commodity prices continue to rise, the business should have no issues producing a continuous profit from its gold mining operations.

4.2 Industry Analysis

Mining, beneficiating, and quarrying of gold is a $3 billion dollar a year business in the United States. Within the industry there are over 200 domestic providers of gold mining operations that operate within 20 states. The industry employs more than 10,000 people and provides adjusted annualized payrolls in excess of $500,000,000 dollars.

The growth rate of this industry has been tremendous with the recent resurgence of inflation. The prices of gold (and other precious metals) have increased substantially as investors have sought the safe haven of commodities in lieu of the falling value of the dollar. Additionally, the greater wealth of developing nations has pushed the per ounce price of gold past $800. This demand is expected to remain strong in the face of inflationary pressures.

4.3 Customer Profile

As Davis Gold Mining intends to sell its gold directly to wholesalers in the open market, is it difficult to determine the "average customer" of the business. Any company engaged in the buying and selling of gold is a potential buyer for the Company.

4.4 Competition

As stated above, the market for gold is conducted on an "open-market" basis. As such, the business will face competition not only from other gold mines but spectulators, hedge funds, and other investment vehicles that are seeking to capitalize on the strong demand for gold as it is considered a safe haven investment during times of economic distress. As such, it has hard to quantify the ongoing competition that the business will face as it divests its inventories of gold. However, Davis Gold Mining will have a very strong competitive advantage in that the business is able to produce its own inventories prior to selling them into the open market. This will create a cost and pricing competitive advantage for the business throughout the life of the Company.

5.0 MARKETING PLAN

The marketing campaigns required by Davis Gold Mining are minimal as the business will sell its mined gold directly to the open market. As such, it is imperative that any marketing expenditures undertaken by the Company focus on developing relationships with gold wholesalers and property management firms that will seek and lease land to the business.

5.1 Marketing Objectives

- Establish relationships with gold wholesalers within the targeted market.

- Develop relationships with specialty property management firms that will lease land to the business for its gold mining operations.

5.2 Marketing Strategies

Prior to the onset of operations, Mr. Hamilton will develop ongoing purchase order relationships (based on market prices) with national and international gold dealers and wholesalers that will acquire the Company's inventory of mined gold. In order to complete this aspect of the marketing operations, Mr. Hamilton will directly contact well-known gold wholesalers. As these buyers are constantly searching for new gold sources, developing these relationships will not be an issue.

Additionally, the Company will make its presence known among real estate agents and property management firms that specialize in the sale and placement of leases for land that is known to carry precious metal deposits. Much like with the gold wholesalers/dealers, Mr. Hamilton will directly contact these companies in order to develop working relationships.

5.3 Pricing

Management anticipates that it will receive approximately $1,000 to $1,200 per troy ounce of gold sold to wholesalers or via spot contracts in the open market.

6.0 ORGANIZATIONAL PLAN AND PERSONNEL SUMMARY

6.1 Corporate Organization

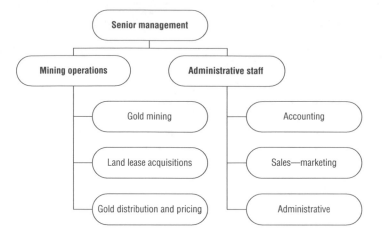

6.2 Organizational Budget

Personnel plan—yearly

Year	1	2	3
Senior management	$150,000	$154,500	$159,135
Foreman	$100,000	$103,000	$106,090
Miners	$232,000	$268,830	$307,661
Accountant	$ 35,000	$ 36,050	$ 37,132
Administrative	$ 44,000	$ 45,320	$ 46,680
Total	**$561,000**	**$607,700**	**$656,697**

Numbers of personnel

Senior management	2	2	2
Foreman	2	2	2
Miners	8	9	10
Accountant	1	1	1
Administrative	2	2	2
Totals	**15**	**16**	**17**

Personnel expense breakdown

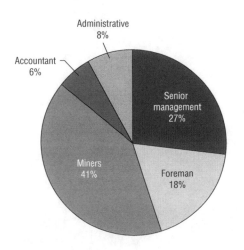

7.0 FINANCIAL PLAN

7.1 Underlying Assumptions

The Company has based its proforma financial statements on the following:

- Davis Gold Mining will have an annual revenue growth rate of 21% per year.

- The Founder will acquire $600,000 of equity funds to develop the business.

- Mr. Hamilton will sell a 40% equity interest in the business in exchange for the requisite capital sought in this business plan.

7.2 Sensitivity Analysis

In the event of an economic downturn, the business may have a decline in its revenues. In an economic recession, the demand for gold decreases as people will have less discretionary income. However, in today's economic climate, inflation has become a serious concern, and investors have driven up the per ounce price of gold substantially as a safe investment to hedge against inflationary risks. As such, the business should have very few issues regarding top line income.

7.3 Source of Funds

Financing

Equity contributions	
Investor(s)	$ 600,000.00
Total equity financing	**$600,000.00**
Banks and lenders	
Total debt financing	**$ 0.00**
Total financing	**$600,000.00**

7.4 General Assumptions

General assumptions

Year	1	2	3
Short term interest rate	9.5%	9.5%	9.5%
Long term interest rate	10.0%	10.0%	10.0%
Federal tax rate	33.0%	33.0%	33.0%
State tax rate	5.0%	5.0%	5.0%
Personnel taxes	15.0%	15.0%	15.0%

7.5 Profit and Loss Statements

Proforma profit and loss (yearly)

Year	1	2	3
Sales	**$2,406,600**	**$2,887,920**	**$3,378,866**
Cost of goods sold	$1,082,970	$1,299,564	$1,520,490
Gross margin	55.00%	55.00%	55.00%
Operating income	**$1,323,630**	**$1,588,356**	**$1,858,377**
Expenses			
Payroll	$ 561,000	$ 607,700	$ 656,697
General and administrative	$ 32,400	$ 33,696	$ 35,044
Distribution expenses	$ 48,132	$ 57,758	$ 67,577
Professional fees and licensure	$ 15,219	$ 15,676	$ 16,146
Insurance costs	$ 21,987	$ 23,086	$ 24,241
Equipment costs	$ 27,596	$ 30,356	$ 33,391
Rent and utilities	$ 44,250	$ 46,463	$ 48,786
Miscellaneous costs	$ 12,033	$ 14,440	$ 16,894
Payroll taxes	$ 84,150	$ 91,155	$ 98,505
Total operating costs	**$ 846,767**	**$ 920,329**	**$ 997,280**
EBITDA	**$ 476,863**	**$ 668,027**	**$ 861,096**
Federal income tax	$ 157,365	$ 220,449	$ 284,162
State income tax	$ 23,843	$ 33,401	$ 43,055
Interest expense	$ 0	$ 0	$ 0
Depreciation expenses	$ 38,214	$ 38,214	$ 38,214
Net profit	**$ 257,441**	**$ 375,962**	**$ 495,665**
Profit margin	**10.70%**	**13.02%**	**14.67%**

Sales, operating costs, and profit forecast

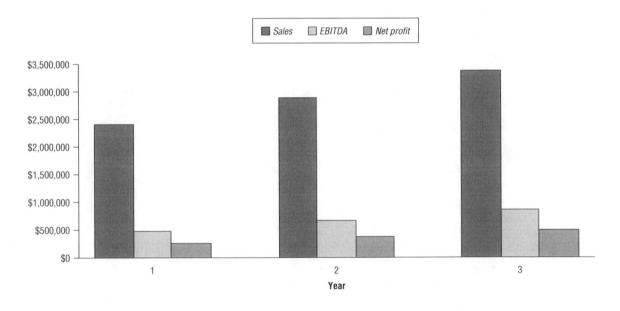

7.6 Cash Flow Analysis

Proforma cash flow analysis—yearly

Year	1	2	3
Cash from operations	$295,655	$414,177	$533,880
Cash from receivables	$ 0	$ 0	$ 0
Operating cash inflow	**$295,655**	**$414,177**	**$533,880**
Other cash inflows			
Equity investment	$600,000	$ 0	$ 0
Increased borrowings	$ 0	$ 0	$ 0
Sales of business assets	$ 0	$ 0	$ 0
A/P increases	$ 37,902	$ 43,587	$ 50,125
Total other cash inflows	**$637,902**	**$ 43,587**	**$ 50,125**
Total cash inflow	**$933,557**	**$457,764**	**$584,005**
Cash outflows			
Repayment of principal	$ 0	$ 0	$ 0
A/P decreases	$ 24,897	$ 29,876	$ 35,852
A/R increases	$ 0	$ 0	$ 0
Asset purchases	$535,000	$207,088	$266,940
Dividends	$133,045	$186,380	$240,246
Total cash outflows	**$692,942**	**$423,344**	**$543,037**
Net cash flow	**$240,615**	**$ 34,420**	**$ 40,968**
Cash balance	**$240,615**	**$275,035**	**$316,003**

Proforma cash flow (yearly)

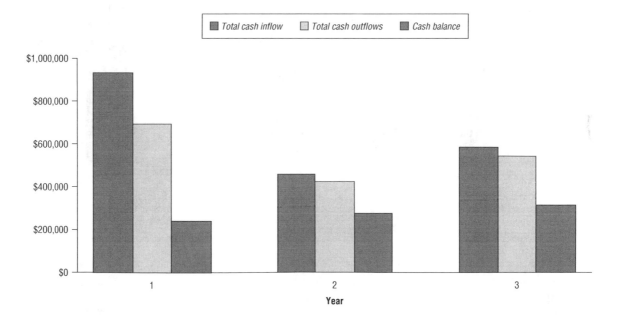

7.7 Balance Sheet

Proforma balance sheet—yearly

Year	1	2	3
Assets			
Cash	$240,615	$275,035	$ 316,003
Amortized development costs	$235,000	$255,709	$ 282,403
Vehicle lease deposits	$ 50,000	$153,544	$ 287,014
FF&E	$250,000	$332,835	$ 439,611
Accumulated depreciation	($ 38,214)	($ 76,429)	($ 114,643)
Total assets	**$737,401**	**$940,695**	**$1,210,388**
Liabilities and equity			
Accounts payable	$ 13,005	$ 26,716	$ 40,990
Long term liabilities	$ 0	$ 0	$ 0
Other liabilities	$ 0	$ 0	$ 0
Total liabilities	**$ 13,005**	**$ 26,716**	**$ 40,990**
Net worth	**$724,396**	**$913,979**	**$1,169,398**
Total liabilities and equity	**$737,401**	**$940,695**	**$1,210,388**

Proforma balance sheet

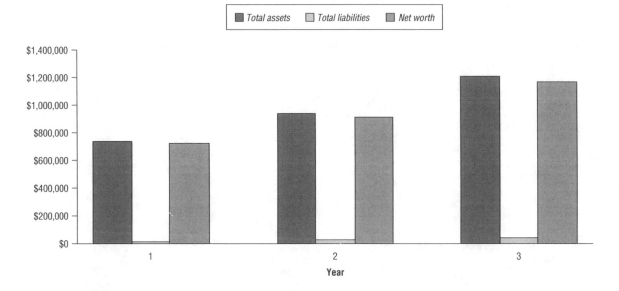

7.8 Breakeven Analysis

Monthly break even analysis

Year	1	2	3
Monthly revenue	$ 128,298	$ 139,444	$ 151,103
Yearly revenue	$1,539,576	$1,673,325	$1,813,237

Break even analysis

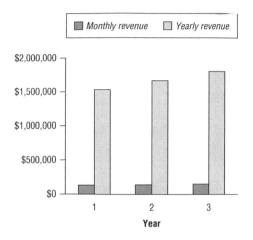

7.9 Business Ratios

Business ratios—yearly

Year	1	2	3
Sales			
Sales growth	0.0%	20.0%	17.0%
Gross margin	55.0%	55.0%	55.0%
Financials			
Profit margin	10.70%	13.02%	14.67%
Assets to liabilities	56.70	35.21	29.53
Equity to liabilities	55.70	34.21	28.53
Assets to equity	1.02	1.03	1.04
Liquidity			
Acid test	18.50	10.29	7.71
Cash to assets	0.33	0.29	0.26

7.10 Three Year Profit and Loss Statement

Profit and loss statement (first year)

Months	1	2	3	4	5	6	7
Sales	$200,000	$200,100	$200,200	$200,300	$200,400	$200,500	$200,600
Cost of goods sold	$ 90,000	$ 90,045	$ 90,090	$ 90,135	$ 90,180	$ 90,225	$ 90,270
Gross margin	55.0%	55.0%	55.0%	55.0%	55.0%	55.0%	55.0%
Operating income	$110,000	$110,055	$110,110	$110,165	$110,220	$110,275	$110,330
Expenses							
Payroll	$ 46,750	$ 46,750	$ 46,750	$ 46,750	$ 46,750	$ 46,750	$ 46,750
General and administrative	$ 2,700	$ 2,700	$ 2,700	$ 2,700	$ 2,700	$ 2,700	$ 2,700
Distribution expenses	$ 4,011	$ 4,011	$ 4,011	$ 4,011	$ 4,011	$ 4,011	$ 4,011
Professional fees and licensure	$ 1,268	$ 1,268	$ 1,268	$ 1,268	$ 1,268	$ 1,268	$ 1,268
Insurance costs	$ 1,832	$ 1,832	$ 1,832	$ 1,832	$ 1,832	$ 1,832	$ 1,832
Equipment costs	$ 2,300	$ 2,300	$ 2,300	$ 2,300	$ 2,300	$ 2,300	$ 2,300
Rent and utilities	$ 3,688	$ 3,688	$ 3,688	$ 3,688	$ 3,688	$ 3,688	$ 3,688
Miscellaneous costs	$ 1,003	$ 1,003	$ 1,003	$ 1,003	$ 1,003	$ 1,003	$ 1,003
Payroll taxes	$ 7,013	$ 7,013	$ 7,013	$ 7,013	$ 7,013	$ 7,013	$ 7,013
Total operating costs	$ 70,564	$ 70,564	$ 70,564	$ 70,564	$ 70,564	$ 70,564	$ 70,564
EBITDA	$ 39,436	$ 39,491	$ 39,546	$ 39,601	$ 39,656	$ 39,711	$ 39,766
Federal income tax	$ 13,078	$ 13,084	$ 13,091	$ 13,097	$ 13,104	$ 13,110	$ 13,117
State income tax	$ 1,981	$ 1,982	$ 1,983	$ 1,984	$ 1,985	$ 1,986	$ 1,987
Interest expense	$ 0	$ 0	$ 0	$ 0	$ 0	$ 0	$ 0
Depreciation expense	$ 3,185	$ 3,185	$ 3,185	$ 3,185	$ 3,185	$ 3,185	$ 3,185
Net profit	$ 21,192	$ 21,240	$ 21,287	$ 21,335	$ 21,382	$ 21,430	$ 21,477

Profit and loss statement (first year cont.)

Months	8	9	10	11	12	1
Sales	$200,700	$ 200,800	$ 200,900	$201,000	$201,100	$2,406,600
Cost of goods sold	$ 90,315	$ 90,360	$ 90,405	$ 90,450	$ 90,495	$1,082,970
Gross margin	55.0%	55.0%	55.0%	55.0%	55.0%	55.0%
Operating income	$110,385	$ 110,440	$ 110,495	$110,550	$110,605	$1,323,630
Expenses						
Payroll	$ 46,750	$ 46,750	$ 46,750	$ 46,750	$ 46,750	$ 561,000
General and administrative	$ 2,700	$ 2,700	$ 2,700	$ 2,700	$ 2,700	$ 32,400
Distribution expenses	$ 4,011	$ 4,011	$ 4,011	$ 4,011	$ 4,011	$ 48,132
Professional fees and licensure	$ 1,268	$ 1,268	$ 1,268	$ 1,268	$ 1,268	$ 15,219
Insurance costs	$ 1,832	$ 1,832	$ 1,832	$ 1,832	$ 1,832	$ 21,987
Equipment costs	$ 2,300	$ 2,300	$ 2,300	$ 2,300	$ 2,300	$ 27,596
Rent and utilities	$ 3,688	$ 3,688	$ 3,688	$ 3,688	$ 3,688	$ 44,250
Miscellaneous costs	$ 1,003	$ 1,003	$ 1,003	$ 1,003	$ 1,003	$ 12,033
Payroll taxes	$ 7,013	$ 7,013	$ 7,013	$ 7,013	$ 7,013	$ 84,150
Total operating costs	$ 70,564	$ 70,564	$ 70,564	$ 70,564	$ 70,564	$ 846,767
EBITDA	$ 39,821	$ 39,876	$ 39,931	$ 39,986	$ 40,041	$ 476,863
Federal income tax	$ 13,124	$ 13,130	$ 13,137	$ 13,143	$ 13,150	$ 157,365
State income tax	$ 1,988	$ 1,989	$ 1,990	$ 1,991	$ 1,992	$ 23,843
Interest expense	$ 0	$ 0	$ 0	$ 0	$ 0	$ 0
Depreciation expense	$ 3,185	$ 3,185	$ 3,185	$ 3,185	$ 3,185	$ 38,214
Net profit	$ 21,525	$ 21,572	$ 21,620	$ 21,667	$ 21,714	$ 257,441

Profit and loss statement (second year)

Quarter	Q1	2 Q2	Q3	Q4	2
Sales	$577,584	$721,980	$779,738	$808,618	$2,887,920
Cost of goods sold	$259,913	$324,891	$350,882	$363,878	$1,299,564
Gross margin	55.0%	55.0%	55.0%	55.0%	55.0%
Operating income	$317,671	$397,089	$428,856	$444,740	$1,588,356
Expenses					
Payroll	$121,540	$151,925	$164,079	$170,156	$ 607,700
General and administrative	$ 6,739	$ 8,424	$ 9,098	$ 9,435	$ 33,696
Distribution expenses	$ 11,552	$ 14,440	$ 15,595	$ 16,172	$ 57,758
Professional fees and licensure	$ 3,135	$ 3,919	$ 4,232	$ 4,389	$ 15,676
Insurance costs	$ 4,617	$ 5,772	$ 6,233	$ 6,464	$ 23,086
Equipment costs	$ 6,071	$ 7,589	$ 8,196	$ 8,500	$ 30,356
Rent and utilities	$ 9,293	$ 11,616	$ 12,545	$ 13,010	$ 46,463
Miscellaneous costs	$ 2,888	$ 3,610	$ 3,899	$ 4,043	$ 14,440
Payroll taxes	$ 18,231	$ 22,789	$ 24,612	$ 25,523	$ 91,155
Total operating costs	$184,066	$230,082	$248,489	$257,692	$ 920,329
EBITDA	$133,605	$167,007	$180,367	$187,048	$ 668,027
Federal income tax	$ 44,090	$ 55,112	$ 59,521	$ 61,726	$ 220,449
State income tax	$ 6,680	$ 8,350	$ 9,018	$ 9,352	$ 33,401
Interest expense	$ 0	$ 0	$ 0	$ 0	$ 0
Depreciation expense	$ 9,554	$ 9,554	$ 9,554	$ 9,554	$ 38,214
Net profit	$ 73,282	$ 93,991	$102,274	$106,416	$ 375,962

Profit and loss statement (third year)

Quarter	Q1	3 Q2	Q3	Q4	3
Sales	$675,773	$844,717	$912,294	$946,083	$3,378,866
Cost of goods sold	$304,098	$380,122	$410,532	$425,737	$1,520,490
Gross margin	55.0%	55.0%	55.0%	55.0%	55.0%
Operating income	$371,675	$464,594	$501,762	$520,345	$1,858,377
Expenses					
Payroll	$131,339	$164,174	$177,308	$183,875	$ 656,697
General and administrative	$ 7,009	$ 8,761	$ 9,462	$ 9,812	$ 35,044
Distribution expenses	$ 13,515	$ 16,894	$ 18,246	$ 18,922	$ 67,577
Professional fees and licensure	$ 3,229	$ 4,036	$ 4,359	$ 4,521	$ 16,146
Insurance costs	$ 4,848	$ 6,060	$ 6,545	$ 6,787	$ 24,241
Equipment costs	$ 6,678	$ 8,348	$ 9,016	$ 9,350	$ 33,391
Rent and utilities	$ 9,757	$ 12,196	$ 13,172	$ 13,660	$ 48,786
Miscellaneous costs	$ 3,379	$ 4,224	$ 4,561	$ 4,730	$ 16,894
Payroll taxes	$ 19,701	$ 24,626	$ 26,596	$ 27,581	$ 98,505
Total operating costs	$199,456	$249,320	$269,266	$279,239	$ 997,280
EBITDA	$172,219	$215,274	$232,496	$241,107	$ 861,096
Federal income tax	$ 56,832	$ 71,040	$ 76,724	$ 79,565	$ 284,162
State income tax	$ 8,611	$ 10,764	$ 11,625	$ 12,055	$ 43,055
Interest expense	$ 0	$ 0	$ 0	$ 0	$ 0
Depreciation expense	$ 9,554	$ 9,554	$ 9,554	$ 9,554	$ 38,214
Net profit	$ 97,222	$123,916	$134,594	$139,933	$ 495,665

7.11 Three Year Cash Flow Analysis

Cash flow analysis (first year)

Month	1	2	3	4	5	6	7	8
Cash from operations	$ 24,377	$ 24,424	$ 24,472	$ 24,519	$ 24,567	$ 24,614	$ 24,662	$ 24,709
Cash from receivables	$ 0	$ 0	$ 0	$ 0	$ 0	$ 0	$ 0	$ 0
Operating cash inflow	**$ 24,377**	**$ 24,424**	**$ 24,472**	**$ 24,519**	**$ 24,567**	**$ 24,614**	**$ 24,662**	**$ 24,709**
Other cash inflows								
Equity investment	$600,000	$ 0	$ 0	$ 0	$ 0	$ 0	$ 0	$ 0
Increased borrowings	$ 0	$ 0	$ 0	$ 0	$ 0	$ 0	$ 0	$ 0
Sales of business assets	$ 0	$ 0	$ 0	$ 0	$ 0	$ 0	$ 0	$ 0
A/P increases	$ 3,159	$ 3,159	$ 3,159	$ 3,159	$ 3,159	$ 3,159	$ 3,159	$ 3,159
Total other cash inflows	**$603,159**	**$ 3,159**	**$ 3,159**	**$ 3,159**	**$ 3,159**	**$ 3,159**	**$ 3,159**	**$ 3,159**
Total cash inflow	**$627,535**	**$ 27,583**	**$ 27,630**	**$ 27,678**	**$ 27,725**	**$ 27,773**	**$ 27,820**	**$ 27,868**
Cash outflows								
Repayment of principal	$ 0	$ 0	$ 0	$ 0	$ 0	$ 0	$ 0	$ 0
A/P decreases	$ 2,075	$ 2,075	$ 2,075	$ 2,075	$ 2,075	$ 2,075	$ 2,075	$ 2,075
A/R increases	$ 0	$ 0	$ 0	$ 0	$ 0	$ 0	$ 0	$ 0
Asset purchases	$535,000	$ 0	$ 0	$ 0	$ 0	$ 0	$ 0	$ 0
Dividends	$ 0	$ 0	$ 0	$ 0	$ 0	$ 0	$ 0	$ 0
Total cash outflows	**$537,075**	**$ 2,075**	**$ 2,075**	**$ 2,075**	**$ 2,075**	**$ 2,075**	**$ 2,075**	**$ 2,075**
Net cash flow	**$ 90,461**	**$ 25,508**	**$ 25,556**	**$ 25,603**	**$ 25,650**	**$ 25,698**	**$ 25,745**	**$ 25,793**
Cash balance	**$ 90,461**	**$115,969**	**$141,524**	**$167,127**	**$192,778**	**$218,476**	**$244,221**	**$270,014**

Cash flow analysis (first year cont.)

Month	9	10	11	12	1
Cash from operations	$ 24,757	$ 24,804	$ 24,852	$ 24,899	$295,655
Cash from receivables	$ 0	$ 0	$ 0	$ 0	$ 0
Operating cash inflow	**$ 24,757**	**$ 24,804**	**$ 24,852**	**$ 24,899**	**$295,655**
Other cash inflows					
Equity investment	$ 0	$ 0	$ 0	$ 0	$600,000
Increased borrowings	$ 0	$ 0	$ 0	$ 0	$ 0
Sales of business assets	$ 0	$ 0	$ 0	$ 0	$ 0
A/P increases	$ 3,159	$ 3,159	$ 3,159	$ 3,159	$ 37,902
Total other cash inflows	**$ 3,159**	**$ 3,159**	**$ 3,159**	**$ 3,159**	**$637,902**
Total cash inflow	**$ 27,915**	**$ 27,963**	**$ 28,010**	**$ 28,058**	**$933,557**
Cash outflows					
Repayment of principal	$ 0	$ 0	$ 0	$ 0	$ 0
A/P decreases	$ 2,075	$ 2,075	$ 2,075	$ 2,075	$ 24,897
A/R increases	$ 0	$ 0	$ 0	$ 0	$ 0
Asset purchases	$ 0	$ 0	$ 0	$ 0	$535,000
Dividends	$ 0	$ 0	$ 0	$133,045	$133,045
Total cash outflows	**$ 2,075**	**$ 2,075**	**$ 2,075**	**$135,120**	**$692,942**
Net cash flow	**$ 25,840**	**$ 25,888**	**$ 25,935**	**−$107,062**	**$240,615**
Cash balance	**$295,854**	**$321,742**	**$347,677**	**$240,615**	**$240,615**

Cash flow analysis (second year)

Quarter	Q1	2 Q2	Q3	Q4	2
Cash from operations	$ 82,835	$103,544	$111,828	$115,969	$414,177
Cash from receivables	$ 0	$ 0	$ 0	$ 0	$ 0
Operating cash inflow	**$ 82,835**	**$103,544**	**$111,828**	**$115,969**	**$414,177**
Other cash inflows					
Equity investment	$ 0	$ 0	$ 0	$ 0	$ 0
Increased borrowings	$ 0	$ 0	$ 0	$ 0	$ 0
Sales of business assets	$ 0	$ 0	$ 0	$ 0	$ 0
A/P increases	$ 8,717	$ 10,897	$ 11,769	$ 12,204	$ 43,587
Total other cash inflows	**$ 8,717**	**$ 10,897**	**$ 11,769**	**$ 12,204**	**$ 43,587**
Total cash inflow	**$ 91,553**	**$114,441**	**$123,596**	**$128,174**	**$457,764**
Cash outflows					
Repayment of principal	$ 0	$ 0	$ 0	$ 0	$ 0
A/P decreases	$ 5,975	$ 7,469	$ 8,067	$ 8,365	$ 29,876
A/R increases	$ 0	$ 0	$ 0	$ 0	$ 0
Asset purchases	$ 41,418	$ 51,772	$ 55,914	$ 57,985	$207,088
Dividends	$ 37,276	$ 46,595	$ 50,322	$ 52,186	$186,380
Total cash outflows	**$ 84,669**	**$105,836**	**$114,303**	**$118,536**	**$423,344**
Net cash flow	**$ 6,884**	**$ 8,605**	**$ 9,293**	**$ 9,638**	**$ 34,420**
Cash balance	**$247,499**	**$256,104**	**$265,397**	**$275,035**	**$275,035**

Cash flow analysis (third year)

Quarter	Q1	3 Q2	Q3	Q4	3
Cash from operations	$106,776	$133,470	$144,147	$149,486	$533,880
Cash from receivables	$ 0	$ 0	$ 0	$ 0	$ 0
Operating cash inflow	**$106,776**	**$133,470**	**$144,147**	**$149,486**	**$533,880**
Other cash inflows					
Equity investment	$ 0	$ 0	$ 0	$ 0	$ 0
Increased borrowings	$ 0	$ 0	$ 0	$ 0	$ 0
Sales of business assets	$ 0	$ 0	$ 0	$ 0	$ 0
A/P increases	$ 10,025	$ 12,531	$ 13,534	$ 14,035	$ 50,125
Total other cash inflows	**$ 10,025**	**$ 12,531**	**$ 13,534**	**$ 14,035**	**$ 50,125**
Total cash inflow	**$116,801**	**$146,001**	**$157,681**	**$163,521**	**$584,005**
Cash outflows					
Repayment of principal	$ 0	$ 0	$ 0	$ 0	$ 0
A/P decreases	$ 7,170	$ 8,963	$ 9,680	$ 10,038	$ 35,852
A/R increases	$ 0	$ 0	$ 0	$ 0	$ 0
Asset purchases	$ 53,388	$ 66,735	$ 72,074	$ 74,743	$266,940
Dividends	$ 48,049	$ 60,061	$ 64,866	$ 67,269	$240,246
Total cash outflows	**$108,607**	**$135,759**	**$146,620**	**$152,050**	**$543,037**
Net cash flow	**$ 8,194**	**$ 10,242**	**$ 11,061**	**$ 11,471**	**$ 40,968**
Cash balance	**$283,229**	**$293,470**	**$304,532**	**$316,003**	**$316,003**

Junk Removal Business

Harry's Haul-Away Service Inc.

2159 Pine Street
Hollywood, Florida 33081

Paul Greenland

Located in Broward County, Florida, Harry's Haul-Away Service Inc. is a new "junk removal" business.

EXECUTIVE SUMMARY

Business Overview

Located in Broward County, Florida, Harry's Haul-Away Service Inc. is a new "junk removal" business. In addition to the removal of construction debris and unwanted items (such as clothing, household items, and old furniture) for individuals and business owners, our enterprise specializes in removing property from foreclosed homes as well as items that evicted tenants have left behind in apartment buildings.

In October of 2010 Harry Smith lost his job as a tool and die maker with ABC Manufacturing Co., where he had been employed for 15 years. Unable to find similar work, Harry decided to take advantage of equipment that he already owned (a full-size pickup truck, 16-foot enclosed trailer, and a large flatbed trailer) and establish his own haul-away service. Harry's 20-year-old son Bill, who also had lost his job at ABC Manufacturing, joined him in the enterprise.

MARKET ANALYSIS

During the late 2000s and early 2010s, home foreclosures reached record levels nationwide. Florida was among the states that were impacted the most severely. According to data from LPS Applied Analytics, among Florida's 67 counties, foreclosures were highest in our home market of southern Florida. In Miami-Dade County alone, foreclosures totaled 94,785, followed by 62,369 in Broward County, and 45,829 in Palm Beach County.

Harry's Haul-Away Service will begin operations by serving the primary service area of Broward County. In 2009 Broward was home to 618,127 households and 81,895 business establishments (including 9,797 finance, insurance & real estate businesses), according to *DemographicsNow* data (SRC LLC).

In addition, Harry's Haul-Away Service also will market its services to older adults and disabled individuals, who may have a difficult time removing and disposing of heavier items. In Broward County alone, *DemographicsNow* indicated that there were 202,964 individuals between the ages of 55 and 64, a total of 119,469 people between the ages of 65 and 74, and 130,137 residents over the age of 75.

PERSONNEL

Harry's Haul-Away Service is owned and operated by Harry Smith. In October 2010 Harry Smith lost his job as a tool and die maker with ABC Manufacturing Co., where he had been employed for 15 years. Unable to find similar work, Harry decided to take advantage of equipment that he already owned (a full-size pickup truck, 16-foot enclosed trailer, and a large flatbed trailer) and establish his own haul-away service. While working for ABC Manufacturing, one of Harry's responsibilities was to transport scrap metal to a local recycling center, and to arrange for the sale and/or disposal of old equipment.

Harry's 20-year-old son Bill, who also had lost his job at ABC Manufacturing, has joined him in the new enterprise. A graduate of Randall Kennedy Community College, Bill has a two-year accounting degree, with practical experience in bookkeeping. In addition to working hand-in-hand with his father, Bill will also manage Harry's Haul-Away Service's books and other administrative tasks associated with the business. What's more, he also has experience buying and selling items on eBay and other popular online sites, which will be useful when the new business decides to refurbish and resell items, rather than dispose of them.

GROWTH STRATEGY

Because home foreclosures will likely be our greatest growth opportunity, we will utilize recent foreclosure data to promote our services to financial institutions in a strategic way. We will begin by concentrating on banks with property holdings in specific Broward County communities from the above listing (report and map available upon request). By reinvesting as much of our profits as we can into the business, our hope is to add two additional staff members and a vehicle-trailer combination during each of our second and third years of operation.

Each year, Harry's Haul-Away Service will expand its services one county at a time. During our second year we will expand our market area to include Miami-Dade County, which in 2009 consisted of 838,027 households and 119,261 business establishments (including 13,694 businesses in the finance, insurance & real estate category). Finally, during our third year we plan to add service in Palm Beach County. In 2009 this larger, three-county market area consisted of 1.97 million households and 264,154 business establishments (including 31,768 businesses in the finance, insurance & real estate category).

As the business expands during years two and three, Harry's Haul-Away Service will continue to market its services to older adults and disabled individuals. In 2009 Miami-Dade County included 267,108 individuals between the ages of 55 and 64, another 182,129 in the 65-to-74 age group, and 174,226 residents over the age of 75. Finally, the larger three-county area included 617,265 individuals between the ages of 55 and 64, another 412,233 in the 65-to-74 age group, and 461,525 residents over the age of 75.

SERVICES

We remove individual items, and also perform room-specific or "whole-house" clean-outs, including:

- Basements
- Attics
- Garages
- Sheds
- Apartments
- Townhouses

- Storage units
- Condominiums
- Warehouses
- Factories
- Offices
- Other commercial structures

Items that we remove include:

- Air-conditioners
- Books
- Bricks
- Carpeting
- Chairs
- Clothing
- Computers
- Concrete
- Construction debris
- Dehumidifiers
- Dirt
- Dryers
- Entertainment centers
- Filing cabinets
- Hot tubs/jacuzzis
- Loveseats
- Mattresses
- Microwaves
- Miscellaneous household items
- Miscellaneous recyclable items
- Monitors
- Moving boxes
- Paper
- Pianos
- Playset demolition/removal
- Radios
- Refrigerators
- Sand
- Sofas

- Storage shed demolition/removal

- Stoves

- Tables

- Televisions

- Tree limbs/stumps

- Washers

- Yard waste

Acknowledging the impact that landfills have on the environment, our business will attempt to recycle, or refurbish and sell, at least 50 percent of the material we haul away from customers.

For liability and licensing reasons, Harry's Haul-Away does not remove hazardous materials or liquids (e.g., gasoline, paints, solvents, oils, pesticides, etc.).

MARKETING & SALES

Harry's Haul-Away will rely upon the following marketing tactics to promote our business:

- A promotional flyer that we will distribute in neighborhoods throughout Broward County.

- Advertisements in print and online yellow page listings.

- A Web site with complete details about Harry's Haul-Away and the services we offer. Our site will include an initial "intake form," which customers can complete and submit to us as part of our free estimate process.

- Videos on YouTube to showcase our professional staff, vehicles, and quality approach to projects. We plan to add video testimonials from customers at the earliest opportunity.

- Direct mailings to rental property owners and finance companies/banks promoting our services, including various discount options.

OPERATIONS

Harry's Haul-Away will operate Monday through Saturday, from 8 AM to 5 PM. As an owner-operated business, we will make every attempt to provide excellent customer service. We will respond to all customer inquiries within three hours. Calls received after normal business hours (e.g., 5 PM) will be returned at the beginning of the next business day.

Harry's Haul-Away Service charges a minimum $75 service fee, which includes one service person removing one item. On average, we charge $75 for a half-vanload and $150 for a full vanload. Our fees will vary depending on the weight of the items that require disposal. Most of the landfills in our area charge $60 per ton for loose material and yard waste (one-ton minimum). Some landfills have drop-off areas where individual items are accepted at a price of $5 per item. In addition, our fees will be higher in the event that two service people are needed, or if items are located in areas that are difficult to access.

In addition to our usual fees for junk removal, special charges will sometimes apply:

- Appliances containing Freon will be disposed of for an additional $30.

- Freon-free appliances will be disposed of for an additional $20.

- Batteries and car tires will carry an additional fee of $5 per item.

LEGAL

Harry's Haul-Away has completed all necessary paperwork with the Board of County Commissioners, Finance and Administrative Services Department, to operate a business in Broward County, Florida. Our employees are bonded and insured, and we have secured appropriate insurance for our vehicles through State Farm (documentation available upon request). We adhere to all regulations set forth by Broward County, Waste and Recycling Services, Solid Waste Operations Division.

FINANCIAL ANALYSIS

Estimated sales and expenses for our first year of operations are available if desired. Sales projections that reflect our expansion plans during years two and three are available upon request, along with detailed monthly cash flow projections for years one through three.

The owners will rely upon $15,000 from personal savings and investments for use as working capital during the first year of business.

SWOT Analysis

Strengths: We own our own vehicle and trailer; no major capital purchases are needed to start the business.

Weaknesses: We are a one-truck operation; business continuity is a concern in the event of a major/expensive breakdown.

Opportunities: The high rate of home foreclosures in our market means there will be ample business opportunities.

Threats: Unpredictable fuel prices are always a concern. In addition, a low cost of entry in this line of business means we will have plenty of competition, requiring us to differentiate our business with professionalism, exceptional service, and competitive pricing.

Media Duplication & Transferring Business

DupliPro Inc.

2117 Smith Ave.
Apple Grove, AZ 85333

Paul Greenland

DupliPro provides audio and video duplication (CDs and DVDs), digital media transferring (analog to digital media), and other ancillary services (disc repair and media destruction/disposal).

EXECUTIVE SUMMARY

Business Overview

By 2011 many types of organizations were in need of an affordable means of duplicating and distributing digital media to their members, employees, and customers. Content included everything from presentations and sermons to meetings and training material. Demand was especially strong among educational institutions, non-profit organizations, healthcare providers, and religious organizations. While some organizations distribute content online, there still is a significant need to distribute information via CDs and DVDs. In addition, consumers and organizations both needed to preserve decaying analog media, such as film, video, photographs, 35mm slides, and transparencies by converting them to a digital format.

DupliPro provides affordable audio and video duplication (CDs and DVDs), digital media transferring (analog to digital media), and other ancillary services (disc repair and media destruction/disposal). We accept original media from customers via pre-arranged pickup (local), courier, mail, UPS/FedEx, or the upload area (FTP) on our Web site.

Our company is a new enterprise established by David Roberts, who has more than 15 years of experience in the media services industry. Until recently, he was employed by Smith & Hampton Worldwide, a diversified conglomerate that decided to outsource its media services. Currently unemployed, Roberts has decided to capitalize on his skill and experience by establishing his own business.

MARKET ANALYSIS

DupliPro is located in Apple Grove, a mid-sized city in Arizona with 6,500 organizations and businesses and 153,000 residents. DupliPro will define its market along the lines of its two primary service offerings, duplication services and transferring services.

Duplication Services

DupliPro will market its duplication services almost exclusively to the commercial market. Specifically, we have classified prospective customers as follows:

- Advertising Agencies (35)

- Churches (213)

- Colleges & Universities (11)

- Conference & Convention Centers (4)

- Education & Library Services (35)

- Entertainment & Recreation Services (92)

- Health & Medical Service Providers (392)

- Hospitals (3)

- Hotels & Lodging (25)

- Legal Services (229)

- Membership Organizations (285)

- Museums & Zoos (15)

- Professional Services (241)

- School Districts (1)

- Social Services (249)

Transfer Services

Although DupliPro will provide transferring services to consumers and organizations, consumers will likely account for the majority of business within this category. Specifically, consumers with household incomes of $50,000 and up will represent our most lucrative prospects. As of 2010, the average household income in Apple Grove was $56,447. According to data from Viking Research Associates, the market can be further sub-divided as follows:

$50,000 - $74,999—10,053 (17.4%)

$75,000 - $99,999—5,570 (9.6%)

$100,000 - $149,999—5,187 (9.0%)

$150,000 +—2,606 (4.5%)

By 2015, the average household income in our market is expected to reach $59,000. At that time, household income will break out as follows:

$50,000 to $74,999—9,980 (16.9%)

$75,000 to $99,999—5,937 (10.1%)

$100,000 to $149,999—6,048 (10.3%)

$150,000 +—2,931 (5.0%)

In addition to income, we anticipate that consumers aged 55 to 74 will account for the majority of our transfer business.

According to Viking Research Associates, our market breaks down according to age as follows:

55 to 64—16,032 (10.5%)

65 to 74—11,229 (7.3%)

These two age brackets are expected to achieve meaningful growth through 2015:

55 to 64—18,250 (11.6%)

65 to 74—13,982 (8.9%)

Competition

According to David Roberts' knowledge of the local market, the majority of organizations in Apple Grove currently handle most of their duplication needs in-house, or utilize large national services. DupliPro will provide the same service at a lower cost and with personalized, local service.

In addition, Apple Grove currently has no media services business that provides transfer services. Customers must travel, or ship their precious original media, to Phoenix (90 minutes away) to have their needs met in this area. Many perform transfers on their own, often with mixed results. DupliPro will provide transfer services of the highest quality directly within Apple Grove at a competitive price.

PERSONNEL

David Roberts has more than 15 years of experience in the media services industry. Until recently, he was employed by Smith & Hampton Worldwide, a diversified conglomerate that decided to outsource its media services. Currently unemployed, Roberts has decided to capitalize on his skill and experience by establishing his own business.

At Smith & Hampton David was a member of the media services department, which included a graphic designer, photographer, videographer, and video editor. David served as the organization's in-house "service bureau." In that role he was responsible for maintaining archives of 35mm slides, photographs, digital images, film, and video. He frequently was called upon to convert analog media to digital formats. His role involved scanning slides and photographs, and performing pre-press services, such as color correction.

Professional & Advisory Support

DupliPro has established a business banking account with Apple Grove Community Bank, as well as a merchant account for accepting credit card payments. Accounting and tax advisory services will be provided by Quality Accounting Services. David Roberts has utilized an online legal document service to prepare the paperwork necessary for incorporating his new business.

GROWTH STRATEGY

Years 1-3: Focus on marketing and sales, with an objective of generating awareness in the local marketplace and building a core base of commercial customers.

Year 4: Potentially relocate operations to leased space in Apple Grove's business district, in order to increase visibility and customer access for transfer services. Consider the addition of one full-time employee to concentrate on production so that Dave Roberts can continue efforts to grow the business.

Your 5: Begin offering specialized, enhanced services, such as media transfers to customized USB flash drives and specialized board packaging for CDs and DVDs, including self-mailers.

PRODUCTS & SERVICES

DupliPro will provide customers with quotes in one business day or less. Quotes will be provided via phone, or the online form on our company's Web site.

Audio & Video Duplication

Customers choose from a series of packaging and disc templates, or we can provide basic graphic design services utilizing a customer's original artwork to create a desired look.

- CD Duplication

- DVD Duplication

Video Transfers (to DVD or external storage media)

- VHS

- 8mm film

- 16 mm film

- 35mm film

- PAL - NTSC

- Beta

- Camcorder

- Digital Files

Audio Transfers (to MP3, MP4, WAV, WMA, CDA format on CD, DVD, or external storage media)

- Cassettes

- Microcassettes

- Records

- Audio Reels

Photo Transfers (to CD, DVD, or external storage media)

- 35mm Slides

- Transparencies

- Prints

- Negatives

Packaging Options

- Paper Window Envelopes (standard)

- Clamshells (plastic cases)

- Jewel Cases

- Standard DVD Cases

- Slim DVD Cases

MARKETING & SALES

DupliPro has developed a marketing plan that includes the following tactics:

- Two four-color sales sheets (one promoting duplication services and one promoting transfer/ancillary services) that can be included in direct mailings, presented during sales calls, and distributed at local and regional events.

- Quarterly public exhibitions at the Apple Grove Mall to promote transfer services. A looping demonstration video will play on a large monitor as part of DupliPro's exhibit, demonstrating how we digitize and color correct old photos and slides, and transfer old film to DVD.

- A sustained (monthly) direct-mail campaign to prospective duplication customers in Apple Grove. A reputable list broker has been identified, along with an area mail house that can prepare the mailings.

- Sales calls to prospective customers, especially religious and educational institutions, which will likely have the greatest need for our duplication services.

- A Web site with complete details about our capabilities and services, as well as a File Transfer Protocol (FTP) area where customers can upload digital files for duplication.

- A Yellow Page advertisement promoting both duplication and transfer services.

- A customer incentive program that provides a 10 percent discount off of a customer's first order.

- Magnetic business cards that will double as advertising specialties.

- Active membership in the local Chamber of Commerce.

OPERATIONS

Facility & Location

DupliPro will begin operations from the owner's home. Areas of the home dedicated to business use will include:

- A finished, 20 x 20 area in the basement. This room will include dedicated areas for disc repair, disc shredding/destruction, disc duplication, completed customer orders, and blank media storage.

- A 12 x 12 upstairs bedroom dedicated to audio and video transferring.

Equipment

DupliPro will utilize the following equipment for operations:

Norazza E23100 Automatic Data Destroyer ($100)
By making thousands of small imprints to CDs or DVDs, this device prevents unauthorized access to data following disposal, thereby preventing identity theft, privacy violations, and corporate espionage. It is capable of destroying discs at a rate of 15 per minute.

Epson Discproducer PP-100N with Security ($8,500)
This device prints and burns as many as 100 discs per minute, utilizing advanced printing and robotics technology. The PP-100N is compatible with any computer network and can receive as many as five jobs at once. A door lock prevents unauthorized access, and further security for published discs is provided by a password protection feature. According to the manufacturer, the Epson DiscProducer is "the professional choice for on-demand CD and DVD disc publishing."

CD Repairman One Step Disc Repair Machine ($2,200)
This programmable device repairs scratched or dirty CDs, DVDs, and videogames, utilizing a polishing pad and a special polishing compound that removes debris.

HP Pavilion Desktop Computer ($500)

Viewsonic 27 inch Widescreen LCD Monitor ($350)

LG 42-Inch 720p Plasma HDTV & Stand ($850)
This will be used for demonstration purposes at events and exhibitions.

Adobe Creative Suite 3 Production Premium Software ($1,600)
Includes the following audio/video applications—Photoshop CS3 extended, Illustrator CS3, Flash CS3 Professional, After Effects CS3 Professional, Premiere Pro CS3, Soundbooth CS3, Encore CS3, On Location, Ultra CS3.

ELMO Dual 8 Movie Projector, Telecine Video Transfer System ($1,500)
This equipment is used to make high-quality transfers of 8mm dual (Regular 8mm and Super 8 Silent) to NTSC or PAL, as well as standard definition or high-definition video.

Seagate 4TB Network Storage Server ($650)

HP Scanjet 8300 4800 dpi 48bit USB Interface Flatbed Scanner ($450)

Cables & Accessories ($500)

Hours of Operation

Although DupliPro is a home-based business, giving the owner the flexibility to perform production work at any time, we will accept e-mails and phone calls from customers during regular business hours:

Monday through Friday—9 am to 5pm

Saturday—9 am to 12 noon

Sunday—Closed

In order to maximize accessibility, DupliPro will have a dedicated telephone number where customers can opt to leave a voicemail message. The owner will attempt to return all routine inquiries within one business day.

Pricing

Audio & Video Duplication
CD Prices (per disc)

1 to 5—$5.36

6 to 24—$3.16

25 to 49—$2.06

50 to 99—$1.84

100 to 199—$1.51

200 to 299—$1.40

300 to 499—$1.29

500+—$1.18

DVD Prices (per disc)

1 to 5—$5.46

6 to 24—$3.26

25 to 49—$2.16

50 to 99—$1.94

100 to 199—$1.61

200 to 299—$1.50

300 to 499—$1.39

500+—$1.28

Prices include art (furnished by customer) inkjet printed onto each CD or DVD, and a paper sleeve. Plastic DVD cases are provided at an additional charge (free quotes provided upon request).

Video Transfers (to DVD or external storage media)
Prices (per-foot)

1 to 999 feet—$.25

1,000 to 4,999 feet—$.24

5,000 to 9,999 feet—$.23

10,000 to 19,999 feet—$.21

20,000+ feet—$.20

We will provide customers with a chart that can be used to estimate the length of their film. For example:

50-foot reel (4 minutes, diameter of 3 inches)

100-foot reel (8 minutes, diameter of 3.75 inches)

200-foot reel (16 minutes, diameter of 5 inches)

400-foot reel (32 minutes, diameter of 7 inches)

Color correction services are provided for an additional $.25 per foot.

Audio Transfers (analog to MP3, MP4, WAV, WMA, CDA format on CD, DVD, or external storage media)
$14.95 per cassette tape, record album, or audio reel.

Photo Scanning/Correction (transfer to CD, DVD, or external storage media)
Basic Scanning (no correction)—$1 per image.

Retouching—$5-$20 (depending on condition of original). Includes red-eye removal, damage repair, cropping, dust/scratch removal, color correction, and re-orientation.

Packaging Options
Many options are available; prices available upon request.

Insurance

DupliPro has secured appropriate business and liability insurance coverage through Thompson Insurance Associates.

LEGAL

DupliPro will adhere to all US and international copyright laws. Duplication only will be provided for individuals or organizations who own the copyright for their material, or for content that is non-copyrighted or in the public domain. Customers will be required to hold DupliPro harmless from allegations of copyright infringement.

All original media provided for duplication or transferring will be returned to the customer following the provision of service. Upon request, we will archive digital master files for customers on our secure, password-protected server, expediting additional duplication services that may be needed at a later time.

FINANCIAL ANALYSIS

DupliPro has prepared the following projections for the first three years of operations. Detailed figures used for estimation purposes are available upon request. David Roberts is seeking a business loan to cover the equipment costs of $17,200. In addition, he will provide $15,000 from his personal savings for general business purposes.

Three-year proforma profit & loss

	2010	2011	2012
Revenue	$65,520	$75,348	$86,650
Expenses			
Advertising & marketing	$ 5,000	$ 3,000	$ 3,000
Miscellaneous items	$ 250	$ 300	$ 350
Legal	$ 1,250	$ 250	$ 250
Accounting	$ 500	$ 500	$ 500
Office supplies	$ 500	$ 550	$ 600
Duplication supplies	$ 7,000	$ 9,000	$11,000
Loan	$ 7,356	$ 7,356	$ 7,356
Equipment repair	$ 1,500	$ 1,500	$ 1,500
Business insurance	$ 500	$ 550	$ 600
Salary	$30,000	$35,000	$40,000
Postage	$ 450	$ 550	$ 650
Telecommunications	$ 500	$ 550	$ 600
Broadband internet	$ 600	$ 650	$ 700
Total expenses	**$55,406**	**$59,756**	**$67,106**
Net income	$10,114	$15,592	$19,544

Summary of proposed financing

Monthly payment	$ 612.98
Total loan amount	$22,067.28
Total payments	36
Total interest paid	$ 2,067.28
Payoff date	12-31-13

Year	Interest	Principal	Balance
2011	$1,116.29	$6,239.47	$13,760.59
2012	$ 698.42	$6,657.34	$ 7,103.19
2013	$ 252.57	$7,103.19	$ 0

Evaluation & Adjustment

This plan will be evaluated on a quarterly basis.

Mobile App Development Business

AppStax LLC

4509 Grand St.
Portland, Oregon 97217

AppStax is a developer of mobile computer applications for both consumer and enterprise markets.

This plan originally appeared in Business Plans Handbook, Volume 1; *it has been updated for this volume.*

EXECUTIVE SUMMARY

Business Overview

Portland, Oregon-based AppStax is a developer of mobile computer applications for both consumer and enterprise markets. Commonly referred to as "apps," mobile applications are software programs designed to run on mobile devices including cell phones and smartphones. Consumers utilize apps for everything from playing games and checking the weather to staying current on the latest news and accessing social media sites. Businesses use "enterprise apps" to provide their employees with a wide range of work-related tools.

Organized as a limited liability company, AppStax is owned by Jeremy Miller, an experienced software developer who has decided to concentrate his efforts mainly on the development of mobile apps. The majority of Jeremy's expertise is related to developing Macintosh applications. For this reason, his business will initially focus on developing apps for the popular Apple iPhone, iPod Touch, and iPad. However, Jeremy also will offer Android app development, which will be outsourced to another developer. AppStax eventually plans to hire a dedicated Android developer.

MARKET ANALYSIS

Data from the research firm Gartner indicated that mobile users would spend more than $6 billion on mobile apps in 2010. A separate analysis conducted by Jupiter Research projected that indirect and direct revenues from mobile applications will exceed $25 billion by 2014.

Apps targeted at individual consumers fall within a large number of different categories, including, but not limited to:

- Books
- Business
- Education
- Entertainment

- Finance

- Games

- Health & Fitness

- Lifestyle

- Medical

- Music

- Navigation

- News

- Productivity

- Reference

- Social Networking

- Sports

- Travel

- Weather

In addition, there is significant market potential for enterprise apps, which organizations utilize for a variety of purposes. Examples include:

- Fleet Vehicle Management

- Sales Force Automation/Field Force Automation

- Customer Service

- Inventory Management

- Property Management

- Professional Reference (e.g., medical/legal)

- Business Intelligence

- Enterprise Resource Planning

INDUSTRY ANALYSIS

Although significant opportunities existed for mobile app developers during the 2010s, the industry climate was extremely competitive. As Deepak Swamy explained in the May 17, 2010, issue of *Total Telecom Online*: "Discovery remains an intractable problem for the bottom 60% of applications. Device fragmentation and app store variations require independent software vendors (ISVs) to take precious resources away from innovation and to put them on the appointment instead of development." For many independent developers and development firms, success or failure was dictated by getting applications on the market quickly.

Enterprise users remained a key market for mobile apps. According to Frost & Sullivan, revenues for mobile workforce management, mobile sales force automation, mobile office, and enhanced fleet management applications alone totaled $2.84 billion in 2009. By 2015 revenues from such applications were forecast to reach $10.87 billion. Businesses stood to reap a return on investment from applications through reductions in employee overtime, speedier sales cycles, reduced paperwork, faster service response times, and improved billing accuracy.

Significant growth was forecast for the mobile app industry during the second and third decades of the 21st century. In the short term, a forecast from Chetan Sharma Consulting indicated that the "global mobile application economy" would be valued at $17.5 billion by 2012. By comparison, compact disc sales were expected to total $13.8 billion at that time. A separate analysis conducted by Jupiter Research projected indirect and direct revenues from mobile applications would exceed $25 billion by 2014.

By 2010 numerous education opportunities existed for developers of mobile apps. For example, the Association of Strategic Marketing offered audio conferences that addressed mobile application development issues for businesses. Topics ranged from differences between platforms and targeting customers with social media and location-based services.

PERSONNEL

Owner Profile

Jermy Miller began his career developing applications for the Apple Macintosh. Most recently, he served as senior software developer with Golden Hammer, a leading publisher of breakthrough educational programs. Over the course of seven years Jeremy utilized his architectural abilities and project management skills to oversee the development of nearly 30 applications, including several English-as-a-second-language (ESL) applications that earned international recognition.

After writing several mobile applications for the Apple iPhone (on a freelance basis), Jeremy was intrigued by the market potential for his work. He has decided to pursue this specific type of development work on a dedicated basis. However, for financial reasons, he will continue developing traditional applications as needed, until he can shift the majority of his project work to the mobile space.

A copy of Jeremy's resume is available upon request, along with a detailed listing of the software applications he has developed throughout his career.

Professional & Advisory Support

Jeremy acknowledges that the work performed by his new business will often involve contracts with clients, including non-compete and non-disclosure agreements. In addition, AppStax will need to ensure that it protects intellectual property rights specific to its own original mobile apps. With this in mind, Jeremy will rely on the law firm of Lee, Norris & Chan, which has specialized expertise in intellectual property law, in the event that counsel is needed. In addition, he has established a business banking account with Fountainhead Community Bank, as well as a merchant account for accepting credit card payments. Tax advisement will be provided by Marsh & Brooks Accounting LLC.

GROWTH STRATEGY

AppStax will begin as a "one-man" development shop. Jeremy Miller will rely upon his individual skills to develop consumer and enterprise-focused mobile apps for the Apple platform. Android development will be offered to customers, but the work initially will be subcontracted to freelance developers with whom Jeremy has established relationships. Generally speaking, reliable subcontractors will be utilized for all types of development work, in order to provide AppStax with flexibility and scalability during its formative years.

During the second year AppStax plans to actually hire an Android developer who, likewise, will have relationships with a network of independent contractors that can be of use to the business. If the Android developer proves to be the right person, Jeremy will consider making this individual a partner in the business.

Android is an important part of the company's growth strategy because it is exploding in popularity worldwide. In fact, some feel that the operating system is poised to be the Windows of the application world. Android is an open source operating system that can be customized as desired. The advantage is that apps can be developed for multiple handsets and multiple mobile carriers, and the developer is not tied to rules and requirements established by a specific company, such as Apple. Although this is an advantage, it also can make development more complex. In some cases, applications must be simplified so that they will work on the greatest number of handsets, for example. Another downside is that the Android Marketplace is more crowded than the Apple App Store, because it is easier to have apps listed there.

Finally, during the third year AppStax will consider offering Blackberry app development. These services also can be offered via the use of independent contractors, or by hiring a dedicated developer with the appropriate skill set. Like Android, Blackberry is a popular platform, especially for the corporate/enterprise market.

SERVICES

Generally speaking, AppStax will provide mobile app development services via one of two models:

Original Application Development

First, AppStax will develop its own "home grown" apps and attempt to market and sell them via leading app marketplaces, such as the Apple App Store and Google's Android Marketplace. By using effective marketing tactics (outlined below), our objective will be to generate a steady stream of revenue from our own software products.

In addition to challenges associated with development and marketing, it can be difficult for developers to have their apps included in the various online marketplaces. For example, Apple maintains control over which apps are included in the Apple App Store; apps must meet the company's specific requirements. Conversely, it is much easier to make an app available via the Android Marketplace. In the latter case, competition is greater due to the larger number of competing apps.

Work-for-Hire Development

AppStax also will develop mobile apps for other clients (e.g., game developers, large corporations, Web developers, interactive marketing agencies, etc.). In some cases we will develop apps on a "work-for-hire" basis, receiving a flat fee for developing the app. In this scenario the client then receives all sales/royalties in connection with the app. Opportunities for updates and enhancements will likely exist in cases such as these. We also will develop apps under a variety of other arrangements, including royalty arrangements, etc.

MARKETING & SALES

AppStax will rely upon the following marketing tactics:

- A Web site promoting AppStax's development capabilities. Our site will include a profile of Jeremy Miller and his capabilities, case study examples of recent mobile app projects he has completed for clients as an independent contractor, customer testimonials, Jeremy's blog, and links to the business' presence on social media outlets such as Facebook and Twitter.

- Search engine optimization (SEO). We will continuously monitor and modify our Web site in order to ensure that content appears in results for leading search engines, including Google and Yahoo!.

- A word-of-mouth marketing strategy that will place a heavy emphasis on networking with other developers and marketing/technology professionals at prospective client organizations (e.g., technology companies, entertainment businesses, video game publishers, etc.)

- A media relations strategy that will involve submitting case studies to technology trade publications, such as *ITProfessional, Computerworld, InformationWeek,* etc., and via leading newswire services like PR Newswire.

- Attendance at leading industry trade shows and seminars. In addition to networking opportunities, Jeremy Miller will make best practices presentations to the development community regarding mobile app development.

OPERATIONS

Location

In order to keep overhead low, AppStax will operate from a home office during the first several years of operations. Jeremy Miller has devoted ample space within his home to be used specifically for business purposes. Although some business travel may be necessary, whenever possible Jeremy will conduct Web-based meetings with clients and other developers. When business travel is required, AppStax is located within close proximity to the Portland International Airport, making business travel convenient anywhere within the continental United States and beyond.

Equipment

Jeremy Miller is fortunate to begin operations with the majority of the equipment that AppStax needs, including two Macintosh computers, several large capacity backup drives, and a laser printer. In addition, he already has broadband Internet service with a dedicated IP-based telephone that can be used for business purposes.

In order to ensure business continuity, Jeremy plans to install a generator that will provide AppStax with an uninterruptible power supply. Additionally, an online data backup solution has been identified to ensure that critical information is not lost in the event of a disaster or other unfortunate occurrence. Finally, the business plans to purchase Xserve, a workgroup server manufactured by Apple. The total investment for these items is approximately $10,000 (detailed equipment/service documentation available upon request).

Development Environment

Whether developing its own original mobile apps, or mobile apps for a client, Jeremy Miller will mainly write in Objective-C (Apple's twist on the C programming language). In addition, he will use an integrated development environment (IDE) called X Code. An IDE is a program used specifically for developing applications. It is the toolset used for writing code.

Development Process

Jeremy Miller will serve as the face of AppStax to customers and will take a consistent approach to every project. Specifically, he will begin by defining project objectives and expectations in as much detail as possible. He will organize projects by building a framework and farming out specific components when needed. In this model, Jeremy maintains control and is able to deliver the same caliber of product as if he had performed all of the development work himself.

Once a mobile app has been developed and tested to satisfaction, AppStax will submit the finished product to the appropriate marketplace for consideration and/or inclusion. Apple maintains control over its App Store, in terms of which apps are made available, while the Android marketplace is much less restrictive. Alternatively, in the event that a mobile app has been developed for another party, this portion of the process may be left to them.

FINANCIAL ANALYSIS

Following is AppStax's projected balance sheet for 2011. Detailed monthly cash flow statements are available upon request. Jeremy Miller anticipates that the company's net income will increase significantly in 2012 and 2013 as he successfully introduces mobile apps to online marketplaces, establishes new client relationships, and expands the types of mobile app platforms for which AppStax will develop (e.g., Apple, Android, and Blackberry).

In addition, Jeremy anticipates that some income will be generated from speaking engagements. However, because estimating such revenue is difficult, it has been excluded from these projections.

	2011
Revenue	**$59,750**
Expenses	
Advertising & marketing	$ 2,000
Miscellaneous items	$ 250
Legal	$ 1,250
Accounting	$ 500
Office supplies	$ 500
Server	$ 3,600
Generator	$ 3,300
Online data backup service	$ 900
Business insurance	$ 650
Salary	$40,000
Postage	$ 250
Business travel	$ 1,000
Telecommunications	$ 300
Broadband internet	$ 500
Total expenses	**$55,000**
Net income	**$ 4,750**

Music Lessons Business

MelodyWorx Inc.

2195 Main St.
Burlington Hills, LA 52605

Paul Greenland

MelodyWorx provides students with quality music lessons from passionate instructors with formal training.

EXECUTIVE SUMMARY

Mission Statement

MelodyWorx is committed to maximizing the musical potential of every student.

Business Overview

MelodyWorx is a music lessons business, which was recently established by classically trained musicians Bill and Tammy Peterson. When a shortage of state funding led to layoffs at the Burlington Hills School District, Tammy lost her job as a music teacher. Similarly, Bill, who works as an independent sales representative for several leading musical instrument manufacturers, saw his job reduced to a part-time position due to decreased demand. Although the chips appeared to be down, the Petersons decided to keep focusing on what they do best: music.

Beyond their personal situations, several recent developments in the local marketplace have resulted in what the Petersons feel is a strong opportunity. These include the closure of Domenico's, a music store serving Burlington Hills and another nearby community. For many years Domenico's was the primary destination for music lessons throughout the region. In addition, several independent instructors have retired or relocated elsewhere. Therefore, MelodyWorx will satisfy unmet demand in the marketplace by becoming the area's premier provider of music lessons.

MARKET ANALYSIS

Although MelodyWorx will provide music lessons to adults, our business will concentrate its marketing efforts mainly on school-aged children.

In 2009 the Burlington Hills population totaled 9,812, a figure that was expected to increase slightly by 2014, at which time the population was projected to reach 10,024, according to Pyramid Research Associates. School-aged children accounted for 19.2 percent of the population. Those aged 5 to 14 accounted for 11.4 percent of the total (1,122), while those in the 15 to 19 segment represented 7.8 percent (768).

Average household income totaled $56,234 in 2009 and was projected to increase 2.7 percent by 2014, at which time the figure would total $57,780. However, strong growth is projected in a number of middle- and upper-income categories. Households with income between $50,000 and $74,999 are expected to increase 11.6 percent between 2009 and 2014. In addition, households with income between $100,000 and $149,999 are expected to increase 34.1 percent during the same timeframe. Finally, households with income exceeding $150,000 are expected to increase 38.9 percent.

Our business is located within 5 miles of the nearby community of Sterling Ridge, which provides additional opportunities. In 2009 the Sterling Ridge population totaled 14,409, which was expected to remain flat through 2014, according to Pyramid Research data. Similar to Burlington Hills, school-aged children in this market accounted for 19.3 percent of the population. Those aged 5 to 14 accounted for 12.7 percent of the total (1,826), while those in the 15 to 19 segment represented 6.6 percent (951). Average household income totals and projections for Sterling Ridge are virtually identical to Burlington Hills.

Competition

MelodyWorx's primary competition will come from independent music instructors who offer lessons in their homes. Although there are several instructors in our primary market area, they offer services on a part-time basis and their availability is somewhat limited. In addition, these independent instructors concentrate almost exclusively on either piano or guitar lessons. Our main differentials will be convenience (greater availability/scheduling flexibility), expertise, and choice (instruction for a greater variety of musical instruments). One initial limitation to our business will be our inability to provide percussion instruction. Currently, one independent instructor in our market provides drum lessons to students from both communities.

INDUSTRY ANALYSIS

Music instruction is a well-established industry. Many instructors are members of the Cincinnati, Ohio-based Music Teachers National Association, which traces its roots back to 1876. The association, whose mission is "to advance the value of music study and music making to society and to support the professionalism of music teachers," included approximately 24,000 independent and collegiate music teachers among its membership in 2011. Members, who were served by 50 state affiliates in seven divisions, benefited from the association's Professional Certification Program, insurance options, and more.

PERSONNEL

MelodyWorx will begin operations with the following staff:

Bill Peterson (co-owner)

Tammy Peterson (co-owner)

Bill and Tammy both have a life-long love of music. They began classical training at early ages and, over time, became proficient with many different kinds of musical instruments. Bill developed exceptional skills with various brass instruments, while Tammy concentrated on keyboard and string instruments.

The Petersons met at Rockport College, where Tammy earned a Bachelor of Music (B.M.) degree with an emphasis on music education. A double major, Bill earned degrees in both business administration and music, with an emphasis on performance. In addition to formal education, over the years the Petersons have lived out their passion for music by playing together in several noteworthy jazz bands that developed strong followings throughout the Midwest.

When a shortage of state funding led to layoffs at the Burlington Hills School District, Tammy lost her job as a music teacher. Similarly, Bill, who works as an independent sales representative for several leading musical instrument manufacturers, saw his job reduced to a part-time position due to decreased demand. Although the chips appeared to be down, the Petersons decided to keep focusing on what they do best: music.

Professional & Advisory Support

MelodyWorx will rely upon Burlington Hills Accounting Services LLC for tax assistance. Legal advice, when needed, will be received from Jonathan R. Smith, an independent attorney in Burlington Hills.

The Petersons plan to secure the following types of insurance coverage through the Music Teachers National Association:

- Comprehensive Healthcare
- Professional Liability
- Private Practice Professional Liability
- Group Disability Income Protection

Finally, MelodyWorx has established both checking and merchant accounts with Burlington Hills Community Bank.

GROWTH STRATEGY

Instruction

During its first year of operation MelodyWorx will focus exclusively on music instruction. During this time period the Petersons well serve as the sole instructors. The addition of independent contractors will be considered during year two. Under this arrangement, MelodyWorx would be able to expand instruction options without hiring additional employees. Independent contractors would pay a commission to MelodyWorx in exchange for lesson space and operational/marketing support.

Instrument Rental & Sales Opportunity

MelodyWorx will consider offering musical instrument rental and sales. The demise of Domenico's (the music store referenced earlier in this plan) was the result of poor management coupled with excess capacity (the store was too large for the marketplace). With this in mind, the Petersons are conducting a feasibility study that should be completed within the next 60 days. If the results of the study are favorable, the owners will discuss leasing additional space to accommodate a rental/retail area (see the Operations section of this plan for facility details), likely during the second half of year one or the first half of year two.

SERVICES

MelodyWorx will take a formal, strategic approach to instruction with every student. This will begin with the completion of a new student questionnaire that will enable us to learn some basic information about our students, including their current skill level, goals, and musical interests. This, combined with our observations during an initial session, will be used to formulate a customized instruction plan. Students with no experience will begin by learning fundamentals, while more experienced students will begin lessons in accordance with their existing skills and abilities.

INSTRUMENTS

Instruction will be provided for the following instruments:

String Instruments

- Acoustic Guitar

- Bass Guitar

- Electric Bass

- Electric Guitar

- String Bass

- Violin

Keyboard

- Electronic Keyboard

- Organ

- Piano

Brass Instruments

- Saxophone

- Trombone

- Trumpet

GENRES

Based on the interests of our students, we will incorporate music from a wide variety of genres into our instructional programs. These include, but are not limited to:

- Alternative

- Bebop

- Baroque

- Big Band

- Bluegrass

- Blues

- Bossa Nova

- Brazilian

- Celtic

- Chamber Music

- Choral

- Christian

- Classical

- Contemporary

- Country

- Dixieland

- Flamenco

- Folk

- Funk

- Hip-Hop
- Gospel
- Jazz
- Latin
- New Age
- Oldies
- Pop
- Renaissance
- R&B
- Reggae
- Rock
- Salsa
- Samba
- Spiritual
- Tango
- World

MARKETING & SALES

MelodyWorx has developed a marketing plan that involves the following tactics:

1. Word-of-mouth marketing, leveraging Tammy Peterson's reputation within the educational community to produce and maintain a steady stream of student referrals.

2. Printed collateral describing our music instruction services for parents of prospective students, as well as referral sources (e.g., music teachers at local schools).

3. A Yellow Page advertisement.

4. Periodic information/demonstration sessions with free refreshments, offered at no cost to attendees, providing information about the lessons we offer, and live demonstrations/testimonials from some of our best students.

5. Presentations to area non-profit organizations (e.g., PTAs, church groups, etc.).

6. A Web site with complete details about our business and the services we offer, including an online "intake form" that parents or prospective students can complete and submit it to us at any time.

7. A customer referral program that provides one free 30-minute music lesson for each new client that is referred.

8. A "your first lesson is free" promotion during our first year of business, in order to provide an incentive for prospective students to check us out.

9. A free holiday recital at the end of every year that will enable our students to perform for the community.

10. Exterior signage identifying/promoting our business.

OPERATIONS

Facility & Location

MelodyWorx has made arrangements to lease a 1,000-square-foot space that is located within close geographic proximity to several elementary schools, as well as a middle school and a high school. This location provides convenient access to several major thoroughfares. Formerly home to a used car dealership, the space is ideal because it offers a decent-sized waiting area and four individual rooms along the perimeter that can be used for music instruction. The space includes a small office space in the front, and the former car lot area provides plenty of parking space. The building owner has agreed to convert an adjoining garage area into additional finished space, should MelodyWorx need to expand (e.g., for musical instrument rental/sales).

Fees

MelodyWorx's standard rate for music instruction is $80 per month, which includes four 30-minute sessions (one per week). When needed, additional 30-minute lessons will be provided at a rate of $20.

Hours of Operation

MelodyWorx will operate from 3 PM to 8 PM Monday through Thursday, and from 8 AM to 4 PM on Saturdays. The business will be closed on Fridays and Sundays. During the day telephone calls will route to Tammy Peterson's cell phone. A drop box will allow customers to drop off payments for lessons when the offices are closed.

FINANCIAL ANALYSIS

During its first year of operations the Petersons anticipate that MelodyWorx will generate a net profit of $15,000. The owners will draw only a small salary from the business and plan to reinvest all net profits into MelodyWorx. Funds may be needed to purchase a small inventory of musical instruments, in the event that expanding into that niche proves to be a viable option.

Startup Expenses

Initially, the Petersons will use two of the four classrooms in their leased facility. They will need to purchase several chairs for these rooms, as well as two couches, a coffee table, and a water cooler for the waiting area. In addition, they will require a desk, filing cabinet, personal computer, and telephone for the office. Finally, funds will be needed to update the signage on the building's exterior. Start-up costs will be an estimated $6,500, which the Petersons will cover from their personal savings.

Financial Statements

Following is MelodyWorx's projected balance sheet for 2011. Detailed monthly cash flow statements and volume projections are available upon request.

Sales	**$75,000**
Operating expenses	
Maintenance	$ 450
Owners' salaries	$30,000
Taxes & licenses	$ 7,500
Office supplies	$ 350
Advertising	$ 2,000
Equipment	$ 1,000
Accounting & legal	$ 1,000
Rent	$11,000
Telephone	$ 1,000
Utilities	$ 2,350
Insurance	$ 2,250
Internet service	$ 1,100
Total	**$60,000**
Net income	**$15,000**

Plant Nursery

Village Garden Center

99901 1st Ave.
New York, NY 11385

BizPlanDB.com

The purpose of this business plan is to raise $150,000 for the development of a plant and tree nursery while showcasing the expected financials and operations over the next three years. Village Garden Center ("the Company") is a New York based corporation that will provide an extensive variety of plants and trees to individuals and landscape contractors in its targeted market. The Company was founded by Carlo Crudo.

1.0 EXECUTIVE SUMMARY

The purpose of this business plan is to raise $150,000 for the development of a plant and tree nursery while showcasing the expected financials and operations over the next three years. Village Garden Center ("the Company") is a New York based corporation that will provide an extensive variety of plants and trees to individuals and landscape contractors in its targeted market. The Company was founded by Carlo Crudo.

1.1 The Products

The primary revenue stream for the business will come from the direct sale of plants and trees from its outdoor and indoor greenhouse facility. The business will carry a number of seasonal and year-round (perennial) species. The Company will sell to both individual customers and landscape contractors.

The Company will also generate secondary revenue streams from arranging the transportation of large orders of trees and plants on behalf of individual customers and landscape contactors.

The third section of the business plan will further describe the services offered by Village Garden Center.

1.2 Financing

Mr. Crudo is seeking to raise $150,000 as a bank loan. The interest rate and loan agreement are to be further discussed during negotiation. This business plan assumes that the business will receive a 10 year loan with a 9% fixed interest rate. The financing will be used for the following:

- Development of the Village Garden Center location.

- Financing for the first six months of operation.

- Capital to purchase the Company's initial inventories of trees and plants.

Mr. Crudo will contribute $25,000 to the venture.

109

1.3 Mission Statement

Management's mission is to develop Village Garden Center into a premier local distributor of plants and trees to the general public and contractors operating within the target market.

1.4 Management Team

The Company was founded by Carlo Crudo. Mr. Crudo has more than 10 years of experience in the landscaping industry. Through his expertise, he will be able to bring the operations of the business to profitability within its first year.

1.5 Sales Forecasts

Mr. Crudo expects a strong rate of growth at the start of operations. Below are the expected financials over the next three years.

Proforma profit and loss (yearly)

Year	1	2	3
Sales	$477,750	$515,970	$557,248
Operating costs	$281,985	$297,292	$309,565
EBITDA	$ 72,915	$ 86,000	$104,391
Taxes, interest, and depreciation	$ 49,564	$ 48,992	$ 55,364
Net profit	$ 23,351	$ 37,008	$ 49,027

Sales, operating costs, and profit forecast

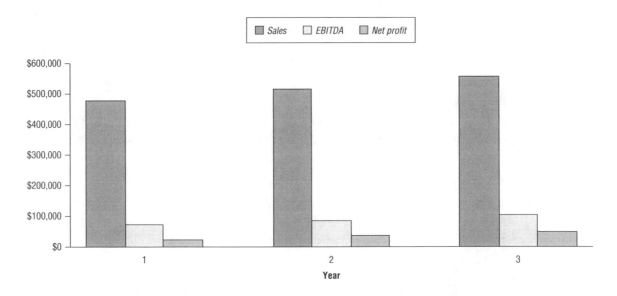

1.6 Expansion Plan

The Founder expects that the business will aggressively expand during the first three years of operation. Mr. Crudo intends to implement marketing campaigns that will effectively target individuals and landscape contractors within the target market.

2.0 COMPANY AND FINANCING SUMMARY

2.1 Registered Name and Corporate Structure

Village Garden Center is registered as a corporation in the State of New York.

2.2 Required Funds

At this time, Village Garden Center requires $150,000 of debt funds. Below is a breakdown of how these funds will be used:

Projected startup costs

Initial lease payments and deposits	$ 10,000
Working capital	$ 35,000
FF&E	$ 45,000
Leasehold improvements	$ 15,000
Security deposits	$ 10,000
Insurance	$ 2,500
Plant and tree inventory	$ 35,000
Marketing budget	$ 17,500
Miscellaneous and unforeseen costs	$ 5,000
Total startup costs	**$175,000**

Use of funds

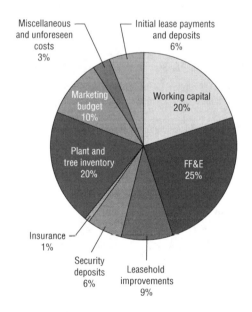

2.3 Investor Equity

Mr. Crudo is not seeking an investment from a third party at this time.

2.4 Management Equity

Carlo Crudo owns 100% of Village Garden Center, Inc.

2.5 Exit Strategy

If the business is very successful, Mr. Crudo may seek to sell the business to a third party for a significant earnings multiple. Most likely, the Company will hire a qualified business broker to sell the business on behalf of Village Garden Center, Inc. Based on historical numbers, the business could fetch a sales premium of up to five to seven times earnings.

3.0 PRODUCTS AND SERVICES

Below is a description of the plant products and related services offered by Village Garden Center.

3.1 Sales of Plants and Trees

As discussed in the executive summary, the primary source of revenue for the business will be the sales of plants and trees to the general public and to contractors. The Company will maintain a large outdoor area where plants are kept and can be selected and purchased by customers. Additionally, the Company will maintain a sizeable greenhouse facility for expensive plants and plants that require careful handling. Additionally, during colder months, all plant sales will be moved indoors to the Company's heated greenhouse facility. Mr. Crudo anticipates that the business will generate margins of approximately 80% on each sale. Additionally, this segment of the business will account for 80% of Village Garden Center's aggregate income.

3.2 Transportation Fees

The Company will also generate secondary revenues from arranging for the transportation and delivery of large orders of plants/trees on behalf of individual and landscape contracting customers. Management anticipates that approximately 20% of the Company's aggregate revenues will come from this service.

4.0 STRATEGIC AND MARKET ANALYSIS

4.1 Economic Outlook

This section of the analysis will detail the economic climate, the plant nursery industry, the customer profile, and the competition that the business will face as it progresses through its business operations.

Currently, the economic market condition in the United States is in recession. Many economists expect that this recession will continue for a significant period of time, at which point the economy will begin a prolonged recovery period. This may have an impact on the Company's ability to generate top line income as plants and trees are not necessities. However, as many people are seeking to sell their homes, these sellers may acquire inventories from the business in order to make their homes more appealing for sale. Furthermore, as more and more people find themselves unable to sell their home for what they owe on it, people are opting to stay in their home longer and spend money to "spruce it up" while they are there.

4.2 Industry Analysis

Aggregately, there are more than 17,000 businesses that operate one or more facilities that sell plants and trees to both individual customers and contractors. In each of the last five years, the industry has generated in excess of $27 billion while providing jobs to more than 150,000 people. Aggregate payrolls in each of the last five years have exceeded $3.5 billion.

This is a mature industry, and the future expected growth rate is expected to mirror that of the general economy. However, with the current economic situation at hand, Mr. Crudo anticipates that the industry will experience sluggish growth as the demand for new housing starts has waned. However, among gardening enthusiasts, Management anticipates that demand will remain strong.

4.3 Customer Profile

The Company will operate among two primary customer bases: individual customers and contractors. Among individual clients, Mr. Crudo expects that the customer base consist of middle to upper middle class men or women living in the Company's target market. Common traits among clients will include:

- Annual household income exceeding $50,000

- Lives or works no more than 15 miles from the Company's location.

- Will spend $25 to $100 per visit to the Village Garden Center.

Among contractors, Management expects that most of these businesses will be actively engaged in landscape contacting. These contractors will have 8 to 10 employees (on average) and aggregate revenues of $250,000 to $1,000,000 per year.

4.4 Competition

The greater New York metropolitan area has more than 200 stores and businesses that operate in a similar capacity to that of the Company. Major competitors include Home Depot and Lowes, which provide plant and tree inventories directly to individuals and contractors. However, the business intends to maintain a competitive advantage by focusing specifically on working with landscape contractors.

5.0 MARKETING PLAN

Village Garden Center intends to maintain an extensive marketing campaign that will ensure maximum visibility for the business in its targeted market. Below is an overview of the marketing strategies and objectives of Village Garden Center.

5.1 Marketing Objectives

- Develop an online presence by creating a website and placing the Company's name and contact information with online directories.

- Implement a local campaign with the Company's targeted market via the use of flyers, local newspaper advertisements, and word-of-mouth advertising.

- Establish relationships with landscape contractors within the target market.

5.2 Marketing Strategies

Mr. Crudo intends to use a number of marketing strategies that will allow Village Garden Center to easily target individuals within the target market. These strategies include traditional print advertisements such as flyers, newspaper advertisements, and Yellow Page listings.

Village Garden Center will also use an Internet-based strategy. This is very important as many people seeking local retailers, such as plant nurseries, now use the Internet to conduct their preliminary searches. Mr. Crudo will register Village Garden Center with online portals so that potential customers can easily reach the business. The Company will also develop its own online website showcasing the operations of the business, its inventory, hours of operation, and other services offered by the business.

Finally, Mr. Crudo will develop ongoing relationships with landscape contractors that will purchase inventories of trees and plants from the business in bulk on a regular basis. In time, these contractors will become an invaluable source of business for Village Garden Center.

5.3 Pricing

As the business intends to carry hundreds of different items within its inventory it is hard to quantify the price of each product sold by the Village Garden Center. However, Management anticipates that each order will generate $100 to $2,000 for the business.

6.0 ORGANIZATIONAL PLAN AND PERSONNEL SUMMARY

6.1 Corporate Organization

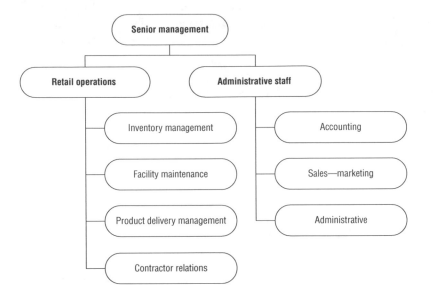

6.2 Organizational Budget

Personnel plan—yearly

Year	1	2	3
Owner	$ 35,000	$ 36,050	$ 37,132
Nursery manager	$ 29,500	$ 30,385	$ 31,297
Nursery employees	$ 70,000	$ 72,100	$ 74,263
Bookkeeper (P/T)	$ 12,500	$ 12,875	$ 13,261
Administrative	$ 20,000	$ 20,600	$ 21,218
Total	**$167,000**	**$172,010**	**$177,170**

Numbers of personnel

Owner	1	1	1
Nursery manager	1	1	1
Nursery employees	4	4	4
Bookkeeper (P/T)	1	1	1
Administrative	1	1	1
Totals	**8**	**8**	**8**

Personnel expense breakdown

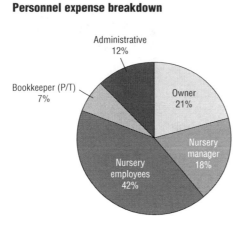

7.0 FINANCIAL PLAN

7.1 Underlying Assumptions

The Company has based its proforma financial statements on the following:

- Village Garden Center will have an annual revenue growth rate of 8% per year.

- The Owner will acquire $150,000 of debt funds to develop the business.

- The loan will have a 10 year term with a 9% interest rate.

7.2 Sensitivity Analysis

In the event of an economic downturn, the business may have a decline in its revenues. The Company's commercial client base of landscape contractors may drastically scale down their purchases as their customer base puts off major landscaping renovations. However, the Company will have a loyal customer base of gardening enthusiasts that will continue to purchase plants and trees on a regular basis. Additionally, the high margin revenues generated by Village Garden Center will allow the business to remain profitable and cash flow positive despite moderate declines in revenue.

7.3 Source of Funds

Financing

Equity contributions	
Management investment	$ 25,000.00
Total equity financing	**$ 25,000.00**
Banks and lenders	
Banks and lenders	$ 150,000.00
Total debt financing	**$150,000.00**
Total financing	**$175,000.00**

7.4 General Assumptions

General assumptions

Year	1	2	3
Short term interest rate	9.5%	9.5%	9.5%
Long term interest rate	10.0%	10.0%	10.0%
Federal tax rate	33.0%	33.0%	33.0%
State tax rate	5.0%	5.0%	5.0%
Personnel taxes	15.0%	15.0%	15.0%

7.5 Profit and Loss Statements

Proforma profit and loss (yearly)

Year	1	2	3
Sales	**$477,750**	**$515,970**	**$557,248**
Cost of goods sold	$122,850	$132,678	$143,292
Gross margin	74.29%	74.29%	74.29%
Operating income	**$354,900**	**$383,292**	**$413,955**
Expenses			
Payroll	$167,000	$172,010	$177,170
General and administrative	$ 14,000	$ 14,560	$ 15,142
Marketing expenses	$ 14,333	$ 15,479	$ 16,717
Professional fees and licensure	$ 5,000	$ 5,150	$ 5,305
Insurance costs	$ 12,000	$ 12,600	$ 13,230
Travel and vehicle costs	$ 17,500	$ 19,250	$ 21,175
Rent and utilities	$ 25,000	$ 26,250	$ 27,563
Miscellaneous costs	$ 2,102	$ 6,192	$ 6,687
Payroll taxes	$ 25,050	$ 25,802	$ 26,576
Total operating costs	**$281,985**	**$297,292**	**$309,565**
EBITDA	**$ 72,915**	**$ 86,000**	**$104,391**
Federal income tax	$ 24,062	$ 24,355	$ 30,752
State income tax	$ 3,646	$ 3,690	$ 4,659
Interest expense	$ 13,107	$ 12,197	$ 11,202
Depreciation expenses	$ 8,750	$ 8,750	$ 8,750
Net profit	**$ 23,351**	**$ 37,008**	**$ 49,027**
Profit margin	**4.89%**	**7.17%**	**8.80%**

Sales, operating costs, and profit forecast

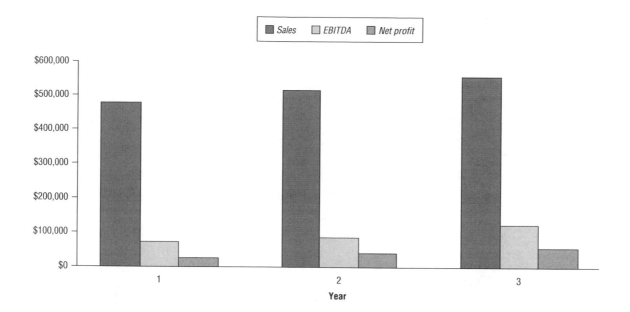

7.6 Cash Flow Analysis

Proforma cash flow analysis—yearly

Year	1	2	3
Cash from operations	$ 32,101	$45,758	$57,777
Cash from receivables	$ 0	$ 0	$ 0
Operating cash inflow	**$ 32,101**	**$45,758**	**$57,777**
Other cash inflows			
Equity investment	$ 25,000	$ 0	$ 0
Increased borrowings	$150,000	$ 0	$ 0
Sales of business assets	$ 0	$ 0	$ 0
A/P increases	$ 5,000	$ 5,750	$ 6,613
Total other cash inflows	**$180,000**	**$ 5,750**	**$ 6,613**
Total cash inflow	**$212,101**	**$51,508**	**$64,389**
Cash outflows			
Repayment of principal	$ 9,695	$10,605	$11,599
A/P decreases	$ 2,400	$ 2,880	$ 3,456
A/R increases	$ 0	$ 0	$ 0
Asset purchases	$122,500	$11,439	$14,444
Dividends	$ 22,471	$22,879	$28,888
Total cash outflows	**$157,066**	**$47,803**	**$58,388**
Net cash flow	**$ 55,035**	**$ 3,705**	**$ 6,001**
Cash balance	**$ 55,035**	**$58,740**	**$64,741**

Proforma cash flow (yearly)

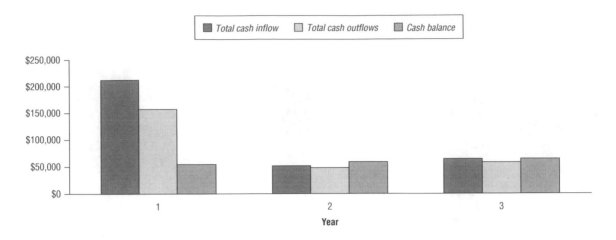

7.7 Balance Sheet

Proforma balance sheet—yearly

Year	1	2	3
Assets			
Cash	$ 55,035	$ 58,740	$ 64,741
Amortized development/expansion costs	$ 42,500	$ 43,644	$ 45,088
Plant and tree inventory	$ 35,000	$ 43,008	$ 53,119
FF&E	$ 45,000	$ 47,288	$ 50,177
Accumulated depreciation	($ 8,750)	($ 17,500)	($ 26,250)
Total assets	**$168,785**	**$175,179**	**$186,875**
Liabilities and equity			
Accounts payable	$ 2,600	$ 5,470	$ 8,627
Long term liabilities	$140,305	$129,700	$119,096
Other liabilities	$ 0	$ 0	$ 0
Total liabilities	**$142,905**	**$135,170**	**$127,722**
Net worth	**$ 25,880**	**$ 40,009**	**$ 59,153**
Total liabilities and equity	**$168,785**	**$175,179**	**$186,875**

Proforma balance sheet

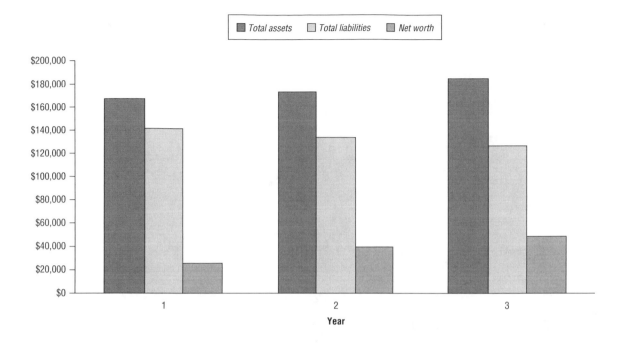

7.8 Breakeven Analysis

Monthly break even analysis

Year	1	2	3
Monthly revenue	$ 31,633	$ 33,350	$ 34,727
Yearly revenue	$379,595	$400,201	$416,722

Break even analysis

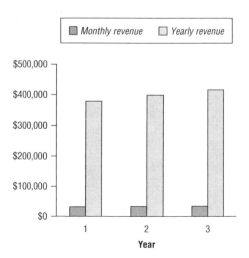

7.9 Business Ratios

Business ratios—yearly

Year	1	2	3
Sales			
Sales growth	0.00%	8.00%	8.00%
Gross margin	74.30%	74.30%	74.30%
Financials			
Profit margin	4.89%	7.17%	8.80%
Assets to liabilities	1.18	1.30	1.46
Equity to liabilities	0.18	0.30	0.46
Assets to equity	6.52	4.38	3.16
Liquidity			
Acid test	0.39	0.43	0.51
Cash to assets	0.33	0.34	0.35

7.10 Three Year Profit and Loss Statement

Profit and loss statement (first year)

Months	1	2	3	4	5	6	7
Sales	**$35,000**	**$35,875**	**$36,750**	**$37,625**	**$38,500**	**$39,375**	**$40,250**
Cost of goods sold	$ 9,000	$ 9,225	$ 9,450	$ 9,675	$ 9,900	$10,125	$10,350
Gross margin	74.3%	74.3%	74.3%	74.3%	74.3%	74.3%	74.3%
Operating income	**$26,000**	**$26,650**	**$27,300**	**$27,950**	**$28,600**	**$29,250**	**$29,900**
Expenses							
Payroll	$13,917	$13,917	$13,917	$13,917	$13,917	$13,917	$13,917
General and administrative	$ 1,167	$ 1,167	$ 1,167	$ 1,167	$ 1,167	$ 1,167	$ 1,167
Marketing expenses	$ 1,194	$ 1,194	$ 1,194	$ 1,194	$ 1,194	$ 1,194	$ 1,194
Professional fees and licensure	$ 417	$ 417	$ 417	$ 417	$ 417	$ 417	$ 417
Insurance costs	$ 1,000	$ 1,000	$ 1,000	$ 1,000	$ 1,000	$ 1,000	$ 1,000
Travel and vehicle costs	$ 1,458	$ 1,458	$ 1,458	$ 1,458	$ 1,458	$ 1,458	$ 1,458
Rent and utilities	$ 2,083	$ 2,083	$ 2,083	$ 2,083	$ 2,083	$ 2,083	$ 2,083
Miscellaneous costs	$ 175	$ 175	$ 175	$ 175	$ 175	$ 175	$ 175
Payroll taxes	$ 2,088	$ 2,088	$ 2,088	$ 2,088	$ 2,088	$ 2,088	$ 2,088
Total operating costs	**$23,499**	**$23,499**	**$23,499**	**$23,499**	**$23,499**	**$23,499**	**$23,499**
EBITDA	**$ 2,501**	**$ 3,151**	**$ 3,801**	**$ 4,451**	**$ 5,101**	**$ 5,751**	**$ 6,401**
Federal income tax	$ 1,763	$ 1,807	$ 1,851	$ 1,895	$ 1,939	$ 1,983	$ 2,027
State income tax	$ 267	$ 274	$ 280	$ 287	$ 294	$ 300	$ 307
Interest expense	$ 1,125	$ 1,119	$ 1,113	$ 1,107	$ 1,101	$ 1,095	$ 1,089
Depreciation expense	$ 729	$ 729	$ 729	$ 729	$ 729	$ 729	$ 729
Net profit	**−$ 1,383**	**−$ 778**	**−$ 173**	**$ 433**	**$ 1,038**	**$ 1,643**	**$ 2,248**

Profit and loss statement (first year cont.)

Month	8	9	10	11	12	1
Sales	$41,125	$42,000	$42,875	$43,750	$44,625	$477,750
Cost of goods sold	$10,575	$10,800	$11,025	$11,250	$11,475	$122,850
Gross margin	74.3%	74.3%	74.3%	74.3%	74.3%	74.3%
Operating income	$30,550	$31,200	$31,850	$32,500	$33,150	$354,900
Expenses						
Payroll	$13,917	$13,917	$13,917	$13,917	$13,917	$167,000
General and administrative	$ 1,167	$ 1,167	$ 1,167	$ 1,167	$ 1,167	$ 14,000
Marketing expenses	$ 1,194	$ 1,194	$ 1,194	$ 1,194	$ 1,194	$ 14,333
Professional fees and licensure	$ 417	$ 417	$ 417	$ 417	$ 417	$ 5,000
Insurance costs	$ 1,000	$ 1,000	$ 1,000	$ 1,000	$ 1,000	$ 12,000
Travel and vehicle costs	$ 1,458	$ 1,458	$ 1,458	$ 1,458	$ 1,458	$ 17,500
Rent and utilities	$ 2,083	$ 2,083	$ 2,083	$ 2,083	$ 2,083	$ 25,000
Miscellaneous costs	$ 175	$ 175	$ 175	$ 175	$ 175	$ 2,102
Payroll taxes	$ 2,088	$ 2,088	$ 2,088	$ 2,088	$ 2,088	$ 25,050
Total operating costs	$23,499	$23,499	$23,499	$23,499	$23,499	$281,985
EBITDA	$ 7,051	$ 7,701	$ 8,351	$ 9,001	$ 9,651	$ 72,915
Federal income tax	$ 2,071	$ 2,115	$ 2,159	$ 2,203	$ 2,248	$ 24,062
State income tax	$ 314	$ 321	$ 327	$ 334	$ 341	$ 3,646
Interest expense	$ 1,083	$ 1,077	$ 1,071	$ 1,065	$ 1,059	$ 13,107
Depreciation expense	$ 729	$ 729	$ 729	$ 729	$ 729	$ 8,750
Net profit	$ 2,854	$ 3,459	$ 4,064	$ 4,670	$ 5,275	$ 23,351

Profit and loss statement (second year)

Quarter	Q1	2 Q2	Q3	Q4	2
Sales	$103,194	$128,993	$139,312	$144,472	$515,970
Cost of goods sold	$ 26,536	$ 33,170	$ 35,823	$ 37,150	$132,678
Gross margin	74.3%	74.3%	74.3%	74.3%	74.3%
Operating income	$ 76,658	$ 95,823	$103,489	$107,322	$383,292
Expenses					
Payroll	$ 34,402	$ 43,003	$ 46,443	$ 48,163	$172,010
General and administrative	$ 2,912	$ 3,640	$ 3,931	$ 4,077	$ 14,560
Marketing expenses	$ 3,096	$ 3,870	$ 4,179	$ 4,334	$ 15,479
Professional fees and licensure	$ 1,030	$ 1,288	$ 1,391	$ 1,442	$ 5,150
Insurance costs	$ 2,520	$ 3,150	$ 3,402	$ 3,528	$ 12,600
Travel and vehicle costs	$ 3,850	$ 4,813	$ 5,198	$ 5,390	$ 19,250
Rent and utilities	$ 5,250	$ 6,563	$ 7,088	$ 7,350	$ 26,250
Miscellaneous costs	$ 1,238	$ 1,548	$ 1,672	$ 1,734	$ 6,192
Payroll taxes	$ 5,160	$ 6,450	$ 6,966	$ 7,224	$ 25,802
Total operating costs	$ 59,458	$ 74,323	$ 80,269	$ 83,242	$297,292
EBITDA	$ 17,200	$ 21,500	$ 23,220	$ 24,080	$ 86,000
Federal income tax	$ 4,871	$ 6,089	$ 6,576	$ 6,819	$ 24,355
State income tax	$ 738	$ 923	$ 996	$ 1,033	$ 3,690
Interest expense	$ 3,138	$ 3,080	$ 3,020	$ 2,959	$ 12,197
Depreciation expense	$ 2,188	$ 2,188	$ 2,188	$ 2,188	$ 8,750
Net profit	$ 6,266	$ 9,222	$ 10,440	$ 11,080	$ 37,008

Profit and loss statement (third year)

Quarter	Q1	3 Q2	Q3	Q4	3
Sales	**$111,450**	**$139,312**	**$150,457**	**$156,029**	**$557,248**
Cost of goods sold	$ 28,658	$ 35,823	$ 38,689	$ 40,122	$143,292
Gross margin	74.3%	74.3%	74.3%	74.3%	74.3%
Operating income	**$ 82,791**	**$103,489**	**$111,768**	**$115,908**	**$413,955**
Expenses					
Payroll	$ 35,434	$ 44,293	$ 47,836	$ 49,608	$177,170
General and administrative	$ 3,028	$ 3,786	$ 4,088	$ 4,240	$ 15,142
Marketing expenses	$ 3,343	$ 4,179	$ 4,514	$ 4,681	$ 16,717
Professional fees and licensure	$ 1,061	$ 1,326	$ 1,432	$ 1,485	$ 5,305
Insurance costs	$ 2,646	$ 3,308	$ 3,572	$ 3,704	$ 13,230
Travel and vehicle costs	$ 4,235	$ 5,294	$ 5,717	$ 5,929	$ 21,175
Rent and utilities	$ 5,513	$ 6,891	$ 7,442	$ 7,718	$ 27,563
Miscellaneous costs	$ 1,337	$ 1,672	$ 1,805	$ 1,872	$ 6,687
Payroll taxes	$ 5,315	$ 6,644	$ 7,175	$ 7,441	$ 26,576
Total operating costs	**$ 61,913**	**$ 77,391**	**$ 83,582**	**$ 86,678**	**$309,565**
EBITDA	**$ 20,878**	**$ 26,098**	**$ 28,185**	**$ 29,229**	**$104,391**
Federal income tax	$ 6,150	$ 7,688	$ 8,303	$ 8,611	$ 30,752
State income tax	$ 932	$ 1,165	$ 1,258	$ 1,305	$ 4,659
Interest expense	$ 2,897	$ 2,834	$ 2,769	$ 2,702	$ 11,202
Depreciation expense	$ 2,188	$ 2,188	$ 2,188	$ 2,188	$ 8,750
Net profit	**$ 8,711**	**$ 12,223**	**$ 13,668**	**$ 14,424**	**$ 49,027**

7.11 Three Year Cash Flow Analysis

Cash flow analysis (first year)

Month	1	2	3	4	5	6	7	8
Cash from operations	−$ 654	−$ 49	$ 557	$ 1,162	$ 1,767	$ 2,372	$ 2,977	$ 3,583
Cash from receivables	$ 0	$ 0	$ 0	$ 0	$ 0	$ 0	$ 0	$ 0
Operating cash inflow	**−$ 654**	**−$ 49**	**$ 557**	**$ 1,162**	**$ 1,767**	**$ 2,372**	**$ 2,977**	**$ 3,583**
Other cash inflows								
Equity investment	$ 25,000	$ 0	$ 0	$ 0	$ 0	$ 0	$ 0	$ 0
Increased borrowings	$150,000	$ 0	$ 0	$ 0	$ 0	$ 0	$ 0	$ 0
Sales of business assets	$ 0	$ 0	$ 0	$ 0	$ 0	$ 0	$ 0	$ 0
A/P increases	$ 417	$ 417	$ 417	$ 417	$ 417	$ 417	$ 417	$ 417
Total other cash inflows	**$175,417**	**$ 417**	**$ 417**	**$ 417**	**$ 417**	**$ 417**	**$ 417**	**$ 417**
Total cash inflow	**$174,763**	**$ 368**	**$ 973**	**$ 1,578**	**$ 2,184**	**$ 2,789**	**$ 3,394**	**$ 3,999**
Cash outflows								
Repayment of principal	$ 775	$ 781	$ 787	$ 793	$ 799	$ 805	$ 811	$ 817
A/P decreases	$ 200	$ 200	$ 200	$ 200	$ 200	$ 200	$ 200	$ 200
A/R increases	$ 0	$ 0	$ 0	$ 0	$ 0	$ 0	$ 0	$ 0
Asset purchases	$122,500	$ 0	$ 0	$ 0	$ 0	$ 0	$ 0	$ 0
Dividends	$ 0	$ 0	$ 0	$ 0	$ 0	$ 0	$ 0	$ 0
Total cash outflows	**$123,475**	**$ 981**	**$ 987**	**$ 993**	**$ 999**	**$ 1,005**	**$ 1,011**	**$ 1,017**
Net cash flow	**$ 51,288**	**−$ 613**	**−$ 14**	**$ 586**	**$ 1,185**	**$ 1,784**	**$ 2,383**	**$ 2,983**
Cash balance	**$ 51,288**	**$50,675**	**$50,662**	**$51,247**	**$52,432**	**$54,216**	**$56,600**	**$59,583**

Cash flow analysis (first year cont.)

Month	9	10	11	12	1
Cash from operations	$ 4,188	$ 4,794	$ 5,399	$ 6,005	$ 32,101
Cash from receivables	$ 0	$ 0	$ 0	$ 0	$ 0
Operating cash inflow	**$ 4,188**	**$ 4,794**	**$ 5,399**	**$ 6,005**	**$ 32,101**
Other cash inflows					
Equity investment	$ 0	$ 0	$ 0	$ 0	$ 25,000
Increased borrowings	$ 0	$ 0	$ 0	$ 0	$150,000
Sales of business assets	$ 0	$ 0	$ 0	$ 0	$ 0
A/P increases	$ 417	$ 417	$ 417	$ 417	$ 5,000
Total other cash inflows	**$ 417**	**$ 417**	**$ 417**	**$ 417**	**$180,000**
Total cash inflow	**$ 4,605**	**$ 5,210**	**$ 5,816**	**$ 6,421**	**$212,101**
Cash outflows					
Repayment of principal	$ 823	$ 829	$ 835	$ 842	$ 9,695
A/P decreases	$ 200	$ 200	$ 200	$ 200	$ 2,400
A/R increases	$ 0	$ 0	$ 0	$ 0	$ 0
Asset purchases	$ 0	$ 0	$ 0	$ 0	$122,500
Dividends	$ 0	$ 0	$ 0	$22,471	$ 22,471
Total cash outflows	**$ 1,023**	**$ 1,029**	**$ 1,035**	**$23,513**	**$157,066**
Net cash flow	**$ 3,582**	**$ 4,181**	**$ 4,780**	**−$17,091**	**$ 55,035**
Cash balance	**$63,165**	**$67,346**	**$72,126**	**$55,035**	**$ 55,035**

Cash flow analysis (second year)

Quarter	Q1	2 Q2	Q3	Q4	2
Cash from operations	$ 9,152	$11,439	$12,355	$12,812	$45,758
Cash from receivables	$ 0	$ 0	$ 0	$ 0	$ 0
Operating cash inflow	**$ 9,152**	**$11,439**	**$12,355**	**$12,812**	**$45,758**
Other cash inflows					
Equity investment	$ 0	$ 0	$ 0	$ 0	$ 0
Increased borrowings	$ 0	$ 0	$ 0	$ 0	$ 0
Sales of business assets	$ 0	$ 0	$ 0	$ 0	$ 0
A/P increases	$ 1,150	$ 1,438	$ 1,553	$ 1,610	$ 5,750
Total other cash inflows	**$ 1,150**	**$ 1,438**	**$ 1,553**	**$ 1,610**	**$ 5,750**
Total cash inflow	**$10,302**	**$12,877**	**$13,907**	**$14,422**	**$51,508**
Cash outflows					
Repayment of principal	$ 2,563	$ 2,621	$ 2,680	$ 2,741	$10,605
A/P decreases	$ 576	$ 720	$ 778	$ 806	$ 2,880
A/R increases	$ 0	$ 0	$ 0	$ 0	$ 0
Asset purchases	$ 2,288	$ 2,860	$ 3,089	$ 3,203	$11,439
Dividends	$ 4,576	$ 5,720	$ 6,177	$ 6,406	$22,879
Total cash outflows	**$10,002**	**$11,920**	**$12,724**	**$13,156**	**$47,803**
Net cash flow	**$ 299**	**$ 957**	**$ 1,183**	**$ 1,266**	**$ 3,705**
Cash balance	**$55,334**	**$56,291**	**$57,474**	**$58,740**	**$58,740**

Cash flow analysis (third year)

Quarter	Q1	3 Q2	Q3	Q4	3
Cash from operations	$11,555	$14,444	$15,600	$16,178	$57,777
Cash from receivables	$ 0	$ 0	$ 0	$ 0	$ 0
Operating cash inflow	**$11,555**	**$14,444**	**$15,600**	**$16,178**	**$57,777**
Other cash inflows					
Equity investment	$ 0	$ 0	$ 0	$ 0	$ 0
Increased borrowings	$ 0	$ 0	$ 0	$ 0	$ 0
Sales of business assets	$ 0	$ 0	$ 0	$ 0	$ 0
A/P increases	$ 1,323	$ 1,653	$ 1,785	$ 1,852	$ 6,613
Total other cash inflows	**$ 1,323**	**$ 1,653**	**$ 1,785**	**$ 1,852**	**$ 6,613**
Total cash inflow	**$12,878**	**$16,097**	**$17,385**	**$18,029**	**$64,389**
Cash outflows					
Repayment of principal	$ 2,803	$ 2,867	$ 2,932	$ 2,998	$11,599
A/P decreases	$ 691	$ 864	$ 933	$ 968	$ 3,456
A/R increases	$ 0	$ 0	$ 0	$ 0	$ 0
Asset purchases	$ 2,889	$ 3,611	$ 3,900	$ 4,044	$14,444
Dividends	$ 5,778	$ 7,222	$ 7,800	$ 8,089	$28,888
Total cash outflows	**$12,161**	**$14,564**	**$15,565**	**$16,099**	**$58,388**
Net cash flow	**$ 717**	**$ 1,534**	**$ 1,821**	**$ 1,930**	**$ 6,001**
Cash balance	**$59,457**	**$60,991**	**$62,811**	**$64,741**	**$64,741**

Printing Business

Big Picture Press Inc.

29 Main St.
Blue Mountain, OR 97200

Paul Greenland

Big Picture Press specializes in large-format printing applications such as vehicle wraps, outdoor banners, posters, and tradeshow graphics.

EXECUTIVE SUMMARY

Business Overview

From museums and sporting arenas to trade shows and hospitals, large-format printing is making a major impact for advertisers and organizations of all types. In recent years large-format printing technology has advanced rapidly, offering customers greater capabilities, higher-quality, and more options. Examples of large-format printing include:

- Backlit Displays
- Murals
- Event Graphics
- Vehicle Graphics
- Signage
- Posters
- Museum Banners
- Point-of-Purchase Displays
- Trade Shows Exhibits
- Wall Graphics
- Floor Graphics
- Yard Signs

Big Picture Press is a new business proposed by Scott Larsen. Scott works for an established printing company in Portland, Oregon, but wishes to open a large-format printing company of his own in the underserved market of Blue Mountain.

In addition to large-format printing, Big Picture Press will offer ancillary services such as basic layout/ graphic design, packaging/shipping, and installation.

MARKET ANALYSIS

Big Picture Press is located in Blue Mountain, a mid-sized Oregon city with approximately 7,000 organizations and businesses and 165,000 residents. The company will market its services to retail and service businesses in the following sub-categories:

Retail Trade

Auto Dealers & Gas Stations (161)

Bars (48)

Building Materials, Hardware & Garden (65)

Clothing Stores (62)

Convenience Stores (21)

Drugstores (25)

Electronics & Computer Stores (35)

Food Markets (39)

Furniture Stores (32)

General Merchandise Stores (35)

Home Furnishings (35)

Liquor Stores (23)

Music Stores (8)

Other Food Service (80)

Other Food Stores (30)

Restaurants (220)

Specialty Stores (240)

Services

Advertising Agencies(40)

Churches (237)

Colleges & Universities (9)

Conference & Convention Centers (5)

Entertainment & Recreation Services (90)

Health & Medical Service Providers (403)

Hospitals (4)

Hotels & Lodging (35)

Legal Services (256)

Membership Organizations (298)

Museums & Zoos (11)

Professional Services (255)

School Districts (2)

*Data obtained from Brooks & Smithers Research Associates

Competition

Big Picture Press will face competition in Blue Mountain. However, based on his industry experience, the owner feels that the market is underserved and could accommodate as many as three additional large-format printing businesses.

According to Scott Larsen's research of the local market, our primary competitors will be:

- Robertson Printing Inc.
- Express Banners Co.
- SignWorks LLC

Big Picture Press will leapfrog the competition by offering more advanced equipment and capabilities (including vehicle wraps) not currently offered in Blue Mountain. In addition, we will offer superior customer service.

INDUSTRY ANALYSIS

According to the trade association Printing Industries of America (PIA), shipments for the printing industry totaled $140.7 billion in 2009. At that time the industry included more than 900,000 employees who worked at approximately 33,500 establishments. Commercial printing accounted for $95.43 billion of total industry revenues. PIA was established in 1887, and by 2011 the association had roughly 10,000 members. The largest graphic arts trade association in the world, PIA "delivers products and services that enhance the growth, efficiency, and profitability of its members and the industry through advocacy, education, research, and technical information."

PERSONNEL

Owner

Scott Larsen has 17 years of experience in the printing industry. During the first 10 years of his career he worked for Pyramid Printing, where he operated a traditional offset press. Larson eventually moved into the large-format printing arena. He currently works for an established printing company in Portland, Oregon, which is recognized as a market leader. The company has achieved significant growth over the last five years, and Larsen has contributed significantly to its success through his attention to quality and detail.

Although Larsen enjoys his current role, he has an entrepreneurial spirit. After earning a business administration degree from Smith College in 2010, he has decided to combine his education with first-hand printing industry skill and knowledge and establish his own enterprise. He foresees tremendous opportunity in the underserved market of Blue Mountain.

Staff

Scott Larsen initially will handle press operations and new business development. To ensure a successful operation, Big Picture Press will need to hire additional staff members for the following positions:

- Sales (prospecting)
- Customer Service (account management)
- Administrative Assistant (production scheduling, payroll, accounts payable/receivable, office operations)
- Production Assistant (assist with press operations, finishing/packaging, installations)

Professional & Advisory Support

Big Picture Press has established a business banking account with Blue Mountain Community Bank, as well as a merchant account for accepting credit card payments. Accounting and tax advisory services will be provided by A-1 Tax & Accounting Services. Scott Larsen has utilized an online legal document service to prepare the paperwork necessary for incorporating his new business.

GROWTH STRATEGY

Years 1-3: Focus heavily on marketing and sales, with an objective of generating awareness in the local marketplace and building a core base of commercial customers.

Year 4-5: Pay off initial financing. Consider the addition of UV flatbed printing capabilities. This major capital expansion would significantly expand the business' capabilities and revenues.

PRODUCTS & SERVICES

Big Picture Press will offer a wide range of large-format printing choices, including:

- Backlit Displays
- Murals
- Event Graphics
- Vehicle Graphics
- Signage
- Posters
- Museum Banners
- Point-of-Purchase Displays
- Trade Shows Exhibits
- Wall Graphics
- Floor Graphics
- Yard Signs

Customers will be provided with quotes in one business day or less. Quotes will be provided via phone, or the online form on the company's Web site.

In addition to large-format printing, Big Picture Press will offer ancillary services such as basic layout/ graphic design, packaging/shipping, and installation.

MARKETING & SALES

Big Picture Press has developed a marketing plan that includes the following tactics:

1. A high-impact vehicle wrap for the company van, which will serve as a "mobile billboard" for the business and demonstrate our capabilities to prospective customers.

2. A glossy, four-color brochure promoting our services/capabilities.

3. A four-color sales sheet that can be used in direct mail campaigns, or left behind with potential clients.

4. A sustained (monthly) direct-mail campaign to prospective large-format printing customers throughout Blue Mountain. A reputable list broker has been identified, along with an area mail house that can prepare the mailings.

5. Sales calls to prospective customers, especially advertising agencies, retailers, hospitals, and other organizations that stand to benefit the most from our large-format printing services.

6. A Web site with complete details about our capabilities and services, as well as a File Transfer Protocol (FTP) area where customers can download design templates for different types of projects, or upload their original art for our production department.

7. A Yellow Page advertisement.

8. A customer incentive program that provides a 10 percent discount off of a customer's first order.

9. Active membership in the local Chamber of Commerce.

OPERATIONS

Facility & Location

Big Picture Press has identified suitable leased space in the Blue Mountain Industrial Park which would meet the company's immediate needs, and also provide room for expansion during subsequent years. A detailed floorplan of this facility is available upon request. This 3,500-square-foot facility includes:

*   Offices (2)

*   Reception Area

*   Conference Room

*   Storage Area

*   Production Area

*   Bathrooms (2)

Other features include convenient rear overhead door access, for shipping and receiving purposes, an existing ventilation system, an existing overhead paging system, and wiring for telephone/data. Minimal modifications will be needed to begin operations.

Equipment

Big Picture Press plans to acquire an Epson Stylus Pro GS6000 large format printer ($25,000). The equipment, which is capable of handling role media up to 64 inches wide, utilizes an eight-color solvent-based ink system. The printer can output onto almost any coated or uncoated type of solvent-based media. By providing faster drying times, this eliminates the need for an external dryer. Another benefit is the fact that the device utilizes less harmful volatile organic compounds, offering printing that is almost odorless. Although the leased facility we have identified includes a ventilation system as an added precaution, the GS6000 requires no special air purification system or ventilation setup. The GS6000 can produce everything from outdoor banners, posters, and signs to tradeshow graphics and vehicle wraps. It is capable of handling almost any print job a customer might want.

In order to ensure smooth operations, Epson offers one year of free warranty coverage for the GS6000 under its Epson Preferred Protection Plan. The plan provides on-site printer repair. Big Picture Press plans to extend this coverage by two years, at an additional cost of $8,725.

Additional supplies needed include:

- Cleaning Cartridges: $500

- Waste Ink Bottle: $40

- Printer Maintenance Kit: $80

- 64-Inch Wide Media Take-up Core: $25

Based on volume, we also will need to purchase ink on a regular basis for the printer. These costs have been calculated into our financial projections (see Financial Analysis section below).

Long-term, Big Picture Press' capital expansion plans include acquisition of a UV flatbed printer that is capable of printing on virtually any substrate up to 1 inch thick. This will require an investment of approximately $85,000.

Hours of Operation
Monday through Friday: 9-5

In order to maximize accessibility, Big Picture Press will have a dedicated telephone number where customers can opt to leave a voicemail message. The owner will attempt to return all routine inquiries within one business day.

Pricing
Large-format printing prices will vary, depending on the size and scope of the project, as well as factors such as shipping and installation. Big Picture Press has prepared a conservative cost/profit estimate based on a labor rate of $25 per hour, and 50 production hours per month for the first year of operations (see Financial Analysis section below).

Insurance
Big Picture Press has received an estimate for appropriate business and liability insurance coverage through Rockwell Insurance Associates.

FINANCIAL ANALYSIS

Big Picture Press has used analysis tools from the manufacturer to estimate monthly and annual profits for the Epson Stylus Pro GS6000. Estimations are conservative, beginning with 2.5 hours of printing per day during year one, 3.5 hours during year two, and 5.0 hours during year three.

The following monthly estimates are specific to costs and profits directly associated with the Epson Stylus Pro GS6000 (e.g., electricity, ink, media, and labor costs). They do not include other business expenses, such as our lease, vehicle, etc. These figures quickly demonstrate the monthly profit potential of the press itself. Big Picture Press has prepared detailed financial estimates in partnership with our accountant (available upon request) that project annual revenues and expenses for our first three years of operation.

THREE YEAR PROFIT ESTIMATE

	2011	2012	2013
Estimated revenue			
Total printed media (square feet)	9,000	12,600	18,000
Sellable output (square feet)	8,550	11,970	17,100
Monthly gross revenue	$ 52,753.50	$ 73,854.90	$ 105,507
Estimated overhead & materials cost			
Ink cost	$ 3,375	$ 4,725	$ 6,750
Media consumption cost	$ 5,400	$ 7,560	$ 10,800
Electricity cost	$ 14.40	$ 20.16	$ 28.80
Monthly labor rate ($25/hour)	$ 1,250	$ 1,750	$ 2,500
Production hours	50	70	100
Total costs	**$10,039.40**	**$14,055.16**	**$ 20,078.80**
Estimated monthly profit	**$42,714.10**	**$59,799.74**	**$ 85,428.20**

Evaluation & Adjustment

This plan will be evaluated on a quarterly basis.

Personal Organizing Consultant

All In Place Inc.

85612 Stony Plain Way
Winnetka, IL 60093

Paul Greenland

All In Place is a professional organization consultancy specializing in upper-income consumers.

EXECUTIVE SUMMARY

Business Overview

All In Place is a newly established professional organization consultancy. As the National Association of Professional Organizers (NAPO) explains, a professional organizer "enhances the lives of clients by designing custom organizing systems and processes and by transferring organizing skills."

In 2010 Claire Richfield, CPO, decided to establish All In Place after assisting a friend who owned a closet organizing business. It was that experience, coupled with a broader interest in home organization, that led her to complete several organization projects for friends and family members. In time, Claire earned voluntary certification from the Board of Certification for Professional Organizers (BCPO) and became a Certified Professional Organizer.

Ultimately, word-of-mouth referrals and encouragement from existing customers prompted her to establish her own professional organization consultancy. Based on her recent experiences and knowledge of the Winnetka market, Claire has decided to target her new business toward upper-income consumers who have the highest levels of disposable income.

MARKET ANALYSIS

All In Place will concentrate its marketing efforts on upper-income consumers. Initially, the business will focus on the immediate Winnetka area. According to data from DemographicsNow, the average household income in Winnetka was $305,131 in 2009. This figure is projected to increase 8.1 percent by 2014, reaching $329,808. Residents earning more than $150,000 annually represented the largest household income category in 2009 (64.6%), followed by those earning between $100,000 and $149,999 (14.1%). Each of these segments is forecast to experience strong growth by 2014 (68% and 12.5%, respectively).

Additional data from DemographicsNow reveals that Winnetka was home to 4,091 households in 2009. At that time total household expenditures averaged $173,470. This figure is forecast to reach $187,703 in 2014. In 2009 average annual expenditures within the household services category totaled about $2,435.

In time, All In Place has the option of broadening its focus beyond the immediate Winnetka area. By simply expanding the radius of the business' primary market area two miles, the number of prospective customers increases significantly. For example, the slightly larger geographic area included 10,955 households in 2009. Household income remains extremely high, with 32 percent of households reporting income above $150,000, and 15.3 percent of households reporting income of between $100,000 and $149,999.

INDUSTRY ANALYSIS

Professional organizers can earn voluntary certification from the Board of Certification for Professional Organizers (BCPO), whose mission is "to advance the credibility and ethical standards of the professional organizing industry through credentialing. In recognizing the experienced organizer, BCPO seeks to inspire organizers to provide superior client services and to continue to develop expertise in the transfer of higher-level organizing skills." Many industry participants also are members of the National Association of Professional Organizers, which had approximately 4,200 members in 2010.

Professional organizers have received significant exposure in recent years. One prime example is A&E's popular program, *Hoarders*, which was in its third season during 2010. As the network explains, the television program "not only captures the drama as experts work to put each hoarder on the road to recovery but also highlights the individual's inner challenges and triumphs."

PERSONNEL

A native of Evanston, Illinois, Claire Richfield, CPO, is a Certified Professional Organizer. All her life, Claire has been known for being neat and organized. With five children close in age, these qualities were invaluable when it came to keeping her household working as a well-oiled machine. With her children in college, Claire began utilizing her natural abilities to help others organize their lives.

In 2010 Claire decided to establish All In Place after assisting a friend who owned a closet organizing business. It was that experience, coupled with a broader interest in home organization, that led her to complete several organization projects for friends and family members. In time, Claire earned voluntary certification from the Board of Certification for Professional Organizers (BCPO) and became a Certified Professional Organizer.

Ultimately, word-of-mouth referrals and encouragement from existing customers prompted her to establish her own professional organization consultancy. Based on her recent experiences and knowledge of the local Winnetka market, Claire has decided to target her services toward upper-income consumers, who have the highest levels of disposable income.

Claire already has the skills needed to succeed as a professional organizer. In addition to having excellent listening and human relations skills, she is:

- Patient
- Efficient
- Organized
- Flexible
- Compassionate
- Professional
- Goal-oriented

Well-established in her community, Claire is confident in her ability to secure a steady stream of organization projects. In addition to her Certified Professional Organizer credentials, she is a member of the National Association of Professional Organizers. While optional, these credentials will go a long way in strengthening Claire's credibility with prospective customers.

Professional & Advisory Support

Claire Richfield has secured a business liability insurance policy for her new company through Professional Insurance Associates, along with a home office rider to her homeowner's insurance policy. She has consulted with the local law firm of Stevens & Welty to prepare basic business agreements that she can use with customers. Additionally, Claire has established a business banking account for All In Place with Winnetka Community Bank, as well as a merchant account for accepting credit card payments. Tax advisory will be provided by North Shore Tax Advisors LLC.

GROWTH STRATEGY

Initially, Claire Richfield plans to operate All In Place as a part-time business. This will allow her to gain experience at a steady, measured pace, and still have time for social and volunteer activities. With this in mind, she will choose her assignments carefully and rely mostly on word-of-mouth marketing/referrals to grow her business.

During All In Place's first several years, Claire Richfield plans to build upon her Certified Professional Organizer status by pursuing continuing education opportunities and strengthening her skills. In terms of *weekly billable hours*, she has established the following targets (based on 48 work weeks per year):

> *Year One*—10 hours (estimated revenue of $72,000)
>
> *Year Two*—15 hours ($108,000)
>
> *Year Three*—20 hours ($144,000)

SERVICES

The actual services performed by All In Place will vary from client to client and project to project. In some cases a project simply may involve helping someone clean up a messy room, while more involved projects may entail space planning for a large area or even preparing a customer for a whole-house move to another location. Claire will offer organization services in a number of different categories, including:

- Closets
- Bedrooms
- Hobby Rooms
- Kitchens/Pantries
- Garages
- Workshops
- Children's Playrooms
- Attics/Basements/Storage Areas
- Home Offices/File Management

- Home Libraries
- Media/Entertainment Collections

Discovery Process

Claire Richfield will begin every new client relationship with a discovery process, during which time she will learn about her new customer's house, condominium, or apartment; identify specific, measurable objectives; and establish concrete project milestones/timelines. This information will then become part of a formal written agreement between her consultancy and the customer.

A key part of the discovery process is learning about the individuals with whom she will be working, and what their hopes, fears, and dreams are. Organizing projects can be highly personal, dealing with the intimate details and sentiments of people's lives. One of Claire Richfield's strong suits is dealing with sensitive situations. She has a calm demeanor and excellent diplomatic skills that will be a tremendous benefit in working with different types of people.

On one recent assignment, Claire worked with a gentleman who grew up during the Great Depression. At the age of 80, his basement was filled with numerous items that the average person would consider to be "disposable." With the help of a trained counselor, Claire was able to help the gentleman realize that it was okay to dispose of these items, so that they would not be a burden to his children in the event that he should become ill or pass away.

Special Populations

Disorganization can be the result of deeply rooted emotional or psychological challenges. One example is "hoarding," which was the subject of a popular television series on A&E during the late 2000s. In its description of the program, the network explains: "Although cleaning marks the first step of tackling this disorder, success is not definite. For some individuals, throwing away the tiniest object is so traumatizing that they will not be able to allow the cleaning process to go on, no matter how it may impact their future. For others, professional help and an organizer's instruction give them the strength to let go."

Claire Richfield has established a referral relationship with Monica Brown, a clinical psychologist in the nearby community of Evanston, in the event that she encounters customers who need assistance that she cannot provide alone. Likewise, Monica Brown has agreed to recommend All In Place to patients who would benefit from the services of a professional organizer.

In addition to hoarding, other examples of populations with specialized needs include senior citizens, as well as individuals with attention deficit disorder, visual impairments, and physical disabilities. When assignments involve serving individuals and families with specialized needs, Claire Richfield will tap into the appropriate community resources, performing research and discussing situations with other professionals when needed, in order to provide customers with the most appropriate and effective organization solutions.

MARKETING & SALES

Because she is well-connected in the community, Claire Richfield plans to promote her services heavily through networking and word-of-mouth marketing. However, she has put together a marketing plan for All In Place that involves the following primary tactics:

1. Presentations to area social clubs and women's groups about organization-related topics.

2. A high-quality, four-color, tri-fold brochure, printed on glossy stock that includes customer testimonials.

3. A Web site with complete details about All In Place.

4. The use of social media channels, including Facebook, to network with potential customers.

5. Attention-getting business cards that include Claire Richfield's photo.

OPERATIONS

Home Office

For the sake of convenience and cost efficiency, Claire Richfield will operate All In Place from her Winnetka home. She has established a home office space that is equipped with a desktop computer, filing cabinets, as well as dedicated phone and fax lines. Claire has purchased a bundle of business productivity software, for which she received training at a local community college. This will enable her to manage contact information for customers, generate invoices, and manage her business' finances.

Equipment

Claire has obtained an Internet-enabled smartphone to stay in communication with prospective and current customers. Her e-mail account will synchronize with her desktop computer, allowing for efficient communications management. Claire also has made several technology investments that are necessary for the operation of the business. These include a digital still camera, as well as a digital video camera, which will be used to document conditions at various client sites.

Fees

Claire Richfield will charge $150 per hour for her services. She typically will bill customers by the hour, but is agreeable to billing on a per-project basis when needed. In addition, she will consider discounts for large/long-term assignments. Based on the size and scope of the job, Claire will require clients to pre-pay for a certain number of hours, or for 30 percent of her total fee when billing per project.

FINANCIAL ANALYSIS

Following is All In Place's projected balance sheet for 2011. Detailed monthly cash flow statements are available upon request. Revenue calculations are conservative, and are based upon 10 hours of billable consulting time per week in 2011. Claire anticipates that her net income will increase significantly in 2012 and 2013 as she increases her average weekly billable consulting hours to 15 and 20 hours, respectively.

Revenue	$72,000
Expenses	
Salary	$45,000
Taxes & licenses	$ 6,500
Health insurance	$ 1,900
Home office	$ 1,375
Accounting & legal	$ 2,000
Insurance	$ 2,125
Office supplies	$ 470
Equipment	$ 2,750
Marketing & advertising	$ 2,000
Telecommunications & internet	$ 1,250
Professional development	$ 1,500
Travel & entertainment	$ 500
Subscriptions & dues	$ 400
Miscellaneous	$ 500
Total expenses	**$68,270**
Net income	**$ 3,730**

Professional Organizing Consultant

Marilyn Ruby Inc.

21 Brook Ave.
Eagan, MN 55121

Paul Greenland

Marilyn Ruby is a professional organization consultant specializing in businesses and organizations.

EXECUTIVE SUMMARY

Business Overview

By 2011 the business community was all too familiar with terms like restructuring, downsizing, consolidation, and reorganization. Intended to save money and, in some cases, "trim the fat" from corporate budgets, one major drawback to these approaches was disorganization. Along with the combination of departments, divisions, facilities, and individual jobs came a fair amount of confusion, resulting from information overload and disrupted processes and workflows.

Employees are now required to process a greater amount of information more quickly than in the past. Despite having exceptional job-related skills, most professionals never received "pile management" training to address the high volume of paper that accumulates on one's desk. Making matters worse is the fact that the average office has decreased in size over the last few decades.

Established in 2010, Marilyn Ruby Inc. is a professional organization consultancy that helps businesses meet the challenges associated with these changes head on and get organized, resulting in:

- Reduced clutter

- Increased control

- Improved efficiency

- Heightened productivity

- Better employee morale

- Increased profitability

- Reduced stress levels

A 1990 graduate of Rydell Business College, Marilyn began her career as an executive secretary. Ultimately, she was chosen to serve as the secretary for the CEO of a leading footwear company. In that role she was responsible for managing the personal and professional calendars of a high-profile business leader and keeping his life organized. In addition, she spearheaded numerous business organization projects.

With 20 years of experience, Marilyn has decided to establish her own consultancy and use her knowledge and skills for the benefit of other organizations, especially small and mid-sized companies that need professional assistance to establish proven, manageable systems for staying organized.

MARKET ANALYSIS

According to a DemographicsNow market report, the Minneapolis-St. Paul area consisted of 30,237 establishments in 2009 (the latest data available). Collectively, these establishments employed approximately 568,131 workers, some 70 percent of whom were white-collar employees. On average, establishments employed 19 people. By employee category, the market breaks down as follows:

- Administrative Support Workers (21%)

- Professional Specialty Occupations (20.2%)

- Executive Managers & Administrators (13.2%)

- Sales Workers & Clerks (7.4%)

- Technologies & Technicians (5.5%)

- Sales Professionals (2.5%)

- Technical Sales & Administrative (0.4%)

Examples of specific jobs/professions that could benefit from Marilyn Ruby's services include:

- Attorneys

- Physicians

- Professors

- Administrators

- Presidents & CEOs

- Administrative assistants

- Executive secretaries

- Project managers

- Department/division managers

Marilyn Ruby Inc. will concentrate its initial marketing efforts on companies with between 20 and 250 employees. Marilyn feels that companies in this size range are excellent prospects because they likely are dealing with organization-related challenges that accompany a growing enterprise. At the same time, they are small enough where she can have a quick and noticeable impact on their operations.

In total, companies in this size range represent 13 percent of the market:

- 20-49 Employees (7.6%)

- 50-99 Employees (3.3%)

- 100-249 Employees (2.1%)

Marilyn Ruby Inc. is in the process of securing a custom report from Dun & Bradstreet in order to identify the enterprises that have achieved the strongest sales growth over the past three to five years, and which are in the strongest financial position.

INDUSTRY ANALYSIS

Good organization has long been the hallmark of successful businesses and companies. Disorganization is a long-time problem. Professional organizers concentrating on the business market have been around for at least 20 years. For example, the November 25, 1991, issue of the *Atlanta Business Chronicle* described a thriving professional organizer named Judith Kohlberg who had been operating a consultancy for three years.

By 2003 productivity issues were costing American businesses approximately 86 workdays annually, according to the National Association of Professional Organizers. By that time the average office worker produced approximately 45 sheets of paper per day and spent six weeks per year "looking for things," according to an article in the January 13, 2003, issue of *The Record* (Stockton, California).

Professional organizers can earn voluntary certification from the Board of Certification for Professional Organizers (BCPO), whose mission is "to advance the credibility and ethical standards of the professional organizing industry through credentialing. In recognizing the experienced organizer, BCPO seeks to inspire organizers to provide superior client services and to continue to develop expertise in the transfer of higher-level organizing skills." Many industry participants also are members of the National Association of Professional Organizers.

PERSONNEL

A native of Minneapolis, Minnesota, Marilyn Ruby, CPO, is a Certified Professional Organizer. She is a 1990 graduate of Rydell Business College. That year, Marilyn began her career as an executive secretary. Ultimately, she was chosen to serve as the secretary for the CEO of a leading footwear company. In that role she was responsible for managing the personal and professional calendars of a high-profile business leader and keeping his life organized.

Over the course of Marilyn's career as an executive secretary, she served on several committees focused on office automation, workflow enhancement, and business process improvement. She oversaw a number of successful initiatives in these areas, including a massive data management initiative following the merger of two companies. Specifically, that project involved taking computer files from both organizations, reorganizing them according to a new structure, and uploading the data onto a new server.

Marilyn Ruby already has the skills needed to succeed as a professional organizer. In addition to having excellent listening and human relations skills, she is:

*   Patient
*   Efficient
*   Organized
*   Professional
*   Goal-oriented
*   Tech savvy

With 20 years of experience, Marilyn has decided to establish her own consultancy and use her knowledge and skills for the benefit of other organizations, especially small and mid-sized companies that need professional assistance to establish proven, manageable systems for staying organized.

She has earned Certified Professional Organizer credentials from the Board of Certification for Professional Organizers, and is a member of the National Association of Professional Organizers. While optional, these credentials will go a long way in strengthening her credibility with prospective customers.

Professional & Advisory Support

Marilyn Ruby has secured a business liability insurance policy for her new company through Fortress Insurance, along with a home office rider to her homeowner's insurance policy. Realizing that her work will often involve exposure to sensitive information, such as trade secrets, she has consulted with the firm of Peters & Stone, which specializes in business law, to prepare agreements covering privacy and nondisclosure. For businesses that do not have standard agreements in areas such as these, this will help to clarify the finer points of their business relationship with Marilyn Ruby Inc. and alleviate any potential concerns and/or ethical issues. In addition, Marilyn Ruby also has established a business banking account with the Greater Twin Cities Bank, as well as a merchant account for accepting credit card payments. Tax advisory will be provided by Luther & Smith Accounting LLC.

GROWTH STRATEGY

After six months of careful planning, Marilyn Ruby began her foray into professional organizing on a freelance basis in 2009. That year, she performed her very first two assignments: helping a local non-profit agency that is close to her heart, as well as a local attorney (who learned about her services while she was volunteering for the non-profit agency). To her admitted surprise, demand among area organizations for a professional organizer was much greater than she had anticipated.

Despite difficult economic conditions, word-of-mouth referrals were enough to keep Marilyn busy on a part-time basis throughout 2010, while she continued to work at her regular full-time job. This, coupled with her recent Certified Professional Organizer status, prompted her to pursue professional organizing as a full-time profession beginning in 2011.

Considering her recent project work, Marilyn Ruby is confident that she will have ample business to support herself as a full-time professional organizer—especially with a deliberate marketing strategy in place. Following a conversation with a fellow NAPO member (in a different market), she learned that this individual increase the size of her business from one employee and $5,000 in revenue in 1998 to five employees and $1 million in revenue in 2008.

Nevertheless, Marilyn Ruby will approach the first three years of her business with cautious optimism and conservative growth projections. For planning purposes she anticipates 15 billable hours of client time per week (based on a 50-week work year) during year one (estimated revenue of $93,750), followed by 25 hours in year two ($156,250), and 35 hours in year three ($218,750).

SERVICES

Marilyn Ruby will begin every new client relationship with a discovery process, during which time she will learn about her new customer's operations; identify specific, measurable objectives; and establish concrete project milestones/timelines. This information will then become part of a formal written agreement between her firm and the customer.

The actual services performed will vary from client to client and project to project. In some cases, a project simply may involve helping someone clean up a messy office space, which could entail sorting a mountain of paper into items that need to be acted upon, filed, or disposed of. Based on prior experience, however, Marilyn realizes that things aren't always that simple. More often than not, clients will need services that involve one or more of the following services:

- Organization skills training
- Paperwork/records management

- Electronic organizing (computer files)
- Workspace planning/design
- Workflow analysis/improvement
- Goal-setting/time management

MARKETING & SALES

In order to promote her new enterprise, Marilyn Ruby has developed a marketing plan that involves the following primary tactics:

1. Membership in area chambers of commerce and local business groups, in an effort to secure new assignments via word-of-mouth marketing/networking.

2. A tri-fold brochure, which can be produced cost-effectively (in small or large quantities) at a local digital printing company. This can be used as a leave-behind when networking, or for direct mail campaigns. Importantly, customer testimonials will be included.

3. Advertisements in print and online materials produced by area chambers of commerce and local business networking groups.

4. A Web site with complete details about her business and the services it offers, as well as a section that includes client testimonials.

5. A monthly e-mail newsletter for businesses in the Twin Cities, offering useful organization tips.

6. The use of social media channels, including LinkedIn, to network with potential customers, as well as fellow industry colleagues.

7. Direct mailings to prospective businesses, per the criteria outlined in the Marketing & Sales section of this plan.

8. A media relations strategy that involves the submission of case studies/success stories to appropriate business and trade magazines.

9. Exhibition at local and regional business expos.

10. Attention-getting business cards that include Marilyn Ruby's photo.

OPERATIONS

Marilyn Ruby will operate her business from an existing home office in order to keep overhead low. She already is equipped with desktop and tablet computers, as well as an Internet-enabled mobile phone, which will enable her to stay in touch with prospective and existing clients and manage her professional and personal calendars efficiently. In addition, she has purchased a basic business productivity software suite that includes applications for contact management and billing.

Marilyn has identified several capital purchases that her business will need to make. These include a digital still camera, as well as a digital video camera, which will be used to document conditions at various client sites.

Fees

Based on conversations with others in the industry, Marilyn Ruby will charge $125 per hour for her services. When working with new consultants, Marilyn has learned that many clients are more comfortable with an hourly rate, versus a project rate. However, she is open to billing on a per-project basis when needed. In addition, she will consider discounts for large/long-term assignments. Based on the size and scope of the job, Marilyn will require clients to pre-pay for a certain number of hours, or for 30 percent of her total fee when billing per project.

FINANCIAL ANALYSIS

Following is Marilyn Ruby's projected balance sheet for 2011. Detailed monthly cash flow statements are available upon request. Revenue calculations are conservative, and are based upon 15 hours of billable consulting time per week in 2011. Marilyn anticipates that her net income will increase significantly in 2012 and 2013 as she increases her average weekly billable consulting hours to 25 and 35 hours, respectively.

Revenue	**$93,750**
Expenses	
Salary	$65,000
Taxes & licenses	$ 8,500
Health insurance	$ 1,800
Home office	$ 875
Accounting & legal	$ 2,000
Insurance	$ 2,125
Office supplies	$ 670
Equipment	$ 2,500
Marketing & advertising	$ 4,500
Telecommunications & internet	$ 1,250
Professional development	$ 850
Travel & entertainment	$ 500
Subscriptions & dues	$ 350
Miscellaneous	$ 500
Total expenses	**$91,420**
Net income	**$ 2,330**

Sharpening Service

The Razor's Edge LLC

4289 Williams Peak Ave.
Raleigh, NC 27607

Paul Greenland

The Razor's Edge provides sharpening services for items in a wide range of categories including kitchen cutlery, woodworking tools, hunting/outdoor items, scissors, and various lawn and garden tools.

EXECUTIVE SUMMARY

Business Overview

The Razor's Edge provides sharpening services for items in a wide range of categories including kitchen cutlery, woodworking tools, hunting/outdoor items, scissors, and various lawn and garden tools. The service is a new business established by Bill Mason, a retired hardware store owner. Mason is interested in beginning a scalable business that he can operate with his son, Jack Mason, initially on a part-time basis. His son, who has a full-time day job in a local machine shop, will initially work for the sharpening service evenings and weekends until the business can sustain him on a full-time basis.

The Razor's Edge will begin operation from a small outbuilding on Bill Mason's property. This location should be suitable for the foreseeable future, as it provides ample space for operations. The owners plan to pick up and deliver items to commercial customers. The Mason property is easily accessible for consumers who wish to drop off items for sharpening.

MARKET ANALYSIS

Overview

The Razor's Edge will focus on five primary target markets: consumers, barbershops/beauty salons, landscaping businesses, tradespeople, and food service/institutional.

In 2010 Raleigh, North Carolina, was home to approximately 371,000 people. Because almost all consumers are in need of sharpening services, there is ample opportunity within this market segment.

Likewise, plenty of opportunity exists for The Razor's Edge within the commercial sector. According to a report from DemographicsNow, our commercial prospects in Raleigh break down as follows:

- Restaurants (592 establishments)

- Beauty & Barbershops (568 establishments)

- Hospitals/Medical (268 establishments)

- Miscellaneous Repair Services (129 establishments)

- Hotels & Lodging (82 establishments)

Landscaping and lawn care businesses fall within the category of "Other Business Services" (902 establishments).

Competition

The Razor's Edge will face competition from a number of different businesses in the Raleigh area. Our primary competitors will be businesses that offer a full range of sharpening services:

- Sharpening Solutions Inc.

- Larsson Enterprises

Competition also will come from businesses that focus on one particular type of sharpening (e.g., saw blades, knives, scissors, etc.):

- Peterson's Outdoor Equipment Inc.

- Raleigh Saw Works

- Municipal Saws & Tools

- Professional Knife Sharpening

- Sharpest Scissors LLC

We will benefit from the fact that there are a limited number of competitors in the marketplace at the present time.

PERSONNEL

Bill Mason

A retired hardware store owner, Bill Mason is well known throughout Raleigh, North Carolina. He operated Mason's Hometown Hardware, a business established by his father in 1938, from 1969 until his retirement in 2005. One of Bill's first jobs, when he worked for his father during high school, was sharpening knives and lawnmower blades. Since his retirement bill has continued to offer occasional sharpening services to his old customers, in order to maintain relationships with them and stay busy. Realizing that there is a strong market opportunity in this area, Bill has decided to capitalize on his reputation in the community and establish a scalable business that he can operate with his son, Jack Mason. Initially, he plans to operate the business with Jack on a part-time basis. During this time he will share his business management knowledge with his son and help him to establish a thriving enterprise.

Jack Mason

Jack currently works full-time for ABC Machine Inc., a local machine shop where he works as a CNC lathe operator. He will initially work for the sharpening service evenings and weekends until the business can sustain him on a full-time basis. Like his father, Jack spent his high school years working at the family hardware store, where he sharpened many a lawnmower blade and knife. With his mechanical skills and hands-on experience, Jack is well-suited for a sharpening business. Best of all, he is eager to learn about business management from his father.

Professional & Advisory Support

The Razor's Edge has established a business banking account with City Credit Union, as well as a merchant account for accepting credit card payments. Rusty Steers, a local accountant, will provide accounting and tax advisory services. The owners have utilized LegalZoom.com, an online legal document service, to prepare the paperwork necessary for establishing their limited liability company.

GROWTH STRATEGY

- *Year One:* Begin as a part-time sharpening service that serves our local market. Develop a core base of repeat commercial customers.

- *Year Two:* Expand our core base of repeat customers and become a full-time operation.

- *Year Three:* Expand the business by adding a mobile/on-site sharpening service and doing demonstrations at local/regional special interest shows (see Marketing & Sales). Consider the addition of a third, part-time employee.

- *Year Four:* Intensify online marketing efforts and begin offering a mail-in sharpening service serving all 50 states.

SERVICES

The Razor's Edge provides sharpening services for items in a wide range of categories including:

Kitchen Cutlery
- Cleavers

- Butcher Knives

- Serrated Knives

- Tourne Knife

- Boning Knife

- Steak Knives

- Utility Knives

- Slicing/Carving Knives

- Cheese Knives

- Chef's Knives

- Deli Knives

- Filet Knives

- Frozen Food Knives

- Mincing Knives

- Paring Knives

Woodworking Tools
- Carving Knives

- Chisels

- Drill Bits

- Woodturning Tools

- Saw Blades
- Plane Blades

Hunting/Outdoor
- Fillet Knives
- Fixed Knives
- Pocket Knives
- Tactical Knives
- Custom Knives
- Machetes
- Folding Knives
- Lock-back Knives
- Serrated Knives
- Fish Hooks
- Axes
- Hatchets

Scissors
- Kitchen Scissors
- Pinking Shears
- Sewing Scissors
- Poultry Shears
- Tin Snips

Lawn & Garden
- Lawnmower Blades (push mower and tractor)
- Pruning Shears
- Loppers
- Edgers
- Clippers
- Sod Cutters

Process

The Razor's Edge will provide all customers with a firm time and cost estimate when they drop off their items for sharpening.

Depending on the items that require sharpening, different types of equipment or tools will be used (see detailed list below). For example, when working with knives we typically use sharpening stones, progressing from coarse stones (for dull or nicked blades) to medium and then fine stones (which produce a sharp edge). There are different types of sharpening stones (e.g., oil stones, water stones, and diamond stones), and some are better suited for specific applications than others. For example, diamond stones are especially effective for sharpening kitchen cutlery.

Beyond sharpening stones, The Razor's Edge will be equipped with other types of sharpening equipment. In some cases, we may use sharpening steels, diamond rod sharpeners, and hand-held or bench mountable leather strops. Sometimes, power equipment may be utilized. Examples include a belt sander equipped with a leather stropping belt, which removes less metal than other methods, a scissor sharpening machine, or a bench grinder.

Typical turnaround time for most jobs will be 3 to 5 business days. For an additional 20 percent charge, we will turn around a customer order in 24 hours or less. All items are cleaned after sharpening and returned in cases/sheathes/containers provided by the customer, or wrapped in plain paper and marked with the customer's last name. All items not claimed within 30 days become the property of The Razor's Edge.

MARKETING & SALES

The Razor's Edge has developed a marketing plan that involves the following primary tactics:

1. A series of five fliers that are customized for each of our primary target markets: consumers, barbershops/beauty salons, landscaping businesses, tradespeople, food service/institutional.

2. Sales calls to prospective accounts (a detailed monthly schedule for our first year of operation is available upon request).

3. A multi-phased direct-mail campaign that initially involves sending fliers to our top commercial prospects.

4. A Yellow Page listing.

5. A Web site with complete details about our business and the services we offer.

6. A customer loyalty program that provides a 10 percent discount to those referring a friend or family member to our business.

7. A "first sharpening is free" (limit two items) incentive to gain new customers.

8. Magnetic signage that can be affixed to our vehicle in order to promote the business.

9. Magnetic business cards that will double as advertising specialties.

10. Active membership in the local Chamber of Commerce.

11. Trade show marketing at the following: Home & Garden Shows; Hunting & Fishing Shows; Knife & Gun Shows; and Cooking Shows

We will begin to use this tactic during our second year of operations, after transitioning to a full-time business. A detailed exhibition schedule will be compiled during year one, at which time we will develop a trade show display with the help of a local large-format graphics company.

OPERATIONS

Location
The Razor's Edge will begin operation from a small outbuilding on Bill Mason's property. This location should be suitable for the foreseeable future, as it provides ample space for operations. The owners anticipate that they will pick up and deliver items to commercial customers. The Mason property is easily accessible for consumers who wish to drop off items for sharpening.

Tools & Equipment
Following is a list of tools and equipment that will be used by The Razor's Edge:

- Belt Sander

- Bench Grinders

- Sharpening Kits/Stones, including: Portable Oil Stone Sharpening System; Oil Stone Kit; Kitchen Sharpening Kit; Woodworking Sharpening Kit

- Electric Sharpeners

- Handheld Sharpeners

- Pocket Sharpeners

- Strops, including: 2" Double Sided Paddle Strop; 8" Double Sided Paddle Strop; 10" Leather Bench Mountable Strop; Leather Razor Strop

- Pastes, including Razor Strop Dressing; Abrasive Powder; Diamond Paste

- Grinding Wheels

- Sharpening Guides

- Sharpening Steels

In addition to the items listed above, The Razor's Edge will occasionally need to purchase various accessories and replacement parts from time to time.

Hours of Operation

During our first year of business, we will adhere to the following schedule:

Monday, Wednesday & Friday: 8 AM to 4:30 PM

Saturday: 8 AM to 12 PM

Closed on Sunday

Pricing

Following is a basic price list for The Razor's Edge:

- Lawnmower Blades (lawn tractor): $7.50 per blade

- Lawnmower Blades (push mower): $10 per blade

- Folding Knives: $7

- Fixed Blade Knives (under 6 inches): $10

- Fixed Blade Knives (6-12 inches): $15

- Fixed Blade Knives (over 12 inches): $20

- Hatchets: $25

- Machetes: $30

- Broken Tip Repair: $25

Additional Charges: $1.50 for 1/2 serrated knives and $3 for completely serrated knives; multi-blade knives are sharpened at a rate of $3 per additional blade.

*Rush charge (24-hour turnaround): 20%

*Free estimates provided for items not listed above

FINANCIAL ANALYSIS

General Overview

The Razor's Edge has prepared detailed financial projections with the help of their accountant, Rusty Steers. These projections, which are available upon request, consider our transition to a full-time operation during year two, the addition of a mobile/on-site sharpening service during year three and our expansion to a mail-in sharpening service serving all 50 states during year four.

Based upon our projections, we anticipate that our net profits will be as follows:

Year 1	Year 2	Year 3	Year 4
$2,000	$10,000	$15,000	$25,000

Capital Purchases

The Razor's Edge already has some of the equipment needed for operations. However, several minor purchases will need to be made. These include:

- Oilstones: $20
- Grinding Wheels: $100
- Knife Sharpener: $45
- Triangle Sharpener: $60
- Scissor Sharpening Machine: $100
- Strops: $60
- Diamond Stone Kit: $225
- Waterstone Kit: $165

Bill Mason will purchase these items from his own personal savings.

Evaluation & Adjustment

This plan will be evaluated on a quarterly basis with accountant Rusty Steers during our first and second years of operation, and semi-annually thereafter.

Soap Making Business

Felson's Homemade Soaps Inc.

8339 Randall Rd.
Wenton, MA 01010

Paul Greenland

Felson's Homemade Soaps produces and markets a wide range of handcrafted soaps for men, women, and children.

EXECUTIVE SUMMARY

Business Overview

Everyone needs soap to stay clean. However, homemade, handcrafted soaps add a little luxury to the equation. By incorporating beautiful combinations of color and scents, they are works of art commonly sold in many high-end boutiques and salons. Felson's Homemade Soaps produces and markets a wide range of handcrafted soaps for men, women, and children. The business produces its products using a number of techniques. These include both "melt & pour" and cold process methods.

Co-owner Carol Felson was introduced to the art of soap making more than five years ago through her daughter Casey's school project. Mother and daughter had so much fun working together on the project that they continued to make specialty soaps for themselves. In time, they perfected their skills and family and friends caught wind after receiving the products as gifts.

Because there are a seemingly endless number of recipes, Carol and Casey were able to make soaps that appealed to just about everyone; women, men, and even children. For this reason, coupled with the popularity of their products, the Felsons have decided to turn their hobby into a profitable part-time business enterprise with full-time potential.

The business is perfectly suited for both women for a number of reasons. The Felsons have a large workspace in their basement (a multi-purpose room equipped with a stove, sink, counter tops, and storage cabinets) that can be used for business purposes. In addition, Casey lives at home while attending community college, and Carol is not currently employed.

MARKET ANALYSIS

Overview

Although products marketed by Felson's Homemade Soaps will appeal to men, women, and children, we are confident that women will be the primary purchasers of our soaps. Specifically, we feel that women aged 35 to 64, with household income of at least $35,000, represent the greatest opportunity. Therefore, we will target our sales and marketing efforts toward this specific demographic segment.

According to ABC Research LLC, in 2010 Wenton was home to approximately 153,000 people (57,900 households). By 2015 the population was expected to reach nearly 157,500 people (approximately 59,000 households).

Females represented 51.6 percent of the population in 2010, a figure that was expected to hold steady through 2015.

In terms of age groupings, the Wenton population broke down as follows in 2010:

35-44: 12.3%

45-54: 12.9%

55-64: 10.5%

Annual household income was categorized this way:

$35,000-$49,999 (15.3%)

$50,000-$74,999 (17.4%)

$75,000-$99,999 (9.6%)

$100,000-$149,999 (9.0%)

$150,000+ (4.5%)

Primary Markets

Felson's Homemade Soaps will initially concentrate on the following primary markets:

Farmers Market

The Wenton Farmers' Market will provide our business with multiple opportunities to exhibit year-round. The market provides exhibitors with indoor and outdoor venues according to the following schedule (2011):

Late Winter Indoor Market
Saturdays, Jan. 8 - Apr. 9
8:00 a.m. - Noon

Summer Outdoor Market
Saturdays
Apr. 16 - Jul. 2
Jul. 16 - Nov. 5

Early Winter
Nov. 12 - Dec. 17

Craft Shows

There are numerous arts and craft shows in our immediate region. After conducting research into shows that have the greatest potential for our type of products, we have selected the following (detailed information regarding each show is available upon request):

Wenton Mall Craft Show (held three times annually)

Valentine's Day Arts & Crafts Spree

Art for the Season

Uptown Craft & Merchandise Show

Annual Mother's Day Craft Show

Summer Festival of Arts & Crafts

Wenton Fall Art & Craft Expo

Jewelry & Accessory Craft Fair

Home Decor Expo (held twice annually)

Wenton Holiday Craft Bazaar

Future Markets

As our business expands, we will consider broadening the scope of our primary market to include the following:

Gift Shop Sales (commission arrangement)

Retail Stores (commission arrangement)

Internet Sales

When we are ready to expand in these areas, detailed market research will be conducted regarding specific gift shops and retail stores that hold the greatest potential in our local and regional areas. However, in 2010 the Wenton area was home to 137 specialty retailers, as well as 74 gift shops.

Competition

Felson's Homemade Soaps will face competition from a number of independent soap makers and small businesses throughout the region. The majority of the competition will likely come from the neighboring communities of Worchester, Newton, and Woonsocket. However, a number also will come from the Boston area.

Because limited data is available, compiling a comprehensive list of other soap makers is not possible. However, three businesses that have attended some of the shows where we plan to exhibit are:

Soap by Sally

L & L Gifts

Tonya's Specialty Products Inc.

We plan to differentiate ourselves by offering soap recipes that our competitors do not.

INDUSTRY

Soap making is a very old profession. During the 21st century, businesses and individual practitioners involved in the production of handcrafted soaps, as well as related suppliers and vendors, were represented by the Handcrafted Soapmakers Guild. Established in 1998, the non-profit trade association's mission is: "To promote the handcrafted soap industry; to act as a center of communication among soapmakers; and to circulate information beneficial to soapmakers."

PERSONNEL

Carol & Casey Felson

Carol Felson was introduced to the art of soap making more than five years ago, through her daughter's school project. Mother and daughter had so much fun working together on the project that they continued to make specialty soaps for themselves. In time, they perfected their skills and family and friends caught wind after receiving the products as gifts. Because there are a seemingly endless number of recipes, Carol and her daughter, Casey, were able to make soaps that appealed to just about everyone; women, men, and even children.

Prior to starting a family, Carol was the assistant manager of an arts and crafts store. Although she is currently unemployed, in recent years Carol worked at Hopson's Crafts, a locally-owned craft store, on a part-time basis. This allowed her to familiarize herself with local crafters, and to gain first-hand knowledge of the best arts and craft shows in the region.

Casey Felson lives at home while attending community college. She is currently pursuing an associate in arts degree, and plans to pursue a four-year degree in business administration at nearby Johnson University. Like her mother, Casey enjoys the arts and crafts scene. She has always been considered to be a creative person by her teachers and friends—a quality that will surely benefit Felson's Homemade Soaps.

Professional & Advisory Support

Felson's Homemade Soaps has established a business banking account with Wenton Community Bank, as well as a merchant account for accepting credit card payments. Janet Stevens, a local accountant, will provide accounting and tax advisory services. The owners have utilized an online legal document service to prepare the paperwork necessary for incorporating their business.

GROWTH STRATEGY

Year One: Focus exclusively on the sale of soap products (individual and combination items, including gift baskets) at local and regional craft shows, farmers markets, festivals, etc. Begin building a customer database to encourage repeat business/individual orders.

Year Two: Expand soap product line based on customer feedback. Implement a basic e-commerce strategy and begin accepting online orders.

Year Three: Begin marketing products through local and regional gift shops and specialty stores.

Year Four: Consider expanding product line to include other products, such as homemade lip balms, hand & foot creams, and lotions, and hiring a part-time employee to help with production.

PRODUCTS

Process & Ingredients

Felson's Homemade Soaps produces its products using a number of techniques. These include both "melt & pour" and cold process methods. While some of the recipes will be familiar, "tried and true" formulations, others will be somewhat unique. We will make our soap using natural ingredients whenever possible. Finally, products will be carefully packaged with unique/attractive wrappings, either for individual sale or as part of a gift basket/collection.

Product Categories

Specialty/Special-Purpose Soaps:

Acne Soap

Flea Repelling Dog Soap

Insecticidal Soap

Lemon Olive Complexion Bar

Shaving Soap

Signature Soaps

Aloe Vera Soap

Bubble Gum Soap (for children)

Citrus Honey Soap

Coffee Soap Recipe

Cucumber Soap

Glycerin Soap Recipe

Honey Soap Recipe

Lavender Soap Recipe

Milk And Honey Bars

Moisturizing Liquid Soap with Jojoba

Nutmeg Butter Soap

Olive Oil (Castile) Soap Recipe

Peppermint Wake Up

Shea Butter Soap

Shea Butter Soap Recipe

Sweet Honey Almond Soap

MARKETING & SALES

A logo for Felson's Homemade Soaps has been developed by Carol Felson's son, Brad, who works as a graphic designer. Brad also has agreed to provide graphic design services for other items listed below. Felson's Homemade Soaps' marketing plan includes the following primary tactics:

1. An attractive sales sheet that can be distributed at craft shows and other venues.

2. During your three, sales calls to prospective retailers will be made to gauge their interest in consignment arrangements.

3. During year two, a Web site with complete details about our business and the services we offer will be established. The site will have basic e-commerce functionality, enabling customers to place online orders.

4. A customer loyalty program that provides a 10 percent discount to those referring a friend or family member to our business.

5. Magnetic signage that can be affixed to our vehicle in order to promote the business.

6. Magnetic business cards that will double as advertising specialties.

7. Active membership in the local Chamber of Commerce.

8. Trade show marketing at the following: Craft Shows, Farmers Markets, and Specialty Shows

OPERATIONS

Location

The Felsons have a large workspace in their basement (a multi-purpose room equipped with a stove, sink, counter tops, and storage cabinets) that can be used for business purposes.

Equipment & Supplies

Following is a list of basic tools and equipment that will be used by Felson's Homemade Soaps:

- Pans
- Spoons
- Molds

In addition to the items listed above, Felson's Homemade Soaps will require an adequate supply of the following materials for soap production:

- Olive Oil
- Palm Oil
- Coconut Oil
- Essential Oils
- Seed Extracts
- Nut Butters
- Jojoba
- Distilled Water
- Sodium Hydroxide
- Lard
- Lye
- Colorants
- Paper (for wrapping)

Hours of Operation

The Felsons will establish a dedicated Internet-based telephone line and e-mail account for their business. When customers or suppliers contact them, Carol will be notified through her smartphone. Inquiries will be returned within one business day. The owners will produce, package, and label soap at times that are mutually convenient.

Pricing

A detailed price list (available upon request) has been developed for the initial products that will be sold by Felson's Homemade Soaps. Although prices vary from item to item, bars of soap typically will retail for $3 per unit, or wholesaled for $2 per unit.

Insurance

Felson's Homemade Soaps has secured appropriate business and liability insurance coverage through Fortress Insurance. This will provide additional coverage for operations, and also any unforeseen issues that arise in connection with the soaps we make.

FINANCIAL ANALYSIS

Carol and Casey Felson have worked with accountant Janet Stevens to develop financial projections for Felson's Homemade Soaps. These projections (available upon request) group products according to two categories (Cold Process Soap and Melt & Pour Soap), and consider factors such as materials, equipment (amortized), preparation time, production time, labor costs, and wrapping. Although actual costs per bar will vary depending based upon the actual recipe, for calculation purposes the Felsons estimate a net profit of $2.00 per bar.

Finalcial projections

Farmers market (100 bars per week × 42 weeks):	$ 8,400
Special events (200 bars per event × 13 events):	$ 5,200
Repeat customer sales (750 bars):	$ 1,500
Total estimated net profit (year one):	**$15,100**

As repeat customer sales increase during year two and the business expands its product line and begins accepting online orders, we anticipate that net profits will increase approximately 25 percent. During year three, the expansion of sales through local and regional gift shops and specialty stores also should have a positive impact on net profits. However, specific projections have not yet been made.

Evaluation & Adjustment

This plan will be evaluated on a semi-annual basis with accountant Janet Stevens during our first and second years of operation, and annually thereafter.

Specialty Bakery

Kate's Cupcakery

999 Main St.
Rocheport, Missouri 65279

Kari Lucke

Kate's Cupcakery strives to offer delicious, beautiful cupcakes to customers looking for a unique way to celebrate special occasions as well as for those looking for an exceptional but affordable culinary indulgence while in downtown Rocheport, Missouri.

1.0. INTRODUCTION

1.1. Mission Statement

Kate's Cupcakery strives to offer delicious, beautiful cupcakes to customers looking for a unique way to celebrate special occasions as well as for those looking for an exceptional but affordable culinary indulgence while in downtown Rocheport, Missouri.

1.2. Executive Summary

Kate's Cupcakery specializes in homemade cupcakes in a wide variety of flavors and designs for special orders as well as for walk-in customers.

1.3. Business Philosophy

Kate's "treat yourself" attitude focuses on affordable indulgence. Typical customers include women looking for a place to share a treat and visit with friends, tourists who stop by for a snack or dessert as part of their Rocheport visit, and hikers and bikers off the Katy Trail who stop for refreshment and rest. Visiting Rocheport is an experience, and Kate's strives to be one of the highlights of that experience by offering a unique environment, friendly and conversational service, and awe-inspiring bakery creations.

1.4. Goals and Objectives

- Break even by the third year of business

- Maintain a high level of product quality and service

- Become known throughout the area as the best cupcake bakery in the mid-Missouri region

1.5. Organization Structure

Katherine (Kate) Patrick is the sole owner and operator of Kate's Cupcakery.

2.0. INDUSTRY AND MARKET

2.1. Industry Analysis

The cupcake bakery industry has taken off in the last few years, as evidenced by the number of shops that have cropped up across the country, from Washington, D.C., and New York City to Los Angeles, California. Mintel Research predicts cupcake sales will increase 20 percent nationwide between 2010 and 2015, as compared to other baked goods, which are expected to show growth rates in the single digits. Other evidence of the growing popularity of the cupcake includes the premiere of the new television show on the Food Network called "The Cupcake Wars," in which four bakers compete to make the most original and tasty mini-cake; the sales numbers for Martha Stewart's new cookbook released in June 2009, *Martha Stewart's Cupcakes*, which spent 11 weeks on the *New York Times* bestseller list; and the creation of several Internet web sites and blogs about cupcakes, including Cupcakes Take the Cake.com and Cupcake-Business.com. In March 2010 Cupcake-Business.com claimed that cupcakes represented a $6 billion industry, with some stores, such as the four branches of Magnolia Bakery in New York, making an average of 5,000 cupcakes a day.

2.2 Market Analysis

Kate's markets to several different categories of customers: (a) brides-to-be (for the wedding market), (b) women ages 21 to 40, including mothers of young children and single women (for the shower/party and special occasion market), (c) tourists and visitors (for the seasonal vacation/day trip market), and (d) Katy Trail users.

2.3. Competition

Kate's Cupcakery is the only cupcake-only bakery in the area. The most direct walk-in competition comes from the other bakery in town, which sells pastries and cookies but not cupcakes, and competitors for special orders include specialty bakers located in Columbia. Two that target the same market as Kate's include Columbia Cakes and Café and Joanne's Bakery.

Columbia Cakes and Cafe makes special-order cupcakes as well as pastries, cookies, and other baked goods. In addition, the establishment serves from a limited breakfast and lunch menu. It is located in downtown Columbia.

Joanne's Bakery offers a variety of baked items by special order as well as over the counter, including cupcakes, cookies, bagels, pastries, and cakes. Joanne's also makes wedding cakes and other special-occasion items. Owner Joanne Blazer has a small on-location shop in the Columbia Mall and does all of the baking off-site.

3.0. PERSONNEL

3.1. Management

Kate's is owned and operated by Katherine (Kate) Patrick. Kate has a bachelor's degree in business from the University of Missouri and thus the skills and knowledge needed to run a small business. She also has experience as a baker, having worked as the head baker for the Downtown Bakery in Green City, Colorado, for five years. Kate has been offering special-order cupcakes for friends, family, and acquaintances out of her home for the past three years and has done several weddings, parties, and showers. The move to the storefront location in Rocheport is a natural expansion of the growing business Kate began in 2007.

3.2. Staffing

Although the store is staffed by Kate herself during the week, extra help for the weekends during the busy months (May through October) is hired in the form of one part-time employee. This person serves walk-in customers, works the cash register, restocks the display case, and performs other duties as needed. Pay is above minimum wage at $8 an hour, and no benefits are provided.

4.0. STRATEGIES

4.1. Business Strategy

For walk-in business, Kate's draws visitors to Rocheport, who are exploring the town's several antique shops and historic sites, and hikers and bikers who use the Katy Trail trailhead as a departure or stopping point. In addition, Kate's is perfect for couples and families who are looking for a place for dessert after dining at the two very popular restaurants in town, Les Bourgeois Winery and Bistro and Abigail's. These two places draw people from Columbia and Booneville as chic alternatives to restaurants in the larger cities. For these customers, Kate's offers a quiet and intimate atmosphere in which to relax with a trendy and affordable treat.

For special order business, such as weddings and bridal showers, Kate's offers unlimited possibilities in terms of design, order size, colors, and so on. For the cupcakes for these special occasions, the presentation is at least as important as the flavor and texture, and Kate's cupcakes are truly "almost too cute to eat."

4.2 Growth Strategy

In the future, Kate's will expand to include a limited lunch menu consisting of soups, sandwiches, and salads. The current physical space and kitchen are adequate to accommodate these additions to the menu; the only increase in investment would include ingredients, cooking supplies, and some additional cutlery and dishes.

5.0. PRODUCTS AND SERVICES

5.1. Description

Kate's Cupcakes offers one product—cupcakes—in a variety of flavors, sizes, and colors/designs. A selection of drinks including bottled water, soda, and juice are available for purchase from a glass-door beverage refrigerator in the store, and both regular and decaffeinated coffee are available. Customers can select the fresh-baked cupcake of their choice from the display case at the front of the store. Kate continually rotates the selection so that there is always a new and interesting choice for regular customers. Basic cupcake flavors such as white and chocolate are always available in both regular size and mini size. Special flavors include seasonal selections (e.g., pumpkin-flavored in the fall) and a wide variety of both traditional and unique selections, from the popular red velvet to the trendy peanut butter chocolate chip. Kate's also promotes a "Cupcake of the Day" flavor. Customers are welcome to eat at one of the several small tables in the store or on the front walk or take their cakes to go.

Kate's also offers special-order cupcakes for any occasion, including weddings, bridal and baby showers, and children's birthday parties. Although Kate offers a printed brochure giving the basic information such as prices, the emphasis is on flexibility and the ability to create anything the customer wants, from a large, elaborate cupcake tower for a wedding, to individually boxed cupcakes for a party, to a tray-full of artfully decorated mini cupcakes for a shower. Kate offers a free one-hour consultation with prospective special-order clients and a contract for any booked event.

5.2. Pricing

The price for a regular-sized cupcake purchased by a walk-in customer is $3.00. Mini-cupcakes are $1.50. For orders over 25 units, the per-cupcake price is reduced 25 cents, and for orders over 50, the price is reduced by 50 cents.

Other prices incurred by the customer may include delivery charge and set-up for special events, which can vary depending on location, or additional fees for special-order flavors that require ingredients not usually stocked.

6.0. MARKETING AND SALES

6.1. Advertising and Promotion

The most important form of advertising for this business is word-of-mouth. As customers visit Kate's or use her services, they pass along the word to their friends, family, and coworkers. In addition, Kate maintains a web site for the business and runs a monthly ad in *Inside Columbia* magazine, a publication that targets the middle to upper class in Columbia and surrounding areas and has a circulation of about 20,000. Kate also uses brochures that promote the bakery's location, focus, and offerings. These are professionally designed and printed using high-quality color, resolution, and paper and placed in businesses around town in Rocheport, Columbia, and Booneville.

6.2. Cost

The cost for the brochure is about 50 cents apiece, with an average run of 200 copies per year, for a total annual cost of $100. The ad in *Inside Columbia* is the highest priced form of advertising used by the business but also one of the most visible to the target market. The cost of the ad runs about $100 a month, for a total of $1,200 a year. Word-of-mouth and the web site are free forms of advertising.

7.0. OPERATIONS

7.1. Customers

The most important walk-in customers for Kate's Cupcakery are visitors to the Rocheport area. Named "One of America's 10 Coolest Small Towns" by Frommer's *Budget Travel* magazine, the town draws people from around the state of Missouri as well as throughout the country.

The other significant customer base for the bakery includes young adult middle- to upper-class residents of surrounding areas, including the cities of Booneville (population: 10,000) and Columbia (population: 94,000). In Booneville, 42 percent of the population is female, and the average resident age is 30 years. Columbia's population is 52 percent female, with an average age of about 26. The median household income in Columbia is $40,326 and in Booneville, $40,397. Women looking for a unique way to celebrate occasions such as weddings, bridal showers, and parties are target customers for the special-order portion of the business, which accounts for the majority of sales.

7.2 Suppliers

The main supplies needed are ingredients for the cupcakes, including flour, sugar, eggs, and so on. These are purchased in bulk from a local wholesaler to save on costs. Other necessary materials such as cupcake liners, cupcake stands, cake-decorating supplies, and embellishments are purchased online from Koyal Wholesale and Wilton, a long-time leader in the cake-decorating business.

7.3. Equipment

Necessary equipment for the bakery includes two industrial baking ovens, mixers, a worktable, bakeware, and related supplies. These items will be purchased used if possible, in order to save on costs.

7.4. Hours

Because a majority of Kate's walk-in business occurs on weekends, the store is open from 10 a.m. to 10 p.m. on Friday and Saturday, 10 a.m. to 5 p.m. on Sundays, and 11 a.m. to 7 p.m. on weekdays. The store is closed on Monday, like many of the other retail businesses in town.

7.5. Facility and Location

Kate's Cupcakery is located on Main Street in downtown Rocheport, Missouri. Rocheport is a small, historical town located along the Missouri River. The town is a popular destination for visitors from the nearby cities of Booneville and Columbia, as well as other towns around the state and even the country, who come to browse antique shops, visit the historic sites or the popular Les Bourgeois Winery, stay in one of the bed and breakfasts, or use the infamous Katy Trail, a state-park-designated walking and biking trail that follows the path of the former Missouri-Kansas-Texas (MKT) Railroad across the state of Missouri.

The store itself is in a restored historic building that was previously used as a café. Therefore, the store has a kitchen in the back, a dining area in the front, and a small customer restroom to one side of the dining area; thus the layout of the store will not need significant renovation. The kitchen will need some modifications in terms of equipment and layout and will be partially renovated to be accommodate the needs of a bakery as well as to meet safety codes, health regulations, and so on. The customer restroom will also receive some renovation to make it more appealing (e.g., new toilet and sink, towel rack, paint, etc.). The interior of the seating area will be maintained as much as possible in its original condition, and the features such as exposed brick walls, tin ceiling, and wood floors add to the historic atmosphere. The end result will be an eclectic and relaxed dining atmosphere supplied by a modern and efficient kitchen. Seating will also be available on the sidewalk outside of the store during temperate weather.

8.0. FINANCIAL ANALYSIS

Kate's will save on start-up costs while preserving the quality and character of the bakery by: buying good-quality used equipment when possible; using an eclectic variety of used coffee mugs from garage sales, donations, etc.; and using disposable serving utensils (e.g., plastic forks and spoons). Because the bakery is housed in a historic building, the materials used to furnish the customer area of the store do not have to be new, and in fact are more appropriately old, to match the historic surroundings. All items will, however, be tasteful and in good condition.

Start-up costs

Equipment (ovens, mixers, etc.)	$ 5,000
Kitchen and customer bathroom remodel	$ 5,000
Tables and chairs	$ 1,000
Counter and cash register	$ 1,000
Work table	$ 500
Display case	$ 500
Beverage refrigerator	$ 500
Petty cash	$ 500
Paper goods (bags, napkins, plastic utensils, etc.)	$ 300
Coffee pots, mugs	$ 300
Business license and fees	$ 200
Bakeware and other kitchen supplies	$ 200
Advertising	$ 200
Beverage stock	$ 100
Ingredients (flour, sugar, butter, etc.)	$ 100
Sign for storefront	$ 100
Menu board	$ 100
Insurance	$ 100
Total	**$15,700**

Start-up expenses will be funded by a three-year small business loan.

Ongoing expenses (per year)

Rent	$12,000
Loan payment	$ 6,000
Part-time help	$ 3,000
Utilities	$ 2,400
Baking and other supplies	$ 1,200
Insurance	$ 1,200
Advertising	$ 1,200
Total	**$27,000**

First-year projected sales are estimated low and could very well be more than stated here. High-traffic months are estimated at an average of 100 cupcakes per week at $3 each, and low traffic months are estimated at half that. Special orders are estimated at an average of two events per month at an average sale of $500 each.

Projected sales, year 1

Walk-in sales, high traffic months (May–October)	$ 7,000
Walk-in sales, low traffic months (November–April)	$ 3,500
Special orders	$12,000
Total	**$22,500**

Sales for the second and third year of business are conservatively projected to grow 10 percent per year, resulting in the following figures:

Projected sales	Year 2	Year 3
Total	$24,750	$27,225

Thus, by Year 3, Kate's should break even. Thereafter, the business will grow with the addition of a lunch menu and other enhancements, as well as an increase in business due to earning a reputation as the best cupcake bakery in the area and the increased popularity of cupcakes.

Transcription Business

Speedy Transcription Services LLC

1870 Willow Tree Dr.
Boulder, CO 80308

Paul Greenland

Speedy Transcription Services provides transcription assistance to businesses and individual professionals on an independent contract basis.

EXECUTIVE SUMMARY

Business Overview

Speedy Transcription Services provides transcription assistance to businesses and individual professionals on an independent contract basis. Services typically are billed by the line. Our business will concentrate on legal and medical transcription, but we will provide general transcription services as well. Although the Internet and adoption of digital voice files enables us to serve customers anywhere in the world, our business initially will market its offerings to independent law and medical offices in the Boulder area.

By 2010 many large hospitals and physician practices had outsourced medical transcription services to large transcription companies. This phenomenon resulted in layoffs for in-house transcriptionists with considerable experience. Speedy Transcription Services is a limited liability company owned by Jane Smith, who formerly worked as a transcriptionist for Boulder General Hospital, and Sharon Nelson, a legal transcriptionist who lost her job when her employer merged with another law firm.

MARKET ANALYSIS

Although the Internet and adoption of digital voice files enables Speedy Transcription Services to serve customers anywhere in the world, the business will initially market its offerings to establishments in the Boulder area. Specifically, Speedy Transcription Services will focus its new client acquisition efforts on businesses in three main categories:

- Health & Medical Services (892 establishments)
- Legal Services (404 establishments)
- Social Services (187 establishments)

As the above data obtained from DemographicsNow (SRC LLC) illustrates, the universe of prospective clients in our local market is quite large. Considering that the very largest or corporately-owned establishments (especially in the Health & Medical Services and Legal Services categories) have likely outsourced their transcription needs to larger service providers, we will strategically concentrate our efforts on smaller and mid-sized medical services providers (e.g., independent physician offices; medical and diagnostic laboratories; physical, occupational, and speech therapy clinics; and audiology offices), law offices, and smaller human services agencies. In addition to the categories listed above, Speedy Transcription also will provide general transcription services to businesses in a variety of industries.

Speedy Transcription Services' owners have prepared a detailed listing of key prospects that is available upon request. We will utilize this in our marketing efforts, which are outlined in this plan.

INDUSTRY

There are different specializations within the transcription field. For example, some practitioners concentrate in specific areas, such as medical, legal, or administrative transcription. According to data from the U.S. Bureau of Labor Statistics' *Occupational Outlook Handbook, 2010-11 Edition,* the field of medical transcription alone employed approximately 105,200 workers in 2008. The majority of these employees (36%) were employed by hospitals, while physician offices were the second-largest employer group (23%).

The owners of Speedy Transcription Services have experienced the effects of outsourcing within the transcription industry first-hand. In recent years, countries such as Canada, Barbados, Pakistan, India, and the Philippines, have begun providing transcription services to U.S. companies. However, the Bureau of Labor Statistics indicates that outsourcing, as well as technological developments, have not impacted the industry to the degree that some may suspect. For example, in the *Occupational Outlook Handbook,* the bureau explains: "Contracting out transcription work overseas and advancements in speech recognition technology are not expected to significantly reduce the need for well-trained medical transcriptionists."

Several different associations exist within the transcription industry. These include the Medical Transcription Industry Association (MTIA), the American Association of Electronic Reporters and Transcribers (AAERT), the Association for Healthcare Documentation Integrity (ADHD), and others. Like most professional organizations, these associations offer their members variety of educational options, networking opportunities, and certifications.

PERSONNEL

Jane Smith, CMT

Jane Smith, CMT, formerly worked as a transcriptionist for Boulder General Hospital. She began her career as a medical transcriptionist in 1998, working for Donald Hiser Surgery Group, a cardiothoracic surgery practice in Denver, Colorado. After holding that position for five years, she worked for Brandenburg Transcription Company until 2007, when she joined Boulder General. In addition to performing actual transcription work, Jane worked in a supervisory capacity, overseeing a staff of nine transcriptionists. In that role, she gained valuable business skills and also served in a mentoring capacity. Jane has earned Certified Medical Transcriptionist certification from the Association for Healthcare Documentation Integrity.

Sharon Nelson

Sharon Nelson began her career as a legal secretary with Hewitt & Jones, a small law firm in Alabama, in 1993. After relocating to Boulder in 1997 she joined Powers, Richfield & Schlichting, a law firm with 26 offices in 17 states. Although she performed other secretarial duties, Sharon developed a reputation as an accurate and proficient transcriptionist. During the last seven years of her career she performed transcription for a group of three real estate attorneys, as well as an environmental attorney. She lost her job in 2010 as part of a restructuring that took place when Powers, Richfield & Schlichting was acquired by a larger law firm.

Résumés for Jane and Sharon are available upon request.

Speedy Transcription Services has established a business banking account with Main Street Credit Union, as well as a merchant account for accepting credit card payments. Holly Weston, a local accountant, will provide accounting and tax advisory services. The owners have utilized LegalZoom. com, an online legal document service, to prepare the paperwork necessary for establishing their limited liability company. In the event that actual legal counsel is required, they will call upon Sherrie McCaskey, an attorney at the Boulder-based firm Johnson & Phelps.

GROWTH STRATEGY

Speedy Transcription Services will begin operation as a part-time business for Jane Smith and Sharon Nelson. Each transcriptionist hopes to devote approximately 20 hours per week to transcription work during the first year, 25 hours during the second year, and 30 hours during the third year. This strategy will enable the owners to devote more time to non-transcription-related activities (e.g., marketing) during the company's formative years. At this point, there are no plans to add additional transcriptionists to the business, although that may change in the future depending on demand. The owners will evaluate their growth strategy on an annual basis and make adjustments as necessary.

SERVICES

Speedy Transcription Services will accept audio recordings for transcription in both analog (e.g. microcassette) and digital (e.g., MP3 and WAV files) formats.

Essentially, our services will fall into one of three main categories:

General & Business Transcription
- Analyst Interviews
- Annual Meetings
- Business Meetings
- Company Reports
- Corporate Conferences
- Corporate Presentations
- Corporate Seminars
- Earnings Calls
- Financial Reports
- Focus Groups
- Interviews
- Press Conferences
- Sales Reports
- Surveys

Medical Transcription

- Advisory Board Meetings
- Grand Rounds
- Lectures
- Panel Discussions
- Pathology Reports
- Physician Dictation
- Roundtable Discussions
- Symposiums

We will perform dictation for a wide range of medical specialties and sub-specialties, including:

- Cardiology
- Family Medicine
- Internal Medicine
- OB/GYN
- Oncology
- Ophthalmology
- Orthopedics
- Otolaryngology
- Pathology
- Pediatrics
- Podiatry
- Surgery

Legal Transcription

- Administrative Hearings
- Arbitrations
- Briefs
- Court Proceedings
- Court Transcripts
- Depositions
- Examinations under Oath
- General Correspondence
- Interviews
- Jury Instruction
- Legal Examinations
- Letters
- Mediation Briefs

- Meeting Minutes
- Memoranda
- Motions
- Pleadings
- Police Interrogations
- Preliminary Hearings
- Proceedings at Meetings/Conferences
- Reports
- Subpoenas
- Summons Notes
- Sworn Statements
- Telephone Conversations
- Testimonies
- Wire Tapes

MARKETING & SALES

Speedy Transcription Services will concentrate its initial marketing efforts on prospective customers who are deemed to be "quick wins." During both of their careers, the owners have developed connections with others in their respective fields (e.g., staff members at area physician offices and law firms). Jane and Sharon will initially reach out to these individuals (a total of 25 area prospects).

After making an initial contact, Jane and Sharon will attempt to set up appointments with practice owners and/or managers of these mostly smaller and mid-sized organizations. They will make a brief presentation about Speedy Transcription Services' capabilities, leave behind literature about the business and, as an incentive, offer a one-time 10 percent discount off a prospective customer's first transcription order.

Speedy Transcription Services will rely upon the following tactics to grow the business:

- Printed collateral describing the business.
- A small Yellow Page listing.
- Relationship building with key prospects in order to build a consistent referral base.
- A Web site with complete details about the business and the services we offer.
- Direct mail campaigns to area healthcare providers, law firms, and social service agencies.

OPERATIONS

Location

Speedy Transcription Services will be a "virtual" business; the owners will each work from home offices. This model has become commonplace, especially in the medical transcription arena. For example, many hospitals now allow their staff transcriptionists to work from home.

Equipment

The owners of Speedy Transcription Services will each need to invest in equipment that is required for performing transcription services in their home offices.

Fortunately, both Sharon and Jane already have desks and personal computers that can be used for business purposes. However, they will need to buy equipment for transcribing microcassette and digital voice files. Specifically, they have decided to purchase the following:

- Sony M2000 Microcassette Transcriber, $250

- WAV Pedal 7 Transcription Kit, $219

These devices each come with headsets and foot controls. In addition, the WAVpedal 7 includes software for transcribing digital files in a variety of formats including WAV, MP3, Sony DVF, Olympus DSS, BCB/PC Dart, DVI Voice Power, Voice-It SRI, and Voxware.

In addition to the transcription equipment listed above, the owners will each need to install dedicated telephone lines for business use and purchase $300 worth of incidental items.

Payment & Fees

Although Speedy Transcription Services' fees are somewhat negotiable, we typically will charge $.17 per line (65 characters). In our view, this will be appealing to customers because they will only pay for the information transcribed, regardless of the actual transcription time involved. If clients prefer to be charged by the minute or by the hour, we will be happy to accommodate them. Rates will vary depending on audio quality. We will accept payments via check, credit card, and PayPal (for Internet transcription orders).

Insurance

Speedy Transcription Services has secured a business liability policy from Stronghold Insurance, as well as specific coverage related to errors and omissions. In addition, the owners will each carry a home office rider to their homeowner's insurance policies.

FINANCIAL ANALYSIS

Following is Speedy Transcription Services projected balance sheet for 2011. Detailed monthly cash flow statements are available upon request. The owners expect that their net income will increase steadily in years two and three as they increase their respective work hours, benefit from new client relationships, and reduce the heavier marketing expenses required during the first year. Although services typically will be billed by the line, for estimation purposes the owners have used an hourly rate of $37 per hour to calculate first-year revenue.

	2011
Revenue	**$74,000**
Expenses	
Advertising & marketing	$ 4,000
Miscellaneous items	$ 600
Legal	$ 1,400
Accounting	$ 800
Office supplies	$ 500
Equipment	$ 770
Business insurance	$ 750
Salaries	$50,000
Postage	$ 300
Telecommunications	$ 1,500
Broadband internet	$ 1,200
Total expenses	**$61,820**
Net income	**$12,180**

Used Records & Collectibles Business

Rudy's Record Shop

46 Market St.
Minneapolis, MN 55402

Paul Greenland

Rudy's Record Shop is an Internet-based used records and collectibles business.

EXECUTIVE SUMMARY

Business Overview

Rudy's Record Shop is an Internet-based used records and collectibles business. The owner, Rudy Paulson, operates the business from two unused bedrooms in his Minneapolis home. He has installed the appropriate climate controls in order to maintain appropriate temperature/humidity levels, so that collectible items do not get damaged. In addition, Rudy has installed a security system and has purchased insurance to cover the maximum value of his collectible inventory.

Being an Internet-based business, the world is Rudy's market. However, he has plans to eventually open an actual brick-and-mortar location to serve music enthusiasts in the Minneapolis area. In this plan, he has outlined a conservative growth strategy to meet this goal.

MARKET ANALYSIS

The market for used records and related collectibles is relatively strong, even in difficult economic times. Recently, Rudy spoke with one record dealer on the West Coast whose record store has annual sales of approximately $500,000, some 20 percent of which is generated online. However, this dealer does not rely on vinyl alone; CDs represent approximately 50 percent of sales, and 20 percent of those CDs are new releases.

Rudy will focus concentrate on two principal markets: collectors and teenagers/young adults.

Collectors

Collectors of all ages will be a prime market for Rudy's Record Shop. In addition to long-time collectors seeking rare/expensive albums, the business will appeal to individuals who are new to record collecting. Such individuals are drawn to the hobby because it is both fun and (in many cases) inexpensive, making steady, regular purchases possible. For example, Rudy recently met a paramedic from Florida who, along with his wife, had "caught the fever." A former baseball card collector, this man regularly visits garage sales and flea markets in search of vinyl bargains. A great many used records can be purchased for less than $2. Although their monetary value is limited, collectors are drawn to warmer sound that record albums offer, interesting album art/jacket design, and a chance to own a piece of history.

Teenagers & Young Adults

Teenagers and young adults were driving the popularity of vinyl during the early 2010s. Although some analysts indicated that 16-to-25-year-olds were a key target market, in some communities children as young as 13 were receiving turntables as gifts and making regular trips to local independent record stores. What's the reason for this phenomenon? In the June 17, 2010, issue of *The Florida Times Union*, one independent record store owner said: "To me, I think a lot of kids don't remember their parents had records. They only remember them having CDs, so they don't want CDs. It's like your etching out your own identity, like wearing a leather jacket and a mohawk when I was in high school. When everyone's walking around with their MP3s, you've got a stack of Ramones and Blondie records."

INDUSTRY ANALYSIS

As digital music has grown in popularity, the number of record stores has plummeted sharply. In fact, according to data from Nielsen Sound Scan, from 2005 through the end of the decade, some 2,680 record stores closed their doors (largely due to lackluster CD sales).

However, vinyl is making a comeback. Beyond collectors interested in record albums from decades past, a growing number of artists are releasing new music on vinyl. For example, Nielsen SoundScan now reports the top vinyl albums, as well as the leading vinyl artists. In its April 16, 2010, issue, the *New York Daily News* cited data from Nielsen SoundScan which revealed that sales of vinyl records increased 89 percent in 2009, and during the early part of 2010 reached their highest level in approximately 20 years.

Evidence of vinyl's popularity is evident by the recent formation of an annual event called Record Store Day. Additionally, in 2010 Gary Calamar and Phil Gallo released their reference book, *Record Store Days: from Vinyl to Digital and Back Again*. In its April 15, 2010, issue, *Library Journal* called the book "An Essential book that both educates and entertains. For music industry history buffs, nostalgic baby boomers, and younger DJs and music nerds." In addition, the industry also has its own publication, *Record Collector*, which is based in Burbank, California, as well as *Goldmine Magazine*.

PERSONNEL

Rudy Paulson has loved music in general, and record albums in particular, as long as he can remember. Early inspiration came from his brother, Joey, who was a DJ at a college radio station in the Twin Cities and later became the entertainment editor of a newspaper in the Chicago area. Thanks to Joey, Rudy amassed a sizable record collection during his high school years. In time, he began buying, selling, and trading records with others. He developed a reputation for his "encyclopedic" knowledge of recording artists in a wide range of genres, from alternative and classic rock to blues and jazz.

Rudy will be the sole employee of Rudy's Record Shop. However, he has secured the services of several professionals to guide him during the formative years of his business. Twin City Accounting will provide tax advisory services. In Addition, Rudy has established a business checking account with Robbins Field Community Bank, as well as a merchant account for accepting credit card purchases.

GROWTH STRATEGY

Rudy's Record Shop will begin as an online enterprise. Based on his past experience selling records online, as well as his knowledge of the industry and conversations with other independent record dealers, Rudy realizes that the Internet will likely generate the majority of his sales. Nevertheless, he hopes to eventually open an actual brick-and-mortar location. To achieve this goal, the owner will reinvest as much of the profits into the business as possible.

Assuming that certain sales targets can be met during the first six months of his new online enterprise, Rudy will pursue conservative expansion plans. To keep costs low and minimize risk, he will first establish a physical retail presence by renting one bay at a popular area flea market (for a monthly cost of $250). If successful, he will consider expanding his presence at the flea market to two bays six months later. After six months of operating a two-bay flea market store, Rudy will attempt to purchase an actual brick-and-mortar location in the Twin Cities (preferably a building with a storefront on the first level and an apartment on the second level, which will help to cover some of his overhead). At that time Rudy will decide whether or not to retain his presence at the flea market.

SERVICES

Rudy's Record Shop will, of course, sell used records including:

- 45s
- EPs
- LPs

However, in order to boost sales, the business also will sell related music merchandise, such as:

- CDs
- Concert/Music Documentary DVDs
- Posters
- Books
- Used Turntables
- T-shirts
- Miscellaneous Memorabilia

MARKETING & SALES

Rudy's Record Shop will rely upon the following marketing tactics:

1. A Web site with e-commerce functionality. Rudy's Record Shop has found an affordable, "off-the-shelf" e-commerce package that will enable the business to list items for sale, along with a complete description of each item's condition, price, etc. Customers will be able to submit questions regarding individual items, purchase via credit card, choose shipping options and insurance.

2. Search engine optimization (SEO). We will continuously monitor and modify our Web site in order to ensure that content appears in results for leading search engines, including Google and Yahoo!

3. Online auction sites. Rudy's Record Shop will place a heavy emphasis on the sale of records and related merchandise via online auction sites, namely eBay.

4. Online video. One of the great things about independent record stores is a social/community element. For example, many music lovers simply enjoy congregating at the local record shop, where they can talk about bands and albums and "chew the fat" with the store owner/employees.

Although an online store cannot offer this experience in its entirety, Rudy's Record Shop will attempt to retain some of the magic by offering online video chats, where customers and music lovers can post questions and comments and have Rudy respond in real-time via online video. Rudy has "propped out" a mock store counter, with records and other merchandise in the background, to add an authentic feel to his video chats.

5. A presence in *Goldmine Magazine*, which includes listings for many used record dealers.

6. A promotional flyer that we will distribute locally, in locations where Twin Cities music lovers congregate (e.g., music clubs, bars, music stores, etc.).

7. Flea market promotions. When our business expands to include a presence at the local flea market, we will pay a marketing fee to be included in promotions offered by the flea market managers (e.g., advertising, circulars, etc.).

OPERATIONS

Generally speaking, Rudy's Record Shop will purchase items (records, CDs, and memorabilia) from the public at "dealer price" and resell them at or below "book price." Items will be purchased from consumers online and in person. A limited number of new items will be purchased at wholesale from several distributors (list available upon request). We will pay the highest percentage (approximately 50%) for items with a high book value. Likewise, a lower percentage will be paid for lower-value items.

Because it will principally be an online business, Rudy's Record Shop will be open 24/7. Rudy typically will answer correspondence from customers Monday through Friday, from 8 AM to 5 PM. However, he will check customer inquiries on the weekends, to identify any urgent issues and maintain excellent customer service. In addition to U.S. mail, arrangements will be made for weekday UPS and FedEx pickups and deliveries. In the case of valuable collectibles, including record albums, Rudy will recommend that all customers purchase the appropriate level of insurance coverage for their purchases.

FINANCIAL ANALYSIS

Rudy's Record Shop will begin operations with $12,250 in assets (the appraised value of used records, CDs, and other collectibles that the owner will make available for sale). Rudy acknowledges that the appraised value of the items within this collection may differ from what he is able to sell them for on the market.

In addition to the aforementioned assets, Rudy will invest $15,000 in cash into the business from his personal savings and investments. Rudy is seeking an additional $25,000 in funding (for operations and merchandise acquisition purposes), which he plans to repay over the course of three years.

Based on his first-hand knowledge of the market and personal experience buying, selling, and trading music-related items, Rudy estimates that his first-year sales will be broken down as follows:

- Used Records (45s, EPs, LPs): 35%

- Used CDs: 30%

- Collectibles/Merchandise: 20%

- New CDs: 15%

During the first year of operations, the owner estimates that Rudy's Record Shop will generate 80% of its sales online and 20% from the flea market. If the record shop grows according to the strategy outlined in this plan, during the second year 65% of sales will likely be made online and 35% will be generated from the flea market. Finally, during the third year Rudy anticipates that 40% of sales will be generated in the brick-and-mortar store, followed by 30% online, and 30% from the flea market.

Detailed sales projections and cash flow statements pertaining to the first three years of operations are available upon request.

SWOT ANALYSIS

Strengths: Rudy's Record Shop will begin with virtually no overhead, and initial inventory will consist of collectibles already in the owner's possession.

Weaknesses: This business will initially have no physical location, which may make it more challenging to develop relationships with repeat customers.

Opportunities: The exploding popularity of vinyl records among teenagers and young adults.

Threats: Record albums and collectibles are discretionary items; changes in the economy can impact demand.

Waste Management

Waste Removal Serivces, Inc.

799 112th St.
New York, NY 10002

BizPlanDB.com

Waste Removal Serivces was developed to provide an extremely comprehensive refuse removal and management service. The business will generate highly recurring streams of revenue from both businesses and residences that use the Waste Removal Serivces for their refuse removal needs.

1.0 EXECUTIVE SUMMARY

The purpose of this business plan is to raise $150,000 for the development of a waste management company while showcasing the expected financials and operations over the next three years. Waste Removal Serivces ("the Company") is a New York based corporation that will provide waste removal services to customers in its targeted market. The Company was founded by Steve Wassef.

1.1 The Services

Waste Removal Serivces was developed to provide an extremely comprehensive refuse removal and management service. The business will generate highly recurring streams of revenue from both businesses and residences that use the Waste Removal Serivces for their refuse removal needs.

At this time, Management is sourcing the two trucks that it will lease in order to provide services to its customer base.

The third section of the business plan will further describe the services offered by Waste Removal Serivces

1.2 Financing

Mr. Wassef is seeking to raise $150,000 from a bank loan. The interest rate and loan agreement are to be further discussed during negotiation. This business plan assumes that the business will receive a 10 year loan with a 9% fixed interest rate. The financing will be used for the following:

- Development of the Company's office location.

- Financing for the first six months of operation.

- Capital to finance deposits for leasing of two waste hauling trucks.

Mr. Wassef will contribute $25,000 to the venture.

1.3 Mission Statement

The mission of Waste Removal Serivces is to become the recognized leader in its targeted market for refuse removal services.

1.4 Management Team

The Company was founded by Steve Wassef. Mr. Wassef has more than 10 years of experience in the waste management industry. Through his expertise, he will be able to bring the operations of the business to profitability within its first year of operations.

1.5 Sales Forecasts

Mr. Wassef expects a strong rate of growth at the start of operations. Below are the expected financials over the next three years.

Proforma profit and loss (yearly)

Year	1	2	3
Sales	$973,590	$1,168,308	$1,366,920
Operating costs	$297,003	$ 310,535	$ 324,590
EBITDA	$ 79,734	$ 141,549	$ 204,349
Taxes, interest, and depreciation	$ 52,155	$ 70,101	$ 93,348
Net profit	**$ 27,579**	**$ 71,448**	**$ 111,001**

Sales, operating costs, and profit forecast

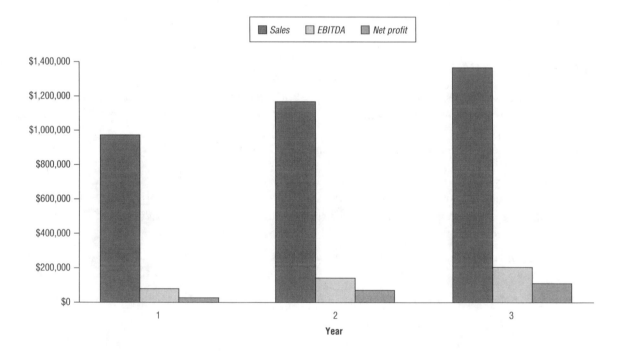

1.6 Expansion Plan

The Founder expects that the business will aggressively expand during the first three years of operation. Mr. Wassef intends to implement marketing campaigns that will effectively target individuals and businesses within the target market.

2.0 COMPANY AND FINANCING SUMMARY

2.1 Registered Name and Corporate Structure

Waste Removal Serivces is registered as a corporation in the State of New York.

2.2 Required Funds

At this time, Waste Removal Serivces requires $150,000 of debt funds. Below is a breakdown of how these funds will be used:

Projected startup costs

Initial lease payments and deposits	$ 15,000
Working capital	$ 35,000
FF&E	$ 25,000
Leasehold improvements	$ 7,500
Security deposits	$ 12,500
Insurance	$ 5,000
Vehicle deposits	$ 50,000
Marketing budget	$ 17,500
Miscellaneous and unforeseen costs	$ 7,500
Total startup costs	**$175,000**

Use of funds

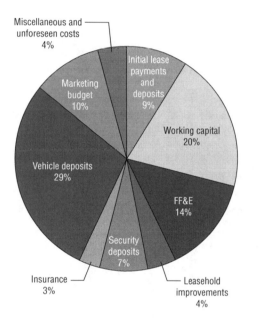

2.3 Investor Equity

Mr. Wassef is not seeking an investment from a third party at this time.

2.4 Management Equity

Steve Wassef owns 100% of Waste Removal Serivces.

2.5 Exit Strategy

If the business is very successful, Mr. Wassef may seek to sell the business to a third party for a significant earnings multiple. Most likely, the Company will hire a qualified business broker to sell the business on behalf of Waste Removal Serivces.

Based on historical numbers, the business could fetch a sales premium of up to 6 times earnings. However, with recent fuel costs rising, the premiums for waste management businesses have declined due to the volatility of the oil markets. It should be noted that Mr. Wassef intends to operate this business for a significant period of time, and a potential exit strategy would not be executed for at least five to seven years.

3.0 PRODUCTS AND SERVICES

Below is a description of the services offered by Waste Removal Serivces

3.1 Waste Management Services

The primary revenue center for the business will come from ongoing hauling of dumpsters, providing waste management services, and hazardous materials disposal. The business will generate substantial fees from housing communities and home owners associations that contract Waste Removal Serivces for their ongoing waste management needs.

The business will also generate significant secondary revenues from the ongoing hauling of large items such as couches, refrigerators, and other large items that require special handing and disposal needs.

4.0 STRATEGIC AND MARKET ANALYSIS

4.1 Economic Outlook

This section of the analysis will detail the economic climate, the waste management industry, the customer profile, and the competition that the business will face as it progresses through its business operations.

Currently, the economic market condition in the United States is in recession. Many economists expect that this recession will continue for a significant period of time (perhaps until 2012), at which point the economy will begin a prolonged recovery period.

A primary concern for the Company is its ability to price its services affordably during times of economic recession or spikes of oil prices. The price of oil and its associated refined energy products have reached multiyear highs. This increase in oil prices has caused the waste management industry's costs to rise significantly. While this is a concern for the business, it is a risk and an issue faced by all other businesses as well. Mr. Wassef will continue to increase prices (at a standardized rate of markup) to ensure the profitability of the business.

4.2 Industry Analysis

Within the United States, there are approximately 8,000 businesses that provide waste management, private recycling, and removal for non-hazardous recyclable waste from construction sites. These companies aggregately generate more than $26 billion dollars per year and provide jobs for more than 160,000 people. The industry is a mature, and the expected future growth rate is anticipated to equal that of the general growth of the US economy.

4.3 Customer Profile

Management anticipates that the following individuals and entities will be customers of Waste Removal Serivces:

- Individual Residences

- Home Owners Associations

- Housing Communities

- Municipal Agencies

- Commercial Enterprises

4.4 Competition

There are a number of waste management businesses that operate throughout towns, cities, and municipalities that provide for the removal of refuse. Within New York, there are approximately 50 independent service providers that work publicly on behalf of the city and state as well as privately for real estate management companies and property owners. It is imperative that the business immediately develop relationships with government organizations and property owners so that the business can begin revenue generating operations.

5.0 MARKETING PLAN

Waste Removal Serivces intends to maintain an extensive marketing campaign that will ensure maximum visibility for the business in its targeted market. Below is an overview of the marketing strategies and objectives of Waste Removal Serivces

5.1 Marketing Objectives

- Develop an online presence by creating a website and placing the Company's name and contact information with online directories.

- Establish relationships with municipal agencies within the targeted market.

- Implement a localized marketing campaign that targets individuals and homeowners associations.

5.2 Marketing Strategies

The Company intends to use a multitude of marketing strategies to promote and expand the waste management businesses operations. The Company will maintain its listing in the Yellow Pages, create marketing campaigns within local newspapers, and promote the business through word-of-mouth advertising. The business actively advertises its affordable contracting services.

Mr. Wassef intends to maintain a website that allows customers to contact Management directly over email for more information regarding the Company's waste management services and pricing quotes. As the Company expands, the business will upgrade the website to include higher levels of functionality and support.

Additionally, Management intends to continually develop a number of referral and contractual relationships within among municipal agencies, commercial enterprises, and housing communities. Since these businesses regularly require waste management services, Management sees a significant opportunity to partner with these firms.

5.3 Pricing

Management anticipates that each end-user customer that uses the Company's waste management services will generate $200 per year of revenue for the business.

6.0 ORGANIZATIONAL PLAN AND PERSONNEL SUMMARY

6.1 Corporate Organization

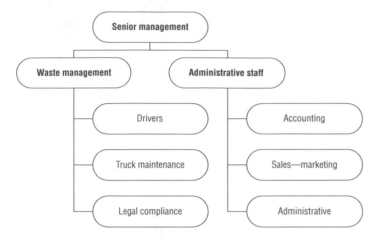

6.2 Organizational Budget

Personnel plan—yearly

Year	1	2	3
Owner	$ 40,000	$ 41,200	$ 42,436
Assistant manager	$ 29,000	$ 29,870	$ 30,766
Drivers	$ 93,000	$ 95,790	$ 98,664
Bookkeeper (P/T)	$ 9,000	$ 9,270	$ 9,548
Administrative (P/T)	$ 17,000	$ 17,510	$ 18,035
Total	**$188,000**	**$193,640**	**$199,449**

Numbers of personnel

Owner	1	1	1
Assistant manager	1	1	1
Drivers	3	3	3
Bookkeeper (P/T)	1	1	1
Administrative (P/T)	1	1	1
Totals	**7**	**7**	**7**

Personnel expense breakdown

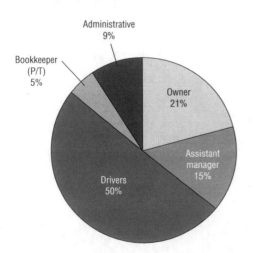

7.0 FINANCIAL PLAN

7.1 Underlying Assumptions

The Company has based its proforma financial statements on the following:

- Waste Removal Serivces will have an annual revenue growth rate of 6% per year.

- The Owner will acquire $150,000 of debt funds to develop the business.

- The loan will have a 10 year term with a 9% interest rate.

7.2 Sensitivity Analysis

The Company's revenues are sensitive to many external factors. Should the cost of oil increase significantly, Management fully expects that its bottom line income will decrease. However, the Company has priced its services so that increases in the price of oil will not severely impact the Company's ability to operate both profitably and cash flow positive. In the event of a dramatic increase in price, Management will seek to increase the price of its waste management services to reflect the higher transportation costs.

7.3 Source of Funds

Financing

Equity contributions	
Management investment	$ 25,000.00
Total equity financing	**$ 25,000.00**
Banks and lenders	
Banks and lenders	$ 150,000.00
Total debt financing	**$150,000.00**
Total financing	**$175,000.00**

7.4 General Assumptions

General assumptions

Year	1	2	3
Short term interest rate	9.5%	9.5%	9.5%
Long term interest rate	10.0%	10.0%	10.0%
Federal tax rate	33.0%	33.0%	33.0%
State tax rate	5.0%	5.0%	5.0%
Personnel taxes	15.0%	15.0%	15.0%

7.5 Profit and Loss Statements

Proforma profit and loss (yearly)

Year	1	2	3
Sales	**$973,590**	**$1,168,308**	**$1,366,920**
Cost of goods sold	$596,853	$ 716,224	$ 837,982
Gross margin	38.70%	38.70%	38.70%
Operating income	**$376,737**	**$ 452,084**	**$ 528,939**
Expenses			
Payroll	$188,000	$ 193,640	$ 199,449
General and administrative	$ 25,200	$ 26,208	$ 27,256
Marketing expenses	$ 4,868	$ 5,842	$ 6,835
Professional fees and licensure	$ 5,219	$ 5,376	$ 5,537
Insurance costs	$ 1,987	$ 2,086	$ 2,191
Truck maintenance costs	$ 17,596	$ 19,356	$ 21,291
Rent and utilities	$ 14,250	$ 14,963	$ 15,711
Miscellaneous costs	$ 11,683	$ 14,020	$ 16,403
Payroll taxes	$ 28,200	$ 29,046	$ 29,917
Total operating costs	**$297,003**	**$ 310,535**	**$ 324,590**
EBITDA	**$ 79,734**	**$ 141,549**	**$ 204,349**
Federal income tax	$ 26,312	$ 42,686	$ 63,738
State income tax	$ 3,987	$ 6,468	$ 9,657
Interest expense	$ 13,107	$ 12,197	$ 11,202
Depreciation expenses	$ 8,750	$ 8,750	$ 8,750
Net profit	**$ 27,579**	**$ 71,448**	**$ 111,001**
Profit margin	**2.83%**	**6.12%**	**8.12%**

Sales, operating costs, and profit forecast

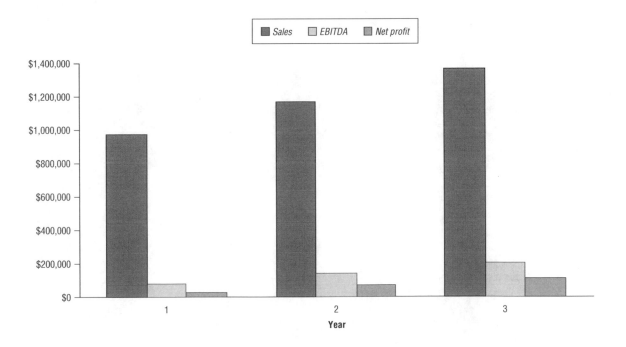

7.6 Cash Flow Analysis

Proforma cash flow analysis—yearly

Year	1	2	3
Cash from operations	$ 36,329	$ 80,198	$119,751
Cash from receivables	$ 0	$ 0	$ 0
Operating cash inflow	**$ 36,329**	**$ 80,198**	**$119,751**
Other cash inflows			
Equity investment	$ 25,000	$ 0	$ 0
Increased borrowings	$150,000	$ 0	$ 0
Sales of business assets	$ 0	$ 0	$ 0
A/P increases	$ 37,902	$ 43,587	$ 50,125
Total other cash inflows	**$212,902**	**$ 43,587**	**$ 50,125**
Total cash inflow	**$249,231**	**$123,786**	**$169,876**
Cash outflows			
Repayment of principal	$ 9,695	$ 10,605	$ 11,599
A/P decreases	$ 24,897	$ 29,876	$ 35,852
A/R increases	$ 0	$ 0	$ 0
Asset purchases	$122,500	$ 20,050	$ 29,938
Dividends	$ 25,430	$ 56,139	$ 83,826
Total cash outflows	**$182,522**	**$116,669**	**$161,214**
Net cash flow	**$ 66,708**	**$ 7,116**	**$ 8,662**
Cash balance	**$ 66,708**	**$ 73,825**	**$ 82,487**

Proforma cash flow (yearly)

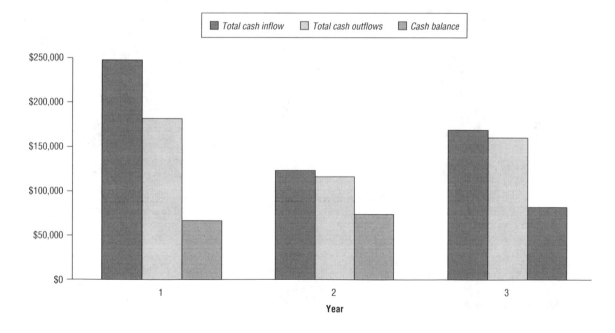

7.7 Balance Sheet

Proforma balance sheet—yearly

Year	1	2	3
Assets			
Cash	$ 66,708	$ 73,825	$ 82,487
Amortized expansion costs	$ 47,500	$ 49,505	$ 52,499
Vehicle deposits	$ 50,000	$ 65,037	$ 87,490
FF&E	$ 25,000	$ 28,007	$ 32,498
Accumulated depreciation	($ 8,750)	($ 17,500)	($ 26,250)
Total assets	**$180,458**	**$198,874**	**$228,724**
Liabilities and equity			
Accounts payable	$ 13,005	$ 26,716	$ 40,990
Long term liabilities	$140,305	$129,700	$119,096
Other liabilities	$ 0	$ 0	$ 0
Total liabilities	**$153,310**	**$156,416**	**$160,085**
Net worth	**$ 27,149**	**$ 42,458**	**$ 68,639**
Total liabilities and equity	**$180,458**	**$198,874**	**$228,724**

Proforma balance sheet

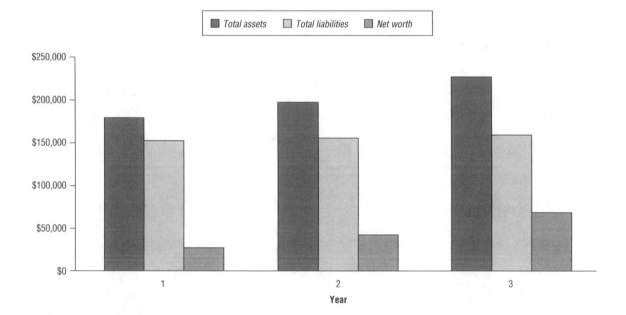

7.8 Breakeven Analysis

Monthly break even analysis

Year	1	2	3
Monthly revenue	$ 63,961	$ 66,876	$ 69,902
Yearly revenue	$767,536	$802,507	$838,828

Break even analysis

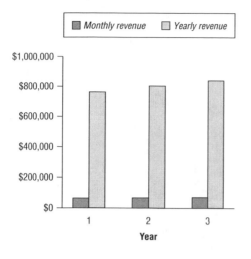

7.9 Business Ratios

Business ratios—yearly

Year	1	2	3
Sales			
Sales growth	0.0%	20.0%	17.0%
Gross margin	38.7%	38.7%	38.7%
Financials			
Profit margin	2.83%	6.12%	8.12%
Assets to liabilities	1.18	1.27	1.43
Equity to liabilities	0.18	0.27	0.43
Assets to equity	6.65	4.68	3.33
Liquidity			
Acid test	0.44	0.47	0.52
Cash to assets	0.37	0.37	0.36

7.10 Three Year Profit and Loss Statement

Profit and loss statement (first year)

Months	1	2	3	4	5	6	7
Sales	$80,500	$80,615	$80,730	$80,845	$80,960	$81,075	$81,190
Cost of goods sold	$49,350	$49,421	$49,491	$49,562	$49,632	$49,703	$49,773
Gross margin	38.7%	38.7%	38.7%	38.7%	38.7%	38.7%	38.7%
Operating income	$31,150	$31,195	$31,239	$31,284	$31,328	$31,373	$31,417
Expenses							
Payroll	$15,667	$15,667	$15,667	$15,667	$15,667	$15,667	$15,667
General and administrative	$ 2,100	$ 2,100	$ 2,100	$ 2,100	$ 2,100	$ 2,100	$ 2,100
Marketing expenses	$ 406	$ 406	$ 406	$ 406	$ 406	$ 406	$ 406
Professional fees and licensure	$ 435	$ 435	$ 435	$ 435	$ 435	$ 435	$ 435
Insurance costs	$ 166	$ 166	$ 166	$ 166	$ 166	$ 166	$ 166
Truck maintenance costs	$ 1,466	$ 1,466	$ 1,466	$ 1,466	$ 1,466	$ 1,466	$ 1,466
Rent and utilities	$ 1,188	$ 1,188	$ 1,188	$ 1,188	$ 1,188	$ 1,188	$ 1,188
Miscellaneous costs	$ 974	$ 974	$ 974	$ 974	$ 974	$ 974	$ 974
Payroll taxes	$ 2,350	$ 2,350	$ 2,350	$ 2,350	$ 2,350	$ 2,350	$ 2,350
Total operating costs	$24,750	$24,750	$24,750	$24,750	$24,750	$24,750	$24,750
EBITDA	$ 6,400	$ 6,444	$ 6,489	$ 6,533	$ 6,578	$ 6,622	$ 6,667
Federal income tax	$ 2,176	$ 2,179	$ 2,182	$ 2,185	$ 2,188	$ 2,191	$ 2,194
State income tax	$ 330	$ 330	$ 331	$ 331	$ 332	$ 332	$ 332
Interest expense	$ 1,125	$ 1,119	$ 1,113	$ 1,107	$ 1,101	$ 1,095	$ 1,089
Depreciation expense	$ 729	$ 729	$ 729	$ 729	$ 729	$ 729	$ 729
Net profit	$ 2,040	$ 2,087	$ 2,134	$ 2,181	$ 2,228	$ 2,274	$ 2,321

Profit and loss statement (first year cont.)

Month	8	9	10	11	12	1
Sales	$81,305	$81,420	$81,535	$81,650	$81,765	$973,590
Cost of goods sold	$49,844	$49,914	$49,985	$50,055	$50,126	$596,853
Gross margin	38.7%	38.7%	38.7%	38.7%	38.7%	38.7%
Operating income	$31,462	$31,506	$31,551	$31,595	$31,640	$376,737
Expenses						
Payroll	$15,667	$15,667	$15,667	$15,667	$15,667	$188,000
General and administrative	$ 2,100	$ 2,100	$ 2,100	$ 2,100	$ 2,100	$ 25,200
Marketing expenses	$ 406	$ 406	$ 406	$ 406	$ 406	$ 4,868
Professional fees and licensure	$ 435	$ 435	$ 435	$ 435	$ 435	$ 5,219
Insurance costs	$ 166	$ 166	$ 166	$ 166	$ 166	$ 1,987
Truck maintenance costs	$ 1,466	$ 1,466	$ 1,466	$ 1,466	$ 1,466	$ 17,596
Rent and utilities	$ 1,188	$ 1,188	$ 1,188	$ 1,188	$ 1,188	$ 14,250
Miscellaneous costs	$ 974	$ 974	$ 974	$ 974	$ 974	$ 11,683
Payroll taxes	$ 2,350	$ 2,350	$ 2,350	$ 2,350	$ 2,350	$ 28,200
Total operating costs	$24,750	$24,750	$24,750	$24,750	$24,750	$297,003
EBITDA	$ 6,711	$ 6,756	$ 6,800	$ 6,845	$ 6,889	$ 79,734
Federal income tax	$ 2,197	$ 2,200	$ 2,204	$ 2,207	$ 2,210	$ 26,312
State income tax	$ 333	$ 333	$ 334	$ 334	$ 335	$ 3,987
Interest expense	$ 1,083	$ 1,077	$ 1,071	$ 1,065	$ 1,059	$ 13,107
Depreciation expense	$ 729	$ 729	$ 729	$ 729	$ 729	$ 8,750
Net profit	$ 2,368	$ 2,415	$ 2,463	$ 2,510	$ 2,557	$ 27,579

Profit and loss statement (second year)

Quarter	Q1	2 Q2	Q3	Q4	2
Sales	**$233,662**	**$292,077**	**$315,443**	**$327,126**	**$1,168,308**
Cost of goods sold	$143,245	$179,056	$193,380	$200,543	$ 716,224
Gross margin	38.7%	38.7%	38.7%	38.7%	38.7%
Operating income	**$ 90,417**	**$113,021**	**$122,063**	**$126,584**	**$ 452,084**
Expenses					
Payroll	$ 38,728	$ 48,410	$ 52,283	$ 54,219	$ 193,640
General and administrative	$ 5,242	$ 6,552	$ 7,076	$ 7,338	$ 26,208
Marketing expenses	$ 1,168	$ 1,460	$ 1,577	$ 1,636	$ 5,842
Professional fees and licensure	$ 1,075	$ 1,344	$ 1,451	$ 1,505	$ 5,376
Insurance costs	$ 417	$ 522	$ 563	$ 584	$ 2,086
Truck maintenance costs	$ 3,871	$ 4,839	$ 5,226	$ 5,420	$ 19,356
Rent and utilities	$ 2,993	$ 3,741	$ 4,040	$ 4,190	$ 14,963
Miscellaneous costs	$ 2,804	$ 3,505	$ 3,785	$ 3,926	$ 14,020
Payroll taxes	$ 5,809	$ 7,262	$ 7,842	$ 8,133	$ 29,046
Total operating costs	**$ 62,107**	**$ 77,634**	**$ 83,845**	**$ 86,950**	**$ 310,535**
EBITDA	**$ 28,310**	**$ 35,387**	**$ 38,218**	**$ 39,634**	**$ 141,549**
Federal income tax	$ 8,537	**$ 10,672**	$ 11,525	$ 11,952	$ 42,686
State income tax	$ 1,294	$ 1,617	$ 1,746	$ 1,811	$ 6,468
Interest expense	$ 3,138	$ 3,080	$ 3,020	$ 2,959	$ 12,197
Depreciation expense	$ 2,188	$ 2,188	$ 2,188	$ 2,188	$ 8,750
Net profit	**$ 13,154**	**$ 17,832**	**$ 19,739**	**$ 20,724**	**$ 71,448**

Profit and loss statement (third year)

Quarter	Q1	3 Q2	Q3	Q4	3
Sales	**$273,384**	**$341,730**	**$369,068**	**$382,738**	**$1,366,920**
Cost of goods sold	$167,596	$209,495	$226,255	$234,635	$ 837,982
Gross margin	38.7%	38.7%	38.7%	38.7%	38.7%
Operating income	**$105,788**	**$132,235**	**$142,813**	**$148,103**	**$ 528,939**
Expenses					
Payroll	$ 39,890	$ 49,862	$ 53,851	$ 55,846	$ 199,449
General and administrative	$ 5,451	$ 6,814	$ 7,359	$ 7,632	$ 27,256
Marketing expenses	$ 1,367	$ 1,709	$ 1,845	$ 1,914	$ 6,835
Professional fees and licensure	$ 1,107	$ 1,384	$ 1,495	$ 1,550	$ 5,537
Insurance costs	$ 438	$ 548	$ 591	$ 613	$ 2,191
Truck maintenance costs	$ 4,258	$ 5,323	$ 5,749	$ 5,962	$ 21,291
Rent and utilities	$ 3,142	$ 3,928	$ 4,242	$ 4,399	$ 15,711
Miscellaneous costs	$ 3,281	$ 4,101	$ 4,429	$ 4,593	$ 16,403
Payroll taxes	$ 5,983	$ 7,479	$ 8,078	$ 8,377	$ 29,917
Total operating costs	**$ 64,918**	**$ 81,147**	**$ 87,639**	**$ 90,885**	**$ 324,590**
EBITDA	**$ 40,870**	**$ 51,087**	**$ 55,174**	**$ 57,218**	**$ 204,349**
Federal income tax	$ 12,748	$ 15,935	$ 17,209	$ 17,847	$ 63,738
State income tax	$ 1,931	$ 2,414	$ 2,607	$ 2,704	$ 9,657
Interest expense	$ 2,897	$ 2,834	$ 2,769	$ 2,702	$ 11,202
Depreciation expense	$ 2,188	$ 2,188	$ 2,188	$ 2,188	$ 8,750
Net profit	**$ 21,106**	**$ 27,717**	**$ 30,401**	**$ 31,777**	**$ 111,001**

7.11 Three Year Cash Flow Analysis

Cash flow analysis (first year)

Month	1	2	3	4	5	6	7	8
Cash from operations	$ 2,770	$ 2,816	$ 2,863	$ 2,910	$ 2,957	$ 3,004	$ 3,051	$ 3,098
Cash from receivables	$ 0	$ 0	$ 0	$ 0	$ 0	$ 0	$ 0	$ 0
Operating cash inflow	**$ 2,770**	**$ 2,816**	**$ 2,863**	**$ 2,910**	**$ 2,957**	**$ 3,004**	**$ 3,051**	**$ 3,098**
Other cash inflows								
Equity investment	$ 25,000	$ 0	$ 0	$ 0	$ 0	$ 0	$ 0	$ 0
Increased borrowings	$150,000	$ 0	$ 0	$ 0	$ 0	$ 0	$ 0	$ 0
Sales of business assets	$ 0	$ 0	$ 0	$ 0	$ 0	$ 0	$ 0	$ 0
A/P increases	$ 3,159	$ 3,159	$ 3,159	$ 3,159	$ 3,159	$ 3,159	$ 3,159	$ 3,159
Total other cash inflows	**$178,159**	**$ 3,159**	**$ 3,159**	**$ 3,159**	**$ 3,159**	**$ 3,159**	**$ 3,159**	**$ 3,159**
Total cash inflow	**$180,928**	**$ 5,975**	**$ 6,022**	**$ 6,068**	**$ 6,115**	**$ 6,162**	**$ 6,209**	**$ 6,256**
Cash outflows								
Repayment of principal	$ 775	$ 781	$ 787	$ 793	$ 799	$ 805	$ 811	$ 817
A/P decreases	$ 2,075	$ 2,075	$ 2,075	$ 2,075	$ 2,075	$ 2,075	$ 2,075	$ 2,075
A/R increases	$ 0	$ 0	$ 0	$ 0	$ 0	$ 0	$ 0	$ 0
Asset purchases	$122,500	$ 0	$ 0	$ 0	$ 0	$ 0	$ 0	$ 0
Dividends	$ 0	$ 0	$ 0	$ 0	$ 0	$ 0	$ 0	$ 0
Total cash outflows	**$125,350**	**$ 2,856**	**$ 2,862**	**$ 2,867**	**$ 2,873**	**$ 2,879**	**$ 2,885**	**$ 2,892**
Net cash flow	**$ 55,578**	**$ 3,119**	**$ 3,160**	**$ 3,201**	**$ 3,242**	**$ 3,283**	**$ 3,324**	**$ 3,365**
Cash balance	**$ 55,578**	**$58,697**	**$61,857**	**$65,058**	**$68,300**	**$71,583**	**$74,906**	**$78,271**

Cash flow analysis (first year cont.)

Month	9	10	11	12	1
Cash from operations	$ 3,145	$ 3,192	$ 3,239	$ 3,286	$ 36,329
Cash from receivables	$ 0	$ 0	$ 0	$ 0	$ 0
Operating cash inflow	**$ 3,145**	**$ 3,192**	**$ 3,239**	**$ 3,286**	**$ 36,329**
Other cash inflows					
Equity investment	$ 0	$ 0	$ 0	$ 0	$ 25,000
Increased borrowings	$ 0	$ 0	$ 0	$ 0	$150,000
Sales of business assets	$ 0	$ 0	$ 0	$ 0	$ 0
A/P increases	$ 3,159	$ 3,159	$ 3,159	$ 3,159	$ 37,902
Total other cash inflows	**$ 3,159**	**$ 3,159**	**$ 3,159**	**$ 3,159**	**$212,902**
Total cash inflow	**$ 6,303**	**$ 6,350**	**$ 6,397**	**$ 6,445**	**$249,231**
Cash outflows					
Repayment of principal	$ 823	$ 829	$ 835	$ 842	$ 9,695
A/P decreases	$ 2,075	$ 2,075	$ 2,075	$ 2,075	$ 24,897
A/R increases	$ 0	$ 0	$ 0	$ 0	$ 0
Asset purchases	$ 0	$ 0	$ 0	$ 0	$122,500
Dividends	$ 0	$ 0	$ 0	$25,430	$ 25,430
Total cash outflows	**$ 2,898**	**$ 2,904**	**$ 2,910**	**$28,346**	**$182,522**
Net cash flow	**$ 3,406**	**$ 3,446**	**$ 3,487**	**−$21,902**	**$ 66,708**
Cash balance	**$81,676**	**$85,123**	**$88,610**	**$66,708**	**$ 66,708**

Cash flow analysis (second year)

Quarter	Q1	2 Q2	Q3	Q4	2
Cash from operations	$16,040	$20,050	$21,654	$22,456	$ 80,198
Cash from receivables	$ 0	$ 0	$ 0	$ 0	$ 0
Operating cash inflow	**$16,040**	**$20,050**	**$21,654**	**$22,456**	**$ 80,198**
Other cash inflows					
Equity investment	$ 0	$ 0	$ 0	$ 0	$ 0
Increased borrowings	$ 0	$ 0	$ 0	$ 0	$ 0
Sales of business assets	$ 0	$ 0	$ 0	$ 0	$ 0
A/P increases	$ 8,717	$10,897	$11,769	$12,204	$ 43,587
Total other cash inflows	**$ 8,717**	**$10,897**	**$11,769**	**$12,204**	**$ 43,587**
Total cash inflow	**$24,757**	**$30,946**	**$33,422**	**$34,660**	**$123,786**
Cash outflows					
Repayment of principal	$ 2,563	$ 2,621	$ 2,680	$ 2,741	$ 10,605
A/P decreases	$ 5,975	$ 7,469	$ 8,067	$ 8,365	$ 29,876
A/R increases	$ 0	$ 0	$ 0	$ 0	$ 0
Asset purchases	$ 4,010	$ 5,012	$ 5,413	$ 5,614	$ 20,050
Dividends	$11,228	$14,035	$15,157	$15,719	$ 56,139
Total cash outflows	**$23,776**	**$29,137**	**$31,318**	**$32,439**	**$116,669**
Net cash flow	**$ 981**	**$ 1,809**	**$ 2,104**	**$ 2,221**	**$ 7,116**
Cash balance	**$67,690**	**$69,499**	**$71,604**	**$73,825**	**$ 73,825**

Cash flow analysis (third year)

Quarter	Q1	3 Q2	Q3	Q4	3
Cash from operations	$23,950	$29,938	$32,333	$33,530	$119,751
Cash from receivables	$ 0	$ 0	$ 0	$ 0	$ 0
Operating cash inflow	**$23,950**	**$29,938**	**$32,333**	**$33,530**	**$119,751**
Other cash inflows					
Equity investment	$ 0	$ 0	$ 0	$ 0	$ 0
Increased borrowings	$ 0	$ 0	$ 0	$ 0	$ 0
Sales of business assets	$ 0	$ 0	$ 0	$ 0	$ 0
A/P increases	$10,025	$12,531	$13,534	$14,035	$ 50,125
Total other cash inflows	**$10,025**	**$12,531**	**$13,534**	**$14,035**	**$ 50,125**
Total cash inflow	**$33,975**	**$42,469**	**$45,867**	**$47,565**	**$169,876**
Cash outflows					
Repayment of principal	$ 2,803	$ 2,867	$ 2,932	$ 2,998	$ 11,599
A/P decreases	$ 7,170	$ 8,963	$ 9,680	$10,038	$ 35,852
A/R increases	$ 0	$ 0	$ 0	$ 0	$ 0
Asset purchases	$ 5,988	$ 7,484	$ 8,083	$ 8,383	$ 29,938
Dividends	$16,765	$20,956	$22,633	$23,471	$ 83,826
Total cash outflows	**$32,726**	**$40,270**	**$43,328**	**$44,890**	**$161,214**
Net cash flow	**$ 1,249**	**$ 2,199**	**$ 2,539**	**$ 2,675**	**$ 8,662**
Cash balance	**$75,074**	**$77,273**	**$79,812**	**$82,487**	**$ 82,487**

Business Plan Template

USING THIS TEMPLATE

A business plan carefully spells out a company's projected course of action over a period of time, usually the first two to three years after the start-up. In addition, banks, lenders, and other investors examine the information and financial documentation before deciding whether or not to finance a new business venture. Therefore, a business plan is an essential tool in obtaining financing and should describe the business itself in detail as well as all important factors influencing the company, including the market, industry, competition, operations and management policies, problem solving strategies, financial resources and needs, and other vital information. The plan enables the business owner to anticipate costs, plan for difficulties, and take advantage of opportunities, as well as design and implement strategies that keep the company running as smoothly as possible.

This template has been provided as a model to help you construct your own business plan. Please keep in mind that there is no single acceptable format for a business plan, and that this template is in no way comprehensive, but serves as an example.

The business plans provided in this section are fictional and have been used by small business agencies as models for clients to use in compiling their own business plans.

GENERIC BUSINESS PLAN

Main headings included below are topics that should be covered in a comprehensive business plan. They include:

Business Summary

Purpose
Provides a brief overview of your business, succinctly highlighting the main ideas of your plan.

Includes

- Name and Type of Business
- Description of Product/Service
- Business History and Development
- Location
- Market

- Competition
- Management
- Financial Information
- Business Strengths and Weaknesses
- Business Growth

Table of Contents

Purpose
Organized in an Outline Format, the Table of Contents illustrates the selection and arrangement of information contained in your plan.

Includes

- Topic Headings and Subheadings
- Page Number References

Business History and Industry Outlook

Purpose

Examines the conception and subsequent development of your business within an industry specific context.

Includes

- Start-up Information
- Owner/Key Personnel Experience
- Location
- Development Problems and Solutions
- Investment/Funding Information

- Future Plans and Goals
- Market Trends and Statistics
- Major Competitors
- Product/Service Advantages
- National, Regional, and Local Economic Impact

Product/Service

Purpose

Introduces, defines, and details the product and/or service that inspired the information of your business.

Includes

- Unique Features
- Niche Served
- Market Comparison
- Stage of Product/Service Development

- Production
- Facilities, Equipment, and Labor
- Financial Requirements
- Product/Service Life Cycle
- Future Growth

Market Examination

Purpose

Assessment of product/service applications in relation to consumer buying cycles.

Includes

- Target Market
- Consumer Buying Habits
- Product/Service Applications
- Consumer Reactions
- Market Factors and Trends

- Penetration of the Market
- Market Share
- Research and Studies
- Cost
- Sales Volume and Goals

Competition

Purpose

Analysis of Competitors in the Marketplace.

Includes

- Competitor Information
- Product/Service Comparison
- Market Niche

- Product/Service Strengths and Weaknesses
- Future Product/Service Development

Marketing

Purpose

Identifies promotion and sales strategies for your product/service.

Includes

- Product/Service Sales Appeal
- Special and Unique Features
- Identification of Customers
- Sales and Marketing Staff
- Sales Cycles
- Type of Advertising/ Promotion
- Pricing
- Competition
- Customer Services

Operations

Purpose

Traces product/service development from production/inception to the market environment.

Includes

- Cost Effective Production Methods
- Facility
- Location
- Equipment
- Labor
- Future Expansion

Administration and Management

Purpose

Offers a statement of your management philosophy with an in-depth focus on processes and procedures.

Includes

- Management Philosophy
- Structure of Organization
- Reporting System
- Methods of Communication
- Employee Skills and Training
- Employee Needs and Compensation
- Work Environment
- Management Policies and Procedures
- Roles and Responsibilities

Key Personnel

Purpose

Describes the unique backgrounds of principle employees involved in business.

Includes

- Owner(s)/Employee Education and Experience
- Positions and Roles
- Benefits and Salary
- Duties and Responsibilities
- Objectives and Goals

Potential Problems and Solutions

Purpose

Discussion of problem solving strategies that change issues into opportunities.

Includes

- Risks
- Litigation
- Future Competition
- Economic Impact
- Problem Solving Skills

Financial Information

Purpose

Secures needed funding and assistance through worksheets and projections detailing financial plans, methods of repayment, and future growth opportunities.

Includes

- Financial Statements
- Bank Loans
- Methods of Repayment
- Tax Returns

- Start-up Costs
- Projected Income (3 years)
- Projected Cash Flow (3 Years)
- Projected Balance Statements (3 years)

Appendices

Purpose

Supporting documents used to enhance your business proposal.

Includes

- Photographs of product, equipment, facilities, etc.
- Copyright/Trademark Documents
- Legal Agreements
- Marketing Materials
- Research and or Studies

- Operation Schedules
- Organizational Charts
- Job Descriptions
- Resumes
- Additional Financial Documentation

Fictional Food Distributor

Commercial Foods, Inc.

3003 Avondale Ave.
Knoxville, TN 37920

This plan demonstrates how a partnership can have a positive impact on a new business. It demonstrates how two individuals can carve a niche in the specialty foods market by offering gourmet foods to upscale restaurants and fine hotels. This plan is fictional and has not been used to gain funding from a bank or other lending institution.

STATEMENT OF PURPOSE

Commercial Foods, Inc. seeks a loan of $75,000 to establish a new business. This sum, together with $5,000 equity investment by the principals, will be used as follows:

- Merchandise inventory $25,000

- Office fixture/equipment $12,000

- Warehouse equipment $14,000

- One delivery truck $10,000

- Working capital $39,000

- Total $100,000

DESCRIPTION OF THE BUSINESS

Commercial Foods, Inc. will be a distributor of specialty food service products to hotels and upscale restaurants in the geographical area of a 50 mile radius of Knoxville. Richard Roberts will direct the sales effort and John Williams will manage the warehouse operation and the office. One delivery truck will be used initially with a second truck added in the third year. We expect to begin operation of the business within 30 days after securing the requested financing.

MANAGEMENT

A. Richard Roberts is a native of Memphis, Tennessee. He is a graduate of Memphis State University with a Bachelor's degree from the School of Business. After graduation, he worked for a major manufacturer of specialty food service products as a detail sales person for five years, and, for the past three years, he has served as a product sales manager for this firm.

B. John Williams is a native of Nashville, Tennessee. He holds a B.S. Degree in Food Technology from the University of Tennessee. His career includes five years as a product development chemist in gourmet food products and five years as operations manager for a food service distributor.

Both men are healthy and energetic. Their backgrounds complement each other, which will ensure the success of Commercial Foods, Inc. They will set policies together and personnel decisions will be made jointly. Initial salaries for the owners will be $1,000 per month for the first few years. The spouses of both principals are successful in the business world and earn enough to support the families.

They have engaged the services of Foster Jones, CPA, and William Hale, Attorney, to assist them in an advisory capacity.

PERSONNEL

The firm will employ one delivery truck driver at a wage of $8.00 per hour. One office worker will be employed at $7.50 per hour. One part-time employee will be used in the office at $5.00 per hour. The driver will load and unload his own trucks. Mr. Williams will assist in the warehouse operation as needed to assist one stock person at $7.00 per hour. An additional delivery truck and driver will be added the third year.

LOCATION

The firm will lease a 20,000 square foot building at 3003 Avondale Ave., in Knoxville, which contains warehouse and office areas equipped with two-door truck docks. The annual rental is $9,000. The building was previously used as a food service warehouse and very little modification to the building will be required.

PRODUCTS AND SERVICES

The firm will offer specialty food service products such as soup bases, dessert mixes, sauce bases, pastry mixes, spices, and flavors, normally used by upscale restaurants and nice hotels. We are going after a niche in the market with high quality gourmet products. There is much less competition in this market than in standard run of the mill food service products. Through their work experiences, the principals have contacts with supply sources and with local chefs.

THE MARKET

We know from our market survey that there are over 200 hotels and upscale restaurants in the area we plan to serve. Customers will be attracted by a direct sales approach. We will offer samples of our products and product application data on use of our products in the finished prepared foods. We will cultivate the chefs in these establishments. The technical background of John Williams will be especially useful here.

COMPETITION

We find that we will be only distributor in the area offering a full line of gourmet food service products. Other foodservice distributors offer only a few such items in conjunction with their standard product line. Our survey shows that many of the chefs are ordering products from Atlanta and Memphis because of a lack of adequate local supply.

SUMMARY

Commercial Foods, Inc. will be established as a foodservice distributor of specialty food in Knoxville. The principals, with excellent experience in the industry, are seeking a $75,000 loan to establish the business. The principals are investing $25,000 as equity capital.

The business will be set up as an S Corporation with each principal owning 50% of the common stock in the corporation.

Fictional Hardware Store

Oshkosh Hardware, Inc.

123 Main St.
Oshkosh, WI 54901

The following plan outlines how a small hardware store can survive competition from large discount chains by offering products and providing expert advice in the use of any product it sells. This plan is fictional and has not been used to gain funding from a bank or other lending institution.

EXECUTIVE SUMMARY

Oshkosh Hardware, Inc. is a new corporation that is going to establish a retail hardware store in a strip mall in Oshkosh, Wisconsin. The store will sell hardware of all kinds, quality tools, paint, and housewares. The business will make revenue and a profit by servicing its customers not only with needed hardware but also with expert advice in the use of any product it sells.

Oshkosh Hardware, Inc. will be operated by its sole shareholder, James Smith. The company will have a total of four employees. It will sell its products in the local market. Customers will buy our products because we will provide free advice on the use of all of our products and will also furnish a full refund warranty.

Oshkosh Hardware, Inc. will sell its products in the Oshkosh store staffed by three sales representatives. No additional employees will be needed to achieve its short and long range goals. The primary short range goal is to open the store by October 1, 1994. In order to achieve this goal a lease must be signed by July 1, 1994 and the complete inventory ordered by August 1, 1994.

Mr. James Smith will invest $30,000 in the business. In addition, the company will have to borrow $150,000 during the first year to cover the investment in inventory, accounts receivable, and furniture and equipment. The company will be profitable after six months of operation and should be able to start repayment of the loan in the second year.

THE BUSINESS

The business will sell hardware of all kinds, quality tools, paint, and housewares. We will purchase our products from three large wholesale buying groups.

In general our customers are homeowners who do their own repair and maintenance, hobbyists, and housewives. Our business is unique in that we will have a complete line of all hardware items and will be able to get special orders by overnight delivery. The business makes revenue and profits by servicing our customers not only with needed hardware but also with expert advice in the use of any product we sell. Our major costs for bringing our products to market are cost of merchandise of 36%, salaries of $45,000, and occupancy costs of $60,000.

Oshkosh Hardware, Inc.'s retail outlet will be located at 1524 Frontage Road, which is in a newly developed retail center of Oshkosh. Our location helps facilitate accessibility from all parts of town and reduces our delivery costs. The store will occupy 7500 square feet of space. The major equipment involved in our business is counters and shelving, a computer, a paint mixing machine, and a truck.

THE MARKET

Oshkosh Hardware, Inc. will operate in the local market. There are 15,000 potential customers in this market area. We have three competitors who control approximately 98% of the market at present. We feel we can capture 25% of the market within the next four years. Our major reason for believing this is that our staff is technically competent to advise our customers in the correct use of all products we sell.

After a careful market analysis, we have determined that approximately 60% of our customers are men and 40% are women. The percentage of customers that fall into the following age categories are:

Under 16: 0%
17-21: 5%
22-30: 30%
31-40: 30%
41-50: 20%
51-60: 10%
61-70: 5%
Over 70: 0%

The reasons our customers prefer our products is our complete knowledge of their use and our full refund warranty.

We get our information about what products our customers want by talking to existing customers. There seems to be an increasing demand for our product. The demand for our product is increasing in size based on the change in population characteristics.

SALES

At Oshkosh Hardware, Inc. we will employ three sales people and will not need any additional personnel to achieve our sales goals. These salespeople will need several years experience in home repair and power tool usage. We expect to attract 30% of our customers from newspaper ads, 5% of our customers from local directories, 5% of our customers from the yellow pages, 10% of our customers from family and friends, and 50% of our customers from current customers. The most cost effect source will be current customers. In general our industry is growing.

MANAGEMENT

We would evaluate the quality of our management staff as being excellent. Our manager is experienced and very motivated to achieve the various sales and quality assurance objectives we have set. We will use a management information system that produces key inventory, quality assurance, and sales data on a weekly basis. All data is compared to previously established goals for that week, and deviations are the primary focus of the management staff.

GOALS IMPLEMENTATION

The short term goals of our business are:

1. Open the store by October 1, 1994
2. Reach our breakeven point in two months
3. Have sales of $100,000 in the first six months

In order to achieve our first short term goal we must:

1. Sign the lease by July 1, 1994
2. Order a complete inventory by August 1, 1994

In order to achieve our second short term goal we must:

1. Advertise extensively in Sept. and Oct.
2. Keep expenses to a minimum

In order to achieve our third short term goal we must:

1. Promote power tool sales for the Christmas season
2. Keep good customer traffic in Jan. and Feb.

The long term goals for our business are:

1. Obtain sales volume of $600,000 in three years
2. Become the largest hardware dealer in the city
3. Open a second store in Fond du Lac

The most important thing we must do in order to achieve the long term goals for our business is to develop a highly profitable business with excellent cash flow.

FINANCE

Oshkosh Hardware, Inc. Faces some potential threats or risks to our business. They are discount house competition. We believe we can avoid or compensate for this by providing quality products complimented by quality advice on the use of every product we sell. The financial projections we have prepared are located at the end of this document.

JOB DESCRIPTION-GENERAL MANAGER

The General Manager of the business of the corporation will be the president of the corporation. He will be responsible for the complete operation of the retail hardware store which is owned by the corporation. A detailed description of his duties and responsibilities is as follows.

Sales

Train and supervise the three sales people. Develop programs to motivate and compensate these employees. Coordinate advertising and sales promotion effects to achieve sales totals as outlined in budget. Oversee purchasing function and inventory control procedures to insure adequate merchandise at all times at a reasonable cost.

Finance

Prepare monthly and annual budgets. Secure adequate line of credit from local banks. Supervise office personnel to insure timely preparation of records, statements, all government reports, control of receivables and payables, and monthly financial statements.

Administration

Perform duties as required in the areas of personnel, building leasing and maintenance, licenses and permits, and public relations.

Organizations, Agencies, & Consultants

A listing of Associations and Consultants of interest to entrepreneurs, followed by the ten Small Business Administration Regional Offices, Small Business Development Centers, Service Corps of Retired Executives offices, and Venture Capital and Finance Companies.

Associations

This section contains a listing of associations and other agencies of interest to the small business owner. Entries are listed alphabetically by organization name.

American Business Women's Association
9100 Ward Pkwy.
PO Box 8728
Kansas City, MO 64114-0728
(800)228-0007
E-mail: abwa@abwa.org
Website: http://www.abwa.org
Jeanne Banks, National President

American Franchisee Association
53 W Jackson Blvd., Ste. 1157
Chicago, IL 60604
(312)431-0545
E-mail: info@franchisee.org
Website: http://www.franchisee.org
Susan P. Kezios, President

American Independent Business Alliance
222 S Black Ave.
Bozeman, MT 59715
(406)582-1255
E-mail: info@amiba.net
Website: http://www.amiba.net
Jennifer Rockne, Director

American Small Businesses Association
206 E College St., Ste. 201
Grapevine, TX 76051
800-942-2722
E-mail: info@asbaonline.org
Website: http://www.asbaonline.org/

American Women's Economic Development Corporation
216 East 45th St., 10th Floor
New York, NY 10017
(917)368-6100

Fax: (212)986-7114
E-mail: info@awed.org
Website: http://www.awed.org
Roseanne Antonucci, Exec. Dir.

Association for Enterprise Opportunity
1601 N Kent St., Ste. 1101
Arlington, VA 22209
(703)841-7760
Fax: (703)841-7748
E-mail: aeo@assoceo.org
Website: http://www.micro enterpriseworks.org
Bill Edwards, Exec.Dir.

Association of Small Business Development Centers
c/o Don Wilson
8990 Burke Lake Rd.
Burke, VA 22015
(703)764-9850
Fax: (703)764-1234
E-mail: info@asbdc-us.org
Website: http://www.asbdc-us.org
Don Wilson, Pres./CEO

BEST Employers Association
2505 McCabe Way
Irvine, CA 92614
(949)253-4080
800-433-0088
Fax: (714)553-0883
E-mail: info@bestlife.com
Website: http://www.bestlife.com
Donald R. Lawrenz, CEO

Center for Family Business
PO Box 24219
Cleveland, OH 44124
(440)460-5409
E-mail: grummi@aol.com
Dr. Leon A. Danco, Chm.

Coalition for Government Procurement
1990 M St. NW, Ste. 400
Washington, DC 20036
(202)331-0975
E-mail: info@thecgp.org
Website: http://www.coalgovpro.org
Paul Caggiano, Pres.

Employers of America
PO Box 1874
Mason City, IA 50402-1874
(641)424 3187
800-728-3187
Fax: (641)424-1673
E-mail: employer@employerhelp.org
Website: http://www.employerhelp.org
Jim Collison, Pres.

Family Firm Institute
200 Lincoln St., Ste. 201
Boston, MA 02111
(617)482-3045
Fax: (617)482-3049
E-mail: ffi@ffi.org
Website: http://www.ffi.org
Judy L. Green, Ph.D., Exec.Dir.

Independent Visually Impaired Enterprisers
500 S 3rd St., Apt. H
Burbank, CA 91502
(818)238-9321
E-mail: abazyn@bazyn communications.com
http://www.acb.org/affiliates
Adris Bazyn, Pres.

International Association for Business Organizations
3 Woodthorn Ct., Ste. 12
Owings Mills, MD 21117
(410)581-1373
E-mail: nahbb@msn.com
Rudolph Lewis, Exec. Officer

International Council for Small Business
The George Washington University
School of Business and Public
Management
2115 G St. NW, Ste. 403
Washington, DC 20052
(202)994-0704
Fax: (202)994-4930
E-mail: icsb@gwu.edu
Website: http://www.icsb.org
Susan G. Duffy. Admin.

International Small Business Consortium
3309 Windjammer St.
Norman, OK 73072
E-mail: sb@isbc.com
Website: http://www.isbc.com

Kauffman Center for Entrepreneurial Leadership
4801 Rockhill Rd.
Kansas City, MO 64110-2046
(816)932-1000
E-mail: info@kauffman.org
Website: http://www.entreworld.org

National Alliance for Fair Competition
3 Bethesda Metro Center, Ste. 1100
Bethesda, MD 20814
(410)235-7116
Fax: (410)235-7116
E-mail: ampesq@aol.com
Tony Ponticelli, Exec.Dir.

National Association for the Self-Employed
PO Box 612067
DFW Airport
Dallas, TX 75261-2067
(800)232-6273
E-mail: mpetron@nase.org
Website: http://www.nase.org
Robert Hughes, Pres.

National Association of Business Leaders
4132 Shoreline Dr., Ste. J & H
Earth City, MO 63045
Fax: (314)298-9110
E-mail: nabl@nabl.com
Website: http://www.nabl.com/
Gene Blumenthal, Contact

National Association of Private Enterprise
PO Box 15550
Long Beach, CA 90815
888-224-0953

Fax: (714)844-4942
Website: http://www.napeonline.net
Laura Squiers, Exec.Dir.

National Association of Small Business Investment Companies
666 11th St. NW, Ste. 750
Washington, DC 20001
(202)628-5055
Fax: (202)628-5080
E-mail: nasbic@nasbic.org
Website: http://www.nasbic.org
Lee W. Mercer, Pres.

National Business Association
PO Box 700728
5151 Beltline Rd., Ste. 1150
Dallas, TX 75370
(972)458-0900
800-456-0440
Fax: (972)960-9149
E-mail: info@nationalbusiness.org
Website: http://www.national
business.org
Raj Nisankarao, Pres.

National Business Owners Association
PO Box 111
Stuart, VA 24171
(276)251-7500
(866)251-7505
Fax: (276)251-2217
E-mail: membershipservices@nboa.org
Website: http://www.rvmdb.com.nboa
Paul LaBarr, Pres.

National Center for Fair Competition
PO Box 220
Annandale, VA 22003
(703)280-4622
Fax: (703)280-0942
E-mail: kentonp1@aol.com
Kenton Pattie, Pres.

National Family Business Council
1640 W. Kennedy Rd.
Lake Forest, IL 60045
(847)295-1040
Fax: (847)295-1898
E-mail: lmsnfbc@email.msn.com
Jogn E. Messervey, Pres.

National Federation of Independent Business
53 Century Blvd., Ste. 250
Nashville, TN 37214
(615)872-5800
800-NFIBNOW
Fax: (615)872-5353
Website: http://www.nfib.org
Jack Faris, Pres. and CEO

National Small Business Association
1156 15th St. NW, Ste. 1100
Washington, DC 20005
(202)293-8830
800-345-6728
Fax: (202)872-8543
E-mail: press@nsba.biz
Website: http://www.nsba.biz
Rob Yunich, Dir. of Communications

PUSH Commercial Division
930 E 50th St.
Chicago, IL 60615-2702
(773)373-3366
Fax: (773)373-3571
E-mail: info@rainbowpush.org
Website: http://www.rainbowpush.org
Rev. Willie T. Barrow, Co-Chm.

Research Institute for Small and Emerging Business
722 12th St. NW
Washington, DC 20005
(202)628-8382
Fax: (202)628-8392
E-mail: info@riseb.org
Website: http://www.riseb.org
Allan Neece, Jr., Chm.

Sales Professionals USA
PO Box 149
Arvada, CO 80001
(303)534-4937
888-736-7767
E-mail: salespro@salesprofessionals-usa.com
Website: http://www.salesprofessionals-usa.com
Sharon Herbert, Natl. Pres.

Score Association - Service Corps of Retired Executives
409 3rd St. SW, 6th Fl.
Washington, DC 20024
(202)205-6762
800-634-0245
Fax: (202)205-7636
E-mail: media@score.org
Website: http://www.score.org
W. Kenneth Yancey, Jr., CEO

Small Business and Entrepreneurship Council
1920 L St. NW, Ste. 200
Washington, DC 20036
(202)785-0238
Fax: (202)822-8118
E-mail: membership@sbec.org
Website: http://www.sbecouncil.org
Karen Kerrigan, Pres./CEO

Small Business in Telecommunications
1331 H St. NW, Ste. 500
Washington, DC 20005
(202)347-4511
Fax: (202)347-8607
E-mail: sbt@sbthome.org
Website: http://www.sbthome.org
Lonnie Danchik, Chm.

Small Business Legislative Council
1010 Massachusetts Ave. NW, Ste. 540
Washington, DC 20005
(202)639-8500
Fax: (202)296-5333
E-mail: email@sblc.org
Website: http://www.sblc.org
John Satagaj, Pres.

Small Business Service Bureau
554 Main St.
PO Box 15014
Worcester, MA 01615-0014
(508)756-3513
800-343-0939
Fax: (508)770-0528
E-mail: membership@sbsb.com
Website: http://www.sbsb.com
Francis R. Carroll, Pres.

**Small Publishers Association
of North America**
1618 W COlorado Ave.
Colorado Springs, CO 80904
(719)475-1726
Fax: (719)471-2182
E-mail: span@spannet.org
Website: http://www.spannet.org
Scott Flora, Exec. Dir.

SOHO America
PO Box 941
Hurst, TX 76053-0941
800-495-SOHO
E-mail: soho@1sas.com
Website: http://www.soho.org

**Structured Employment Economic
Development Corporation**
915 Broadway, 17th Fl.
New York, NY 10010
(212)473-0255
Fax: (212)473-0357
E-mail: info@seedco.org
Website: http://www.seedco.org
William Grinker, CEO

Support Services Alliance
107 Prospect St.
Schoharie, NY 12157
800-836-4772

E-mail: info@ssamembers.com
Website: http://www.ssainfo.com
Steve COle, Pres.

**United States Association for Small
Business and Entrepreneurship**
975 University Ave., No. 3260
Madison, WI 53706
(608)262-9982
Fax: (608)263-0818
E-mail: jgillman@wisc.edu
Website: http://www.ususbe.org
Joan Gillman, Exec. Dir.

Consultants

This section contains a listing of consultants specializing in small business development. It is arranged alphabetically by country, then by state or province, then by city, then by firm name.

Canada

Alberta

Common Sense Solutions
3405 16A Ave.
Edmonton, AB, Canada
(403)465-7330
Fax: (403)465-7380
E-mail: gcoulson@comsense
solutions.com
Website: http://www.comsense
solutions.com

Varsity Consulting Group
School of Business
University of Alberta
Edmonton, AB, Canada T6G 2R6
(780)492-2994
Fax: (780)492-5400
Website: http://www.bus.ualberta.ca/vcg

Viro Hospital Consulting
42 Commonwealth Bldg., 9912 - 106
St. NW
Edmonton, AB, Canada T5K 1C5
(403)425-3871
Fax: (403)425-3871
E-mail: rpb@freenet.edmonton.ab.ca

British Columbia

SRI Strategic Resources Inc.
4330 Kingsway, Ste. 1600
Burnaby, BC, Canada V5H 4G7
(604)435-0627
Fax: (604)435-2782

E-mail: inquiry@sri.bc.ca
Website: http://www.sri.com

Andrew R. De Boda Consulting
1523 Milford Ave.
Coquitlam, BC, Canada V3J 2V9
(604)936-4527
Fax: (604)936-4527
E-mail: deboda@intergate.bc.ca
Website: http://www.ourworld.
compuserve.com/homepages/deboda

The Sage Group Ltd.
980 - 355 Burrard St.
744 W Haistings, Ste. 410
Vancouver, BC, Canada V6C 1A5
(604)669-9269
Fax: (604)669-6622

Tikkanen-Bradley
1345 Nelson St., Ste. 202
Vancouver, BC, Canada V6E 1J8
(604)669-0583
E-mail: webmaster@tikkanen
bradley.com
Website: http://www.tikkanenbradley.com

Ontario

The Cynton Co.
17 Massey St.
Brampton, ON, Canada L6S 2V6
(905)792-7769
Fax: (905)792-8116
E-mail: cynton@home.com
Website: http://www.cynton.com

Begley & Associates
RR 6
Cambridge, ON, Canada N1R 5S7
(519)740-3629
Fax: (519)740-3629
E-mail: begley@in.on.ca
Website: http://www.in.on.ca/~begley/
index.htm

CRO Engineering Ltd.
1895 William Hodgins Ln.
Carp, ON, Canada K0A 1L0
(613)839-1108
Fax: (613)839-1406
E-mail: J.Grefford@ieee.ca
Website: http://www.geocities.com/
WallStreet/District/7401/

Task Enterprises
Box 69, RR 2 Hamilton
Flamborough, ON, Canada L8N 2Z7
(905)659-0153
Fax: (905)659-0861

HST Group Ltd.
430 Gilmour St.
Ottawa, ON, Canada K2P 0R8
(613)236-7303
Fax: (613)236-9893

Harrison Associates
BCE Pl.
181 Bay St., Ste. 3740
PO Box 798
Toronto, ON, Canada M5J 2T3
(416)364-5441
Fax: (416)364-2875

TCI Convergence Ltd. Management Consultants
99 Crown's Ln.
Toronto, ON, Canada M5R 3P4
(416)515-4146
Fax: (416)515-2097
E-mail: tci@inforamp.net
Website: http://tciconverge.com/index.1.html

Ken Wyman & Associates Inc.
64B Shuter St., Ste. 200
Toronto, ON, Canada M5B 1B1
(416)362-2926
Fax: (416)362-3039
E-mail: kenwyman@compuserve.com

JPL Business Consultants
82705 Metter Rd.
Wellandport, ON, Canada L0R 2J0
(905)386-7450
Fax: (905)386-7450
E-mail: plamarch@freenet.npiec.on.ca

Quebec

The Zimmar Consulting Partnership Inc.
Westmount
PO Box 98
Montreal, QC, Canada H3Z 2T1
(514)484-1459
Fax: (514)484-3063

Saskatchewan

Trimension Group
No. 104-110 Research Dr.
Innovation Place, SK, Canada S7N 3R3
(306)668-2560
Fax: (306)975-1156
E-mail: trimension@trimension.ca
Website: http://www.trimension.ca

Corporate Management Consultants
40 Government Road - PO Box 185
Prud Homme, SK, Canada, S0K 3K0
(306)654-4569
Fax: (650)618-2742

E-mail: cmccorporatemanagement@shaw.ca
Website: http://www.Corporate managementconsultants.com
Gerald Rekve

United States

Alabama

Business Planning Inc.
300 Office Park Dr.
Birmingham, AL 35223-2474
(205)870-7090
Fax: (205)870-7103

Tradebank of Eastern Alabama
546 Broad St., Ste. 3
Gadsden, AL 35901
(205)547-8700
Fax: (205)547-8718
E-mail: mansion@webex.com
Website: http://www.webex.com/~tea

Alaska

AK Business Development Center
3335 Arctic Blvd., Ste. 203
Anchorage, AK 99503
(907)562-0335
Free: 800-478-3474
Fax: (907)562-6988
E-mail: abdc@gci.net
Website: http://www.abdc.org

Business Matters
PO Box 287
Fairbanks, AK 99707
(907)452-5650

Arizona

Carefree Direct Marketing Corp.
8001 E Serene St.
PO Box 3737
Carefree, AZ 85377-3737
(480)488-4227
Fax: (480)488-2841

Trans Energy Corp.
1739 W 7th Ave.
Mesa, AZ 85202
(480)827-7915
Fax: (480)967-6601
E-mail: aha@clean-air.org
Website: http://www.clean-air.org

CMAS
5125 N 16th St.
Phoenix, AZ 85016

(602)395-1001
Fax: (602)604-8180

Comgate Telemanagement Ltd.
706 E Bell Rd., Ste. 105
Phoenix, AZ 85022
(602)485-5708
Fax: (602)485-5709
E-mail: comgate@netzone.com
Website: http://www.comgate.com

Moneysoft Inc.
1 E Camelback Rd. #550
Phoenix, AZ 85012
Free: 800-966-7797
E-mail: mbray@moneysoft.com

Harvey C. Skoog
PO Box 26439
Prescott Valley, AZ 86312
(520)772-1714
Fax: (520)772-2814

LMC Services
8711 E Pinnacle Peak Rd., No. 340
Scottsdale, AZ 85255-3555
(602)585-7177
Fax: (602)585-5880
E-mail: louws@earthlink.com

Sauerbrun Technology Group Ltd.
7979 E Princess Dr., Ste. 5
Scottsdale, AZ 85255-5878
(602)502-4950
Fax: (602)502-4292
E-mail: info@sauerbrun.com
Website: http://www.sauerbrun.com

Gary L. McLeod
PO Box 230
Sonoita, AZ 85637
Fax: (602)455-5661

Van Cleve Associates
6932 E 2nd St.
Tucson, AZ 85710
(520)296-2587
Fax: (520)296-3358

California

Acumen Group Inc.
(650)949-9349
Fax: (650)949-4845
E-mail: acumen-g@ix.netcom.com
Website: http://pw2.netcom.com/~janed/acumen.html

On-line Career and Management Consulting
420 Central Ave., No. 314
Alameda, CA 94501

(510)864-0336
Fax: (510)864-0336
E-mail: career@dnai.com
Website: http://www.dnai.com/~career

Career Paths-Thomas E. Church & Associates Inc.
PO Box 2439
Aptos, CA 95001
(408)662-7950
Fax: (408)662-7955
E-mail: church@ix.netcom.com
Website: http://www.careerpaths-tom.com

Keck & Co. Business Consultants
410 Walsh Rd.
Atherton, CA 94027
(650)854-9588
Fax: (650)854-7240
E-mail: info@keckco.com
Website: http://www.keckco.com

Ben W. Laverty III, PhD, REA, CEI
4909 Stockdale Hwy., Ste. 132
Bakersfield, CA 93309
(661)283-8300
Free: 800-833-0373
Fax: (661)283-8313
E-mail: cstc@cstcsafety.com
Website: http://www.cstcsafety.com/cstc

Lindquist Consultants-Venture Planning
225 Arlington Ave.
Berkeley, CA 94707
(510)524-6685
Fax: (510)527-6604

Larson Associates
PO Box 9005
Brea, CA 92822
(714)529-4121
Fax: (714)572-3606
E-mail: ray@consultlarson.com
Website: http://www.consultlarson.com

Kremer Management Consulting
PO Box 500
Carmel, CA 93921
(408)626-8311
Fax: (408)624-2663
E-mail: ddkremer@aol.com

W and J PARTNERSHIP
PO Box 2499
18876 Edwin Markham Dr.
Castro Valley, CA 94546
(510)583-7751
Fax: (510)583-7645
E-mail: wamorgan@wjpartnership.com
Website: http://www.wjpartnership.com

JB Associates
21118 Gardena Dr.
Cupertino, CA 95014
(408)257-0214
Fax: (408)257-0216
E-mail: semarang@sirius.com

House Agricultural Consultants
PO Box 1615
Davis, CA 95617-1615
(916)753-3361
Fax: (916)753-0464
E-mail: infoag@houseag.com
Website: http://www.houseag.com/

3C Systems Co.
16161 Ventura Blvd., Ste. 815
Encino, CA 91436
(818)907-1302
Fax: (818)907-1357
E-mail: mark@3CSysCo.com
Website: http://www.3CSysCo.com

Technical Management Consultants
3624 Westfall Dr.
Encino, CA 91436-4154
(818)784-0626
Fax: (818)501-5575
E-mail: tmcrs@aol.com

RAINWATER-GISH & Associates, Business Finance & Development
317 3rd St., Ste. 3
Eureka, CA 95501
(707)443-0030
Fax: (707)443-5683

Global Tradelinks
451 Pebble Beach Pl.
Fullerton, CA 92835
(714)441-2280
Fax: (714)441-2281
E-mail: info@globaltradelinks.com
Website: http://www.globaltradelinks.com

Strategic Business Group
800 Cienaga Dr.
Fullerton, CA 92835-1248
(714)449-1040
Fax: (714)525-1631

Burnes Consulting
20537 Wolf Creek Rd.
Grass Valley, CA 95949
(530)346-8188
Free: 800-949-9021
Fax: (530)346-7704
E-mail: kent@burnesconsulting.com
Website: http://www.burnesconsulting.com

Pioneer Business Consultants
9042 Garfield Ave., Ste. 312
Huntington Beach, CA 92646
(714)964-7600

Beblie, Brandt & Jacobs Inc.
16 Technology, Ste. 164
Irvine, CA 92618
(714)450-8790
Fax: (714)450-8799
E-mail: darcy@bbjinc.com
Website: http://198.147.90.26

Fluor Daniel Inc.
3353 Michelson Dr.
Irvine, CA 92612-0650
(949)975-2000
Fax: (949)975-5271
E-mail: sales.consulting@fluordaniel.com
Website: http://www.fluordaniel
consulting.com

MCS Associates
18300 Von Karman, Ste. 710
Irvine, CA 92612
(949)263-8700
Fax: (949)263-0770
E-mail: info@mcsassociates.com
Website: http://www.mcsassociates.com

Inspired Arts Inc.
4225 Executive Sq., Ste. 1160
La Jolla, CA 92037
(619)623-3525
Free: 800-851-4394
Fax: (619)623-3534
E-mail: info@inspiredarts.com
Website: http://www.inspiredarts.com

The Laresis Companies
PO Box 3284
La Jolla, CA 92038
(619)452-2720
Fax: (619)452-8744

RCL & Co.
PO Box 1143
737 Pearl St., Ste. 201
La Jolla, CA 92038
(619)454-8883
Fax: (619)454-8880

Comprehensive Business Services
3201 Lucas Cir.
Lafayette, CA 94549
(925)283-8272
Fax: (925)283-8272

The Ribble Group
27601 Forbes Rd., Ste. 52
Laguna Niguel, CA 92677

(714)582-1085
Fax: (714)582-6420
E-mail: ribble@deltanet.com

Norris Bernstein, CMC
9309 Marina Pacifica Dr. N
Long Beach, CA 90803
(562)493-5458
Fax: (562)493-5459
E-mail: norris@ctecomputer.com
Website: http://foodconsultants.com/
bernstein/

Horizon Consulting Services
1315 Garthwick Dr.
Los Altos, CA 94024
(415)967-0906
Fax: (415)967-0906

Brincko Associates Inc.
1801 Avenue of the Stars, Ste. 1054
Los Angeles, CA 90067
(310)553-4523
Fax: (310)553-6782

**Rubenstein/Justman Management
Consultants**
2049 Century Park E, 24th Fl.
Los Angeles, CA 90067
(310)282-0800
Fax: (310)282-0400
E-mail: info@rjmc.net
Website: http://www.rjmc.net

F.J. Schroeder & Associates
1926 Westholme Ave.
Los Angeles, CA 90025
(310)470-2655
Fax: (310)470-6378
E-mail: fjsacons@aol.com
Website: http://www.mcninet.com/
GlobalLook/Fjschroe.html

Western Management Associates
5959 W Century Blvd., Ste. 565
Los Angeles, CA 90045-6506
(310)645-1091
Free: (888)788-6534
Fax: (310)645-1092
E-mail: gene@cfoforrent.com
Website: http://www.cfoforrent.com

Darrell Sell and Associates
Los Gatos, CA 95030
(408)354-7794
E-mail: darrell@netcom.com

Leslie J. Zambo
3355 Michael Dr.
Marina, CA 93933
(408)384-7086

Fax: (408)647-4199
E-mail: 104776.1552@compuserve.com

Marketing Services Management
PO Box 1377
Martinez, CA 94553
(510)370-8527
Fax: (510)370-8527
E-mail: markserve@biotechnet.com

William M. Shine Consulting Service
PO Box 127
Moraga, CA 94556-0127
(510)376-6516

Palo Alto Management Group Inc.
2672 Bayshore Pky., Ste. 701
Mountain View, CA 94043
(415)968-4374
Fax: (415)968-4245
E-mail: mburwen@pamg.com

BizplanSource
1048 Irvine Ave., Ste. 621
Newport Beach, CA 92660
Free: 888-253-0974
Fax: 800-859-8254
E-mail: info@bizplansource.com
Website: http://www.bizplansource.com
Adam Greengrass, President

The Market Connection
4020 Birch St., Ste. 203
Newport Beach, CA 92660
(714)731-6273
Fax: (714)833-0253

Muller Associates
PO Box 7264
Newport Beach, CA 92658
(714)646-1169
Fax: (714)646-1169

International Health Resources
PO Box 329
North San Juan, CA 95960-0329
(530)292-1266
Fax: (530)292-1243
Website: http://www.futureof
healthcare.com

NEXUS - Consultants to Management
PO Box 1531
Novato, CA 94948
(415)897-4400
Fax: (415)898-2252
E-mail: jimnexus@aol.com

Aerospcace.Org
PO Box 28831
Oakland, CA 94604-8831

(510)530-9169
Fax: (510)530-3411
Website: http://www.aerospace.org

Intelequest Corp.
722 Gailen Ave.
Palo Alto, CA 94303
(415)968-3443
Fax: (415)493-6954
E-mail: frits@iqix.com

McLaughlin & Associates
66 San Marino Cir.
Rancho Mirage, CA 92270
(760)321-2932
Fax: (760)328-2474
E-mail: jackmcla@msn.com

**Carrera Consulting Group, a division
of Maximus**
2110 21st St., Ste. 400
Sacramento, CA 95818
(916)456-3300
Fax: (916)456-3306
E-mail: central@carreraconsulting.com
Website: http://www.carreraconsulting.com

**Bay Area Tax Consultants and Bayhill
Financial Consultants**
1150 Bayhill Dr., Ste. 1150
San Bruno, CA 94066-3004
(415)952-8786
Fax: (415)588-4524
E-mail: baytax@compuserve.com
Website: http://www.baytax.com/

AdCon Services, LLC
8871 Hillery Dr.
Dan Diego, CA 92126
(858)433-1411
E-mail: adam@adconservices.com
Website: http://www.adconservices.com
Adam Greengrass

California Business Incubation Network
101 W Broadway, No. 480
San Diego, CA 92101
(619)237-0559
Fax: (619)237-0521

G.R. Gordetsky Consultants Inc.
11414 Windy Summit Pl.
San Diego, CA 92127
(619)487-4939
Fax: (619)487-5587
E-mail: gordet@pacbell.net

Freeman, Sullivan & Co.
131 Steuart St., Ste. 500
San Francisco, CA 94105
(415)777-0707

Free: 800-777-0737
Fax: (415)777-2420
Website: http://www.fsc-research.com

Ideas Unlimited
2151 California St., Ste. 7
San Francisco, CA 94115
(415)931-0641
Fax: (415)931-0880

Russell Miller Inc.
300 Montgomery St., Ste. 900
San Francisco, CA 94104
(415)956-7474
Fax: (415)398-0620
E-mail: rmi@pacbell.net
Website: http://www.rmisf.com

PKF Consulting
425 California St., Ste. 1650
San Francisco, CA 94104
(415)421-5378
Fax: (415)956-7708
E-mail: callahan@pkfc.com
Website: http://www.pkfonline.com

Welling & Woodard Inc.
1067 Broadway
San Francisco, CA 94133
(415)776-4500
Fax: (415)776-5067

Highland Associates
16174 Highland Dr.
San Jose, CA 95127
(408)272-7008
Fax: (408)272-4040

ORDIS Inc.
6815 Trinidad Dr.
San Jose, CA 95120-2056
(408)268-3321
Free: 800-446-7347
Fax: (408)268-3582
E-mail: ordis@ordis.com
Website: http://www.ordis.com

Stanford Resources Inc.
20 Great Oaks Blvd., Ste. 200
San Jose, CA 95119
(408)360-8400
Fax: (408)360-8410
E-mail: sales@stanfordsources.com
Website: http://www.stanfordresources.com

Technology Properties Ltd. Inc.
PO Box 20250
San Jose, CA 95160
(408)243-9898
Fax: (408)296-6637
E-mail: sanjose@tplnet.com

Helfert Associates
1777 Borel Pl., Ste. 508
San Mateo, CA 94402-3514
(650)377-0540
Fax: (650)377-0472

Mykytyn Consulting Group Inc.
185 N Redwood Dr., Ste. 200
San Rafael, CA 94903
(415)491-1770
Fax: (415)491-1251
E-mail: info@mcgi.com
Website: http://www.mcgi.com

Omega Management Systems Inc.
3 Mount Darwin Ct.
San Rafael, CA 94903-1109
(415)499-1300
Fax: (415)492-9490
E-mail: omegamgt@ix.netcom.com

The Information Group Inc.
4675 Stevens Creek Blvd., Ste. 100
Santa Clara, CA 95051
(408)985-7877
Fax: (408)985-2945
E-mail: dvincent@tig-usa.com
Website: http://www.tig-usa.com

Cast Management Consultants
1620 26th St., Ste. 2040N
Santa Monica, CA 90404
(310)828-7511
Fax: (310)453-6831

Cuma Consulting Management
Box 724
Santa Rosa, CA 95402
(707)785-2477
Fax: (707)785-2478

The E-Myth Academy
131B Stony Cir., Ste. 2000
Santa Rosa, CA 95401
(707)569-5600
Free: 800-221-0266
Fax: (707)569-5700
E-mail: info@e-myth.com
Website: http://www.e-myth.com

Reilly, Connors & Ray
1743 Canyon Rd.
Spring Valley, CA 91977
(619)698-4808
Fax: (619)460-3892
E-mail: davidray@adnc.com

Management Consultants
Sunnyvale, CA 94087-4700
(408)773-0321

RJR Associates
1639 Lewiston Dr.
Sunnyvale, CA 94087
(408)737-7720
E-mail: bobroy@rjrassoc.com
Website: http://www.rjrassoc.com

Schwafel Associates
333 Cobalt Way, Ste. 21
Sunnyvale, CA 94085
(408)720-0649
Fax: (408)720-1796
E-mail: schwafel@ricochet.net
Website: http://www.patca.org

Staubs Business Services
23320 S Vermont Ave.
Torrance, CA 90502-2940
(310)830-9128
Fax: (310)830-9128
E-mail: Harry_L_Staubs@Lamg.com

Out of Your Mind... and Into the Marketplace
13381 White Sands Dr.
Tustin, CA 92780-4565
(714)544-0248
Free: 800-419-1513
Fax: (714)730-1414
E-mail: lpinson@aol.com
Website: http://www.business-plan.com

Independent Research Services
PO Box 2426
Van Nuys, CA 91404-2426
(818)993-3622

Ingman Company Inc.
7949 Woodley Ave., Ste. 120
Van Nuys, CA 91406-1232
(818)375-5027
Fax: (818)894-5001

Innovative Technology Associates
3639 E Harbor Blvd., Ste. 203E
Ventura, CA 93001
(805)650-9353

Grid Technology Associates
20404 Tufts Cir.
Walnut, CA 91789
(909)444-0922
Fax: (909)444-0922
E-mail: grid_technology@msn.com

Ridge Consultants Inc.
100 Pringle Ave., Ste. 580
Walnut Creek, CA 94596
(925)274-1990
Fax: (510)274-1956
E-mail: info@ridgecon.com
Website: http://www.ridgecon.com

Bell Springs Publishing
PO Box 1240
Willits, CA 95490
(707)459-6372
E-mail: bellsprings@sabernet
Website: http://www.bellsprings.com

Hutchinson Consulting and Appraisal
23245 Sylvan St., Ste. 103
Woodland Hills, CA 91367
(818)888-8175
Free: 800-977-7548
Fax: (818)888-8220
E-mail: r.f.hutchinson-cpa@worldnet.
att.net

Colorado

Sam Boyer & Associates
4255 S Buckley Rd., No. 136
Aurora, CO 80013
Free: 800-785-0485
Fax: (303)766-8740
E-mail: samboyer@samboyer.com
Website: http://www.samboyer.com/

Ameriwest Business Consultants Inc.
PO Box 26266
Colorado Springs, CO 80936
(719)380-7096
Fax: (719)380-7096
E-mail: email@abchelp.com
Website: http://www.abchelp.com

GVNW Consulting Inc.
2270 La Montana Way
Colorado Springs, CO 80936
(719)594-5800
Fax: (719)594-5803
Website: http://www.gvnw.com

M-Squared Inc.
755 San Gabriel Pl.
Colorado Springs, CO 80906
(719)576-2554
Fax: (719)576-2554

Thornton Financial FNIC
1024 Centre Ave., Bldg. E
Fort Collins, CO 80526-1849
(970)221-2089
Fax: (970)484-5206

TenEyck Associates
1760 Cherryville Rd.
Greenwood Village, CO 80121-1503
(303)758-6129
Fax: (303)761-8286

Associated Enterprises Ltd.
13050 W Ceder Dr., Unit 11
Lakewood, CO 80228

(303)988-6695
Fax: (303)988-6739
E-mail: ael1@classic.msn.com

The Vincent Company Inc.
200 Union Blvd., Ste. 210
Lakewood, CO 80228
(303)989-7271
Free: 800-274-0733
Fax: (303)989-7570
E-mail: vincent@vincentco.com
Website: http://www.vincentco.com

Johnson & West Management Consultants Inc.
7612 S Logan Dr.
Littleton, CO 80122
(303)730-2810
Fax: (303)730-3219

Western Capital Holdings Inc.
10050 E Applwood Dr.
Parker, CO 80138
(303)841-1022
Fax: (303)770-1945

Connecticut

Stratman Group Inc.
40 Tower Ln.
Avon, CT 06001-4222
(860)677-2898
Free: 800-551-0499
Fax: (860)677-8210

Cowherd Consulting Group Inc.
106 Stephen Mather Rd.
Darien, CT 06820
(203)655-2150
Fax: (203)655-6427

Greenwich Associates
8 Greenwich Office Park
Greenwich, CT 06831-5149
(203)629-1200
Fax: (203)629-1229
E-mail: lisa@greenwich.com
Website: http://www.greenwich.com

Follow-up News
185 Pine St., Ste. 818
Manchester, CT 06040
(860)647-7542
Free: 800-708-0696
Fax: (860)646-6544
E-mail: Followupnews@aol.com

Lovins & Associates Consulting
309 Edwards St.
New Haven, CT 06511
(203)787-3367

Fax: (203)624-7599
E-mail: Alovinsphd@aol.com
Website: http://www.lovinsgroup.com

JC Ventures Inc.
4 Arnold St.
Old Greenwich, CT 06870-1203
(203)698-1990
Free: 800-698-1997
Fax: (203)698-2638

Charles L. Hornung Associates
52 Ned's Mountain Rd.
Ridgefield, CT 06877
(203)431-0297

Manus
100 Prospect St., S Tower
Stamford, CT 06901
(203)326-3880
Free: 800-445-0942
Fax: (203)326-3890
E-mail: manus1@aol.com
Website: http://www.RightManus.com

RealBusinessPlans.com
156 Westport Rd.
Wilton, CT 06897
(914)837-2886
E-mail: ct@realbusinessplans.com
Website: http://www.RealBusinessPlans.com
Tony Tecce

Delaware

Focus Marketing
61-7 Habor Dr.
Claymont, DE 19703
(302)793-3064

Daedalus Ventures Ltd.
PO Box 1474
Hockessin, DE 19707
(302)239-6758
Fax: (302)239-9991
E-mail: daedalus@mail.del.net

The Formula Group
PO Box 866
Hockessin, DE 19707
(302)456-0952
Fax: (302)456-1354
E-mail: formula@netaxs.com

Selden Enterprises Inc.
2502 Silverside Rd., Ste. 1
Wilmington, DE 19810-3740
(302)529-7113
Fax: (302)529-7442
E-mail: selden2@bellatlantic.net
Website: http://www.seldenenterprises.com

District of Columbia

Bruce W. McGee and Associates
7826 Eastern Ave. NW, Ste. 30
Washington, DC 20012
(202)726-7272
Fax: (202)726-2946

McManis Associates Inc.
1900 K St. NW, Ste. 700
Washington, DC 20006
(202)466-7680
Fax: (202)872-1898
Website: http://www.mcmanis-mmi.com

Smith, Dawson & Andrews Inc.
1000 Connecticut Ave., Ste. 302
Washington, DC 20036
(202)835-0740
Fax: (202)775-8526
E-mail: webmaster@sda-inc.com
Website: http://www.sda-inc.com

Florida

BackBone, Inc.
20404 Hacienda Court
Boca Raton, FL 33498
(561)470-0965
Fax: 516-908-4038
E-mail: BPlans@backboneinc.com
Website: http://www.backboneinc.com
Charles Epstein, President

Whalen & Associates Inc.
4255 Northwest 26 Ct.
Boca Raton, FL 33434
(561)241-5950
Fax: (561)241-7414
E-mail: drwhalen@ix.netcom.com

E.N. Rysso & Associates
180 Bermuda Petrel Ct.
Daytona Beach, FL 32119
(386)760-3028
E-mail: erysso@aol.com

Virtual Technocrats LLC
560 Lavers Circle, #146
Delray Beach, FL 33444
(561)265-3509
E-mail: josh@virtualtechnocrats.com;
info@virtualtechnocrats.com
Website: http://www.virtualtechno
crats.com
Josh Eikov, Managing Director

Eric Sands Consulting Services
6193 Rock Island Rd., Ste. 412
Fort Lauderdale, FL 33319
(954)721-4767

Fax: (954)720-2815
E-mail: easands@aol.com
Website: http://www.ericsandsconsultig.com

Professional Planning Associates, Inc.
1975 E. Sunrise Blvd. Suite 607
Fort Lauderdale, FL 33304
(954)764-5204
Fax: 954-463-4172
E-mail: Mgoldstein@proplana.com
Website: http://proplana.com
Michael Goldstein, President

Host Media Corp.
3948 S 3rd St., Ste. 191
Jacksonville Beach, FL 32250
(904)285-3239
Fax: (904)285-5618
E-mail: msconsulting@compuserve.com
Website: http://www.media
servicesgroup.com

William V. Hall
1925 Brickell, Ste. D-701
Miami, FL 33129
(305)856-9622
Fax: (305)856-4113
E-mail: williamvhall@compuserve.com

F.A. McGee Inc.
800 Claughton Island Dr., Ste. 401
Miami, FL 33131
(305)377-9123

Taxplan Inc.
Mirasol International Ctr.
2699 Collins Ave.
Miami Beach, FL 33140
(305)538-3303

T.C. Brown & Associates
8415 Excalibur Cir., Apt. B1
Naples, FL 34108
(941)594-1949
Fax: (941)594-0611
E-mail: tcater@naples.net.com

RLA International Consulting
713 Lagoon Dr.
North Palm Beach, FL 33408
(407)626-4258
Fax: (407)626-5772

Comprehensive Franchising Inc.
2465 Ridgecrest Ave.
Orange Park, FL 32065
(904)272-6567
Free: 800-321-6567
Fax: (904)272-6750
E-mail: theimp@cris.com
Website: http://www.franchise411.com

Hunter G. Jackson Jr. - Consulting Environmental Physicist
PO Box 618272
Orlando, FL 32861-8272
(407)295-4188
E-mail: hunterjackson@juno.com

F. Newton Parks
210 El Brillo Way
Palm Beach, FL 33480
(561)833-1727
Fax: (561)833-4541

Avery Business Development Services
2506 St. Michel Ct.
Ponte Vedra Beach, FL 32082
(904)285-6033
Fax: (904)285-6033

Strategic Business Planning Co.
PO Box 821006
South Florida, FL 33082-1006
(954)704-9100
Fax: (954)438-7333
E-mail: info@bizplan.com
Website: http://www.bizplan.com

Dufresne Consulting Group Inc.
10014 N Dale Mabry, Ste. 101
Tampa, FL 33618-4426
(813)264-4775
Fax: (813)264-9300
Website: http://www.dcgconsult.com

Agrippa Enterprises Inc.
PO Box 175
Venice, FL 34284-0175
(941)355-7876
E-mail: webservices@agrippa.com
Website: http://www.agrippa.com

Center for Simplified Strategic Planning Inc.
PO Box 3324
Vero Beach, FL 32964-3324
(561)231-3636
Fax: (561)231-1099
Website: http://www.cssp.com

Georgia

Marketing Spectrum Inc.
115 Perimeter Pl., Ste. 440
Atlanta, GA 30346
(770)395-7244
Fax: (770)393-4071

Business Ventures Corp.
1650 Oakbrook Dr., Ste. 405
Norcross, GA 30093
(770)729-8000
Fax: (770)729-8028

Informed Decisions Inc.
100 Falling Cheek
Sautee Nacoochee, GA 30571
(706)878-1905
Fax: (706)878-1802
E-mail: skylake@compuserve.com

Tom C. Davis & Associates, P.C.
3189 Perimeter Rd.
Valdosta, GA 31602
(912)247-9801
Fax: (912)244-7704
E-mail: mail@tcdcpa.com
Website: http://www.tcdcpa.com/

Illinois

TWD and Associates
431 S Patton
Arlington Heights, IL 60005
(847)398-6410
Fax: (847)255-5095
E-mail: tdoo@aol.com

Management Planning Associates Inc.
2275 Half Day Rd., Ste. 350
Bannockburn, IL 60015-1277
(847)945-2421
Fax: (847)945-2425

Phil Faris Associates
86 Old Mill Ct.
Barrington, IL 60010
(847)382-4888
Fax: (847)382-4890
E-mail: pfaris@meginsnet.net

Seven Continents Technology
787 Stonebridge
Buffalo Grove, IL 60089
(708)577-9653
Fax: (708)870-1220

Grubb & Blue Inc.
2404 Windsor Pl.
Champaign, IL 61820
(217)366-0052
Fax: (217)356-0117

ACE Accounting Service Inc.
3128 N Bernard St.
Chicago, IL 60618
(773)463-7854
Fax: (773)463-7854

AON Consulting Worldwide
200 E Randolph St., 10th Fl.
Chicago, IL 60601
(312)381-4800
Free: 800-438-6487
Fax: (312)381-0240
Website: http://www.aon.com

FMS Consultants
5801 N Sheridan Rd., Ste. 3D
Chicago, IL 60660
(773)561-7362
Fax: (773)561-6274

Grant Thornton
800 1 Prudential Plz.
130 E Randolph St.
Chicago, IL 60601
(312)856-0001
Fax: (312)861-1340
E-mail: gtinfo@gt.com
Website: http://www.grantthornton.com

Kingsbury International Ltd.
5341 N Glenwood Ave.
Chicago, IL 60640
(773)271-3030
Fax: (773)728-7080
E-mail: jetlag@mcs.com
Website: http://www.kingbiz.com

MacDougall & Blake Inc.
1414 N Wells St., Ste. 311
Chicago, IL 60610-1306
(312)587-3330
Fax: (312)587-3699
E-mail: jblake@compuserve.com

James C. Osburn Ltd.
6445 N. Western Ave., Ste. 304
Chicago, IL 60645
(773)262-4428
Fax: (773)262-6755
E-mail: osburnltd@aol.com

Tarifero & Tazewell Inc.
211 S Clark
Chicago, IL 60690
(312)665-9714
Fax: (312)665-9716

Human Energy Design Systems
620 Roosevelt Dr.
Edwardsville, IL 62025
(618)692-0258
Fax: (618)692-0819

China Business Consultants Group
931 Dakota Cir.
Naperville, IL 60563
(630)778-7992
Fax: (630)778-7915
E-mail: cbcq@aol.com

Center for Workforce Effectiveness
500 Skokie Blvd., Ste. 222
Northbrook, IL 60062
(847)559-8777
Fax: (847)559-8778

E-mail: office@cwelink.com
Website: http://www.cwelink.com

Smith Associates
1320 White Mountain Dr.
Northbrook, IL 60062
(847)480-7200
Fax: (847)480-9828

Francorp Inc.
20200 Governors Dr.
Olympia Fields, IL 60461
(708)481-2900
Free: 800-372-6244
Fax: (708)481-5885
E-mail: francorp@aol.com
Website: http://www.francorpinc.com

Camber Business Strategy Consultants
1010 S Plum Tree Ct
Palatine, IL 60078-0986
(847)202-0101
Fax: (847)705-7510
E-mail: camber@ameritech.net

Partec Enterprise Group
5202 Keith Dr.
Richton Park, IL 60471
(708)503-4047
Fax: (708)503-9468

Rockford Consulting Group Ltd.
Century Plz., Ste. 206
7210 E State St.
Rockford, IL 61108
(815)229-2900
Free: 800-667-7495
Fax: (815)229-2612
E-mail: rligus@RockfordConsulting.com
Website: http://www.Rockford
Consulting.com

RSM McGladrey Inc.
1699 E Woodfield Rd., Ste. 300
Schaumburg, IL 60173-4969
(847)413-6900
Fax: (847)517-7067
Website: http://www.rsmmcgladrey.com

A.D. Star Consulting
320 Euclid
Winnetka, IL 60093
(847)446-7827
Fax: (847)446-7827
E-mail: startwo@worldnet.att.net

Indiana

Modular Consultants Inc.
3109 Crabtree Ln.
Elkhart, IN 46514

(219)264-5761
Fax: (219)264-5761
E-mail: sasabo5313@aol.com

Midwest Marketing Research
PO Box 1077
Goshen, IN 46527
(219)533-0548
Fax: (219)533-0540
E-mail: 103365.654@compuserve

Ketchum Consulting Group
8021 Knue Rd., Ste. 112
Indianapolis, IN 46250
(317)845-5411
Fax: (317)842-9941

MDI Management Consulting
1519 Park Dr.
Munster, IN 46321
(219)838-7909
Fax: (219)838-7909

Iowa

McCord Consulting Group Inc.
4533 Pine View Dr. NE
PO Box 11024
Cedar Rapids, IA 52410
(319)378-0077
Fax: (319)378-1577
E-mail: smmccord@hom.com
Website: http://www.mccordgroup.com

Management Solutions L.C.
3815 Lincoln Pl. Dr.
Des Moines, IA 50312
(515)277-6408
Fax: (515)277-3506
E-mail: wasunimers@uswest.net

Grandview Marketing
15 Red Bridge Dr.
Sioux City, IA 51104
(712)239-3122
Fax: (712)258-7578
E-mail: eandrews@pionet.net

Kansas

Assessments in Action
513A N Mur-Len
Olathe, KS 66062
(913)764-6270
Free: (888)548-1504
Fax: (913)764-6495
E-mail: lowdene@qni.com
Website: http://www.assessments-in-action.com

Maine

Edgemont Enterprises
PO Box 8354
Portland, ME 04104
(207)871-8964
Fax: (207)871-8964

Pan Atlantic Consultants
5 Milk St.
Portland, ME 04101
(207)871-8622
Fax: (207)772-4842
E-mail: pmurphy@maine.rr.com
Website: http://www.panatlantic.net

Maryland

Clemons & Associates Inc.
5024-R Campbell Blvd.
Baltimore, MD 21236
(410)931-8100
Fax: (410)931-8111
E-mail: info@clemonsmgmt.com
Website: http://www.clemonsmgmt.com

Imperial Group Ltd.
305 Washington Ave., Ste. 204
Baltimore, MD 21204-6009
(410)337-8500
Fax: (410)337-7641

Leadership Institute
3831 Yolando Rd.
Baltimore, MD 21218
(410)366-9111
Fax: (410)243-8478
E-mail: behconsult@aol.com

Burdeshaw Associates Ltd.
4701 Sangamore Rd.
Bethesda, MD 20816-2508
(301)229-5800
Fax: (301)229-5045
E-mail: jstacy@burdeshaw.com
Website: http://www.burdeshaw.com

Michael E. Cohen
5225 Pooks Hill Rd., Ste. 1119 S
Bethesda, MD 20814
(301)530-5738
Fax: (301)530-2988
E-mail: mecohen@crosslink.net

World Development Group Inc.
5272 River Rd., Ste. 650
Bethesda, MD 20816-1405
(301)652-1818
Fax: (301)652-1250
E-mail: wdg@has.com
Website: http://www.worlddg.com

Swartz Consulting
PO Box 4301
Crofton, MD 21114-4301
(301)262-6728

Software Solutions International Inc.
9633 Duffer Way
Gaithersburg, MD 20886
(301)330-4136
Fax: (301)330-4136

Strategies Inc.
8 Park Center Ct., Ste. 200
Owings Mills, MD 21117
(410)363-6669
Fax: (410)363-1231
E-mail: strategies@strat1.com
Website: http://www.strat1.com

Hammer Marketing Resources
179 Inverness Rd.
Severna Park, MD 21146
(410)544-9191
Fax: (305)675-3277
E-mail: info@gohammer.com
Website: http://www.gohammer.com

Andrew Sussman & Associates
13731 Kretsinger
Smithsburg, MD 21783
(301)824-2943
Fax: (301)824-2943

Massachusetts

Geibel Marketing and Public Relations
PO Box 611
Belmont, MA 02478-0005
(617)484-8285
Fax: (617)489-3567
E-mail: jgeibel@geibelpr.com
Website: http://www.geibelpr.com

Bain & Co.
2 Copley Pl.
Boston, MA 02116
(617)572-2000
Fax: (617)572-2427
E-mail: corporate.inquiries@bain.com
Website: http://www.bain.com

Mehr & Co.
62 Kinnaird St.
Cambridge, MA 02139
(617)876-3311
Fax: (617)876-3023
E-mail: mehrco@aol.com

Monitor Company Inc.
2 Canal Park
Cambridge, MA 02141

(617)252-2000
Fax: (617)252-2100
Website: http://www.monitor.com

Information & Research Associates
PO Box 3121
Framingham, MA 01701
(508)788-0784

Walden Consultants Ltd.
252 Pond St.
Hopkinton, MA 01748
(508)435-4882
Fax: (508)435-3971
Website: http://www.waldencon
sultants.com

Jeffrey D. Marshall
102 Mitchell Rd.
Ipswich, MA 01938-1219
(508)356-1113
Fax: (508)356-2989

Consulting Resources Corp.
6 Northbrook Park
Lexington, MA 02420
(781)863-1222
Fax: (781)863-1441
E-mail: res@consultingresources.net
Website: http://www.consulting
resources.net

Planning Technologies Group L.L.C.
92 Hayden Ave.
Lexington, MA 02421
(781)778-4678
Fax: (781)861-1099
E-mail: ptg@plantech.com
Website: http://www.plantech.com

Kalba International Inc.
23 Sandy Pond Rd.
Lincoln, MA 01773
(781)259-9589
Fax: (781)259-1460
E-mail: info@kalbainternational.com
Website: http://www.kalbainter
national.com

VMB Associates Inc.
115 Ashland St.
Melrose, MA 02176
(781)665-0623
Fax: (425)732-7142
E-mail: vmbinc@aol.com

The Company Doctor
14 Pudding Stone Ln.
Mendon, MA 01756
(508)478-1747
Fax: (508)478-0520

Data and Strategies Group Inc.
190 N Main St.
Natick, MA 01760
(508)653-9990
Fax: (508)653-7799
E-mail: dsginc@dsggroup.com
Website: http://www.dsggroup.com

The Enterprise Group
73 Parker Rd.
Needham, MA 02494
(617)444-6631
Fax: (617)433-9991
E-mail: lsacco@world.std.com
Website: http://www.enterprise-group.com

PSMJ Resources Inc.
10 Midland Ave.
Newton, MA 02458
(617)965-0055
Free: 800-537-7765
Fax: (617)965-5152
E-mail: psmj@tiac.net
Website: http://www.psmj.com

Scheur Management Group Inc.
255 Washington St., Ste. 100
Newton, MA 02458-1611
(617)969-7500
Fax: (617)969-7508
E-mail: smgnow@scheur.com
Website: http://www.scheur.com

I.E.E.E., Boston Section
240 Bear Hill Rd., 202B
Waltham, MA 02451-1017
(781)890-5294
Fax: (781)890-5290

**Business Planning and Consulting
Services**
20 Beechwood Ter.
Wellesley, MA 02482
(617)237-9151
Fax: (617)237-9151

Michigan

Walter Frederick Consulting
1719 South Blvd.
Ann Arbor, MI 48104
(313)662-4336
Fax: (313)769-7505

Fox Enterprises
6220 W Freeland Rd.
Freeland, MI 48623
(517)695-9170
Fax: (517)695-9174
E-mail: foxjw@concentric.net
Website: http://www.cris.com/~foxjw

G.G.W. and Associates
1213 Hampton
Jackson, MI 49203
(517)782-2255
Fax: (517)782-2255

Altamar Group Ltd.
6810 S Cedar, Ste. 2-B
Lansing, MI 48911
(517)694-0910
Free: 800-443-2627
Fax: (517)694-1377

Sheffieck Consultants Inc.
23610 Greening Dr.
Novi, MI 48375-3130
(248)347-3545
Fax: (248)347-3530
E-mail: cfsheff@concentric.net

Rehmann, Robson PC
5800 Gratiot
Saginaw, MI 48605
(517)799-9580
Fax: (517)799-0227
Website: http://www.rrpc.com

Francis & Co.
17200 W 10 Mile Rd., Ste. 207
Southfield, MI 48075
(248)559-7600
Fax: (248)559-5249

Private Ventures Inc.
16000 W 9 Mile Rd., Ste. 504
Southfield, MI 48075
(248)569-1977
Free: 800-448-7614
Fax: (248)569-1838
E-mail: pventuresi@aol.com

JGK Associates
14464 Kerner Dr.
Sterling Heights, MI 48313
(810)247-9055
Fax: (248)822-4977
E-mail: kozlowski@home.com

Minnesota

Health Fitness Corp.
3500 W 80th St., Ste. 130
Bloomington, MN 55431
(612)831-6830
Fax: (612)831-7264

Consatech Inc.
PO Box 1047
Burnsville, MN 55337
(612)953-1088
Fax: (612)435-2966

Robert F. Knotek
14960 Ironwood Ct.
Eden Prairie, MN 55346
(612)949-2875

DRI Consulting
7715 Stonewood Ct.
Edina, MN 55439
(612)941-9656
Fax: (612)941-2693
E-mail: dric@dric.com
Website: http://www.dric.com

Markin Consulting
12072 87th Pl. N
Maple Grove, MN 55369
(612)493-3568
Fax: (612)493-5744
E-mail: markin@markinconsulting.com
Website: http://www.markin
consulting.com

Minnesota Cooperation Office for Small Business & Job Creation Inc.
5001 W 80th St., Ste. 825
Minneapolis, MN 55437
(612)830-1230
Fax: (612)830-1232
E-mail: mncoop@msn.com
Website: http://www.mnco.org

Enterprise Consulting Inc.
PO Box 1111
Minnetonka, MN 55345
(612)949-5909
Fax: (612)906-3965

Amdahl International
724 1st Ave. SW
Rochester, MN 55902
(507)252-0402
Fax: (507)252-0402
E-mail: amdahl@best-service.com
Website: http://www.wp.com/amdahl_int

Power Systems Research
1365 Corporate Center Curve, 2nd Fl.
St. Paul, MN 55121
(612)905-8400
Free: (888)625-8612
Fax: (612)454-0760
E-mail: Barb@Powersys.com
Website: http://www.powersys.com

Missouri

Business Planning and Development Corp.
4030 Charlotte St.
Kansas City, MO 64110
(816)753-0495

E-mail: humph@bpdev.demon.co.uk
Website: http://www.bpdev.demon.co.uk

CFO Service
10336 Donoho
St. Louis, MO 63131
(314)750-2940
E-mail: jskae@cfoservice.com
Website: http://www.cfoservice.com

Nebraska

International Management Consulting Group Inc.
1309 Harlan Dr., Ste. 205
Bellevue, NE 68005
(402)291-4545
Frcc: 800-665-IMCG
Fax: (402)291-4343
E-mail: imcg@neonramp.com
Website: http://www.mgtcon
sulting.com

Heartland Management Consulting Group
1904 Barrington Pky.
Papillion, NE 68046
(402)339-2387
Fax: (402)339-1319

Nevada

The DuBois Group
865 Tahoe Blvd., Ste. 108
Incline Village, NV 89451
(775)832-0550
Free: 800-375-2935
Fax: (775)832-0556
E-mail: DuBoisGrp@aol.com

New Hampshire

Wolff Consultants
10 Buck Rd.
Hanover, NH 03755
(603)643-6015

BPT Consulting Associates Ltd.
12 Parmenter Rd., Ste. B-6
Londonderry, NH 03053
(603)437-8484
Free: (888)278-0030
Fax: (603)434-5388
E-mail: bptcons@tiac.net
Website: http://www.bptconsulting.com

New Jersey

Bedminster Group Inc.
1170 Rte. 22 E
Bridgewater, NJ 08807

(908)500-4155
Fax: (908)766-0780
E-mail: info@bedminstergroup.com
Website: http://www.bedminster
group.com
Fax: (202)806-1777
Terry Strong, Acting Regional Dir.

Delta Planning Inc.
PO Box 425
Denville, NJ 07834
(913)625-1742
Free: 800-672-0762
Fax: (973)625-3531
E-mail: DeltaP@worldnet.att.net
Website: http://deltaplanning.com

Kumar Associates Inc.
1004 Cumbermeade Rd.
Fort Lee, NJ 07024
(201)224-9480
Fax: (201)585-2343
E-mail: mail@kumarassociates.com
Website: http://kumarassociates.com

John Hall & Company Inc.
PO Box 187
Glen Ridge, NJ 07028
(973)680-4449
Fax: (973)680-4581
E-mail: jhcompany@aol.com

Market Focus
PO Box 402
Maplewood, NJ 07040
(973)378-2470
Fax: (973)378-2470
E-mail: mcss66@marketfocus.com

Vanguard Communications Corp.
100 American Rd.
Morris Plains, NJ 07950
(973)605-8000
Fax: (973)605-8329
Website: http://www.vanguard.net/

ConMar International Ltd.
1901 US Hwy. 130
North Brunswick, NJ 08902
(732)940-8347
Fax: (732)274-1199

KLW New Products
156 Cedar Dr.
Old Tappan, NJ 07675
(201)358-1300
Fax: (201)664-2594
E-mail: lrlarsen@usa.net
Website: http://www.klwnew
products.com

PA Consulting Group
315A Enterprise Dr.
Plainsboro, NJ 08536
(609)936-8300
Fax: (609)936-8811
E-mail: info@paconsulting.com
Website: http://www.pa-consulting.com

Aurora Marketing Management Inc.
66 Witherspoon St., Ste. 600
Princeton, NJ 08542
(908)904-1125
Fax: (908)359-1108
E-mail: aurora2@voicenet.com
Website: http://www.auroramarketing.net

Smart Business Supersite
88 Orchard Rd., CN-5219
Princeton, NJ 08543
(908)321-1924
Fax: (908)321-5156
E-mail: irv@smartbiz.com
Website: http://www.smartbiz.com

Tracelin Associates
1171 Main St., Ste. 6K
Rahway, NJ 07065
(732)381-3288

Schkeeper Inc.
130-6 Bodman Pl.
Red Bank, NJ 07701
(732)219-1965
Fax: (732)530-3703

Henry Branch Associates
2502 Harmon Cove Twr.
Secaucus, NJ 07094
(201)866-2008
Fax: (201)601-0101
E-mail: hbranch161@home.com

Robert Gibbons & Company Inc.
46 Knoll Rd.
Tenafly, NJ 07670-1050
(201)871-3933
Fax: (201)871-2173
E-mail: crisisbob@aol.com

PMC Management Consultants Inc.
6 Thistle Ln.
Three Bridges, NJ 08887-0332
(908)788-1014
Free: 800-PMC-0250
Fax: (908)806-7287
E-mail: int@pmc-management.com
Website: http://www.pmc-management.com

R.W. Bankart & Associates
20 Valley Ave., Ste. D-2
Westwood, NJ 07675-3607
(201)664-7672

New Mexico

Vondle & Associates Inc.
4926 Calle de Tierra, NE
Albuquerque, NM 87111
(505)292-8961
Fax: (505)296-2790
E-mail: vondle@aol.com

InfoNewMexico
2207 Black Hills Rd., NE
Rio Rancho, NM 87124
(505)891-2462
Fax: (505)896-8971

New York

Powers Research and Training Institute
PO Box 78
Bayville, NY 11709
(516)628-2250
Fax: (516)628-2252
E-mail: powercocch@compuserve.com
Website: http://www.nancypowers.com

Consortium House
296 Wittenberg Rd.
Bearsville, NY 12409
(845)679-8867
Fax: (845)679-9248
E-mail: eugenegs@aol.com
Website: http://www.chpub.com

Progressive Finance Corp.
3549 Tiemann Ave.
Bronx, NY 10469
(718)405-9029
Free: 800-225-8381
Fax: (718)405-1170

Wave Hill Associates Inc.
2621 Palisade Ave., Ste. 15-C
Bronx, NY 10463
(718)549-7368
Fax: (718)601-9670
E-mail: pepper@compuserve.com

Management Insight
96 Arlington Rd.
Buffalo, NY 14221
(716)631-3319
Fax: (716)631-0203
E-mail: michalski@foodservice insight.com
Website: http://www.foodservice insight.com

Samani International Enterprises, Marions Panyaught Consultancy
2028 Parsons
Flushing, NY 11357-3436
(917)287-8087
Fax: 800-873-8939
E-mail: vjp2@biostrategist.com
Website: http://www.biostrategist.com

Marketing Resources Group
71-58 Austin St.
Forest Hills, NY 11375
(718)261-8882

Mangabay Business Plans & Development Subsidiary of Innis Asset Allocation
125-10 Queens Blvd., Ste. 2202
Kew Gardens, NY 11415
(905)527-1947
Fax: 509-472-1935
E-mail: mangabay@mangabay.com
Website: http://www.mangabay.com
Lee Toh, Managing Partner

ComputerEase Co.
1301 Monmouth Ave.
Lakewood, NY 08701
(212)406-9464
Fax: (914)277-5317
E-mail: crawfordc@juno.com

Boice Dunham Group
30 W 13th St.
New York, NY 10011
(212)924-2200
Fax: (212)924-1108

Elizabeth Capen
27 E 95th St.
New York, NY 10128
(212)427-7654
Fax: (212)876-3190

Haver Analytics
60 E 42nd St., Ste. 2424
New York, NY 10017
(212)986-9300
Fax: (212)986-5857
E-mail: data@haver.com
Website: http://www.haver.com

The Jordan, Edmiston Group Inc.
150 E 52nd Ave., 18th Fl.
New York, NY 10022
(212)754-0710
Fax: (212)754-0337

KPMG International
345 Park Ave.
New York, NY 10154-0102
(212)758-9700

Fax: (212)758-9819
Website: http://www.kpmg.com

Mahoney Cohen Consulting Corp.
111 W 40th St., 12th Fl.
New York, NY 10018
(212)490-8000
Fax: (212)790-5913

Management Practice Inc.
342 Madison Ave.
New York, NY 10173-1230
(212)867-7948
Fax: (212)972-5188
Website: http://www.mpiweb.com

Moseley Associates Inc.
342 Madison Ave., Ste. 1414
New York, NY 10016
(212)213-6673
Fax: (212)687-1520

Practice Development Counsel
60 Sutton Pl. S
New York, NY 10022
(212)593-1549
Fax: (212)980-7940
E-mail: pwhaserot@pdcounsel.com
Website: http://www.pdcounsel.com

Unique Value International Inc.
575 Madison Ave., 10th Fl.
New York, NY 10022-1304
(212)605-0590
Fax: (212)605-0589

The Van Tulleken Co.
126 E 56th St.
New York, NY 10022
(212)355-1390
Fax: (212)755-3061
E-mail: newyork@vantulleken.com

Vencon Management Inc.
301 W 53rd St.
New York, NY 10019
(212)581-8787
Fax: (212)397-4126
Website: http://www.venconinc.com

Werner International Inc.
55 E 52nd, 29th Fl.
New York, NY 10055
(212)909-1260
Fax: (212)909-1273
E-mail: richard.downing@rgh.com
Website: http://www.wernertex.com

Zimmerman Business Consulting Inc.
44 E 92nd St., Ste. 5-B
New York, NY 10128

(212)860-3107
Fax: (212)860-7730
E-mail: ljzzbci@aol.com
Website: http://www.zbcinc.com

Overton Financial
7 Allen Rd.
Peekskill, NY 10566
(914)737-4649
Fax: (914)737-4696

Stromberg Consulting
2500 Westchester Ave.
Purchase, NY 10577
(914)251-1515
Fax: (914)251-1562
E-mail: strategy@stromberg_consulting.com
Website: http://www.stromberg_consulting.com

Innovation Management Consulting Inc.
209 Dewitt Rd.
Syracuse, NY 13214-2006
(315)425-5144
Fax: (315)445-8989
E-mail: missonneb@axess.net

M. Clifford Agress
891 Fulton St.
Valley Stream, NY 11580
(516)825-8955
Fax: (516)825-8955

Destiny Kinal Marketing Consultancy
105 Chemung St.
Waverly, NY 14892
(607)565-8317
Fax: (607)565-4083

Valutis Consulting Inc.
5350 Main St., Ste. 7
Williamsville, NY 14221-5338
(716)634-2553
Fax: (716)634-2554
E-mail: valutis@localnet.com
Website: http://www.valutisconsulting.com

North Carolina

Best Practices L.L.C.
6320 Quadrangle Dr., Ste. 200
Chapel Hill, NC 27514
(919)403-0251
Fax: (919)403-0144
E-mail: best@best:in/class
Website: http://www.best-in-class.com

Norelli & Co.
Bank of America Corporate Ctr.
100 N Tyron St., Ste. 5160

Charlotte, NC 28202-4000
(704)376-5484
Fax: (704)376-5485
E-mail: consult@norelli.com
Website: http://www.norelli.com

North Dakota

Center for Innovation
4300 Dartmouth Dr.
PO Box 8372
Grand Forks, ND 58202
(701)777-3132
Fax: (701)777-2339
E-mail: bruce@innovators.net
Website: http://www.innovators.net

Ohio

Transportation Technology Services
208 Harmon Rd.
Aurora, OH 44202
(330)562-3596

Empro Systems Inc.
4777 Red Bank Expy., Ste. 1
Cincinnati, OH 45227-1542
(513)271-2042
Fax: (513)271-2042

Alliance Management International Ltd.
1440 Windrow Ln.
Cleveland, OH 44147-3200
(440)838-1922
Fax: (440)838-0979
E-mail: bgruss@amiltd.com
Website: http://www.amiltd.com

Bozell Kamstra Public Relations
1301 E 9th St., Ste. 3400
Cleveland, OH 44114
(216)623-1511
Fax: (216)623-1501
E-mail: jfeniger@cleveland.bozellkamstra.com
Website: http://www.bozellkamstra.com

Cory Dillon Associates
111 Schreyer Pl. E
Columbus, OH 43214
(614)262-8211
Fax: (614)262-3806

Holcomb Gallagher Adams
300 Marconi, Ste. 303
Columbus, OH 43215
(614)221-3343
Fax: (614)221-3367
E-mail: riadams@acme.freenet.oh.us

Young & Associates
PO Box 711
Kent, OH 44240
(330)678-0524
Free: 800-525-9775
Fax: (330)678-6219
E-mail: online@younginc.com
Website: http://www.younginc.com

Robert A. Westman & Associates
8981 Inversary Dr. SE
Warren, OH 44484-2551
(330)856-4149
Fax: (330)856-2564

Oklahoma

Innovative Partners L.L.C.
4900 Richmond Sq., Ste. 100
Oklahoma City, OK 73118
(405)840-0033
Fax: (405)843-8359
E-mail: ipartners@juno.com

Oregon

INTERCON - The International Converting Institute
5200 Badger Rd.
Crooked River Ranch, OR 97760
(541)548-1447
Fax: (541)548-1618
E-mail: johnbowler@
crookedriverranch.com

Talbott ARM
HC 60, Box 5620
Lakeview, OR 97630
(541)635-8587
Fax: (503)947-3482

Management Technology Associates Ltd.
2768 SW Sherwood Dr, Ste. 105
Portland, OR 97201-2251
(503)224-5220
Fax: (503)224-5334
E-mail: lcuster@mta-ltd.com
Website: http://www.mgmt-tech.com

Pennsylvania

Healthscope Inc.
400 Lancaster Ave.
Devon, PA 19333
(610)687-6199
Fax: (610)687-6376
E-mail: health@voicenet.com
Website: http://www.healthscope.net/

Elayne Howard & Associates Inc.
3501 Masons Mill Rd., Ste. 501

Huntingdon Valley, PA 19006-3509
(215)657-9550

GRA Inc.
115 West Ave., Ste. 201
Jenkintown, PA 19046
(215)884-7500
Fax: (215)884-1385
E-mail: gramail@gra-inc.com
Website: http://www.gra-inc.com

Mifflin County Industrial Development Corp.
Mifflin County Industrial Plz.
6395 SR 103 N
Bldg. 50
Lewistown, PA 17044
(717)242-0393
Fax: (717)242-1842
E-mail: mcide@acsworld.net

Autech Products
1289 Revere Rd.
Morrisville, PA 19067
(215)493-3759
Fax: (215)493-9791
E-mail: autech4@yahoo.com

Advantage Associates
434 Avon Dr.
Pittsburgh, PA 15228
(412)343-1558
Fax: (412)362-1684
E-mail: ecocba1@aol.com

Regis J. Sheehan & Associates
Pittsburgh, PA 15220
(412)279-1207

James W. Davidson Company Inc.
23 Forest View Rd.
Wallingford, PA 19086
(610)566-1462

Puerto Rico

Diego Chevere & Co.
Metro Parque 7, Ste. 204
Metro Office
Caparra Heights, PR 00920
(787)774-9595
Fax: (787)774-9566
E-mail: dcco@coqui.net

Manuel L. Porrata and Associates
898 Munoz Rivera Ave., Ste. 201
San Juan, PR 00927
(787)765-2140
Fax: (787)754-3285
E-mail: m_porrata@manuelporrata.com
Website: http://manualporrata.com

South Carolina

Aquafood Business Associates
PO Box 13267
Charleston, SC 29422
(843)795-9506
Fax: (843)795-9477
E-mail: rraba@aol.com

Profit Associates Inc.
PO Box 38026
Charleston, SC 29414
(803)763-5718
Fax: (803)763-5719
E-mail: bobrog@awod.com
Website: http://www.awod.com/gallery/
business/proasc

Strategic Innovations International
12 Executive Ct.
Lake Wylie, SC 29710
(803)831-1225
Fax: (803)831-1177
E-mail: stratinnov@aol.com
Website: http://www.
strategicinnovations.com

Minus Stage
Box 4436
Rock Hill, SC 29731
(803)328-0705
Fax: (803)329-9948

Tennessee

Daniel Petchers & Associates
8820 Fernwood CV
Germantown, TN 38138
(901)755-9896

Business Choices
1114 Forest Harbor, Ste. 300
Hendersonville, TN 37075-9646
(615)822-8692
Free: 800-737-8382
Fax: (615)822-8692
E-mail: bz-ch@juno.com

RCFA Healthcare Management Services L.L.C.
9648 Kingston Pke., Ste. 8
Knoxville, TN 37922
(865)531-0176
Free: 800-635-4040
Fax: (865)531-0722
E-mail: info@rcfa.com
Website: http://www.rcfa.com

Growth Consultants of America
3917 Trimble Rd.
Nashville, TN 37215

(615)383-0550
Fax: (615)269-8940
E-mail: 70244.451@compuserve.com

Texas

**Integrated Cost Management
Systems Inc.**
2261 Brookhollow Plz. Dr., Ste. 104
Arlington, TX 76006
(817)633-2873
Fax: (817)633-3781
E-mail: abm@icms.net
Website: http://www.icms.net

Lori Williams
1000 Leslie Ct.
Arlington, TX 76012
(817)459-3934
Fax: (817)459-3934

Business Resource Software Inc.
2013 Wells Branch Pky., Ste. 305
Austin, TX 78728
Free: 800-423-1228
Fax: (512)251-4401
E-mail: info@brs-inc.com
Website: http://www.brs-inc.com

Erisa Adminstrative Services Inc.
12325 Hymeadow Dr., Bldg. 4
Austin, TX 78750-1847
(512)250-9020
Fax: (512)250-9487
Website: http://www.cserisa.com

R. Miller Hicks & Co.
1011 W 11th St.
Austin, TX 78703
(512)477-7000
Fax: (512)477-9697
E-mail: millerhicks@rmhicks.com
Website: http://www.rmhicks.com

Pragmatic Tactics Inc.
3303 Westchester Ave.
College Station, TX 77845
(409)696-5294
Free: 800-570-5294
Fax: (409)696-4994
E-mail: ptactics@aol.com
Website: http://www.ptatics.com

Perot Systems
12404 Park Central Dr.
Dallas, TX 75251
(972)340-5000
Free: 800-688-4333
Fax: (972)455-4100
E-mail: corp.comm@ps.net
Website: http://www.perotsystems.com

ReGENERATION Partners
3838 Oak Lawn Ave.
Dallas, TX 75219
(214)559-3999
Free: 800-406-1112
E-mail: info@regeneration-partner.com
Website: http://www.regeneration-partners.com

**High Technology Associates - Division
of Global Technologies Inc.**
1775 St. James Pl., Ste. 105
Houston, TX 77056
(713)963-9300
Fax: (713)963-8341
E-mail: hta@infohwy.com

MasterCOM
103 Thunder Rd.
Kerrville, TX 78028
(830)895-7990
Fax: (830)443-3428
E-mail: jmstubblefield@master
training.com
Website: http://www.mastertraining.com

PROTEC
4607 Linden Pl.
Pearland, TX 77584
(281)997-9872
Fax: (281)997-9895
E-mail: p.oman@ix.netcom.com

Alpha Quadrant Inc.
10618 Auldine
San Antonio, TX 78230
(210)344-3330
Fax: (210)344-8151
E-mail: mbussone@sbcglobal.net
Website:http://www.a-quadrant.com
Michele Bussone

Bastian Public Relations
614 San Dizier
San Antonio, TX 78232
(210)404-1839
E-mail: lisa@bastianpr.com
Website: http://www.bastianpr.com
Lisa Bastian CBC

**Business Strategy Development
Consultants**
PO Box 690365
San Antonio, TX 78269
(210)696-8000
Free: 800-927-BSDC
Fax: (210)696-8000

Tom Welch, CPC
6900 San Pedro Ave., Ste. 147
San Antonio, TX 78216-6207

(210)737-7022
Fax: (210)737-7022
E-mail: bplan@iamerica.net
Website: http://www.moneywords.com

Utah

Business Management Resource
PO Box 521125
Salt Lake City, UT 84152-1125
(801)272-4668
Fax: (801)277-3290
E-mail: pingfong@worldnet.att.net

Virginia

Tindell Associates
209 Oxford Ave.
Alexandria, VA 22301
(703)683-0109
Fax: 703-783-0219
E-mail: scott@tindell.net
Website: http://www.tindell.net
Scott Lockett, President

Elliott B. Jaffa
2530-B S Walter Reed Dr.
Arlington, VA 22206
(703)931-0040
E-mail: thetrainingdoctor@excite.com
Website: http://www.tregistry.com/
jaffa.htm

Koach Enterprises - USA
5529 N 18th St.
Arlington, VA 22205
(703)241-8361
Fax: (703)241-8623

Federal Market Development
5650 Chapel Run Ct.
Centreville, VA 20120-3601
(703)502-8930
Free: 800-821-5003
Fax: (703)502-8929

Huff, Stuart & Carlton
2107 Graves Mills Rd., Ste. C
Forest, VA 24551
(804)316-9356
Free: (888)316-9356
Fax: (804)316-9357
Website: http://www.wealthmgt.net

AMX International Inc.
1420 Spring Hill Rd. , Ste. 600
McLean, VA 22102-3006
(703)690-4100
Fax: (703)643-1279
E-mail: amxmail@amxi.com
Website: http://www.amxi.com

Charles Scott Pugh (Investor)
4101 Pittaway Dr.
Richmond, VA 23235-1022
(804)560-0979
Fax: (804)560-4670

John C. Randall and Associates Inc.
PO Box 15127
Richmond, VA 23227
(804)746-4450
Fax: (804)730-8933
E-mail: randalljcx@aol.com
Website: http://www.johncrandall.com

McLeod & Co.
410 1st St.
Roanoke, VA 24011
(540)342-6911
Fax: (540)344-6367
Website: http://www.mcleodco.com/

Salzinger & Company Inc.
8000 Towers Crescent Dr., Ste. 1350
Vienna, VA 22182
(703)442-5200
Fax: (703)442-5205
E-mail: info@salzinger.com
Website: http://www.salzinger.com

The Small Business Counselor
12423 Hedges Run Dr., Ste. 153
Woodbridge, VA 22192
(703)490-6755
Fax: (703)490-1356

Washington

Burlington Consultants
10900 NE 8th St., Ste. 900
Bellevue, WA 98004
(425)688-3060
Fax: (425)454-4383
E-mail: partners@burlington
consultants.com
Website: http://www.burlington
consultants.com

Perry L. Smith Consulting
800 Bellevue Way NE, Ste. 400
Bellevue, WA 98004-4208
(425)462-2072
Fax: (425)462-5638

St. Charles Consulting Group
1420 NW Gilman Blvd.
Issaquah, WA 98027
(425)557-8708
Fax: (425)557-8731
E-mail: info@stcharlesconsulting.com
Website: http://www.stcharlescon
sulting.com

Independent Automotive Training Services
PO Box 334
Kirkland, WA 98083
(425)822-5715
E-mail: ltunney@autosvccon.com
Website: http://www.autosvccon.com

Kahle Associate Inc.
6203 204th Dr. NE
Redmond, WA 98053
(425)836-8763
Fax: (425)868-3770
E-mail: randykahle@kahleassociates.com
Website: http://www.kahleassociates.com

Dan Collin
3419 Wallingord Ave N, No. 2
Seattle, WA 98103
(206)634-9469
E-mail: dc@dancollin.com
Website: http://members.home.net/
dcollin/

ECG Management Consultants Inc.
1111 3rd Ave., Ste. 2700
Seattle, WA 98101-3201
(206)689-2200
Fax: (206)689-2209
E-mail: ecg@ecgmc.com
Website: http://www.ecgmc.com

Northwest Trade Adjustment Assistance Center
900 4th Ave., Ste. 2430
Seattle, WA 98164-1001
(206)622-2730
Free: 800-667-8087
Fax: (206)622-1105
E-mail: matchingfunds@nwtaac.org
Website: http://www.taacenters.org

Business Planning Consultants
S 3510 Ridgeview Dr.
Spokane, WA 99206
(509)928-0332
Fax: (509)921-0842
E-mail: bpci@nextdim.com

West Virginia

**Stanley & Associates Inc./
BusinessandMarketingPlans.com**
1687 Robert C. Byrd Dr.
Beckley, WV 25801
(304)252-0324
Free: 888-752-6720
Fax: (304)252-0470
E-mail: cclay@charterinternet.com

Website: http://www.Businessand
MarketingPlans.com
Christopher Clay

Wisconsin

White & Associates Inc.
5349 Somerset Ln. S
Greenfield, WI 53221
(414)281-7373
Fax: (414)281-7006
E-mail: wnaconsult@aol.com

Small business administration regional offices

This section contains a listing of Small Business Administration offices arranged numerically by region. Service areas are provided. Contact the appropriate office for a referral to the nearest field office, or visit the Small Business Administration online at www.sba.gov.

Region 1

U.S. Small Business Administration
Region I Office
10 Causeway St., Ste. 812
Boston, MA 02222-1093
Phone: (617)565-8415
Fax: (617)565-8420
Serves Connecticut, Maine, Massachusetts, New Hampshire, Rhode Island, and Vermont.

Region 2

U.S. Small Business Administration
Region II Office
26 Federal Plaza, Ste. 3108
New York, NY 10278
Phone: (212)264-1450
Fax: (212)264-0038
Serves New Jersey, New York, Puerto Rico, and the Virgin Islands.

Region 3

U.S. Small Business Administration
Region III Office
Robert N C Nix Sr. Federal Building
900 Market St., 5th Fl.
Philadelphia, PA 19107
(215)580-2807
Serves Delaware, the District of Columbia, Maryland, Pennsylvania, Virginia, and West Virginia.

Region 4

U.S. Small Business Administration
Region IV Office
233 Peachtree St. NE
Harris Tower 1800
Atlanta, GA 30303
Phone: (404)331-4999
Fax: (404)331-2354
Serves Alabama, Florida, Georgia,
Kentucky, Mississippi, North
Carolina, South Carolina, and
Tennessee.

Region 5

U.S. Small Business Administration
Region V Office
500 W. Madison St.
Citicorp Center, Ste. 1240
Chicago, IL 60661-2511
Phone: (312)353-0357
Fax: (312)353-3426
Serves Illinois, Indiana, Michigan,
Minnesota, Ohio, and Wisconsin.

Region 6

U.S. Small Business Administration
Region VI Office
4300 Amon Carter Blvd., Ste. 108
Fort Worth, TX 76155
Phone: (817)684-5581
Fax: (817)684-5588
Serves Arkansas, Louisiana, New Mexico,
Oklahoma, and Texas.

Region 7

U.S. Small Business Administration
Region VII Office
323 W. 8th St., Ste. 307
Kansas City, MO 64105-1500
Phone: (816)374-6380
Fax: (816)374-6339
Serves Iowa, Kansas, Missouri, and
Nebraska.

Region 8

U.S. Small Business Administration
Region VIII Office
721 19th St., Ste. 400
Denver, CO 80202
Phone: (303)844-0500
Fax: (303)844-0506
Serves Colorado, Montana, North
Dakota, South Dakota, Utah, and
Wyoming.

Region 9

U.S. Small Business Administration
Region IX Office
330 N Brand Blvd., Ste. 1270
Glendale, CA 91203-2304
Phone: (818)552-3434
Fax: (818)552-3440
Serves American Samoa, Arizona,
California, Guam, Hawaii, Nevada, and
the Trust Territory of the Pacific
Islands.

Region 10

U.S. Small Business Administration
Region X Office
2401 Fourth Ave., Ste. 400
Seattle, WA 98121
Phone: (206)553-5676
Fax: (206)553-4155
Serves Alaska, Idaho, Oregon, and
Washington.

Small business development centers

This section contains a listing of all Small Business Development Centers, organized alphabetically by state/U.S. territory, then by city, then by agency name.

Alabama

Alabama SBDC
UNIVERSITY OF ALABAMA
2800 Milan Court Suite 124
Birmingham, AL 35211-6908
Phone: 205-943-6750
Fax: 205-943-6752
E-Mail: wcampbell@provost.uab.edu
Website: http://www.asbdc.org
Mr. William Campbell Jr, State Director

Alaska

Alaska SBDC
**UNIVERSITY OF ALASKA -
ANCHORAGE**
430 West Seventh Avenue, Suite 110
Anchorage, AK 99501
Phone: 907-274 -7232
Fax: 907-274-9524
E-Mail: anerw@uaa.alaska.edu
Website: http://www.aksbdc.org
Ms. Jean R. Wall, State Director

American Samoa

American Samoa SBDC
**AMERICAN SAMOA COMMUNITY
COLLEGE**
P.O. Box 2609
Pago Pago, American Samoa 96799
Phone: 011-684-699-4830
Fax: 011-684-699-6132
E-Mail: htalex@att.net
Mr. Herbert Thweatt, Director

Arizona

Arizona SBDC
**MARICOPA COUNTY COMMUNITY
COLLEGE**
2411 West 14th Street, Suite 132
Tempe, AZ 85281
Phone: 480-731-8720
Fax: 480-731-8729
E-Mail: mike.york@domail.
maricopa.edu
Website: http://www.dist.maricopa.
edu.sbdc
Mr. Michael York, State Director

Arkansas

Arkansas SBDC
UNIVERSITY OF ARKANSAS
2801 South University Avenue
Little Rock, AR 72204
Phone: 501-324-9043
Fax: 501-324-9049
E-Mail: jmroderick@ualr.edu
Website: http://asbdc.ualr.edu
Ms. Janet M. Roderick, State Director

California

California - San Francisco SBDC
Northern California SBDC Lead Center
HUMBOLDT STATE UNIVERSITY
Office of Economic Development
1 Harpst Street 2006A, Siemens Hall
Arcata, CA, 95521
Phone: 707-826-3922
Fax: 707-826-3206
E-Mail: gainer@humboldt.edu
Ms. Margaret A. Gainer, Regional
Director

California - Sacramento SBDC
**CALIFORNIA STATE UNIVERSITY -
CHICO**
Chico, CA 95929-0765
Phone: 530-898-4598
Fax: 530-898-4734

E-Mail: dripke@csuchico.edu
Website: http://gsbdc.csuchico.edu
Mr. Dan Ripke, Interim Regional Director

California - San Diego SBDC
SOUTHWESTERN COMMUNITY
COLLEGE DISTRICT
900 Otey Lakes Road
Chula Vista, CA 91910
Phone: 619-482-6388
Fax: 619-482-6402
E-Mail: dtrujillo@swc.cc.ca.us
Website: http://www.sbditc.org
Ms. Debbie P. Trujillo, Regional Director

California - Fresno SBDC
UC Merced Lead Center
UNIVERSITY OF CALIFORNIA -
MERCED
550 East Shaw, Suite 105A
Fresno, CA 93710
Phone: 559-241-6590
Fax: 559-241-7422
E-Mail: crosander@ucmerced.edu
Website: http://sbdc.ucmerced.edu
Mr. Chris Rosander, State Director

California - Santa Ana SBDC
Tri-County Lead SBDC
CALIFORNIA STATE UNIVERSITY -
FULLERTON
800 North State College Boulevard, LH640
Fullerton, CA 92834
Phone: 714-278-2719
Fax: 714-278-7858
E-Mail: vpham@fullerton.edu
Website: http://www.leadsbdc.org
Ms. Vi Pham, Lead Center Director

California - Los Angeles Region SBDC
LONG BEACH COMMUNITY
COLLEGE DISTRICT
3950 Paramount Boulevard, Ste 101
Lakewood, CA 90712
Phone: 562-938-5004
Fax: 562-938-5030
E-Mail: ssloan@lbcc.edu
Ms. Sheneui Sloan, Interim Lead Center
Director

Colorado

Colorado SBDC
OFFICE OF ECONOMIC
DEVELOPMENT
1625 Broadway, Suite 170
Denver, CO 80202
Phone: 303-892-3864
Fax: 303-892-3848
E-Mail: Kelly.Manning@state.co.us

Website: http://www.state.co.us/oed/sbdc
Ms. Kelly Manning, State Director

Connecticut

Connecticut SBDC
UNIVERSITY OF CONNECTICUT
1376 Storrs Road, Unit 4094
Storrs, CT 06269-1094
Phone: 860-870-6370
Fax: 860-870-6374
E-Mail: richard.cheney@uconn.edu
Website: http://www.sbdc.uconn.edu
Mr. Richard Cheney, Interim State Director

Delaware

Delaware SBDC
DELAWARE TECHNOLOGY PARK
1 Innovation Way, Suite 301
Newark, DE 19711
Phone: 302-831-2747
Fax: 302-831-1423
E-Mail: Clinton.tymes@mvs.udel.edu
Website: http://www.delawaresbdc.org
Mr. Clinton Tymes, State Director

District of Columbia

District of Columbia SBDC
HOWARD UNIVERSITY
2600 6th Street, NW Room 128
Washington, DC 20059
Phone: 202-806-1550
Fax: 202-806-1777
E-Mail: hturner@howard.edu
Website: http://www.dcsbdc.com/
Mr. Henry Turner, Executive Director

Florida

Florida SBDC
UNIVERSITY OF WEST FLORIDA
401 East Chase Street, Suite 100
Pensacola, FL 32502
Phone: 850-473-7800
Fax: 850-473-7813
E-Mail: jcartwri@uwf.edu
Website: http://www.floridasbdc.com
Mr. Jerry Cartwright, State Director

Georgia

Georgia SBDC
UNIVERSITY OF GEORGIA
1180 East Broad Street
Athens, GA 30602
Phone: 706-542-6762
Fax: 706-542-6776
E-mail: aadams@sbdc.uga.edu

Website: http://www.sbdc.uga.edu
Mr. Allan Adams, Interim State Director

Guam

Guam Small Business Development
Center
UNIVERSITY OF GUAM
Pacific Islands SBDC
P.O. Box 5014 - U.O.G. Station
Mangilao, GU 96923
Phone: 671-735-2590
Fax: 671-734-2002
E-mail: casey@pacificsbdc.com
Website: http://www.uog.edu/sbdc
Mr. Casey Jeszenka, Director

Hawaii

Hawaii SBDC
UNIVERSITY OF HAWAII - HILO
308 Kamehameha Avenue, Suite 201
Hilo, HI 96720
Phone: 808-974-7515
Fax: 808-974-7683
E-Mail: darrylm@interpac.net
Website: http://www.hawaii-sbdc.org
Mr. Darryl Mleynek, State Director

Idaho

Idaho SBDC
BOISE STATE UNIVERSITY
1910 University Drive
Boise, ID 83725
Phone: 208-426-3799
Fax: 208-426-3877
E-mail: jhogge@boisestate.edu
Website: http://www.idahosbdc.org
Mr. Jim Hogge, State Director

Illinois

Illinois SBDC
DEPARTMENT OF COMMERCE
AND ECONOMIC OPPORTUNITY
620 E. Adams, S-4
Springfield, IL 62701
Phone: 217-524-5700
Fax: 217-524-0171
E-mail: mpatrilli@ildceo.net
Website: http://www.ilsbdc.biz
Mr. Mark Petrilli, State Director

Indiana

Indiana SBDC
INDIANA ECONOMIC
DEVELOPMENT CORPORATION
One North Capitol, Suite 900
Indianapolis, IN 46204

Phone: 317-234-8872
Fax: 317-232-8874
E-mail: dtrocha@isbdc.org
Website: http://www.isbdc.org
Ms. Debbie Bishop Trocha, State
Director

Iowa

Iowa SBDC
IOWA STATE UNIVERSITY
340 Gerdin Business Bldg.
Ames, IA 50011-1350
Phone: 515-294-2037
Fax: 515-294-6522
E-mail: jonryan@iastate.edu
Website: http://www.iabusnet.org
Mr. Jon Ryan, State Director

Kansas

Kansas SBDC
FORT HAYS STATE UNIVERSITY
214 SW Sixth Street, Suite 301
Topeka, KS 66603
Phone: 785-296-6514
Fax: 785-291-3261
E-mail: ksbdc.wkearns@fhsu.edu
Website: http://www.fhsu.edu/ksbdc
Mr. Wally Kearns, State Director

Kentucky

Kentucky SBDC
UNIVERSITY OF KENTUCKY
225 Gatton College of Business
Economics Building
Lexington, KY 40506-0034
Phone: 859-257-7668
Fax: 859-323-1907
E-mail: lrnaug0@pop.uky.edu
Website: http://www.ksbdc.org
Ms. Becky Naugle, State Director

Louisiana

Louisiana SBDC
**UNIVERSITY OF LOUISIANA -
MONROE**
College of Business Administration
700 University Avenue
Monroe, LA 71209
Phone: 318-342-5506
Fax: 318-342-5510
E-mail: wilkerson@ulm.edu
Website: http://www.lsbdc.org
Ms. Mary Lynn Wilkerson, State
Director

Maine

Maine SBDC
**UNIVERSITY OF SOUTHERN
MAINE**
96 Falmouth Street P.O. Box 9300
Portland, ME 04103
Phone: 207-780-4420
Fax: 207-780-4810
E-mail: jrmassaua@maine.edu
Website: http://www.mainesbdc.org
Mr. John Massaua, State Director

Maryland

Maryland SBDC
UNIVERSITY OF MARYLAND
7100 Baltimore Avenue, Suite 401
College Park, MD 20742
Phone: 301-403-8300
Fax: 301-403-8303
E-mail: rsprow@mdsbdc.umd.edu
Website: http://www.mdsbdc.umd.edu
Ms. Renee Sprow, State Director

Massachusetts

Massachusetts SBDC
UNIVERSITY OF MASSACHUSETTS
School of Management, Room 205
Amherst, MA 01003-4935
Phone: 413-545-6301
Fax: 413-545-1273
E-mail: gep@msbdc.umass.edu
Website: http://msbdc.som.umass.edu
Ms. Georgianna Parkin, State Director

Michigan

Michigan SBTDC
**GRAND VALLEY STATE
UNIVERSITY**
510 West Fulton Avenue
Grand Rapids, MI 49504
Phone: 616-331-7485
Fax: 616-331-7389
E-mail: lopuckic@gvsu.edu
Website: http://www.misbtdc.org
Ms. Carol Lopucki, State Director

Minnesota

Minnesota SBDC
**MINNESOTA SMALL BUSINESS
DEVELOPMENT CENTER**
1st National Bank Building
332 Minnesota Street, Suite E200
St. Paul, MN 55101-1351
Phone: 651-297-5773
Fax: 651-296-5287

E-mail: michael.myhre@state.mn.us
Website: http://www.mnsbdc.com
Mr. Michael Myhre, State Director

Mississippi

Mississippi SBDC
UNIVERSITY OF MISSISSIPPI
B-19 Jeanette Phillips Drive
P.O. Box 1848
University, MS 38677
Phone: 662-915-5001
Fax: 662-915-5650
E-mail: wgurley@olemiss.edu
Website: http://www.olemiss.edu/depts/
mssbdc
Mr. Doug Gurley, Jr., State Director

Missouri

Missouri SBDC
UNIVERSITY OF MISSOURI
1205 University Avenue, Suite 300
Columbia, MO 65211
Phone: 573-882-1348
Fax: 573-884-4297
E-mail: summersm@missouri.edu
Website: http://www.mo-sbdc.org/
index.shtml
Mr. Max Summers, State Director

Montana

Montana SBDC
DEPARTMENT OF COMMERCE
301 South Park Avenue, Room 114 /
P.O. Box 200505
Helena, MT 59620
Phone: 406-841-2746
Fax: 406-444-1872
E-mail: adesch@state.mt.us
Website: http://commerce.state.mt.us/
brd/BRD_SBDC.html
Ms. Ann Desch, State Director

Nebraska

Nebraska SBDC
**UNIVERSITY OF NEBRASKA -
OMAHA**
60th & Dodge Street, CBA Room 407
Omaha, NE 68182
Phone: 402-554-2521
Fax: 402-554-3473
E-mail: rbernier@unomaha.edu
Website: http://nbdc.unomaha.edu
Mr. Robert Bernier, State Director

Nevada

Nevada SBDC
UNIVERSITY OF NEVADA - RENO
Reno College of Business
Administration, Room 411
Reno, NV 89557-0100
Phone: 775-784-1717
Fax: 775-784-4337
E-mail: males@unr.edu
Website: http://www.nsbdc.org
Mr. Sam Males, State Director

New Hampshire

New Hampshire SBDC
UNIVERSITY OF NEW HAMPSHIRE
108 McConnell Hall
Durham, NH 03824-3593
Phone: 603-862-4879
Fax: 603-862-4876
E-mail: Mary.Collins@unh.edu
Website: http://www.nhsbdc.org
Ms. Mary Collins, State Director

New Jersey

New Jersey SBDC
RUTGERS UNIVERSITY
49 Bleeker Street
Newark, NJ 07102-1993
Phone: 973-353-5950
Fax: 973-353-1110
E-mail: bhopper@njsbdc.com
Website: http://www.njsbdc.com/home
Ms. Brenda Hopper, State Director

New Mexico

New Mexico SBDC
SANTA FE COMMUNITY COLLEGE
6401 Richards Avenue
Santa Fe, NM 87505
Phone: 505-428-1362
Fax: 505-471-9469
E-mail: rmiller@santa-fe.cc.nm.us
Website: http://www.nmsbdc.org
Mr. Roy Miller, State Director

New York

New York SBDC
STATE UNIVERSITY OF NEW YORK
SUNY Plaza, S-523
Albany, NY 12246
Phone: 518-443-5398
Fax: 518-443-5275
E-mail: j.king@nyssbdc.org
Website: http://www.nyssbdc.org
Mr. Jim King, State Director

North Carolina

North Carolina SBDTC
UNIVERSITY OF NORTH CAROLINA
5 West Hargett Street, Suite 600
Raleigh, NC 27601
Phone: 919-715-7272
Fax: 919-715-7777
E-mail: sdaugherty@sbtdc.org
Website: http://www.sbtdc.org
Mr. Scott Daugherty, State Director

North Dakota

North Dakota SBDC
UNIVERSITY OF NORTH DAKOTA
1600 E. Century Avenue, Suite 2
Bismarck, ND 58503
Phone: 701-328-5375
Fax: 701-328-5320
E-mail: christine.martin@und.nodak.edu
Website: http://www.ndsbdc.org
Ms. Christine Martin-Goldman, State
Director

Ohio

Ohio SBDC
OHIO DEPARTMENT
OF DEVELOPMENT
77 South High Street
Columbus, OH 43216
Phone: 614-466-5102
Fax: 614-466-0829
E-mail: mabraham@odod.state.oh.us
Website: http://www.ohiosbdc.org
Ms. Michele Abraham, State Director

Oklahoma

Oklahoma SBDC
SOUTHEAST OKLAHOMA STATE
UNIVERSITY
517 University, Box 2584, Station A
Durant, OK 74701
Phone: 580-745-7577
Fax: 580-745-7471
E-mail: gpennington@sosu.edu
Website: http://www.osbdc.org
Mr. Grady Pennington, State Director

Oregon

Oregon SBDC
LANE COMMUNITY COLLEGE
99 West Tenth Avenue, Suite 390
Eugene, OR 97401-3021
Phone: 541-463-5250
Fax: 541-345-6006
E-mail: carterb@lanecc.edu

Website: http://www.bizcenter.org
Mr. William Carter, State Director

Pennsylvania

Pennsylvania SBDC
UNIVERSITY OF PENNSYLVANIA
The Wharton School
3733 Spruce Street
Philadelphia, PA 19104-6374
Phone: 215-898-1219
Fax: 215-573-2135
E-mail: ghiggins@wharton.upenn.edu
Website: http://pasbdc.org
Mr. Gregory Higgins, State Director

Puerto Rico

Puerto Rico SBDC
INTER-AMERICAN UNIVERSITY
OF PUERTO RICO
416 Ponce de Leon Avenue, Union Plaza,
Seventh Floor
Hato Rey, PR 00918
Phone: 787-763-6811
Fax: 787-763-4629
E-mail: cmarti@prsbdc.org
Website: http://www.prsbdc.org
Ms. Carmen Marti, Executive Director

Rhode Island

Rhode Island SBDC
BRYANT UNIVERSITY
1150 Douglas Pike
Smithfield, RI 02917
Phone: 401-232-6923
Fax: 401-232-6933
E-mail: adawson@bryant.edu
Website: http://www.risbdc.org
Ms. Diane Fournaris, Interim State Director

South Carolina

South Carolina SBDC
UNIVERSITY OF SOUTH CAROLINA
College of Business Administration
1710 College Street
Columbia, SC 29208
Phone: 803-777-4907
Fax: 803-777-4403
E-mail: lenti@moore.sc.edu
Website: http://scsbdc.moore.sc.edu
Mr. John Lenti, State Director

South Dakota

South Dakota SBDC
UNIVERSITY OF SOUTH DAKOTA
414 East Clark Street, Patterson Hall
Vermillion, SD 57069

Phone: 605-677-6256
Fax: 605-677-5427
E-mail: jshemmin@usd.edu
Website: http://www.sdsbdc.org
Mr. John S. Hemmingstad, State
Director

Tennessee

Tennessee SBDC
TENNESSEE BOARD OF REGENTS
1415 Murfressboro Road, Suite 540
Nashville, TN 37217-2833
Phone: 615-898-2745
Fax: 615-893-7089
E-mail: pgeho@mail.tsbdc.org
Website: http://www.tsbdc.org
Mr. Patrick Geho, State Director

Texas

Texas-North SBDC
**DALLAS COUNTY COMMUNITY
COLLEGE**
1402 Corinth Street
Dallas, TX 75215
Phone: 214-860-5835
Fax: 214-860-5813
E-mail: cmk9402@dcccd.edu
Website: http://www.ntsbdc.org
Ms. Liz Klimback, Region Director

Texas-Houston SBDC
UNIVERSITY OF HOUSTON
2302 Fannin, Suite 200
Houston, TX 77002
Phone: 713-752-8425
Fax: 713-756-1500
E-mail: fyoung@uh.edu
Website: http://sbdcnetwork.uh.edu
Mr. Mike Young, Executive Director

Texas-NW SBDC
TEXAS TECH UNIVERSITY
2579 South Loop 289, Suite 114
Lubbock, TX 79423
Phone: 806-745-3973
Fax: 806-745-6207
E-mail: c.bean@nwtsbdc.org
Website: http://www.nwtsbdc.org
Mr. Craig Bean, Executive Director

**Texas-South-West Texas Border
Region SBDC**
**UNIVERSITY OF TEXAS -
SAN ANTONIO**
501 West Durango Boulevard
San Antonio, TX 78207-4415
Phone: 210-458-2742
Fax: 210-458-2464

E-mail: albert.salgado@utsa.edu
Website: http://www.iedtexas.org
Mr. Alberto Salgado, Region Director

Utah

Utah SBDC
SALT LAKE COMMUNITY COLLEGE
9750 South 300 West
Sandy, UT 84070
Phone: 801-957-3493
Fax: 801-957-3488
E-mail: Greg.Panichello@slcc.edu
Website:http://www.slcc.edu/sbdc
Mr. Greg Panichello, State Director

Vermont

Vermont SBDC
VERMONT TECHNICAL COLLEGE
PO Box 188, 1 Main Street
Randolph Center, VT 05061-0188
Phone: 802-728-9101
Fax: 802-728-3026
E-mail: lquillen@vtc.edu
Website: http://www.vtsbdc.org
Ms. Lenae Quillen-Blume, State Director

Virgin Islands

Virgin Islands SBDC
**UNIVERSITY OF THE VIRGIN
ISLANDS**
8000 Nisky Center, Suite 720
St. Thomas, VI 00802-5804
Phone: 340-776-3206
Fax: 340-775-3756
E-mail: wbush@webmail.uvi.edu
Website: http://rps.uvi.edu/SBDC
Mr. Warren Bush, State Director

Virginia

Virginia SBDC
GEORGE MASON UNIVERSITY
4031 University Drive, Suite 200
Fairfax, VA 22030-3409
Phone: 703-277-7727
Fax: 703-352-8515
E-mail: jkeenan@gmu.edu
Website: http://www.virginiasbdc.org
Ms. Jody Keenan, Director

Washington

Washington SBDC
WASHINGTON STATE UNIVERSITY
534 E. Trent Avenue
P.O. Box 1495
Spokane, WA 99210-1495

Phone: 509-358-7765
Fax: 509-358-7764
E-mail: barogers@wsu.edu
Website: http://www.wsbdc.org
Mr. Brett Rogers, State Director

West Virginia

West Virginia SBDC
**WEST VIRGINIA DEVELOPMENT
OFFICE**
Capital Complex, Building 6, Room 652
Charleston, WV 25301
Phone: 304-558-2960
Fax: 304-558-0127
E-mail: csalyer@wvsbdc.org
Website: http://www.wvsbdc.org
Mr. Conley Salyor, State Director

Wisconsin

Wisconsin SBDC
UNIVERSITY OF WISCONSIN
432 North Lake Street, Room 423
Madison, WI 53706
Phone: 608-263-7794
Fax: 608-263-7830
E-mail: erica.kauten@uwex.edu
Website: http://www.wisconsinsbdc.org
Ms. Erica Kauten, State Director

Wyoming

Wyoming SBDC
UNIVERSITY OF WYOMING
P.O. Box 3922
Laramie, WY 82071-3922
Phone: 307-766-3505
Fax: 307-766-3406
E-mail: DDW@uwyo.edu
Website: http://www.uwyo.edu/sbdc
Ms. Debbie Popp, Acting State Director

Service corps of retired executives (score) offices

*This section contains a listing of all
SCORE offices organized alphabetically by
state/U.S. territory, then by city, then by
agency name.*

Alabama

SCORE Office (Northeast Alabama)
1330 Quintard Ave.
Anniston, AL 36202
(256)237-3536

SCORE Office (North Alabama)
901 South 15th St, Rm. 201
Birmingham, AL 35294-2060
(205)934-6868
Fax: (205)934-0538

SCORE Office (Baldwin County)
29750 Larry Dee Cawyer Dr.
Daphne, AL 36526
(334)928-5838

SCORE Office (Shoals)
612 S. COurt
Florence, AL 35630
(256)764-4661
Fax: (256)766-9017
E-mail: shoals@shoalschamber.com

SCORE Office (Mobile)
600 S Court St.
Mobile, AL 36104
(334)240-6868
Fax: (334)240-6869

SCORE Office (Alabama Capitol City)
600 S. Court St.
Montgomery, AL 36104
(334)240-6868
Fax: (334)240-6869

SCORE Office (East Alabama)
601 Ave. A
Opelika, AL 36801
(334)745-4861
E-mail: score636@hotmail.com
Website: http://www.angelfire.com/sc/
score636/

SCORE Office (Tuscaloosa)
2200 University Blvd.
Tuscaloosa, AL 35402
(205)758-7588

Alaska

SCORE Office (Anchorage)
510 L St., Ste. 310
Anchorage, AK 99501
(907)271-4022
Fax: (907)271-4545

Arizona

SCORE Office (Lake Havasu)
10 S. Acoma Blvd.
Lake Havasu City, AZ 86403
(520)453-5951
E-mail: SCORE@ctaz.com
Website: http://www.scorearizona.org/
lake_havasu/

SCORE Office (East Valley)
Federal Bldg., Rm. 104
26 N. MacDonald St.
Mesa, AZ 85201
(602)379-3100
Fax: (602)379-3143
E-mail: 402@aol.com
Website: http://www.scorearizona.
org/mesa/

SCORE Office (Phoenix)
2828 N. Central Ave., Ste. 800
Central & One Thomas
Phoenix, AZ 85004
(602)640-2329
Fax: (602)640-2360
E-mail: e-mail@SCORE-phoenix.org
Website: http://www.score-phoenix.org/

SCORE Office (Prescott Arizona)
1228 Willow Creek Rd., Ste. 2
Prescott, AZ 86301
(520)778-7438
Fax: (520)778-0812
E-mail: score@northlink.com
Website: http://www.scorearizona.org/
prescott/

SCORE Office (Tucson)
110 E. Pennington St.
Tucson, AZ 85702
(520)670-5008
Fax: (520)670-5011
E-mail: score@azstarnet.com
Website: http://www.scorearizona.org/
tucson/

SCORE Office (Yuma)
281 W. 24th St., Ste. 116
Yuma, AZ 85364
(520)314-0480
E-mail: score@C2i2.com
Website: http://www.scorearizona.org/
yuma

Arkansas

SCORE Office (South Central)
201 N. Jackson Ave.
El Dorado, AR 71730-5803
(870)863-6113
Fax: (870)863-6115

SCORE Office (Ozark)
Fayetteville, AR 72701
(501)442-7619

SCORE Office (Northwest Arkansas)
Glenn Haven Dr., No. 4
Ft. Smith, AR 72901
(501)783-3556

SCORE Office (Garland County)
Grand & Ouachita
PO Box 6012
Hot Springs Village, AR 71902
(501)321-1700

SCORE Office (Little Rock)
2120 Riverfront Dr., Rm. 100
Little Rock, AR 72202-1747
(501)324-5893
Fax: (501)324-5199

SCORE Office (Southeast Arkansas)
121 W. 6th
Pine Bluff, AR 71601
(870)535-7189
Fax: (870)535-1643

California

SCORE Office (Golden Empire)
1706 Chester Ave., No. 200
Bakersfield, CA 93301
(805)322-5881
Fax: (805)322-5663

SCORE Office (Greater Chico Area)
1324 Mangrove St., Ste. 114
Chico, CA 95926
(916)342-8932
Fax: (916)342-8932

SCORE Office (Concord)
2151-A Salvio St., Ste. B
Concord, CA 94520
(510)685-1181
Fax: (510)685-5623

SCORE Office (Covina)
935 W. Badillo St.
Covina, CA 91723
(818)967-4191
Fax: (818)966-9660

SCORE Office (Rancho Cucamonga)
8280 Utica, Ste. 160
Cucamonga, CA 91730
(909)987-1012
Fax: (909)987-5917

SCORE Office (Culver City)
PO Box 707
Culver City, CA 90232-0707
(310)287-3850
Fax: (310)287-1350

SCORE Office (Danville)
380 Diablo Rd., Ste. 103
Danville, CA 94526
(510)837-4400

SCORE Office (Downey)
11131 Brookshire Ave.
Downey, CA 90241
(310)923-2191
Fax: (310)864-0461

SCORE Office (El Cajon)
109 Rea Ave.
El Cajon, CA 92020
(619)444-1327
Fax: (619)440-6164

SCORE Office (El Centro)
1100 Main St.
El Centro, CA 92243
(619)352-3681
Fax: (619)352-3246

SCORE Office (Escondido)
720 N. Broadway
Escondido, CA 92025
(619)745-2125
Fax: (619)745-1183

SCORE Office (Fairfield)
1111 Webster St.
Fairfield, CA 94533
(707)425-4625
Fax: (707)425-0826

SCORE Office (Fontana)
17009 Valley Blvd., Ste. B
Fontana, CA 92335
(909)822-4433
Fax: (909)822-6238

SCORE Office (Foster City)
1125 E. Hillsdale Blvd.
Foster City, CA 94404
(415)573-7600
Fax: (415)573-5201

SCORE Office (Fremont)
2201 Walnut Ave., Ste. 110
Fremont, CA 94538
(510)795-2244
Fax: (510)795-2240

SCORE Office (Central California)
2719 N. Air Fresno Dr., Ste. 200
Fresno, CA 93727-1547
(559)487-5605
Fax: (559)487-5636

SCORE Office (Gardena)
1204 W. Gardena Blvd.
Gardena, CA 90247
(310)532-9905
Fax: (310)515-4893

SCORE Office (Lompoc)
330 N. Brand Blvd., Ste. 190
Glendale, CA 91203-2304

(818)552-3206
Fax: (818)552-3323

SCORE Office (Los Angeles)
330 N. Brand Blvd., Ste. 190
Glendale, CA 91203-2304
(818)552-3206
Fax: (818)552-3323

SCORE Office (Glendora)
131 E. Foothill Blvd.
Glendora, CA 91740
(818)963-4128
Fax: (818)914-4822

SCORE Office (Grover Beach)
177 S. 8th St.
Grover Beach, CA 93433
(805)489-9091
Fax: (805)489-9091

SCORE Office (Hawthorne)
12477 Hawthorne Blvd.
Hawthorne, CA 90250
(310)676-1163
Fax: (310)676-7661

SCORE Office (Hayward)
22300 Foothill Blvd., Ste. 303
Hayward, CA 94541
(510)537-2424

SCORE Office (Hemet)
1700 E. Florida Ave.
Hemet, CA 92544-4679
(909)652-4390
Fax: (909)929-8543

SCORE Office (Hesperia)
16367 Main St.
PO Box 403656
Hesperia, CA 92340
(619)244-2135

SCORE Office (Holloster)
321 San Felipe Rd., No. 11
Hollister, CA 95023

SCORE Office (Hollywood)
7018 Hollywood Blvd.
Hollywood, CA 90028
(213)469-8311
Fax: (213)469-2805

SCORE Office (Indio)
82503 Hwy. 111
PO Drawer TTT
Indio, CA 92202
(619)347-0676

SCORE Office (Inglewood)
330 Queen St.

Inglewood, CA 90301
(818)552-3206

SCORE Office (La Puente)
218 N. Grendanda St. D.
La Puente, CA 91744
(818)330-3216
Fax: (818)330-9524

SCORE Office (La Verne)
2078 Bonita Ave.
La Verne, CA 91750
(909)593-5265
Fax: (714)929-8475

SCORE Office (Lake Elsinore)
132 W. Graham Ave.
Lake Elsinore, CA 92530
(909)674-2577

SCORE Office (Lakeport)
PO Box 295
Lakeport, CA 95453
(707)263-5092

SCORE Office (Lakewood)
5445 E. Del Amo Blvd., Ste. 2
Lakewood, CA 90714
(213)920-7737

SCORE Office (Long Beach)
1 World Trade Center
Long Beach, CA 90831

SCORE Office (Los Alamitos)
901 W. Civic Center Dr., Ste. 160
Los Alamitos, CA 90720

SCORE Office (Los Altos)
321 University Ave.
Los Altos, CA 94022
(415)948-1455

SCORE Office (Manhattan Beach)
PO Box 3007
Manhattan Beach, CA 90266
(310)545-5313
Fax: (310)545-7203

SCORE Office (Merced)
1632 N. St.
Merced, CA 95340
(209)725-3800
Fax: (209)383-4959

SCORE Office (Milpitas)
75 S. Milpitas Blvd., Ste. 205
Milpitas, CA 95035
(408)262-2613
Fax: (408)262-2823

SCORE Office (Yosemite)
1012 11th St., Ste. 300
Modesto, CA 95354
(209)521-9333

SCORE Office (Montclair)
5220 Benito Ave.
Montclair, CA 91763

SCORE Office (Monterey Bay)
380 Alvarado St.
PO Box 1770
Monterey, CA 93940-1770
(408)649-1770

SCORE Office (Moreno Valley)
25480 Alessandro
Moreno Valley, CA 92553

SCORE Office (Morgan Hill)
25 W. 1st St.
PO Box 786
Morgan Hill, CA 95038
(408)779-9444
Fax: (408)778-1786

SCORE Office (Morro Bay)
880 Main St.
Morro Bay, CA 93442
(805)772-4467

SCORE Office (Mountain View)
580 Castro St.
Mountain View, CA 94041
(415)968-8378
Fax: (415)968-5668

SCORE Office (Napa)
1556 1st St.
Napa, CA 94559
(707)226-7455
Fax: (707)226-1171

SCORE Office (North Hollywood)
5019 Lankershim Blvd.
North Hollywood, CA 91601
(818)552-3206

SCORE Office (Northridge)
8801 Reseda Blvd.
Northridge, CA 91324
(818)349-5676

SCORE Office (Novato)
807 De Long Ave.
Novato, CA 94945
(415)897-1164
Fax: (415)898-9097

SCORE Office (East Bay)
519 17th St.
Oakland, CA 94612

(510)273-6611
Fax: (510)273-6015
E-mail: webmaster@eastbayscore.org
Website: http://www.eastbayscore.org

SCORE Office (Oceanside)
928 N. Coast Hwy.
Oceanside, CA 92054
(619)722-1534

SCORE Office (Ontario)
121 West B. St.
Ontario, CA 91762
Fax: (714)984-6439

SCORE Office (Oxnard)
PO Box 867
Oxnard, CA 93032
(805)385-8860
Fax: (805)487-1763

SCORE Office (Pacifica)
450 Dundee Way, Ste. 2
Pacifica, CA 94044
(415)355-4122

SCORE Office (Palm Desert)
72990 Hwy. 111
Palm Desert, CA 92260
(619)346-6111
Fax: (619)346-3463

SCORE Office (Palm Springs)
650 E. Tahquitz Canyon Way Ste. D
Palm Springs, CA 92262-6706
(760)320-6682
Fax: (760)323-9426

SCORE Office (Lakeside)
2150 Low Tree
Palmdale, CA 93551
(805)948-4518
Fax: (805)949-1212

SCORE Office (Palo Alto)
325 Forest Ave.
Palo Alto, CA 94301
(415)324-3121
Fax: (415)324-1215

SCORE Office (Pasadena)
117 E. Colorado Blvd., Ste. 100
Pasadena, CA 91105
(818)795-3355
Fax: (818)795-5663

SCORE Office (Paso Robles)
1225 Park St.
Paso Robles, CA 93446-2234
(805)238-0506
Fax: (805)238-0527

SCORE Office (Petaluma)
799 Baywood Dr., Ste. 3
Petaluma, CA 94954
(707)762-2785
Fax: (707)762-4721

SCORE Office (Pico Rivera)
9122 E. Washington Blvd.
Pico Rivera, CA 90660

SCORE Office (Pittsburg)
2700 E. Leland Rd.
Pittsburg, CA 94565
(510)439-2181
Fax: (510)427-1599

SCORE Office (Pleasanton)
777 Peters Ave.
Pleasanton, CA 94566
(510)846-9697

SCORE Office (Monterey Park)
485 N. Garey
Pomona, CA 91769

SCORE Office (Pomona)
485 N. Garey Ave.
Pomona, CA 91766
(909)622-1256

SCORE Office (Antelope Valley)
4511 West Ave. M-4
Quartz Hill, CA 93536
(805)272-0087
E-mail: avscore@ptw.com
Website: http://www.score.av.org/

SCORE Office (Shasta)
737 Auditorium Dr.
Redding, CA 96099
(916)225-2770

SCORE Office (Redwood City)
1675 Broadway
Redwood City, CA 94063
(415)364-1722
Fax: (415)364-1729

SCORE Office (Richmond)
3925 MacDonald Ave.
Richmond, CA 94805

SCORE Office (Ridgecrest)
PO Box 771
Ridgecrest, CA 93555
(619)375-8331
Fax: (619)375-0365

SCORE Office (Riverside)
3685 Main St., Ste. 350
Riverside, CA 92501
(909)683-7100

SCORE Office (Sacramento)
9845 Horn Rd., 260-B
Sacramento, CA 95827
(916)361-2322
Fax: (916)361-2164
E-mail: sacchapter@directcon.net

SCORE Office (Salinas)
PO Box 1170
Salinas, CA 93902
(408)424-7611
Fax: (408)424-8639

SCORE Office (Inland Empire)
777 E. Rialto Ave.
Purchasing
San Bernardino, CA 92415-0760
(909)386-8278

SCORE Office (San Carlos)
San Carlos Chamber of Commerce
PO Box 1086
San Carlos, CA 94070
(415)593-1068
Fax: (415)593-9108

SCORE Office (Encinitas)
550 W. C St., Ste. 550
San Diego, CA 92101-3540
(619)557-7272
Fax: (619)557-5894

SCORE Office (San Diego)
550 West C. St., Ste. 550
San Diego, CA 92101-3540
(619)557-7272
Fax: (619)557-5894
Website: http://www.score-sandiego.org

SCORE Office (Menlo Park)
1100 Merrill St.
San Francisco, CA 94105
(415)325-2818
Fax: (415)325-0920

SCORE Office (San Francisco)
455 Market St., 6th Fl.
San Francisco, CA 94105
(415)744-6827
Fax: (415)744-6750
E-mail: sfscore@sfscore.
Website: http://www.sfscore.com

SCORE Office (San Gabriel)
401 W. Las Tunas Dr.
San Gabriel, CA 91776
(818)576-2525
Fax: (818)289-2901

SCORE Office (San Jose)
Deanza College
208 S. 1st. St., Ste. 137
San Jose, CA 95113
(408)288-8479
Fax: (408)535-5541

SCORE Office (Silicon Valley)
84 W. Santa Clara St., Ste. 100
San Jose, CA 95113
(408)288-8479
Fax: (408)535-5541
E-mail: info@svscore.org
Website: http://www.svscore.org

SCORE Office (San Luis Obispo)
3566 S. Hiquera, No. 104
San Luis Obispo, CA 93401
(805)547-0779

SCORE Office (San Mateo)
1021 S. El Camino, 2nd Fl.
San Mateo, CA 94402
(415)341-5679

SCORE Office (San Pedro)
390 W. 7th St.
San Pedro, CA 90731
(310)832-7272

SCORE Office (Orange County)
200 W. Santa Anna Blvd., Ste. 700
Santa Ana, CA 92701
(714)550-7369
Fax: (714)550-0191
Website: http://www.score114.org

SCORE Office (Santa Barbara)
3227 State St.
Santa Barbara, CA 93130
(805)563-0084

SCORE Office (Central Coast)
509 W. Morrison Ave.
Santa Maria, CA 93454
(805)347-7755

SCORE Office (Santa Maria)
614 S. Broadway
Santa Maria, CA 93454-5111
(805)925-2403
Fax: (805)928-7559

SCORE Office (Santa Monica)
501 Colorado, Ste. 150
Santa Monica, CA 90401
(310)393-9825
Fax: (310)394-1868

SCORE Office (Santa Rosa)
777 Sonoma Ave., Rm. 115E
Santa Rosa, CA 95404

(707)571-8342
Fax: (707)541-0331
Website: http://www.pressdemo.com/community/score/score.html

SCORE Office (Scotts Valley)
4 Camp Evers Ln.
Scotts Valley, CA 95066
(408)438-1010
Fax: (408)438-6544

SCORE Office (Simi Valley)
40 W. Cochran St., Ste. 100
Simi Valley, CA 93065
(805)526-3900
Fax: (805)526-6234

SCORE Office (Sonoma)
453 1st St. E
Sonoma, CA 95476
(707)996-1033

SCORE Office (Los Banos)
222 S. Shepard St.
Sonora, CA 95370
(209)532-4212

SCORE Office (Tuolumne County)
39 North Washington St.
Sonora, CA 95370
(209)588-0128
E-mail: score@mlode.com

SCORE Office (South San Francisco)
445 Market St., Ste. 6th Fl.
South San Francisco, CA 94105
(415)744-6827
Fax: (415)744-6812

SCORE Office (Stockton)
401 N. San Joaquin St., Rm. 215
Stockton, CA 95202
(209)946-6293

SCORE Office (Taft)
314 4th St.
Taft, CA 93268
(805)765-2165
Fax: (805)765-6639

SCORE Office (Conejo Valley)
625 W. Hillcrest Dr.
Thousand Oaks, CA 91360
(805)499-1993
Fax: (805)498-7264

SCORE Office (Torrance)
3400 Torrance Blvd., Ste. 100
Torrance, CA 90503
(310)540-5858
Fax: (310)540-7662

SCORE Office (Truckee)
PO Box 2757
Truckee, CA 96160
(916)587-2757
Fax: (916)587-2439

SCORE Office (Visalia)
113 S. M St,
Tulare, CA 93274
(209)627-0766
Fax: (209)627-8149

SCORE Office (Upland)
433 N. 2nd Ave.
Upland, CA 91786
(909)931-4108

SCORE Office (Vallejo)
2 Florida St.
Vallejo, CA 94590
(707)644-5551
Fax: (707)644-5590

SCORE Office (Van Nuys)
14540 Victory Blvd.
Van Nuys, CA 91411
(818)989-0300
Fax: (818)989-3836

SCORE Office (Ventura)
5700 Ralston St., Ste. 310
Ventura, CA 93001
(805)658-2688
Fax: (805)658-2252
E-mail: scoreven@jps.net
Website: http://www.jps.net/scoreven

SCORE Office (Vista)
201 E. Washington St.
Vista, CA 92084
(619)726-1122
Fax: (619)226-8654

SCORE Office (Watsonville)
PO Box 1748
Watsonville, CA 95077
(408)724-3849
Fax: (408)728-5300

SCORE Office (West Covina)
811 S. Sunset Ave.
West Covina, CA 91790
(818)338-8496
Fax: (818)960-0511

SCORE Office (Westlake)
30893 Thousand Oaks Blvd.
Westlake Village, CA 91362
(805)496-5630
Fax: (818)991-1754

Colorado

SCORE Office (Colorado Springs)
2 N. Cascade Ave., Ste. 110
Colorado Springs, CO 80903
(719)636-3074
Website: http://www.cscc.org/score02/
index.html

SCORE Office (Denver)
US Custom's House, 4th Fl.
721 19th St.
Denver, CO 80201-0660
(303)844-3985
Fax: (303)844-6490
E-mail: score62@csn.net
Website: http://www.sni.net/score62

SCORE Office (Tri-River)
1102 Grand Ave.
Glenwood Springs, CO 81601
(970)945-6589

SCORE Office (Grand Junction)
2591 B & 3/4 Rd.
Grand Junction, CO 81503
(970)243-5242

SCORE Office (Gunnison)
608 N. 11th
Gunnison, CO 81230
(303)641-4422

SCORE Office (Montrose)
1214 Peppertree Dr.
Montrose, CO 81401
(970)249-6080

SCORE Office (Pagosa Springs)
PO Box 4381
Pagosa Springs, CO 81157
(970)731-4890

SCORE Office (Rifle)
0854 W. Battlement Pky., Apt. C106
Parachute, CO 81635
(970)285-9390

SCORE Office (Pueblo)
302 N. Santa Fe
Pueblo, CO 81003
(719)542-1704
Fax: (719)542-1624
E-mail: mackey@iex.net
Website: http://www.pueblo.org/score

SCORE Office (Ridgway)
143 Poplar Pl.
Ridgway, CO 81432

SCORE Office (Silverton)
PO Box 480

Silverton, CO 81433
(303)387-5430

SCORE Office (Minturn)
PO Box 2066
Vail, CO 81658
(970)476-1224

Connecticut

SCORE Office (Greater Bridgeport)
230 Park Ave.
Bridgeport, CT 06601-0999
(203)576-4369
Fax: (203)576-4388

SCORE Office (Bristol)
10 Main St. 1st. Fl.
Bristol, CT 06010
(203)584-4718
Fax: (203)584-4722

SCORE office (Greater Danbury)
246 Federal Rd.
Unit LL2, Ste. 7
Brookfield, CT 06804
(203)775-1151

SCORE Office (Greater Danbury)
246 Federal Rd., Unit LL2, Ste. 7
Brookfield, CT 06804
(203)775-1151

SCORE Office (Eastern Connecticut)
Administration Bldg., Rm. 313
PO 625
61 Main St. (Chapter 579)
Groton, CT 06475
(203)388-9508

SCORE Office (Greater Hartford County)
330 Main St.
Hartford, CT 06106
(860)548-1749
Fax: (860)240-4659
Website: http://www.score56.org

SCORE Office (Manchester)
20 Hartford Rd.
Manchester, CT 06040
(203)646-2223
Fax: (203)646-5871

SCORE Office (New Britain)
185 Main St., Ste. 431
New Britain, CT 06051
(203)827-4492
Fax: (203)827-4480

SCORE Office (New Haven)
25 Science Pk., Bldg. 25, Rm. 366

New Haven, CT 06511
(203)865-7645

SCORE Office (Fairfield County)
24 Beldon Ave., 5th Fl.
Norwalk, CT 06850
(203)847-7348
Fax: (203)849-9308

SCORE Office (Old Saybrook)
146 Main St.
Old Saybrook, CT 06475
(860)388-9508

SCORE Office (Simsbury)
Box 244
Simsbury, CT 06070
(203)651-7307
Fax: (203)651-1933

SCORE Office (Torrington)
23 North Rd.
Torrington, CT 06791
(203)482-6586

Delaware

SCORE Office (Dover)
Treadway Towers
PO Box 576
Dover, DE 19903
(302)678-0892
Fax: (302)678-0189

SCORE Office (Lewes)
PO Box 1
Lewes, DE 19958
(302)645-8073
Fax: (302)645-8412

SCORE Office (Milford)
204 NE Front St.
Milford, DE 19963
(302)422-3301

SCORE Office (Wilmington)
824 Market St., Ste. 610
Wilmington, DE 19801
(302)573-6652
Fax: (302)573-6092
Website: http://www.scoredelaware.com

District of Columbia

SCORE Office (George Mason University)
409 3rd St. SW, 4th Fl.
Washington, DC 20024
800-634-0245

SCORE Office (Washington DC)
1110 Vermont Ave. NW, 9th Fl.

Washington, DC 20043
(202)606-4000
Fax: (202)606-4225
E-mail: dcscore@hotmail.com
Website: http://www.scoredc.org/

Florida

SCORE Office (Desota County Chamber of Commerce)
16 South Velucia Ave.
Arcadia, FL 34266
(941)494-4033

SCORE Office (Suncoast/Pinellas)
Airport Business Ctr.
4707 - 140th Ave. N, No. 311
Clearwater, FL 33755
(813)532-6800
Fax: (813)532-6800

SCORE Office (DeLand)
336 N. Woodland Blvd.
DeLand, FL 32720
(904)734-4331
Fax: (904)734-4333

SCORE Office (South Palm Beach)
1050 S. Federal Hwy., Ste. 132
Delray Beach, FL 33483
(561)278-7752
Fax: (561)278-0288

SCORE Office (Ft. Lauderdale)
Federal Bldg., Ste. 123
299 E. Broward Blvd.
Ft. Lauderdale, FL 33301
(954)356-7263
Fax: (954)356-7145

SCORE Office (Southwest Florida)
The Renaissance
8695 College Pky., Ste. 345 & 346
Ft. Myers, FL 33919
(941)489-2935
Fax: (941)489-1170

SCORE Office (Treasure Coast)
Professional Center, Ste. 2
3220 S. US, No. 1
Ft. Pierce, FL 34982
(561)489-0548

SCORE Office (Gainesville)
101 SE 2nd Pl., Ste. 104
Gainesville, FL 32601
(904)375-8278

SCORE Office (Hialeah Dade Chamber)
59 W. 5th St.
Hialeah, FL 33010

(305)887-1515
Fax: (305)887-2453

SCORE Office (Daytona Beach)
921 Nova Rd., Ste. A
Holly Hills, FL 32117
(904)255-6889
Fax: (904)255-0229
E-mail: score87@dbeach.com

SCORE Office (South Broward)
3475 Sheridian St., Ste. 203
Hollywood, FL 33021
(305)966-8415

SCORE Office (Citrus County)
5 Poplar Ct.
Homosassa, FL 34446
(352)382-1037

SCORE Office (Jacksonville)
7825 Baymeadows Way, Ste. 100-B
Jacksonville, FL 32256
(904)443-1911
Fax: (904)443-1980
E-mail: scorejax@juno.com
Website: http://www.scorejax.org/

SCORE Office (Jacksonville Satellite)
3 Independent Dr.
Jacksonville, FL 32256
(904)366-6600
Fax: (904)632-0617

SCORE Office (Central Florida)
5410 S. Florida Ave., No. 3
Lakeland, FL 33801
(941)687-5783
Fax: (941)687-6225

SCORE Office (Lakeland)
100 Lake Morton Dr.
Lakeland, FL 33801
(941)686-2168

SCORE Office (St. Petersburg)
800 W. Bay Dr., Ste. 505
Largo, FL 33712
(813)585-4571

SCORE Office (Leesburg)
9501 US Hwy. 441
Leesburg, FL 34788-8751
(352)365-3556
Fax: (352)365-3501

SCORE Office (Cocoa)
1600 Farno Rd., Unit 205
Melbourne, FL 32935
(407)254-2288

SCORE Office (Melbourne)
Melbourne Professional Complex
1600 Sarno, Ste. 205
Melbourne, FL 32935
(407)254-2288
Fax: (407)245-2288

SCORE Office (Merritt Island)
1600 Sarno Rd., Ste. 205
Melbourne, FL 32935
(407)254-2288
Fax: (407)254-2288

SCORE Office (Space Coast)
Melbourn Professional Complex
1600 Sarno, Ste. 205
Melbourne, FL 32935
(407)254-2288
Fax: (407)254-2288

SCORE Office (Dade)
49 NW 5th St.
Miami, FL 33128
(305)371-6889
Fax: (305)374-1882
E-mail: score@netrox.net
Website: http://www.netrox.net/~score/

SCORE Office (Naples of Collier)
International College
2654 Tamiami Trl. E
Naples, FL 34112
(941)417-1280
Fax: (941)417-1281
E-mail: score@naples.net
Website: http://www.naples.net/clubs/
score/index.htm

SCORE Office (Pasco County)
6014 US Hwy. 19, Ste. 302
New Port Richey, FL 34652
(813)842-4638

SCORE Office (Southeast Volusia)
115 Canal St.
New Smyrna Beach, FL 32168
(904)428-2449
Fax: (904)423-3512

SCORE Office (Ocala)
110 E. Silver Springs Blvd.
Ocala, FL 34470
(352)629-5959

Clay County SCORE Office
Clay County Chamber of Commerce
1734 Kingsdey Ave.
PO Box 1441
Orange Park, FL 32073
(904)264-2651
Fax: (904)269-0363

SCORE Office (Orlando)
80 N. Hughey Ave.
Rm. 445 Federal Bldg.
Orlando, FL 32801
(407)648-6476
Fax: (407)648-6425

SCORE Office (Emerald Coast)
19 W. Garden St., No. 325
Pensacola, FL 32501
(904)444-2060
Fax: (904)444-2070

SCORE Office (Charlotte County)
201 W. Marion Ave., Ste. 211
Punta Gorda, FL 33950
(941)575-1818
E-mail: score@gls3c.com
Website: http://www.charlotte-
florida.com/business/scorepg01.htm

SCORE Office (St. Augustine)
1 Riberia St.
St. Augustine, FL 32084
(904)829-5681
Fax: (904)829-6477

SCORE Office (Bradenton)
2801 Fruitville, Ste. 280
Sarasota, FL 34237
(813)955-1029

SCORE Office (Manasota)
2801 Fruitville Rd., Ste. 280
Sarasota, FL 34237
(941)955-1029
Fax: (941)955-5581
E-mail: score116@gte.net
Website: http://www.score-suncoast.org/

SCORE Office (Tallahassee)
200 W. Park Ave.
Tallahassee, FL 32302
(850)487-2665

SCORE Office (Hillsborough)
4732 Dale Mabry Hwy. N, Ste. 400
Tampa, FL 33614-6509
(813)870-0125

SCORE Office (Lake Sumter)
122 E. Main St.
Tavares, FL 32778-3810
(352)365-3556

SCORE Office (Titusville)
2000 S. Washington Ave.
Titusville, FL 32780
(407)267-3036
Fax: (407)264-0127

SCORE Office (Venice)
257 N. Tamiami Trl.
Venice, FL 34285
(941)488-2236
Fax: (941)484-5903

SCORE Office (Palm Beach)
500 Australian Ave. S, Ste. 100
West Palm Beach, FL 33401
(561)833-1672
Fax: (561)833-1712

SCORE Office (Wildwood)
103 N. Webster St.
Wildwood, FL 34785

Georgia

SCORE Office (Atlanta)
Harris Tower, Suite 1900
233 Peachtree Rd., NE
Atlanta, GA 30309
(404)347-2442
Fax: (404)347-1227

SCORE Office (Augusta)
3126 Oxford Rd.
Augusta, GA 30909
(706)869-9100

SCORE Office (Columbus)
School Bldg.
PO Box 40
Columbus, GA 31901
(706)327-3654

SCORE Office (Dalton-Whitfield)
305 S. Thorton Ave.
Dalton, GA 30720
(706)279-3383

SCORE Office (Gainesville)
PO Box 374
Gainesville, GA 30503
(770)532-6206
Fax: (770)535-8419

SCORE Office (Macon)
711 Grand Bldg.
Macon, GA 31201
(912)751-6160

SCORE Office (Brunswick)
4 Glen Ave.
St. Simons Island, GA 31520
(912)265-0620
Fax: (912)265-0629

SCORE Office (Savannah)
111 E. Liberty St., Ste. 103
Savannah, GA 31401
(912)652-4335

Fax: (912)652-4184
E-mail: info@scoresav.org
Website: http://www.coastalempire.com/
score/index.htm

Guam

SCORE Office (Guam)
Pacific News Bldg., Rm. 103
238 Archbishop Flores St.
Agana, GU 96910-5100
(671)472-7308

Hawaii

SCORE Office (Hawaii, Inc.)
1111 Bishop St., Ste. 204
PO Box 50207
Honolulu, HI 96813
(808)522-8132
Fax: (808)522-8135
E-mail: hnlscore@juno.com

SCORE Office (Kahului)
250 Alamaha, Unit N16A
Kahului, HI 96732
(808)871-7711

SCORE Office (Maui, Inc.)
590 E. Lipoa Pkwy., Ste. 227
Kihei, HI 96753
(808)875-2380

Idaho

SCORE Office (Treasure Valley)
1020 Main St., No. 290
Boise, ID 83702
(208)334-1696
Fax: (208)334-9353

SCORE Office (Eastern Idaho)
2300 N. Yellowstone, Ste. 119
Idaho Falls, ID 83401
(208)523-1022
Fax: (208)528-7127

Illinois

SCORE Office (Fox Valley)
40 W. Downer Pl.
PO Box 277
Aurora, IL 60506
(630)897-9214
Fax: (630)897-7002

SCORE Office (Greater Belvidere)
419 S. State St.
Belvidere, IL 61008
(815)544-4357
Fax: (815)547-7654

SCORE Office (Bensenville)
1050 Busse Hwy. Suite 100
Bensenville, IL 60106
(708)350-2944
Fax: (708)350-2979

SCORE Office (Central Illinois)
402 N. Hershey Rd.
Bloomington, IL 61704
(309)644-0549
Fax: (309)663-8270
E-mail: webmaster@central-illinois-
score.org
Website: http://www.central-illinois-
score.org/

SCORE Office (Southern Illinois)
150 E. Pleasant Hill Rd.
Box 1
Carbondale, IL 62901
(618)453-6654
Fax: (618)453-5040

SCORE Office (Chicago)
Northwest Atrium Ctr.
500 W. Madison St., No. 1250
Chicago, IL 60661
(312)353-7724
Fax: (312)886-5688
Website: http://www.mcs.net/~bic/

**SCORE Office (Chicago–Oliver Harvey
College)**
Pullman Bldg.
1000 E. 11th St., 7th Fl.
Chicago, IL 60628
Fax: (312)468-8086

SCORE Office (Danville)
28 W. N. Street
Danville, IL 61832
(217)442-7232
Fax: (217)442-6228

SCORE Office (Decatur)
Milliken University
1184 W. Main St.
Decatur, IL 62522
(217)424-6297
Fax: (217)424-3993
E-mail: charding@mail.millikin.edu
Website: http://www.millikin.edu/
academics/Tabor/score.html

SCORE Office (Downers Grove)
925 Curtis
Downers Grove, IL 60515
(708)968-4050
Fax: (708)968-8368

SCORE Office (Elgin)
24 E. Chicago, 3rd Fl.
PO Box 648
Elgin, IL 60120
(847)741-5660
Fax: (847)741-5677

SCORE Office (Freeport Area)
26 S. Galena Ave.
Freeport, IL 61032
(815)233-1350
Fax: (815)235-4038

SCORE Office (Galesburg)
292 E. Simmons St.
PO Box 749
Galesburg, IL 61401
(309)343-1194
Fax: (309)343-1195

SCORE Office (Glen Ellyn)
500 Pennsylvania
Glen Ellyn, IL 60137
(708)469-0907
Fax: (708)469-0426

SCORE Office (Greater Alton)
Alden Hall
5800 Godfrey Rd.
Godfrey, IL 62035-2466
(618)467-2280
Fax: (618)466-8289
Website: http://www.altonweb.com/
score/

SCORE Office (Grayslake)
19351 W. Washington St.
Grayslake, IL 60030
(708)223-3633
Fax: (708)223-9371

SCORE Office (Harrisburg)
303 S. Commercial
Harrisburg, IL 62946-1528
(618)252-8528
Fax: (618)252-0210

SCORE Office (Joliet)
100 N. Chicago
Joliet, IL 60432
(815)727-5371
Fax: (815)727-5374

SCORE Office (Kankakee)
101 S. Schuyler Ave.
Kankakee, IL 60901
(815)933-0376
Fax: (815)933-0380

SCORE Office (Macomb)
216 Seal Hall, Rm. 214

Macomb, IL 61455
(309)298-1128
Fax: (309)298-2520

SCORE Office (Matteson)
210 Lincoln Mall
Matteson, IL 60443
(708)709-3750
Fax: (708)503-9322

SCORE Office (Mattoon)
1701 Wabash Ave.
Mattoon, IL 61938
(217)235-5661
Fax: (217)234-6544

SCORE Office (Quad Cities)
622 19th St.
Moline, IL 61265
(309)797-0082
Fax: (309)757-5435
E-mail: score@qconline.com
Website: http://www.qconline.com/
business/score/

SCORE Office (Naperville)
131 W. Jefferson Ave.
Naperville, IL 60540
(708)355-4141
Fax: (708)355-8355

SCORE Office (Northbrook)
2002 Walters Ave.
Northbrook, IL 60062
(847)498-5555
Fax: (847)498-5510

SCORE Office (Palos Hills)
10900 S. 88th Ave.
Palos Hills, IL 60465
(847)974-5468
Fax: (847)974-0078

SCORE Office (Peoria)
124 SW Adams, Ste. 300
Peoria, IL 61602
(309)676-0755
Fax: (309)676-7534

SCORE Office (Prospect Heights)
1375 Wolf Rd.
Prospect Heights, IL 60070
(847)537-8660
Fax: (847)537-7138

SCORE Office (Quincy Tri-State)
300 Civic Center Plz., Ste. 245
Quincy, IL 62301
(217)222-8093
Fax: (217)222-3033

SCORE Office (River Grove)
2000 5th Ave.
River Grove, IL 60171
(708)456-0300
Fax: (708)583-3121

SCORE Office (Northern Illinois)
515 N. Court St.
Rockford, IL 61103
(815)962-0122
Fax: (815)962-0122

SCORE Office (St. Charles)
103 N. 1st Ave.
St. Charles, IL 60174-1982
(847)584-8384
Fax: (847)584-6065

SCORE Office (Springfield)
511 W. Capitol Ave., Ste. 302
Springfield, IL 62704
(217)492-4416
Fax: (217)492-4867

SCORE Office (Sycamore)
112 Somunak St.
Sycamore, IL 60178
(815)895-3456
Fax: (815)895-0125

SCORE Office (University)
Hwy. 50 & Stuenkel Rd. Ste. C3305
University Park, IL 60466
(708)534-5000
Fax: (708)534-8457

Indiana

SCORE Office (Anderson)
205 W. 11th St.
Anderson, IN 46015
(317)642-0264

SCORE Office (Bloomington)
Star Center
216 W. Allen
Bloomington, IN 47403
(812)335-7334
E-mail: wtfische@indiana.edu
Website: http://www.brainfreezemedia.
com/score527/

SCORE Office (South East Indiana)
500 Franklin St.
Box 29
Columbus, IN 47201
(812)379-4457

SCORE Office (Corydon)
310 N. Elm St.
Corydon, IN 47112

(812)738-2137
Fax: (812)738-6438

SCORE Office (Crown Point)
Old Courthouse Sq. Ste. 206
PO Box 43
Crown Point, IN 46307
(219)663-1800

SCORE Office (Elkhart)
418 S. Main St.
Elkhart, IN 46515
(219)293-1531
Fax: (219)294-1859

SCORE Office (Evansville)
1100 W. Lloyd Expy., Ste. 105
Evansville, IN 47708
(812)426-6144

SCORE Office (Fort Wayne)
1300 S. Harrison St.
Ft. Wayne, IN 46802
(219)422-2601
Fax: (219)422-2601

SCORE Office (Gary)
973 W. 6th Ave., Rm. 326
Gary, IN 46402
(219)882-3918

SCORE Office (Hammond)
7034 Indianapolis Blvd.
Hammond, IN 46324
(219)931-1000
Fax: (219)845-9548

SCORE Office (Indianapolis)
429 N. Pennsylvania St., Ste. 100
Indianapolis, IN 46204-1873
(317)226-7264
Fax: (317)226-7259
E-mail: inscore@indy.net
Website: http://www.score-
indianapolis.org/

SCORE Office (Jasper)
PO Box 307
Jasper, IN 47547-0307
(812)482-6866

**SCORE Office (Kokomo/Howard
Counties)**
106 N. Washington St.
Kokomo, IN 46901
(765)457-5301
Fax: (765)452-4564

SCORE Office (Logansport)
300 E. Broadway, Ste. 103
Logansport, IN 46947
(219)753-6388

SCORE Office (Madison)
301 E. Main St.
Madison, IN 47250
(812)265-3135
Fax: (812)265-2923

SCORE Office (Marengo)
Rt. 1 Box 224D
Marengo, IN 47140
Fax: (812)365-2793

SCORE Office (Marion/Grant Counties)
215 S. Adams
Marion, IN 46952
(765)664-5107

SCORE Office (Merrillville)
255 W. 80th Pl.
Merrillville, IN 46410
(219)769-8180
Fax: (219)736-6223

SCORE Office (Michigan City)
200 E. Michigan Blvd.
Michigan City, IN 46360
(219)874-6221
Fax: (219)873-1204

SCORE Office (South Central Indiana)
4100 Charleston Rd.
New Albany, IN 47150-9538
(812)945-0066

SCORE Office (Rensselaer)
104 W. Washington
Rensselaer, IN 47978

SCORE Office (Salem)
210 N. Main St.
Salem, IN 47167
(812)883-4303
Fax: (812)883-1467

SCORE Office (South Bend)
300 N. Michigan St.
South Bend, IN 46601
(219)282-4350
E-mail: chair@southbend-score.org
Website: http://www.southbend-score.org/

SCORE Office (Valparaiso)
150 Lincolnway
Valparaiso, IN 46383
(219)462-1105
Fax: (219)469-5710

SCORE Office (Vincennes)
27 N. 3rd
PO Box 553
Vincennes, IN 47591
(812)882-6440
Fax: (812)882-6441

SCORE Office (Wabash)
PO Box 371
Wabash, IN 46992
(219)563-1168
Fax: (219)563-6920

Iowa

SCORE Office (Burlington)
Federal Bldg.
300 N. Main St.
Burlington, IA 52601
(319)752-2967

SCORE Office (Cedar Rapids)
2750 1st Ave. NE, Ste 350
Cedar Rapids, IA 52401-1806
(319)362-6405
Fax: (319)362-7861
E:mail: score@scorecr.org
Website: http://www.scorecr.org

SCORE Office (Illowa)
333 4th Ave. S
Clinton, IA 52732
(319)242-5702

SCORE Office (Council Bluffs)
7 N. 6th St.
Council Bluffs, IA 51502
(712)325-1000

SCORE Office (Northeast Iowa)
3404 285th St.
Cresco, IA 52136
(319)547-3377

SCORE Office (Des Moines)
Federal Bldg., Rm. 749
210 Walnut St.
Des Moines, IA 50309-2186
(515)284-4760

SCORE Office (Ft. Dodge)
Federal Bldg., Rm. 436
205 S. 8th St.
Ft. Dodge, IA 50501
(515)955-2622

SCORE Office (Independence)
110 1st. St. east
Independence, IA 50644
(319)334-7178
Fax: (319)334-7179

SCORE Office (Iowa City)
210 Federal Bldg.
PO Box 1853
Iowa City, IA 52240-1853
(319)338-1662

SCORE Office (Keokuk)
401 Main St.
Pierce Bldg., No. 1
Keokuk, IA 52632
(319)524-5055

SCORE Office (Central Iowa)
Fisher Community College
709 S. Center
Marshalltown, IA 50158
(515)753-6645

SCORE Office (River City)
15 West State St.
Mason City, IA 50401
(515)423-5724

SCORE Office (South Central)
SBDC, Indian Hills Community College
525 Grandview Ave.
Ottumwa, IA 52501
(515)683-5127
Fax: (515)683-5263

SCORE Office (Dubuque)
10250 Sundown Rd.
Peosta, IA 52068
(319)556-5110

SCORE Office (Southwest Iowa)
614 W. Sheridan
Shenandoah, IA 51601
(712)246-3260

SCORE Office (Sioux City)
Federal Bldg.
320 6th St.
Sioux City, IA 51101
(712)277-2324
Fax: (712)277-2325

SCORE Office (Iowa Lakes)
122 W. 5th St.
Spencer, IA 51301
(712)262-3059

SCORE Office (Vista)
119 W. 6th St.
Storm Lake, IA 50588
(712)732-3780

SCORE Office (Waterloo)
215 E. 4th
Waterloo, IA 50703
(319)233-8431

Kansas

SCORE Office (Southwest Kansas)
501 W. Spruce
Dodge City, KS 67801
(316)227-3119

SCORE Office (Emporia)
811 Homewood
Emporia, KS 66801
(316)342-1600

SCORE Office (Golden Belt)
1307 Williams
Great Bend, KS 67530
(316)792-2401

SCORE Office (Hays)
PO Box 400
Hays, KS 67601
(913)625-6595

SCORE Office (Hutchinson)
1 E. 9th St.
Hutchinson, KS 67501
(316)665-8468
Fax: (316)665-7619

SCORE Office (Southeast Kansas)
404 Westminster Pl.
PO Box 886
Independence, KS 67301
(316)331-4741

SCORE Office (McPherson)
306 N. Main
PO Box 616
McPherson, KS 67460
(316)241-3303

SCORE Office (Salina)
120 Ash St.
Salina, KS 67401
(785)243-4290
Fax: (785)243-1833

SCORE Office (Topeka)
1700 College
Topeka, KS 66621
(785)231-1010

SCORE Office (Wichita)
100 E. English, Ste. 510
Wichita, KS 67202
(316)269-6273
Fax: (316)269-6499

SCORE Office (Ark Valley)
205 E. 9th St.
Winfield, KS 67156
(316)221-1617

Kentucky

SCORE Office (Ashland)
PO Box 830
Ashland, KY 41105
(606)329-8011
Fax: (606)325-4607

SCORE Office (Bowling Green)
812 State St.
PO Box 51
Bowling Green, KY 42101
(502)781-3200
Fax: (502)843-0458

SCORE Office (Tri-Lakes)
508 Barbee Way
Danville, KY 40422-1548
(606)231-9902

SCORE Office (Glasgow)
301 W. Main St.
Glasgow, KY 42141
(502)651-3161
Fax: (502)651-3122

SCORE Office (Hazard)
B & I Technical Center
100 Airport Gardens Rd.
Hazard, KY 41701
(606)439-5856
Fax: (606)439-1808

SCORE Office (Lexington)
410 W. Vine St., Ste. 290, Civic C
Lexington, KY 40507
(606)231-9902
Fax: (606)253-3190
E-mail: scorelex@uky.campus.mci.net

SCORE Office (Louisville)
188 Federal Office Bldg.
600 Dr. Martin L. King Jr. Pl.
Louisville, KY 40202
(502)582-5976

SCORE Office (Madisonville)
257 N. Main
Madisonville, KY 42431
(502)825-1399
Fax: (502)825-1396

SCORE Office (Paducah)
Federal Office Bldg.
501 Broadway, Rm. B-36
Paducah, KY 42001
(502)442-5685

Louisiana

SCORE Office (Central Louisiana)
802 3rd St.
Alexandria, LA 71309
(318)442-6671

SCORE Office (Baton Rouge)
564 Laurel St.
PO Box 3217
Baton Rouge, LA 70801

(504)381-7130
Fax: (504)336-4306

SCORE Office (North Shore)
2 W. Thomas
Hammond, LA 70401
(504)345-4457
Fax: (504)345-4749

SCORE Office (Lafayette)
804 St. Mary Blvd.
Lafayette, LA 70505-1307
(318)233-2705
Fax: (318)234-8671
E-mail: score302@aol.com

SCORE Office (Lake Charles)
120 W. Pujo St.
Lake Charles, LA 70601
(318)433-3632

SCORE Office (New Orleans)
365 Canal St., Ste. 3100
New Orleans, LA 70130
(504)589-2356
Fax: (504)589-2339

SCORE Office (Shreveport)
400 Edwards St.
Shreveport, LA 71101
(318)677-2536
Fax: (318)677-2541

Maine

SCORE Office (Augusta)
40 Western Ave.
Augusta, ME 04330
(207)622-8509

SCORE Office (Bangor)
Peabody Hall, Rm. 229
One College Cir.
Bangor, ME 04401
(207)941-9707

SCORE Office (Central & Northern Arroostock)
111 High St.
Caribou, ME 04736
(207)492-8010
Fax: (207)492-8010

SCORE Office (Penquis)
South St.
Dover Foxcroft, ME 04426
(207)564-7021

SCORE Office (Maine Coastal)
Mill Mall
Box 1105
Ellsworth, ME 04605-1105

(207)667-5800
E-mail: score@arcadia.net

SCORE Office (Lewiston-Auburn)
BIC of Maine-Bates Mill Complex
35 Canal St.
Lewiston, ME 04240-7764
(207)782-3708
Fax: (207)783-7745

SCORE Office (Portland)
66 Pearl St., Rm. 210
Portland, ME 04101
(207)772-1147
Fax: (207)772-5581
E-mail: Score53@score.maine.org
Website: http://www.score.maine.org/
chapter53/

SCORE Office (Western Mountains)
255 River St.
PO Box 252
Rumford, ME 04257-0252
(207)369-9976

SCORE Office (Oxford Hills)
166 Main St.
South Paris, ME 04281
(207)743-0499

Maryland

SCORE Office (Southern Maryland)
2525 Riva Rd., Ste. 110
Annapolis, MD 21401
(410)266-9553
Fax: (410)573-0981
E-mail: score390@aol.com
Website: http://members.aol.com/
score390/index.htm

SCORE Office (Baltimore)
The City Crescent Bldg., 6th Fl.
10 S. Howard St.
Baltimore, MD 21201
(410)962-2233
Fax: (410)962-1805

SCORE Office (Bel Air)
108 S. Bond St.
Bel Air, MD 21014
(410)838-2020
Fax: (410)893-4715

SCORE Office (Bethesda)
7910 Woodmont Ave., Ste. 1204
Bethesda, MD 20814
(301)652-4900
Fax: (301)657-1973

SCORE Office (Bowie)
6670 Race Track Rd.
Bowie, MD 20715
(301)262-0920
Fax: (301)262-0921

SCORE Office (Dorchester County)
203 Sunburst Hwy.
Cambridge, MD 21613
(410)228-3575

SCORE Office (Upper Shore)
210 Marlboro Ave.
Easton, MD 21601
(410)822-4606
Fax: (410)822-7922

SCORE Office (Frederick County)
43A S. Market St.
Frederick, MD 21701
(301)662-8723
Fax: (301)846-4427

SCORE Office (Gaithersburg)
9 Park Ave.
Gaithersburg, MD 20877
(301)840-1400
Fax: (301)963-3918

SCORE Office (Glen Burnie)
103 Crain Hwy. SE
Glen Burnie, MD 21061
(410)766-8282
Fax: (410)766-9722

SCORE Office (Hagerstown)
111 W. Washington St.
Hagerstown, MD 21740
(301)739-2015
Fax: (301)739-1278

SCORE Office (Laurel)
7901 Sandy Spring Rd. Ste. 501
Laurel, MD 20707
(301)725-4000
Fax: (301)725-0776

SCORE Office (Salisbury)
300 E. Main St.
Salisbury, MD 21801
(410)749-0185
Fax: (410)860-9925

Massachusetts

SCORE Office (NE Massachusetts)
100 Cummings Ctr., Ste. 101 K
Beverly, MA 01923
(978)922-9441
Website: http://www1.shore.net/~score/

SCORE Office (Boston)
10 Causeway St., Rm. 265
Boston, MA 02222-1093
(617)565-5591
Fax: (617)565-5598
E-mail: boston-score-20@worldnet.att.net
Website: http://www.scoreboston.org/

SCORE office (Bristol/Plymouth County)
53 N. 6th St., Federal Bldg.
Bristol, MA 02740
(508)994-5093

SCORE Office (SE Massachusetts)
60 School St.
Brockton, MA 02401
(508)587-2673
Fax: (508)587-1340
Website: http://www.metrosouth
chamber.com/score.html

SCORE Office (North Adams)
820 N. State Rd.
Cheshire, MA 01225
(413)743-5100

SCORE Office (Clinton Satellite)
1 Green St.
Clinton, MA 01510
Fax: (508)368-7689

SCORE Office (Greenfield)
PO Box 898
Greenfield, MA 01302
(413)773-5463
Fax: (413)773-7008

SCORE Office (Haverhill)
87 Winter St.
Haverhill, MA 01830
(508)373-5663
Fax: (508)373-8060

SCORE Office (Hudson Satellite)
PO Box 578
Hudson, MA 01749
(508)568-0360
Fax: (508)568-0360

SCORE Office (Cape Cod)
Independence Pk., Ste. 5B
270 Communications Way
Hyannis, MA 02601
(508)775-4884
Fax: (508)790-2540

SCORE Office (Lawrence)
264 Essex St.
Lawrence, MA 01840
(508)686-0900
Fax: (508)794-9953

SCORE Office (Leominster Satellite)
110 Erdman Way
Leominster, MA 01453
(508)840-4300
Fax: (508)840-4896

SCORE Office (Bristol/Plymouth Counties)
53 N. 6th St., Federal Bldg.
New Bedford, MA 02740
(508)994-5093

SCORE Office (Newburyport)
29 State St.
Newburyport, MA 01950
(617)462-6680

SCORE Office (Pittsfield)
66 West St.
Pittsfield, MA 01201
(413)499-2485

SCORE Office (Haverhill-Salem)
32 Derby Sq.
Salem, MA 01970
(508)745-0330
Fax: (508)745-3855

SCORE Office (Springfield)
1350 Main St.
Federal Bldg.
Springfield, MA 01103
(413)785-0314

SCORE Office (Carver)
12 Taunton Green, Ste. 201
Taunton, MA 02780
(508)824-4068
Fax: (508)824-4069

SCORE Office (Worcester)
33 Waldo St.
Worcester, MA 01608
(508)753-2929
Fax: (508)754-8560

Michigan

SCORE Office (Allegan)
PO Box 338
Allegan, MI 49010
(616)673-2479

SCORE Office (Ann Arbor)
425 S. Main St., Ste. 103
Ann Arbor, MI 48104
(313)665-4433

SCORE Office (Battle Creek)
34 W. Jackson Ste. 4A
Battle Creek, MI 49017-3505

(616)962-4076
Fax: (616)962-6309

SCORE Office (Cadillac)
222 Lake St.
Cadillac, MI 49601
(616)775-9776
Fax: (616)768-4255

SCORE Office (Detroit)
477 Michigan Ave., Rm. 515
Detroit, MI 48226
(313)226-7947
Fax: (313)226-3448

SCORE Office (Flint)
708 Root Rd., Rm. 308
Flint, MI 48503
(810)233-6846

SCORE Office (Grand Rapids)
111 Pearl St. NW
Grand Rapids, MI 49503-2831
(616)771-0305
Fax: (616)771-0328
E-mail: scoreone@iserv.net
Website: http://www.iserv.net/
~scoreone/

SCORE Office (Holland)
480 State St.
Holland, MI 49423
(616)396-9472

SCORE Office (Jackson)
209 East Washington
PO Box 80
Jackson, MI 49204
(517)782-8221
Fax: (517)782-0061

SCORE Office (Kalamazoo)
345 W. Michigan Ave.
Kalamazoo, MI 49007
(616)381-5382
Fax: (616)384-0096
E-mail: score@nucleus.net

SCORE Office (Lansing)
117 E. Allegan
PO Box 14030
Lansing, MI 48901
(517)487-6340
Fax: (517)484-6910

SCORE Office (Livonia)
15401 Farmington Rd.
Livonia, MI 48154
(313)427-2122
Fax: (313)427-6055

SCORE Office (Madison Heights)
26345 John R
Madison Heights, MI 48071
(810)542-5010
Fax: (810)542-6821

SCORE Office (Monroe)
111 E. 1st
Monroe, MI 48161
(313)242-3366
Fax: (313)242-7253

SCORE Office (Mt. Clemens)
58 S/B Gratiot
Mt. Clemens, MI 48043
(810)463-1528
Fax: (810)463-6541

SCORE Office (Muskegon)
PO Box 1087
230 Terrace Plz.
Muskegon, MI 49443
(616)722-3751
Fax: (616)728-7251

SCORE Office (Petoskey)
401 E. Mitchell St.
Petoskey, MI 49770
(616)347-4150

SCORE Office (Pontiac)
Executive Office Bldg.
1200 N. Telegraph Rd.
Pontiac, MI 48341
(810)975-9555

SCORE Office (Pontiac)
PO Box 430025
Pontiac, MI 48343
(810)335-9600

SCORE Office (Port Huron)
920 Pinegrove Ave.
Port Huron, MI 48060
(810)985-7101

SCORE Office (Rochester)
71 Walnut Ste. 110
Rochester, MI 48307
(810)651-6700
Fax: (810)651-5270

SCORE Office (Saginaw)
901 S. Washington Ave.
Saginaw, MI 48601
(517)752-7161
Fax: (517)752-9055

SCORE Office (Upper Peninsula)
2581 I-75 Business Spur
Sault Ste. Marie, MI 49783
(906)632-3301

SCORE Office (Southfield)
21000 W. 10 Mile Rd.
Southfield, MI 48075
(810)204-3050
Fax: (810)204-3099

SCORE Office (Traverse City)
202 E. Grandview Pkwy.
PO Box 387
Traverse City, MI 49685
(616)947-5075
Fax: (616)946-2565

SCORE Office (Warren)
30500 Van Dyke, Ste. 118
Warren, MI 48093
(810)751-3939

Minnesota

SCORE Office (Aitkin)
Aitkin, MN 56431
(218)741-3906

SCORE Office (Albert Lea)
202 N. Broadway Ave.
Albert Lea, MN 56007
(507)373-7487

SCORE Office (Austin)
PO Box 864
Austin, MN 55912
(507)437-4561
Fax: (507)437-4869

SCORE Office (South Metro)
Ames Business Ctr.
2500 W. County Rd., No. 42
Burnsville, MN 55337
(612)898-5645
Fax: (612)435-6972
E-mail: southmetro@scoreminn.org
Website: http://www.scoreminn.org/
southmetro/

SCORE Office (Duluth)
1717 Minnesota Ave.
Duluth, MN 55802
(218)727-8286
Fax: (218)727-3113
E-mail: duluth@scoreminn.org
Website: http://www.scoreminn.org

SCORE Office (Fairmont)
PO Box 826
Fairmont, MN 56031
(507)235-5547
Fax: (507)235-8411

SCORE Office (Southwest Minnesota)
112 Riverfront St.

Box 999
Mankato, MN 56001
(507)345-4519
Fax: (507)345-4451
Website: http://www.scoreminn.org/

SCORE Office (Minneapolis)
North Plaza Bldg., Ste. 51
5217 Wayzata Blvd.
Minneapolis, MN 55416
(612)591-0539
Fax: (612)544-0436
Website: http://www.scoreminn.org/

SCORE Office (Owatonna)
PO Box 331
Owatonna, MN 55060
(507)451-7970
Fax: (507)451-7972

SCORE Office (Red Wing)
2000 W. Main St., Ste. 324
Red Wing, MN 55066
(612)388-4079

SCORE Office (Southeastern Minnesota)
220 S. Broadway, Ste. 100
Rochester, MN 55901
(507)288-1122
Fax: (507)282-8960
Website: http://www.scoreminn.org/

SCORE Office (Brainerd)
St. Cloud, MN 56301

SCORE Office (Central Area)
1527 Northway Dr.
St. Cloud, MN 56301
(320)240-1332
Fax: (320)255-9050
Website: http://www.scoreminn.org/

SCORE Office (St. Paul)
350 St. Peter St., No. 295
Lowry Professional Bldg.
St. Paul, MN 55102
(651)223-5010
Fax: (651)223-5048
Website: http://www.scoreminn.org/

SCORE Office (Winona)
Box 870
Winona, MN 55987
(507)452-2272
Fax: (507)454-8814

SCORE Office (Worthington)
1121 3rd Ave.
Worthington, MN 56187
(507)372-2919
Fax: (507)372-2827

Mississippi

SCORE Office (Delta)
915 Washington Ave.
PO Box 933
Greenville, MS 38701
(601)378-3141

SCORE Office (Gulfcoast)
1 Government Plaza
2909 13th St., Ste. 203
Gulfport, MS 39501
(228)863-0054

SCORE Office (Jackson)
1st Jackson Center, Ste. 400
101 W. Capitol St.
Jackson, MS 39201
(601)965-5533

SCORE Office (Meridian)
5220 16th Ave.
Meridian, MS 39305
(601)482-4412

Missouri

SCORE Office (Lake of the Ozark)
University Extension
113 Kansas St.
PO Box 1405
Camdenton, MO 65020
(573)346-2644
Fax: (573)346-2694
E-mail: score@cdoc.net
Website: http://sites.cdoc.net/score/

Chamber of Commerce (Cape Girardeau)
PO Box 98
Cape Girardeau, MO 63702-0098
(314)335-3312

SCORE Office (Mid-Missouri)
1705 Halstead Ct.
Columbia, MO 65203
(573)874-1132

SCORE Office (Ozark-Gateway)
1486 Glassy Rd.
Cuba, MO 65453-1640
(573)885-4954

SCORE Office (Kansas City)
323 W. 8th St., Ste. 104
Kansas City, MO 64105
(816)374-6675
Fax: (816)374-6692
E-mail: SCOREBIC@AOL.COM
Website: http://www.crn.org/score/

SCORE Office (Sedalia)
Lucas Place
323 W. 8th St., Ste.104
Kansas City, MO 64105
(816)374-6675

SCORE office (Tri-Lakes)
PO Box 1148
Kimberling, MO 65686
(417)739-3041

SCORE Office (Tri-Lakes)
HCRI Box 85
Lampe, MO 65681
(417)858-6798

SCORE Office (Mexico)
111 N. Washington St.
Mexico, MO 65265
(314)581-2765

SCORE Office (Southeast Missouri)
Rte. 1, Box 280
Neelyville, MO 63954
(573)989-3577

SCORE office (Poplar Bluff Area)
806 Emma St.
Poplar Bluff, MO 63901
(573)686-8892

SCORE Office (St. Joseph)
3003 Frederick Ave.
St. Joseph, MO 64506
(816)232-4461

SCORE Office (St. Louis)
815 Olive St., Rm. 242
St. Louis, MO 63101-1569
(314)539-6970
Fax: (314)539-3785
E-mail: info@stlscore.org
Website: http://www.stlscore.org/

SCORE Office (Lewis & Clark)
425 Spencer Rd.
St. Peters, MO 63376
(314)928-2900
Fax: (314)928-2900
E-mail: score01@mail.win.org

SCORE Office (Springfield)
620 S. Glenstone, Ste. 110
Springfield, MO 65802-3200
(417)864-7670
Fax: (417)864-4108

SCORE office (Southeast Kansas)
1206 W. First St.
Webb City, MO 64870
(417)673-3984

Montana

SCORE Office (Billings)
815 S. 27th St.
Billings, MT 59101
(406)245-4111

SCORE Office (Bozeman)
1205 E. Main St.
Bozeman, MT 59715
(406)586-5421

SCORE Office (Butte)
1000 George St.
Butte, MT 59701
(406)723-3177

SCORE Office (Great Falls)
710 First Ave. N
Great Falls, MT 59401
(406)761-4434
E-mail: scoregtf@in.tch.com

SCORE Office (Havre, Montana)
518 First St.
Havre, MT 59501
(406)265-4383

SCORE Office (Helena)
Federal Bldg.
301 S. Park
Helena, MT 59626-0054
(406)441-1081

SCORE Office (Kalispell)
2 Main St.
Kalispell, MT 59901
(406)756-5271
Fax: (406)752-6665

SCORE Office (Missoula)
723 Ronan
Missoula, MT 59806
(406)327-8806
E-mail: score@safeshop.com
Website: http://missoula.bigsky.net/
score/

Nebraska

SCORE Office (Columbus)
Columbus, NE 68601
(402)564-2769

SCORE Office (Fremont)
92 W. 5th St.
Fremont, NE 68025
(402)721-2641

SCORE Office (Hastings)
Hastings, NE 68901
(402)463-3447

SCORE Office (Lincoln)
8800 O St.
Lincoln, NE 68520
(402)437-2409

SCORE Office (Panhandle)
150549 CR 30
Minatare, NE 69356
(308)632-2133
Website: http://www.tandt.com/
SCORE

SCORE Office (Norfolk)
3209 S. 48th Ave.
Norfolk, NE 68106
(402)564-2769

SCORE Office (North Platte)
3301 W. 2nd St.
North Platte, NE 69101
(308)532-4466

SCORE Office (Omaha)
11145 Mill Valley Rd.
Omaha, NE 68154
(402)221-3606
Fax: (402)221-3680
E-mail: infoctr@ne.uswest.net
Website: http://www.tandt.com/score/

Nevada

SCORE Office (Incline Village)
969 Tahoe Blvd.
Incline Village, NV 89451
(702)831-7327
Fax: (702)832-1605

SCORE Office (Carson City)
301 E. Stewart
PO Box 7527
Las Vegas, NV 89125
(702)388-6104

SCORE Office (Las Vegas)
300 Las Vegas Blvd. S, Ste. 1100
Las Vegas, NV 89101
(702)388-6104

SCORE Office (Northern Nevada)
SBDC, College of Business
Administration
Univ. of Nevada
Reno, NV 89557-0100
(702)784-4436
Fax: (702)784-4337

New Hampshire

SCORE Office (North Country)
PO Box 34

Berlin, NH 03570
(603)752-1090

SCORE Office (Concord)
143 N. Main St., Rm. 202A
PO Box 1258
Concord, NH 03301
(603)225-1400
Fax: (603)225-1409

SCORE Office (Dover)
299 Central Ave.
Dover, NH 03820
(603)742-2218
Fax: (603)749-6317

SCORE Office (Monadnock)
34 Mechanic St.
Keene, NH 03431-3421
(603)352-0320

SCORE Office (Lakes Region)
67 Water St., Ste. 105
Laconia, NH 03246
(603)524-9168

SCORE Office (Upper Valley)
Citizens Bank Bldg., Rm. 310
20 W. Park St.
Lebanon, NH 03766
(603)448-3491
Fax: (603)448-1908
E-mail: billt@valley.net
Website: http://www.valley.net/~score/

SCORE Office (Merrimack Valley)
275 Chestnut St., Rm. 618
Manchester, NH 03103
(603)666-7561
Fax: (603)666-7925

SCORE Office (Mt. Washington Valley)
PO Box 1066
North Conway, NH 03818
(603)383-0800

SCORE Office (Seacoast)
195 Commerce Way, Unit-A
Portsmouth, NH 03801-3251
(603)433-0575

New Jersey

SCORE Office (Somerset)
Paritan Valley Community College,
Rte. 28
Branchburg, NJ 08807
(908)218-8874
E-mail: nj-score@grizbiz.com.
Website: http://www.nj-score.org/

SCORE Office (Chester)
5 Old Mill Rd.
Chester, NJ 07930
(908)879-7080

SCORE Office (Greater Princeton)
4 A George Washington Dr.
Cranbury, NJ 08512
(609)520-1776

SCORE Office (Freehold)
36 W. Main St.
Freehold, NJ 07728
(908)462-3030
Fax: (908)462-2123

SCORE Office (North West)
Picantinny Innovation Ctr.
3159 Schrader Rd.
Hamburg, NJ 07419
(973)209-8525
Fax: (973)209-7252
E-mail: nj-score@grizbiz.com
Website: http://www.nj-score.org/

SCORE Office (Monmouth)
765 Newman Springs Rd.
Lincroft, NJ 07738
(908)224-2573
E-mail: nj-score@grizbiz.com
Website: http://www.nj-score.org/

SCORE Office (Manalapan)
125 Symmes Dr.
Manalapan, NJ 07726
(908)431-7220

SCORE Office (Jersey City)
2 Gateway Ctr., 4th Fl.
Newark, NJ 07102
(973)645-3982
Fax: (973)645-2375

SCORE Office (Newark)
2 Gateway Center, 15th Fl.
Newark, NJ 07102-5553
(973)645-3982
Fax: (973)645-2375
E-mail: nj-score@grizbiz.com
Website: http://www.nj-score.org

SCORE Office (Bergen County)
327 E. Ridgewood Ave.
Paramus, NJ 07652
(201)599-6090
E-mail: nj-score@grizbiz.com
Website: http://www.nj-score.org/

SCORE Office (Pennsauken)
4900 Rte. 70

Pennsauken, NJ 08109
(609)486-3421

SCORE Office (Southern New Jersey)
4900 Rte. 70
Pennsauken, NJ 08109
(609)486-3421
E-mail: nj-score@grizbiz.com
Website: http://www.nj-score.org/

SCORE Office (Greater Princeton)
216 Rockingham Row
Princeton Forrestal Village
Princeton, NJ 08540
(609)520-1776
Fax: (609)520-9107
E-mail: nj-score@grizbiz.com
Website: http://www.nj-score.org/

SCORE Office (Shrewsbury)
Hwy. 35
Shrewsbury, NJ 07702
(908)842-5995
Fax: (908)219-6140

SCORE Office (Ocean County)
33 Washington St.
Toms River, NJ 08754
(732)505-6033
E-mail: nj-score@grizbiz.com
Website: http://www.nj-score.org/

SCORE Office (Wall)
2700 Allaire Rd.
Wall, NJ 07719
(908)449-8877

SCORE Office (Wayne)
2055 Hamburg Tpke.
Wayne, NJ 07470
(201)831-7788
Fax: (201)831-9112

New Mexico

SCORE Office (Albuquerque)
525 Buena Vista, SE
Albuquerque, NM 87106
(505)272-7999
Fax: (505)272-7963

SCORE Office (Las Cruces)
Loretto Towne Center
505 S. Main St., Ste. 125
Las Cruces, NM 88001
(505)523-5627
Fax: (505)524-2101
E-mail: score.397@zianet.com

SCORE Office (Roswell)
Federal Bldg., Rm. 237

Roswell, NM 88201
(505)625-2112
Fax: (505)623-2545

SCORE Office (Santa Fe)
Montoya Federal Bldg.
120 Federal Place, Rm. 307
Santa Fe, NM 87501
(505)988-6302
Fax: (505)988-6300

New York

SCORE Office (Northeast)
1 Computer Dr. S
Albany, NY 12205
(518)446-1118
Fax: (518)446-1228

SCORE Office (Auburn)
30 South St.
PO Box 675
Auburn, NY 13021
(315)252-7291

SCORE Office (South Tier Binghamton)
Metro Center, 2nd Fl.
49 Court St.
PO Box 995
Binghamton, NY 13902
(607)772-8860

SCORE Office (Queens County City)
12055 Queens Blvd., Rm. 333
Borough Hall, NY 11424
(718)263-8961

SCORE Office (Buffalo)
Federal Bldg., Rm. 1311
111 W. Huron St.
Buffalo, NY 14202
(716)551-4301
Website: http://www2.pcom.net/score/buf45.html

SCORE Office (Canandaigua)
Chamber of Commerce Bldg.
113 S. Main St.
Canandaigua, NY 14424
(716)394-4400
Fax: (716)394-4546

SCORE Office (Chemung)
333 E. Water St., 4th Fl.
Elmira, NY 14901
(607)734-3358

SCORE Office (Geneva)
Chamber of Commerce Bldg.
PO Box 587

Geneva, NY 14456
(315)789-1776
Fax: (315)789-3993

SCORE Office (Glens Falls)
84 Broad St.
Glens Falls, NY 12801
(518)798-8463
Fax: (518)745-1433

SCORE Office (Orange County)
40 Matthews St.
Goshen, NY 10924
(914)294-8080
Fax: (914)294-6121

SCORE Office (Huntington Area)
151 W. Carver St.
Huntington, NY 11743
(516)423-6100

SCORE Office (Tompkins County)
904 E. Shore Dr.
Ithaca, NY 14850
(607)273-7080

SCORE Office (Long Island City)
120-55 Queens Blvd.
Jamaica, NY 11424
(718)263-8961
Fax: (718)263-9032

SCORE Office (Chatauqua)
101 W. 5th St.
Jamestown, NY 14701
(716)484-1103

SCORE Office (Westchester)
2 Caradon Ln.
Katonah, NY 10536
(914)948-3907
Fax: (914)948-4645
E-mail: score@w-w-w.com
Website: http://w-w-w.com/score/

SCORE Office (Queens County)
Queens Borough Hall
120-55 Queens Blvd. Rm. 333
Kew Gardens, NY 11424
(718)263-8961
Fax: (718)263-9032

SCORE Office (Brookhaven)
3233 Rte. 112
Medford, NY 11763
(516)451-6563
Fax: (516)451-6925

SCORE Office (Melville)
35 Pinelawn Rd., Rm. 207-W
Melville, NY 11747
(516)454-0771

SCORE Office (Nassau County)
400 County Seat Dr., No. 140
Mineola, NY 11501
(516)571-3303
E-mail: Counse1998@aol.com
Website: http://members.aol.com/Counse1998/Default.htm

SCORE Office (Mt. Vernon)
4 N. 7th Ave.
Mt. Vernon, NY 10550
(914)667-7500

SCORE Office (New York)
26 Federal Plz., Rm. 3100
New York, NY 10278
(212)264-4507
Fax: (212)264-4963
E-mail: score1000@erols.com
Website: http://users.erols.com/score-nyc/

SCORE Office (Newburgh)
47 Grand St.
Newburgh, NY 12550
(914)562-5100

SCORE Office (Owego)
188 Front St.
Owego, NY 13827
(607)687-2020

SCORE Office (Peekskill)
1 S. Division St.
Peekskill, NY 10566
(914)737-3600
Fax: (914)737-0541

SCORE Office (Penn Yan)
2375 Rte. 14A
Penn Yan, NY 14527
(315)536-3111

SCORE Office (Dutchess)
110 Main St.
Poughkeepsie, NY 12601
(914)454-1700

SCORE Office (Rochester)
601 Keating Federal Bldg., Rm. 410
100 State St.
Rochester, NY 14614
(716)263-6473
Fax: (716)263-3146
Website: http://www.ggw.org/score/

SCORE Office (Saranac Lake)
30 Main St.
Saranac Lake, NY 12983
(315)448-0415

SCORE Office (Suffolk)
286 Main St.
Setauket, NY 11733
(516)751-3886

SCORE Office (Staten Island)
130 Bay St.
Staten Island, NY 10301
(718)727-1221

SCORE Office (Ulster)
Clinton Bldg., Rm. 107
Stone Ridge, NY 12484
(914)687-5035
Fax: (914)687-5015
Website: http://www.scoreulster.org/

SCORE Office (Syracuse)
401 S. Salina, 5th Fl.
Syracuse, NY 13202
(315)471-9393

SCORE Office (Utica)
SUNY Institute of Technology, Route 12
Utica, NY 13504-3050
(315)792-7553

SCORE Office (Watertown)
518 Davidson St.
Watertown, NY 13601
(315)788-1200
Fax: (315)788-8251

North Carolina

SCORE office (Asheboro)
317 E. Dixie Dr.
Asheboro, NC 27203
(336)626-2626
Fax: (336)626-7077

SCORE Office (Asheville)
Federal Bldg., Rm. 259
151 Patton
Asheville, NC 28801-5770
(828)271-4786
Fax: (828)271-4009

SCORE Office (Chapel Hill)
104 S. Estes Dr.
PO Box 2897
Chapel Hill, NC 27514
(919)967-7075

SCORE Office (Coastal Plains)
PO Box 2897
Chapel Hill, NC 27515
(919)967-7075
Fax: (919)968-6874

SCORE Office (Charlotte)
200 N. College St., Ste. A-2015

Charlotte, NC 28202
(704)344-6576
Fax: (704)344-6769
E-mail: CharlotteSCORE47@AOL.com
Website: http://www.charweb.org/
business/score/

SCORE Office (Durham)
411 W. Chapel Hill St.
Durham, NC 27707
(919)541-2171

SCORE Office (Gastonia)
PO Box 2168
Gastonia, NC 28053
(704)864-2621
Fax: (704)854-8723

SCORE Office (Greensboro)
400 W. Market St., Ste. 103
Greensboro, NC 27401-2241
(910)333-5399

SCORE Office (Henderson)
PO Box 917
Henderson, NC 27536
(919)492-2061
Fax: (919)430-0460

SCORE Office (Hendersonville)
Federal Bldg., Rm. 108
W. 4th Ave. & Church St.
Hendersonville, NC 28792
(828)693-8702
E-mail: score@circle.net
Website: http://www.wncguide.com/
score/Welcome.html

SCORE Office (Unifour)
PO Box 1828
Hickory, NC 28603
(704)328-6111

SCORE Office (High Point)
1101 N. Main St.
High Point, NC 27262
(336)882-8625
Fax: (336)889-9499

SCORE Office (Outer Banks)
Collington Rd. and Mustain
Kill Devil Hills, NC 27948
(252)441-8144

SCORE Office (Down East)
312 S. Front St., Ste. 6
New Bern, NC 28560
(252)633-6688
Fax: (252)633-9608

SCORE Office (Kinston)
PO Box 95

New Bern, NC 28561
(919)633-6688

SCORE Office (Raleigh)
Century Post Office Bldg., Ste. 306
300 Federal St. Mall
Raleigh, NC 27601
(919)856-4739
E-mail: jendres@ibm.net
Website: http://www.intrex.net/score96/
score96.htm

SCORE Office (Sanford)
1801 Nash St.
Sanford, NC 27330
(919)774-6442
Fax: (919)776-8739

SCORE Office (Sandhills Area)
1480 Hwy. 15-501
PO Box 458
Southern Pines, NC 28387
(910)692-3926

SCORE Office (Wilmington)
Corps of Engineers Bldg.
96 Darlington Ave., Ste. 207
Wilmington, NC 28403
(910)815-4576
Fax: (910)815-4658

North Dakota

**SCORE Office
(Bismarck-Mandan)**
700 E. Main Ave., 2nd Fl.
PO Box 5509
Bismarck, ND 58506-5509
(701)250-4303

SCORE Office (Fargo)
657 2nd Ave., Rm. 225
Fargo, ND 58108-3083
(701)239-5677

SCORE Office (Upper Red River)
4275 Technology Dr., Rm. 156
Grand Forks, ND 58202-8372
(701)777-3051

SCORE Office (Minot)
100 1st St. SW
Minot, ND 58701-3846
(701)852-6883
Fax: (701)852-6905

Ohio

SCORE Office (Akron)
1 Cascade Plz., 7th Fl.
Akron, OH 44308

(330)379-3163
Fax: (330)379-3164

SCORE Office (Ashland)
Gill Center
47 W. Main St.
Ashland, OH 44805
(419)281-4584

SCORE Office (Canton)
116 Cleveland Ave. NW, Ste. 601
Canton, OH 44702-1720
(330)453-6047

SCORE Office (Chillicothe)
165 S. Paint St.
Chillicothe, OH 45601
(614)772-4530

SCORE Office (Cincinnati)
Ameritrust Bldg., Rm. 850
525 Vine St.
Cincinnati, OH 45202
(513)684-2812
Fax: (513)684-3251
Website: http://www.score.
chapter34.org/

SCORE Office (Cleveland)
Eaton Center, Ste. 620
1100 Superior Ave.
Cleveland, OH 44114-2507
(216)522-4194
Fax: (216)522-4844

SCORE Office (Columbus)
2 Nationwide Plz., Ste. 1400
Columbus, OH 43215-2542
(614)469-2357
Fax: (614)469-2391
E-mail: info@scorecolumbus.org
Website: http://www.scorecolumbus.org/

SCORE Office (Dayton)
Dayton Federal Bldg., Rm. 505
200 W. Second St.
Dayton, OH 45402-1430
(513)225-2887
Fax: (513)225-7667

SCORE Office (Defiance)
615 W. 3rd St.
PO Box 130
Defiance, OH 43512
(419)782-7946

SCORE Office (Findlay)
123 E. Main Cross St.
PO Box 923
Findlay, OH 45840
(419)422-3314

SCORE Office (Lima)
147 N. Main St.
Lima, OH 45801
(419)222-6045
Fax: (419)229-0266

SCORE Office (Mansfield)
55 N. Mulberry St.
Mansfield, OH 44902
(419)522-3211

SCORE Office (Marietta)
Thomas Hall
Marietta, OH 45750
(614)373-0268

SCORE Office (Medina)
County Administrative Bldg.
144 N. Broadway
Medina, OH 44256
(216)764-8650

SCORE Office (Licking County)
50 W. Locust St.
Newark, OH 43055
(614)345-7458

SCORE Office (Salem)
2491 State Rte. 45 S
Salem, OH 44460
(216)332-0361

SCORE Office (Tiffin)
62 S. Washington St.
Tiffin, OH 44883
(419)447-4141
Fax: (419)447-5141

SCORE Office (Toledo)
608 Madison Ave, Ste. 910
Toledo, OH 43624
(419)259-7598
Fax: (419)259-6460

SCORE Office (Heart of Ohio)
377 W. Liberty St.
Wooster, OH 44691
(330)262-5735
Fax: (330)262-5745

SCORE Office (Youngstown)
306 Williamson Hall
Youngstown, OH 44555
(330)746-2687

Oklahoma

SCORE Office (Anadarko)
PO Box 366
Anadarko, OK 73005
(405)247-6651

SCORE Office (Ardmore)
410 W. Main
Ardmore, OK 73401
(580)226-2620

SCORE Office (Northeast Oklahoma)
210 S. Main
Grove, OK 74344
(918)787-2796
Fax: (918)787-2796
E-mail: Score595@greencis.net

SCORE Office (Lawton)
4500 W. Lee Blvd., Bldg. 100, Ste. 107
Lawton, OK 73505
(580)353-8727
Fax: (580)250-5677

SCORE Office (Oklahoma City)
210 Park Ave., No. 1300
Oklahoma City, OK 73102
(405)231-5163
Fax: (405)231-4876
E-mail: score212@usa.net

SCORE Office (Stillwater)
439 S. Main
Stillwater, OK 74074
(405)372-5573
Fax: (405)372-4316

SCORE Office (Tulsa)
616 S. Boston, Ste. 406
Tulsa, OK 74119
(918)581-7462
Fax: (918)581-6908
Website: http://www.ionet.net/~tulscore/

Oregon

SCORE Office (Bend)
63085 N. Hwy. 97
Bend, OR 97701
(541)923-2849
Fax: (541)330-6900

SCORE Office (Willamette)
1401 Willamette St.
PO Box 1107
Eugene, OR 97401-4003
(541)465-6600
Fax: (541)484-4942

SCORE Office (Florence)
3149 Oak St.
Florence, OR 97439
(503)997-8444
Fax: (503)997-8448

SCORE Office (Southern Oregon)
33 N. Central Ave., Ste. 216

Medford, OR 97501
(541)776-4220
E mail: pgr134f@prodigy.com

SCORE Office (Portland)
1515 SW 5th Ave., Ste. 1050
Portland, OR 97201
(503)326-3441
Fax: (503)326-2808
E-mail: gr134@prodigy.com

SCORE Office (Salem)
416 State St. (corner of Liberty)
Salem, OR 97301
(503)370-2896

Pennsylvania

SCORE Office (Altoona-Blair)
1212 12th Ave.
Altoona, PA 16601-3493
(814)943-8151

SCORE Office (Lehigh Valley)
Rauch Bldg. 37
Lehigh University
621 Taylor St.
Bethlehem, PA 18015
(610)758-4496
Fax: (610)758-5205

SCORE Office (Butler County)
100 N. Main St.
PO Box 1082
Butler, PA 16003
(412)283-2222
Fax: (412)283-0224

SCORE Office (Harrisburg)
4211 Trindle Rd.
Camp Hill, PA 17011
(717)761-4304
Fax: (717)761-4315

SCORE Office (Cumberland Valley)
75 S. 2nd St.
Chambersburg, PA 17201
(717)264-2935

SCORE Office (Monroe County-Stroudsburg)
556 Main St.
East Stroudsburg, PA 18301
(717)421-4433

SCORE Office (Erie)
120 W. 9th St.
Erie, PA 16501
(814)871-5650
Fax: (814)871-7530

SCORE Office (Bucks County)
409 Hood Blvd.
Fairless Hills, PA 19030
(215)943-8850
Fax: (215)943-7404

SCORE Office (Hanover)
146 Broadway
Hanover, PA 17331
(717)637-6130
Fax: (717)637-9127

SCORE Office (Harrisburg)
100 Chestnut, Ste. 309
Harrisburg, PA 17101
(717)782-3874

SCORE Office (East Montgomery County)
Baederwood Shopping Center
1653 The Fairways, Ste. 204
Jenkintown, PA 19046
(215)885-3027

SCORE Office (Kittanning)
2 Butler Rd.
Kittanning, PA 16201
(412)543-1305
Fax: (412)543-6206

SCORE Office (Lancaster)
118 W. Chestnut St.
Lancaster, PA 17603
(717)397-3092

SCORE Office (Westmoreland County)
300 Fraser Purchase Rd.
Latrobe, PA 15650-2690
(412)539-7505
Fax: (412)539-1850

SCORE Office (Lebanon)
252 N. 8th St.
PO Box 899
Lebanon, PA 17042-0899
(717)273-3727
Fax: (717)273-7940

SCORE Office (Lewistown)
3 W. Monument Sq., Ste. 204
Lewistown, PA 17044
(717)248-6713
Fax: (717)248-6714

SCORE Office (Delaware County)
602 E. Baltimore Pike
Media, PA 19063
(610)565-3677
Fax: (610)565-1606

SCORE Office (Milton Area)
112 S. Front St.
Milton, PA 17847

(717)742-7341
Fax: (717)792-2008

SCORE Office (Mon-Valley)
435 Donner Ave.
Monessen, PA 15062
(412)684-4277
Fax: (412)684-7688

SCORE Office (Monroeville)
William Penn Plaza
2790 Mosside Blvd., Ste. 295
Monroeville, PA 15146
(412)856-0622
Fax: (412)856-1030

SCORE Office (Airport Area)
986 Brodhead Rd.
Moon Township, PA 15108-2398
(412)264-6270
Fax: (412)264-1575

SCORE Office (Northeast)
8601 E. Roosevelt Blvd.
Philadelphia, PA 19152
(215)332-3400
Fax: (215)332-6050

SCORE Office (Philadelphia)
1315 Walnut St., Ste. 500
Philadelphia, PA 19107
(215)790-5050
Fax: (215)790-5057
E-mail: score46@bellatlantic.net
Website: http://www.pgweb.net/score46/

SCORE Office (Pittsburgh)
1000 Liberty Ave., Rm. 1122
Pittsburgh, PA 15222
(412)395-6560
Fax: (412)395-6562

SCORE Office (Tri-County)
801 N. Charlotte St.
Pottstown, PA 19464
(610)327-2673

SCORE Office (Reading)
601 Penn St.
Reading, PA 19601
(610)376-3497

SCORE Office (Scranton)
Oppenheim Bldg.
116 N. Washington Ave., Ste. 650
Scranton, PA 18503
(717)347-4611
Fax: (717)347-4611

SCORE Office (Central Pennsylvania)
200 Innovation Blvd., Ste. 242-B
State College, PA 16803

(814)234-9415
Fax: (814)238-9686
Website: http://countrystore.org/
business/score.htm

SCORE Office (Monroe-Stroudsburg)
556 Main St.
Stroudsburg, PA 18360
(717)421-4433

SCORE Office (Uniontown)
Federal Bldg.
Pittsburg St.
PO Box 2065 DTS
Uniontown, PA 15401
(412)437-4222
E-mail: uniontownscore@lcsys.net

SCORE Office (Warren County)
315 2nd Ave.
Warren, PA 16365
(814)723-9017

SCORE Office (Waynesboro)
323 E. Main St.
Waynesboro, PA 17268
(717)762-7123
Fax: (717)962-7124

SCORE Office (Chester County)
Government Service Center, Ste. 281
601 Westtown Rd.
West Chester, PA 19382-4538
(610)344-6910
Fax: (610)344-6919
E-mail: score@locke.ccil.org

SCORE Office (Wilkes-Barre)
7 N. Wilkes-Barre Blvd.
Wilkes Barre, PA 18702-5241
(717)826-6502
Fax: (717)826-6287

SCORE Office (North Central Pennsylvania)
240 W. 3rd St., Rm. 227
PO Box 725
Williamsport, PA 17703
(717)322-3720
Fax: (717)322-1607
E-mail: score234@mail.csrlink.net
Website: http://www.lycoming.org/
score/

SCORE Office (York)
Cyber Center
2101 Pennsylvania Ave.
York, PA 17404
(717)845-8830
Fax: (717)854-9333

Puerto Rico

SCORE Office (Puerto Rico & Virgin Islands)
PO Box 12383-96
San Juan, PR 00914-0383
(787)726-8040
Fax: (787)726-8135

Rhode Island

SCORE Office (Barrington)
281 County Rd.
Barrington, RI 02806
(401)247-1920
Fax: (401)247-3763

SCORE Office (Woonsocket)
640 Washington Hwy.
Lincoln, RI 02865
(401)334-1000
Fax: (401)334-1009

SCORE Office (Wickford)
8045 Post Rd.
North Kingstown, RI 02852
(401)295-5566
Fax: (401)295-8987

SCORE Office (J.G.E. Knight)
380 Westminster St.
Providence, RI 02903
(401)528-4571
Fax: (401)528-4539
Website: http://www.riscore.org

SCORE Office (Warwick)
3288 Post Rd.
Warwick, RI 02886
(401)732-1100
Fax: (401)732-1101

SCORE Office (Westerly)
74 Post Rd.
Westerly, RI 02891
(401)596-7761
800-732-7636
Fax: (401)596-2190

South Carolina

SCORE Office (Aiken)
PO Box 892
Aiken, SC 29802
(803)641-1111
800-542-4536
Fax: (803)641-4174

SCORE Office (Anderson)
Anderson Mall
3130 N. Main St.

Anderson, SC 29621
(864)224-0453

SCORE Office (Coastal)
284 King St.
Charleston, SC 29401
(803)727-4778
Fax: (803)853-2529

SCORE Office (Midlands)
Strom Thurmond Bldg., Rm. 358
1835 Assembly St., Rm 358
Columbia, SC 29201
(803)765-5131
Fax: (803)765-5962
Website: http://www.scoremid
lands.org/

SCORE Office (Piedmont)
Federal Bldg., Rm. B-02
300 E. Washington St.
Greenville, SC 29601
(864)271-3638

SCORE Office (Greenwood)
PO Drawer 1467
Greenwood, SC 29648
(864)223-8357

SCORE Office (Hilton Head Island)
52 Savannah Trail
Hilton Head, SC 29926
(803)785-7107
Fax: (803)785-7110

SCORE Office (Grand Strand)
937 Broadway
Myrtle Beach, SC 29577
(803)918-1079
Fax: (803)918-1083
E-mail: score381@aol.com

SCORE Office (Spartanburg)
PO Box 1636
Spartanburg, SC 29304
(864)594-5000
Fax: (864)594-5055

South Dakota

SCORE Office (West River)
Rushmore Plz. Civic Ctr.
444 Mount Rushmore Rd., No. 209
Rapid City, SD 57701
(605)394-5311
E-mail: score@gwtc.net

SCORE Office (Sioux Falls)
First Financial Center
110 S. Phillips Ave., Ste. 200
Sioux Falls, SD 57104-6727

(605)330-4231
Fax: (605)330-4231

Tennessee

SCORE Office (Chattanooga)
Federal Bldg., Rm. 26
900 Georgia Ave.
Chattanooga, TN 37402
(423)752-5190
Fax: (423)752-5335

SCORE Office (Cleveland)
PO Box 2275
Cleveland, TN 37320
(423)472-6587
Fax: (423)472-2019

SCORE Office (Upper Cumberland Center)
1225 S. Willow Ave.
Cookeville, TN 38501
(615)432-4111
Fax: (615)432-6010

SCORE Office (Unicoi County)
PO Box 713
Erwin, TN 37650
(423)743-3000
Fax: (423)743-0942

SCORE Office (Greeneville)
115 Academy St.
Greeneville, TN 37743
(423)638-4111
Fax: (423)638-5345

SCORE Office (Jackson)
194 Auditorium St.
Jackson, TN 38301
(901)423-2200

SCORE Office (Northeast Tennessee)
1st Tennessee Bank Bldg.
2710 S. Roan St., Ste. 584
Johnson City, TN 37601
(423)929-7686
Fax: (423)461-8052

SCORE Office (Kingsport)
151 E. Main St.
Kingsport, TN 37662
(423)392-8805

SCORE Office (Greater Knoxville)
Farragot Bldg., Ste. 224
530 S. Gay St.
Knoxville, TN 37902
(423)545-4203
E-mail: scoreknox@ntown.com
Website: http://www.scoreknox.org/

SCORE Office (Maryville)
201 S. Washington St.
Maryville, TN 37804-5728
(423)983-2241
800-525-6834
Fax: (423)984-1386

SCORE Office (Memphis)
Federal Bldg., Ste. 390
167 N. Main St.
Memphis, TN 38103
(901)544-3588

SCORE Office (Nashville)
50 Vantage Way, Ste. 201
Nashville, TN 37228-1500
(615)736-7621

Texas

SCORE Office (Abilene)
2106 Federal Post Office and Court Bldg.
Abilene, TX 79601
(915)677-1857

SCORE Office (Austin)
2501 S. Congress
Austin, TX 78701
(512)442-7235
Fax: (512)442-7528

SCORE Office (Golden Triangle)
450 Boyd St.
Beaumont, TX 77704
(409)838-6581
Fax: (409)833-6718

SCORE Office (Brownsville)
3505 Boca Chica Blvd., Ste. 305
Brownsville, TX 78521
(210)541-4508

SCORE Office (Brazos Valley)
3000 Briarcrest, Ste. 302
Bryan, TX 77802
(409)776-8876
E-mail: 102633.2612@compuserve.com

SCORE Office (Cleburne)
Watergarden Pl., 9th Fl., Ste. 400
Cleburne, TX 76031
(817)871-6002

SCORE Office (Corpus Christi)
651 Upper North Broadway, Ste. 654
Corpus Christi, TX 78477
(512)888-4322
Fax: (512)888-3418

SCORE Office (Dallas)
6260 E. Mockingbird
Dallas, TX 75214-2619

(214)828-2471
Fax: (214)821-8033

SCORE Office (El Paso)
10 Civic Center Plaza
El Paso, TX 79901
(915)534-0541
Fax: (915)534-0513

SCORE Office (Bedford)
100 E. 15th St., Ste. 400
Ft. Worth, TX 76102
(817)871-6002

SCORE Office (Ft. Worth)
100 E. 15th St., No. 24
Ft. Worth, TX 76102
(817)871-6002
Fax: (817)871-6031
E-mail: fwbac@onramp.net

SCORE Office (Garland)
2734 W. Kingsley Rd.
Garland, TX 75041
(214)271-9224

SCORE Office (Granbury Chamber of Commerce)
416 S. Morgan
Granbury, TX 76048
(817)573-1622
Fax: (817)573-0805

SCORE Office (Lower Rio Grande Valley)
222 E. Van Buren, Ste. 500
Harlingen, TX 78550
(956)427-8533
Fax: (956)427-8537

SCORE Office (Houston)
9301 Southwest Fwy., Ste. 550
Houston, TX 77074
(713)773-6565
Fax: (713)773-6550

SCORE Office (Irving)
3333 N. MacArthur Blvd., Ste. 100
Irving, TX 75062
(214)252-8484
Fax: (214)252-6710

SCORE Office (Lubbock)
1205 Texas Ave., Rm. 411D
Lubbock, TX 79401
(806)472-7462
Fax: (806)472-7487

SCORE Office (Midland)
Post Office Annex
200 E. Wall St., Rm. P121
Midland, TX 79701
(915)687-2649

SCORE Office (Orange)
1012 Green Ave.
Orange, TX 77630-5620
(409)883-3536
800-528-4906
Fax: (409)886-3247

SCORE Office (Plano)
1200 E. 15th St.
PO Drawer 940287
Plano, TX 75094-0287
(214)424-7547
Fax: (214)422-5182

SCORE Office (Port Arthur)
4749 Twin City Hwy., Ste. 300
Port Arthur, TX 77642
(409)963-1107
Fax: (409)963-3322

SCORE Office (Richardson)
411 Belle Grove
Richardson, TX 75080
(214)234-4141
800-777-8001
Fax: (214)680-9103

SCORE Office (San Antonio)
Federal Bldg., Rm. A527
727 E. Durango
San Antonio, TX 78206
(210)472-5931
Fax: (210)472-5935

SCORE Office (Texarkana State College)
819 State Line Ave.
Texarkana, TX 75501
(903)792-7191
Fax: (903)793-4304

SCORE Office (East Texas)
RTDC
1530 SSW Loop 323, Ste. 100
Tyler, TX 75701
(903)510-2975
Fax: (903)510-2978

SCORE Office (Waco)
401 Franklin Ave.
Waco, TX 76701
(817)754-8898
Fax: (817)756-0776
Website: http://www.brc-waco.com/

SCORE Office (Wichita Falls)
Hamilton Bldg.
900 8th St.
Wichita Falls, TX 76307
(940)723-2741
Fax: (940)723-8773

Utah

SCORE Office (Northern Utah)
160 N. Main
Logan, UT 84321
(435)746-2269

SCORE Office (Ogden)
1701 E. Windsor Dr.
Ogden, UT 84604
(801)629-8613
E-mail: score158@netscape.net

SCORE Office (Central Utah)
1071 E. Windsor Dr.
Provo, UT 84604
(801)373-8660

SCORE Office (Southern Utah)
225 South 700 East
St. George, UT 84770
(435)652-7751

SCORE Office (Salt Lake)
310 S Main St.
Salt Lake City, UT 84101
(801)746-2269
Fax: (801)746-2273

Vermont

SCORE Office (Champlain Valley)
Winston Prouty Federal Bldg.
11 Lincoln St., Rm. 106
Essex Junction, VT 05452
(802)951-6762

SCORE Office (Montpelier)
87 State St., Rm. 205
PO Box 605
Montpelier, VT 05601
(802)828-4422
Fax: (802)828-4485

SCORE Office (Marble Valley)
256 N. Main St.
Rutland, VT 05701-2413
(802)773-9147

SCORE Office (Northeast Kingdom)
20 Main St.
PO Box 904
St. Johnsbury, VT 05819
(802)748-5101

Virgin Islands

SCORE Office (St. Croix)
United Plaza Shopping Center
PO Box 4010, Christiansted
St. Croix, VI 00822
(809)778-5380

SCORE Office (St. Thomas-St. John)
Federal Bldg., Rm. 21
Veterans Dr.
St. Thomas, VI 00801
(809)774-8530

Virginia

SCORE Office (Arlington)
2009 N. 14th St., Ste. 111
Arlington, VA 22201
(703)525-2400

SCORE Office (Blacksburg)
141 Jackson St.
Blacksburg, VA 24060
(540)552-4061

SCORE Office (Bristol)
20 Volunteer Pkwy.
Bristol, VA 24203
(540)989-4850

SCORE Office (Central Virginia)
1001 E. Market St., Ste. 101
Charlottesville, VA 22902
(804)295-6712
Fax: (804)295-7066

SCORE Office (Alleghany Satellite)
241 W. Main St.
Covington, VA 24426
(540)962-2178
Fax: (540)962-2179

SCORE Office (Central Fairfax)
3975 University Dr., Ste. 350
Fairfax, VA 22030
(703)591-2450

SCORE Office (Falls Church)
PO Box 491
Falls Church, VA 22040
(703)532-1050
Fax: (703)237-7904

SCORE Office (Glenns)
Glenns Campus
Box 287
Glenns, VA 23149
(804)693-9650

SCORE Office (Peninsula)
6 Manhattan Sq.
PO Box 7269
Hampton, VA 23666
(757)766-2000
Fax: (757)865-0339
E-mail: score100@seva.net

SCORE Office (Tri-Cities)
108 N. Main St.

Hopewell, VA 23860
(804)458-5536

SCORE Office (Lynchburg)
Federal Bldg.
1100 Main St.
Lynchburg, VA 24504-1714
(804)846-3235

SCORE Office (Greater Prince William)
8963 Center St
Manassas, VA 20110
(703)368-4813
Fax: (703)368-4733

SCORE Office (Martinsville)
115 Broad St.
Martinsville, VA 24112-0709
(540)632-6401
Fax: (540)632-5059

SCORE Office (Hampton Roads)
Federal Bldg., Rm. 737
200 Grandby St.
Norfolk, VA 23510
(757)441-3733
Fax: (757)441-3733
E-mail: scorehr60@juno.com

SCORE Office (Norfolk)
Federal Bldg., Rm. 737
200 Granby St.
Norfolk, VA 23510
(757)441-3733
Fax: (757)441-3733

SCORE Office (Virginia Beach)
Chamber of Commerce
200 Grandby St., Rm 737
Norfolk, VA 23510
(804)441-3733

SCORE Office (Radford)
1126 Norwood St.
Radford, VA 24141
(540)639-2202

SCORE Office (Richmond)
Federal Bldg.
400 N. 8th St., Ste. 1150
PO Box 10126
Richmond, VA 23240-0126
(804)771-2400
Fax: (804)771-8018
E-mail: scorechapter12@yahoo.com
Website: http://www.cvco.org/score/

SCORE Office (Roanoke)
Federal Bldg., Rm. 716
250 Franklin Rd.
Roanoke, VA 24011

(540)857-2834
Fax: (540)857-2043
E-mail: scorerva@juno.com
Website: http://hometown.aol.com/
scorerv/Index.html

SCORE Office (Fairfax)
8391 Old Courthouse Rd., Ste. 300
Vienna, VA 22182
(703)749-0400

SCORE Office (Greater Vienna)
513 Maple Ave. West
Vienna, VA 22180
(703)281-1333
Fax: (703)242-1482

SCORE Office (Shenandoah Valley)
301 W. Main St.
Waynesboro, VA 22980
(540)949-8203
Fax: (540)949-7740
E-mail: score427@intelos.net

SCORE Office (Williamsburg)
201 Penniman Rd.
Williamsburg, VA 23185
(757)229-6511
E-mail: wacc@williamsburgcc.com

SCORE Office (Northern Virginia)
1360 S. Pleasant Valley Rd.
Winchester, VA 22601
(540)662-4118

Washington

SCORE Office (Gray's Harbor)
506 Duffy St.
Aberdeen, WA 98520
(360)532-1924
Fax: (360)533-7945

SCORE Office (Bellingham)
101 E. Holly St.
Bellingham, WA 98225
(360)676-3307

SCORE Office (Everett)
2702 Hoyt Ave.
Everett, WA 98201-3556
(206)259-8000

SCORE Office (Gig Harbor)
3125 Judson St.
Gig Harbor, WA 98335
(206)851-6865

SCORE Office (Kennewick)
PO Box 6986
Kennewick, WA 99336
(509)736-0510

SCORE Office (Puyallup)
322 2nd St. SW
PO Box 1298
Puyallup, WA 98371
(206)845-6755
Fax: (206)848-6164

SCORE Office (Seattle)
1200 6th Ave., Ste. 1700
Seattle, WA 98101
(206)553-7320
Fax: (206)553-7044
E-mail: score55@aol.com
Website: http://www.scn.org/civic/score-online/index55.html

SCORE Office (Spokane)
801 W. Riverside Ave., No. 240
Spokane, WA 99201
(509)353-2820
Fax: (509)353-2600
E-mail: score@dmi.net
Website: http://www.dmi.net/score/

SCORE Office (Clover Park)
PO Box 1933
Tacoma, WA 98401-1933
(206)627-2175

SCORE Office (Tacoma)
1101 Pacific Ave.
Tacoma, WA 98402
(253)274-1288
Fax: (253)274-1289

SCORE Office (Fort Vancouver)
1701 Broadway, S-1
Vancouver, WA 98663
(360)699-1079

SCORE Office (Walla Walla)
500 Tausick Way
Walla Walla, WA 99362
(509)527-4681

SCORE Office (Mid-Columbia)
1113 S. 14th Ave.
Yakima, WA 98907
(509)574-4944
Fax: (509)574-2943
Website: http://www.ellensburg.com/
~score/

West Virginia

SCORE Office (Charleston)
1116 Smith St.
Charleston, WV 25301
(304)347-5463
E-mail: score256@juno.com

SCORE Office (Virginia Street)
1116 Smith St., Ste. 302
Charleston, WV 25301
(304)347-5463

SCORE Office (Marion County)
PO Box 208
Fairmont, WV 26555-0208
(304)363-0486

SCORE Office (Upper Monongahela Valley)
1000 Technology Dr., Ste. 1111
Fairmont, WV 26555
(304)363-0486
E-mail: score537@hotmail.com

SCORE Office (Huntington)
1101 6th Ave., Ste. 220
Huntington, WV 25701-2309
(304)523-4092

SCORE Office (Wheeling)
1310 Market St.
Wheeling, WV 26003
(304)233-2575
Fax: (304)233-1320

Wisconsin

SCORE Office (Fox Cities)
227 S. Walnut St.
Appleton, WI 54913
(920)734-7101
Fax: (920)734-7161

SCORE Office (Beloit)
136 W. Grand Ave., Ste. 100
PO Box 717
Beloit, WI 53511
(608)365-8835
Fax: (608)365-9170

SCORE Office (Eau Claire)
Federal Bldg., Rm. B11
510 S. Barstow St.
Eau Claire, WI 54701
(715)834-1573
E-mail: score@ecol.net
Website: http://www.ecol.net/~score/

SCORE Office (Fond du Lac)
207 N. Main St.
Fond du Lac, WI 54935
(414)921-9500
Fax: (414)921-9559

SCORE Office (Green Bay)
835 Potts Ave.
Green Bay, WI 54304
(414)496-8930
Fax: (414)496-6009

SCORE Office (Janesville)
20 S. Main St., Ste. 11
PO Box 8008
Janesville, WI 53547
(608)757-3160
Fax: (608)757-3170

SCORE Office (La Crosse)
712 Main St.
La Crosse, WI 54602-0219
(608)784-4880

SCORE Office (Madison)
505 S. Rosa Rd.
Madison, WI 53719
(608)441-2820

SCORE Office (Manitowoc)
1515 Memorial Dr.
PO Box 903
Manitowoc, WI 54221-0903
(414)684-5575
Fax: (414)684-1915

SCORE Office (Milwaukee)
310 W. Wisconsin Ave., Ste. 425
Milwaukee, WI 53203
(414)297-3942
Fax: (414)297-1377

SCORE Office (Central Wisconsin)
1224 Lindbergh Ave.
Stevens Point, WI 54481
(715)344-7729

SCORE Office (Superior)
Superior Business Center Inc.
1423 N. 8th St.
Superior, WI 54880
(715)394-7388
Fax: (715)393-7414

SCORE Office (Waukesha)
223 Wisconsin Ave.
Waukesha, WI 53186-4926
(414)542-4249

SCORE Office (Wausau)
300 3rd St., Ste. 200
Wausau, WI 54402-6190
(715)845-6231

SCORE Office (Wisconsin Rapids)
2240 Kingston Rd.
Wisconsin Rapids, WI 54494
(715)423-1830

Wyoming

SCORE Office (Casper)
Federal Bldg., No. 2215
100 East B St.

Casper, WY 82602
(307)261-6529
Fax: (307)261-6530

Venture capital & financing companies

This section contains a listing of financing and loan companies in the United States and Canada. These listing are arranged alphabetically by country, then by state or province, then by city, then by organization name.

Canada

Alberta

Launchworks Inc.
1902J 11th St., S.E.
Calgary, AB, Canada T2G 3G2
(403)269-1119
Fax: (403)269-1141
Website: http://www.launchworks.com

Native Venture Capital Company, Inc.
21 Artist View Point, Box 7
Site 25, RR 12
Calgary, AB, Canada T3E 6W3
(903)208-5380

Miralta Capital Inc.
4445 Calgary Trail South
888 Terrace Plaza Alberta
Edmonton, AB, Canada T6H 5R7
(780)438-3535
Fax: (780)438-3129

Vencap Equities Alberta Ltd.
10180-101st St., Ste. 1980
Edmonton, AB, Canada T5J 3S4
(403)420-1171
Fax: (403)429-2541

British Columbia

Discovery Capital
5th Fl., 1199 West Hastings
Vancouver, BC, Canada V6E 3T5
(604)683-3000
Fax: (604)662-3457
E-mail: info@discoverycapital.com
Website: http://www.discoverycapital.com

Greenstone Venture Partners
1177 West Hastings St.
Ste. 400
Vancouver, BC, Canada V6E 2K3
(604)717-1977
Fax: (604)717-1976
Website: http://www.greenstonevc.com

Growthworks Capital
2600-1055 West Georgia St.
Box 11170 Royal Centre
Vancouver, BC, Canada V6E 3R5
(604)895-7259
Fax: (604)669-7605
Website: http://www.wofund.com

MDS Discovery Venture Management, Inc.
555 W. Eighth Ave., Ste. 305
Vancouver, BC, Canada V5Z 1C6
(604)872-8464
Fax: (604)872-2977
E-mail: info@mds-ventures.com

Ventures West Management Inc.
1285 W. Pender St., Ste. 280
Vancouver, BC, Canada V6E 4B1
(604)688-9495
Fax: (604)687-2145
Website: http://www.ventureswest.com

Nova Scotia

ACF Equity Atlantic Inc.
Purdy's Wharf Tower II
Ste. 2106
Halifax, NS, Canada B3J 3R7
(902)421-1965
Fax: (902)421-1808

Montgomerie, Huck & Co.
146 Bluenose Dr.
PO Box 538
Lunenburg, NS, Canada B0J 2C0
(902)634-7125
Fax: (902)634-7130

Ontario

IPS Industrial Promotion Services Ltd.
60 Columbia Way, Ste. 720
Markham, ON, Canada L3R 0C9
(905)475-9400
Fax: (905)475-5003

Betwin Investments Inc.
Box 23110
Sault Ste. Marie, ON, Canada P6A 6W6
(705)253-0744
Fax: (705)253-0744

Bailey & Company, Inc.
594 Spadina Ave.
Toronto, ON, Canada M5S 2H4
(416)921-6930
Fax: (416)925-4670

BCE Capital
200 Bay St.

South Tower, Ste. 3120
Toronto, ON, Canada M5J 2J2
(416)815-0078
Fax: (416)941-1073
Website: http://www.bcecapital.com

Castlehill Ventures
55 University Ave., Ste. 500
Toronto, ON, Canada M5J 2H7
(416)862-8574
Fax: (416)862-8875

CCFL Mezzanine Partners of Canada
70 University Ave.
Ste. 1450
Toronto, ON, Canada M5J 2M4
(416)977-1450
Fax: (416)977-6764
E-mail: info@ccfl.com
Website: http://www.ccfl.com

Celtic House International
100 Simcoe St., Ste. 100
Toronto, ON, Canada M5H 3G2
(416)542-2436
Fax: (416)542-2435
Website: http://www.celtic-house.com

Clairvest Group Inc.
22 St. Clair Ave. East
Ste. 1700
Toronto, ON, Canada M4T 2S3
(416)925-9270
Fax: (416)925-5753

Crosbie & Co., Inc.
One First Canadian Place
9th Fl.
PO Box 116
Toronto, ON, Canada M5X 1A4
(416)362-7726
Fax: (416)362-3447
E-mail: info@crosbieco.com
Website: http://www.crosbieco.com

Drug Royalty Corp.
Eight King St. East
Ste. 202
Toronto, ON, Canada M5C 1B5
(416)863-1865
Fax: (416)863-5161

Grieve, Horner, Brown & Asculai
8 King St. E, Ste. 1704
Toronto, ON, Canada M5C 1B5
(416)362-7668
Fax: (416)362-7660

Jefferson Partners
77 King St. West
Ste. 4010

PO Box 136
Toronto, ON, Canada M5K 1H1
(416)367-1533
Fax: (416)367-5827
Website: http://www.jefferson.com

J.L. Albright Venture Partners
Canada Trust Tower, 161 Bay St.
Ste. 4440
PO Box 215
Toronto, ON, Canada M5J 2S1
(416)367-2440
Fax: (416)367-4604
Website: http://www.jlaventures.com

McLean Watson Capital Inc.
One First Canadian Place
Ste. 1410
PO Box 129
Toronto, ON, Canada M5X 1A4
(416)363-2000
Fax: (416)363-2010
Website: http://www.mcleanwatson.com

Middlefield Capital Fund
One First Canadian Place
85th Fl.
PO Box 192
Toronto, ON, Canada M5X 1A6
(416)362-0714
Fax: (416)362-7925
Website: http://www.middlefield.com

Mosaic Venture Partners
24 Duncan St.
Ste. 300
Toronto, ON, Canada M5V 3M6
(416)597-8889
Fax: (416)597-2345

Onex Corp.
161 Bay St.
PO Box 700
Toronto, ON, Canada M5J 2S1
(416)362-7711
Fax: (416)362-5765

Penfund Partners Inc.
145 King St. West
Ste. 1920
Toronto, ON, Canada M5H 1J8
(416)865-0300
Fax: (416)364-6912
Website: http://www.penfund.com

Primaxis Technology Ventures Inc.
1 Richmond St. West, 8th Fl.
Toronto, ON, Canada M5H 3W4
(416)313-5210
Fax: (416)313-5218
Website: http://www.primaxis.com

Priveq Capital Funds
240 Duncan Mill Rd., Ste. 602
Toronto, ON, Canada M3B 3P1
(416)447-3330
Fax: (416)447-3331
E-mail: priveq@sympatico.ca

Roynat Ventures
40 King St. West, 26th Fl.
Toronto, ON, Canada M5H 1H1
(416)933-2667
Fax: (416)933-2783
Website: http://www.roynatcapital.com

Tera Capital Corp.
366 Adelaide St. East, Ste. 337
Toronto, ON, Canada M5A 3X9
(416)368-1024
Fax: (416)368-1427

Working Ventures Canadian Fund Inc.
250 Bloor St. East, Ste. 1600
Toronto, ON, Canada M4W 1E6
(416)934-7718
Fax: (416)929-0901
Website: http://www.workingventures.ca

Quebec

Altamira Capital Corp.
202 University
Niveau de Maisoneuve, Bur. 201
Montreal, QC, Canada H3A 2A5
(514)499-1656
Fax: (514)499-9570

Federal Business Development Bank
Venture Capital Division
Five Place Ville Marie, Ste. 600
Montreal, QC, Canada H3B 5E7
(514)283-1896
Fax: (514)283-5455

Hydro-Quebec Capitech Inc.
75 Boul, Rene Levesque Quest
Montreal, QC, Canada H2Z 1A4
(514)289-4783
Fax: (514)289-5420
Website: http://www.hqcapitech.com

Investissement Desjardins
2 complexe Desjardins
C.P. 760
Montreal, QC, Canada H5B 1B8
(514)281-7131
Fax: (514)281-7808
Website: http://www.desjardins.com/id

Marleau Lemire Inc.
One Place Ville-Marie, Ste. 3601
Montreal, QC, Canada H3B 3P2

(514)877-3800
Fax: (514)875-6415

Speirs Consultants Inc.
365 Stanstead
Montreal, QC, Canada H3R 1X5
(514)342-3858
Fax: (514)342-1977

Tecnocap Inc.
4028 Marlowe
Montreal, QC, Canada H4A 3M2
(514)483-6009
Fax: (514)483-6045
Website: http://www.technocap.com

Telsoft Ventures
1000, Rue de la Gauchetiere
Quest, 25eme Etage
Montreal, QC, Canada H3B 4W5
(514)397-8450
Fax: (514)397-8451

Saskatchewan

Saskatchewan Government Growth Fund
1801 Hamilton St., Ste. 1210
Canada Trust Tower
Regina, SK, Canada S4P 4B4
(306)787-2994
Fax: (306)787-2086

United states

Alabama

FHL Capital Corp.
600 20th Street North
Suite 350
Birmingham, AL 35203
(205)328-3098
Fax: (205)323-0001

Harbert Management Corp.
One Riverchase Pkwy. South
Birmingham, AL 35244
(205)987-5500
Fax: (205)987-5707
Website: http://www.harbert.net

Jefferson Capital Fund
PO Box 13129
Birmingham, AL 35213
(205)324-7709

Private Capital Corp.
100 Brookwood Pl., 4th Fl.
Birmingham, AL 35209
(205)879-2722
Fax: (205)879-5121

21st Century Health Ventures
One Health South Pkwy.
Birmingham, AL 35243
(256)268-6250
Fax: (256)970-8928

FJC Growth Capital Corp.
200 W. Side Sq., Ste. 340
Huntsville, AL 35801
(256)922-2918
Fax: (256)922-2909

Hickory Venture Capital Corp.
301 Washington St. NW
Suite 301
Huntsville, AL 35801
(256)539-1931
Fax: (256)539-5130
E-mail: hvcc@hvcc.com
Website: http://www.hvcc.com

Southeastern Technology Fund
7910 South Memorial Pkwy., Ste. F
Huntsville, AL 35802
(256)883-8711
Fax: (256)883-8558

Cordova Ventures
4121 Carmichael Rd., Ste. 301
Montgomery, AL 36106
(334)271-6011
Fax: (334)260-0120
Website: http://www.cordova
ventures.com

Small Business Clinic of Alabama/AG Bartholomew & Associates
PO Box 231074
Montgomery, AL 36123-1074
(334)284-3640

Arizona

Miller Capital Corp.
4909 E. McDowell Rd.
Phoenix, AZ 85008
(602)225-0504
Fax: (602)225-9024
Website: http://www.themiller
group.com

The Columbine Venture Funds
9449 North 90th St., Ste. 200
Scottsdale, AZ 85258
(602)661-9222
Fax: (602)661-6262

Koch Ventures
17767 N. Perimeter Dr., Ste. 101
Scottsdale, AZ 85255
(480)419-3600

Fax: (480)419-3606
Website: http://www.kochventures.com

McKee & Co.
7702 E. Doubletree Ranch Rd.
Suite 230
Scottsdale, AZ 85258
(480)368-0333
Fax: (480)607-7446

Merita Capital Ltd.
7350 E. Stetson Dr., Ste. 108-A
Scottsdale, AZ 85251
(480)947-8700
Fax: (480)947-8766

Valley Ventures / Arizona Growth Partners L.P.
6720 N. Scottsdale Rd., Ste. 208
Scottsdale, AZ 85253
(480)661-6600
Fax: (480)661-6262

Estreetcapital.com
660 South Mill Ave., Ste. 315
Tempe, AZ 85281
(480)968-8400
Fax: (480)968-8480
Website: http://www.estreetcapital.com

Coronado Venture Fund
PO Box 65420
Tucson, AZ 85728-5420
(520)577-3764
Fax: (520)299-8491

Arkansas

Arkansas Capital Corp.
225 South Pulaski St.
Little Rock, AR 72201
(501)374-9247
Fax: (501)374-9425
Website: http://www.arcapital.com

California

Sundance Venture Partners, L.P.
100 Clocktower Place, Ste. 130
Carmel, CA 93923
(831)625-6500
Fax: (831)625-6590

Westar Capital (Costa Mesa)
949 South Coast Dr., Ste. 650
Costa Mesa, CA 92626
(714)481-5160
Fax: (714)481-5166
E-mail: mailbox@westarcapital.com
Website: http://www.westarcapital.com

Alpine Technology Ventures
20300 Stevens Creek Boulevard, Ste. 495
Cupertino, CA 95014
(408)725-1810
Fax: (408)725-1207
Website: http://www.alpineventures.com

Bay Partners
10600 N. De Anza Blvd.
Cupertino, CA 95014-2031
(408)725-2444
Fax: (408)446-4502
Website: http://www.baypartners.com

Novus Ventures
20111 Stevens Creek Blvd., Ste. 130
Cupertino, CA 95014
(408)252-3900
Fax: (408)252-1713
Website: http://www.novusventures.com

Triune Capital
19925 Stevens Creek Blvd., Ste. 200
Cupertino, CA 95014
(310)284-6800
Fax: (310)284-3290

Acorn Ventures
268 Bush St., Ste. 2829
Daly City, CA 94014
(650)994-7801
Fax: (650)994-3305
Website: http://www.acornventures.com

Digital Media Campus
2221 Park Place
El Segundo, CA 90245
(310)426-8000
Fax: (310)426-8010
E-mail: info@thecampus.com
Website: http://www.digital
mediacampus.com

BankAmerica Ventures / BA Venture Partners
950 Tower Ln., Ste. 700
Foster City, CA 94404
(650)378-6000
Fax: (650)378-6040
Website: http://
www.baventurepartners.com

Starting Point Partners
666 Portofino Lane
Foster City, CA 94404
(650)722-1035
Website: http://www.startingpoint
partners.com

Opportunity Capital Partners
2201 Walnut Ave., Ste. 210

Fremont, CA 94538
(510)795-7000
Fax: (510)494-5439
Website: http://www.ocpcapital.com

Imperial Ventures Inc.
9920 S. La Cienega Boulevar, 14th Fl.
Inglewood, CA 90301
(310)417-5409
Fax: (310)338-6115

Ventana Global (Irvine)
18881 Von Karman Ave., Ste. 1150
Irvine, CA 92612
(949)476-2204
Fax: (949)752-0223
Website: http://www.ventanaglobal.com

Integrated Consortium Inc.
50 Ridgecrest Rd.
Kentfield, CA 94904
(415)925-0386
Fax: (415)461-2726

Enterprise Partners
979 Ivanhoe Ave., Ste. 550
La Jolla, CA 92037
(858)454-8833
Fax: (858)454-2489
Website: http://www.epvc.com

Domain Associates
28202 Cabot Rd., Ste. 200
Laguna Niguel, CA 92677
(949)347-2446
Fax: (949)347-9720
Website: http://www.domainvc.com

Cascade Communications Ventures
60 E. Sir Francis Drake Blvd., Ste. 300
Larkspur, CA 94939
(415)925-6500
Fax: (415)925-6501

Allegis Capital
One First St., Ste. Two
Los Altos, CA 94022
(650)917-5900
Fax: (650)917-5901
Website: http://www.allegiscapital.com

Aspen Ventures
1000 Fremont Ave., Ste. 200
Los Altos, CA 94024
(650)917-5670
Fax: (650)917-5677
Website: http://www.aspenventures.com

AVI Capital L.P.
1 First St., Ste. 2
Los Altos, CA 94022

Organizations, Agencies, & Consultants

(650)949-9862
Fax: (650)949-8510
Website: http://www.avicapital.com

Bastion Capital Corp.
1999 Avenue of the Stars, Ste. 2960
Los Angeles, CA 90067
(310)788-5700
Fax: (310)277-7582
E-mail: ga@bastioncapital.com
Website: http://www.bastioncapital.com

Davis Group
PO Box 69953
Los Angeles, CA 90069-0953
(310)659-6327
Fax: (310)659-6337

Developers Equity Corp.
1880 Century Park East, Ste. 211
Los Angeles, CA 90067
(213)277-0300

Far East Capital Corp.
350 S. Grand Ave., Ste. 4100
Los Angeles, CA 90071
(213)687-1361
Fax: (213)617-7939
E-mail: free@fareastnationalbank.com

Kline Hawkes & Co.
11726 San Vicente Blvd., Ste. 300
Los Angeles, CA 90049
(310)442-4700
Fax: (310)442-4707
Website: http://www.klinehawkes.com

Lawrence Financial Group
701 Teakwood
PO Box 491773
Los Angeles, CA 90049
(310)471-4060
Fax: (310)472-3155

Riordan Lewis & Haden
300 S. Grand Ave., 29th Fl.
Los Angeles, CA 90071
(213)229-8500
Fax: (213)229-8597

Union Venture Corp.
445 S. Figueroa St., 9th Fl.
Los Angeles, CA 90071
(213)236-4092
Fax: (213)236-6329

Wedbush Capital Partners
1000 Wilshire Blvd.
Los Angeles, CA 90017
(213)688-4545
Fax: (213)688-6642
Website: http://www.wedbush.com

Advent International Corp.
2180 Sand Hill Rd., Ste. 420
Menlo Park, CA 94025
(650)233-7500
Fax: (650)233-7515
Website: http://www.adventinter
national.com

Altos Ventures
2882 Sand Hill Rd., Ste. 100
Menlo Park, CA 94025
(650)234-9771
Fax: (650)233-9821
Website: http://www.altosvc.com

Applied Technology
1010 El Camino Real, Ste. 300
Menlo Park, CA 94025
(415)326-8622
Fax: (415)326-8163

APV Technology Partners
535 Middlefield, Ste. 150
Menlo Park, CA 94025
(650)327-7871
Fax: (650)327-7631
Website: http://www.apvtp.com

August Capital Management
2480 Sand Hill Rd., Ste. 101
Menlo Park, CA 94025
(650)234-9900
Fax: (650)234-9910
Website: http://www.augustcap.com

Baccharis Capital Inc.
2420 Sand Hill Rd., Ste. 100
Menlo Park, CA 94025
(650)324-6844
Fax: (650)854-3025

Benchmark Capital
2480 Sand Hill Rd., Ste. 200
Menlo Park, CA 94025
(650)854-8180
Fax: (650)854-8183
E-mail: info@benchmark.com
Website: http://www.benchmark.com

Bessemer Venture Partners (Menlo Park)
535 Middlefield Rd., Ste. 245
Menlo Park, CA 94025
(650)853-7000
Fax: (650)853-7001
Website: http://www.bvp.com

The Cambria Group
1600 El Camino Real Rd., Ste. 155
Menlo Park, CA 94025
(650)329-8600

Fax: (650)329-8601
Website: http://www.cambriagroup.com

Canaan Partners
2884 Sand Hill Rd., Ste. 115
Menlo Park, CA 94025
(650)854-8092
Fax: (650)854-8127
Website: http://www.canaan.com

Capstone Ventures
3000 Sand Hill Rd., Bldg. One, Ste. 290
Menlo Park, CA 94025
(650)854-2523
Fax: (650)854-9010
Website: http://www.capstonevc.com

Comdisco Venture Group (Silicon Valley)
3000 Sand Hill Rd., Bldg. 1, Ste. 155
Menlo Park, CA 94025
(650)854-9484
Fax: (650)854-4026

Commtech International
535 Middlefield Rd., Ste. 200
Menlo Park, CA 94025
(650)328-0190
Fax: (650)328-6442

Compass Technology Partners
1550 El Camino Real, Ste. 275
Menlo Park, CA 94025-4111
(650)322-7595
Fax: (650)322-0588
Website: http://www.compass
techpartners.com

Convergence Partners
3000 Sand Hill Rd., Ste. 235
Menlo Park, CA 94025
(650)854-3010
Fax: (650)854-3015
Website: http://www.conver
gencepartners.com

The Dakota Group
PO Box 1025
Menlo Park, CA 94025
(650)853-0600
Fax: (650)851-4899
E-mail: info@dakota.com

Delphi Ventures
3000 Sand Hill Rd.
Bldg. One, Ste. 135
Menlo Park, CA 94025
(650)854-9650
Fax: (650)854-2961
Website: http://www.delphiventures.com

El Dorado Ventures
2884 Sand Hill Rd., Ste. 121
Menlo Park, CA 94025
(650)854-1200
Fax: (650)854-1202
Website: http://www.eldorado
ventures.com

Glynn Ventures
3000 Sand Hill Rd., Bldg. 4, Ste. 235
Menlo Park, CA 94025
(650)854-2215

Indosuez Ventures
2180 Sand Hill Rd., Ste. 450
Menlo Park, CA 94025
(650)854-0587
Fax: (650)323-5561
Website: http://www.indosuez
ventures.com

Institutional Venture Partners
3000 Sand Hill Rd., Bldg. 2, Ste. 290
Menlo Park, CA 94025
(650)854-0132
Fax: (650)854-5762
Website: http://www.ivp.com

Interwest Partners (Menlo Park)
3000 Sand Hill Rd., Bldg. 3, Ste. 255
Menlo Park, CA 94025-7112
(650)854-8585
Fax: (650)854-4706
Website: http://www.interwest.com

**Kleiner Perkins Caufield & Byers
(Menlo Park)**
2750 Sand Hill Rd.
Menlo Park, CA 94025
(650)233-2750
Fax: (650)233-0300
Website: http://www.kpcb.com

Magic Venture Capital LLC
1010 El Camino Real, Ste. 300
Menlo Park, CA 94025
(650)325-4149

Matrix Partners
2500 Sand Hill Rd., Ste. 113
Menlo Park, CA 94025
(650)854-3131
Fax: (650)854-3296
Website: http://www.matrixpartners.com

Mayfield Fund
2800 Sand Hill Rd.
Menlo Park, CA 94025
(650)854-5560
Fax: (650)854-5712
Website: http://www.mayfield.com

**McCown De Leeuw and Co. (Menlo
Park)**
3000 Sand Hill Rd., Bldg. 3, Ste. 290
Menlo Park, CA 94025-7111
(650)854-6000
Fax: (650)854-0853
Website: http://www.mdcpartners.com

Menlo Ventures
3000 Sand Hill Rd., Bldg. 4, Ste. 100
Menlo Park, CA 94025
(650)854-8540
Fax: (650)854-7059
Website: http://www.menloventures.com

Merrill Pickard Anderson & Eyre
2480 Sand Hill Rd., Ste. 200
Menlo Park, CA 94025
(650)854-8600
Fax: (650)854-0345

**New Enterprise Associates (Menlo
Park)**
2490 Sand Hill Rd.
Menlo Park, CA 94025
(650)854-9499
Fax: (650)854-9397
Website: http://www.nea.com

Onset Ventures
2400 Sand Hill Rd., Ste. 150
Menlo Park, CA 94025
(650)529-0700
Fax: (650)529-0777
Website: http://www.onset.com

Paragon Venture Partners
3000 Sand Hill Rd., Bldg. 1, Ste. 275
Menlo Park, CA 94025
(650)854-8000
Fax: (650)854-7260

**Pathfinder Venture Capital Funds
(Menlo Park)**
3000 Sand Hill Rd., Bldg. 3, Ste. 255
Menlo Park, CA 94025
(650)854-0650
Fax: (650)854-4706

Rocket Ventures
3000 Sandhill Rd., Bldg. 1, Ste. 170
Menlo Park, CA 94025
(650)561-9100
Fax: (650)561-9183
Website: http://www.rocketventures.com

Sequoia Capital
3000 Sand Hill Rd., Bldg. 4, Ste. 280
Menlo Park, CA 94025
(650)854-3927
Fax: (650)854-2977

E-mail: sequoia@sequioacap.com
Website: http://www.sequoiacap.com

Sierra Ventures
3000 Sand Hill Rd., Bldg. 4, Ste. 210
Menlo Park, CA 94025
(650)854-1000
Fax: (650)854-5593
Website: http://www.sierraventures.com

Sigma Partners
2884 Sand Hill Rd., Ste. 121
Menlo Park, CA 94025-7022
(650)853-1700
Fax: (650)853-1717
E-mail: info@sigmapartners.com
Website: http://www.sigmapartners.com

Sprout Group (Menlo Park)
3000 Sand Hill Rd.
Bldg. 3, Ste. 170
Menlo Park, CA 94025
(650)234-2700
Fax: (650)234-2779
Website: http://www.sproutgroup.com

TA Associates (Menlo Park)
70 Willow Rd., Ste. 100
Menlo Park, CA 94025
(650)328-1210
Fax: (650)326-4933
Website: http://www.ta.com

Thompson Clive & Partners Ltd.
3000 Sand Hill Rd., Bldg. 1, Ste. 185
Menlo Park, CA 94025-7102
(650)854-0314
Fax: (650)854-0670
E-mail: mail@tcvc.com
Website: http://www.tcvc.com

Trinity Ventures Ltd.
3000 Sand Hill Rd., Bldg. 1, Ste. 240
Menlo Park, CA 94025
(650)854-9500
Fax: (650)854-9501
Website: http://www.trinityventures.com

U.S. Venture Partners
2180 Sand Hill Rd., Ste. 300
Menlo Park, CA 94025
(650)854-9080
Fax: (650)854-3018
Website: http://www.usvp.com

USVP-Schlein Marketing Fund
2180 Sand Hill Rd., Ste. 300
Menlo Park, CA 94025
(415)854-9080
Fax: (415)854-3018
Website: http://www.usvp.com

Venrock Associates
2494 Sand Hill Rd., Ste. 200
Menlo Park, CA 94025
(650)561-9580
Fax: (650)561-9180
Website: http://www.venrock.com

Brad Peery Capital Inc.
145 Chapel Pkwy.
Mill Valley, CA 94941
(415)389-0625
Fax: (415)389-1336

Dot Edu Ventures
650 Castro St., Ste. 270
Mountain View, CA 94041
(650)575-5638
Fax: (650)325-5247
Website: http://www.dotedu
ventures.com

Forrest, Binkley & Brown
840 Newport Ctr. Dr., Ste. 480
Newport Beach, CA 92660
(949)729-3222
Fax: (949)729-3226
Website: http://www.fbbvc.com

Marwit Capital LLC
180 Newport Center Dr., Ste. 200
Newport Beach, CA 92660
(949)640-6234
Fax: (949)720-8077
Website: http://www.marwit.com

**Kaiser Permanente / National Venture
Development**
1800 Harrison St., 22nd Fl.
Oakland, CA 94612
(510)267-4010
Fax: (510)267-4036
Website: http://www.kpventures.com

Nu Capital Access Group, Ltd.
7677 Oakport St., Ste. 105
Oakland, CA 94621
(510)635-7345
Fax: (510)635-7068

Inman and Bowman
4 Orinda Way, Bldg. D, Ste. 150
Orinda, CA 94563
(510)253-1611
Fax: (510)253-9037

Accel Partners (San Francisco)
428 University Ave.
Palo Alto, CA 94301
(650)614-4800
Fax: (650)614-4880
Website: http://www.accel.com

Advanced Technology Ventures
485 Ramona St., Ste. 200
Palo Alto, CA 94301
(650)321-8601
Fax: (650)321-0934
Website: http://www.atvcapital.com

Anila Fund
400 Channing Ave.
Palo Alto, CA 94301
(650)833-5790
Fax: (650)833-0590
Website: http://www.anila.com

**Asset Management Company Venture
Capital**
2275 E. Bayshore, Ste. 150
Palo Alto, CA 94303
(650)494-7400
Fax: (650)856-1826
E-mail: postmaster@assetman.com
Website: http://www.assetman.com

**BancBoston Capital / BancBoston
Ventures**
435 Tasso St., Ste. 250
Palo Alto, CA 94305
(650)470-4100
Fax: (650)853-1425
Website: http://www.bancboston
capital.com

Charter Ventures
525 University Ave., Ste. 1400
Palo Alto, CA 94301
(650)325-6953
Fax: (650)325-4762
Website: http://www.charterventures.com

Communications Ventures
505 Hamilton Avenue, Ste. 305
Palo Alto, CA 94301
(650)325-9600
Fax: (650)325-9608
Website: http://www.comven.com

HMS Group
2468 Embarcadero Way
Palo Alto, CA 94303-3313
(650)856-9862
Fax: (650)856-9864

Jafco America Ventures, Inc.
505 Hamilton Ste. 310
Palto Alto, CA 94301
(650)463-8800
Fax: (650)463-8801
Website: http://www.jafco.com

New Vista Capital
540 Cowper St., Ste. 200

Palo Alto, CA 94301
(650)329-9333
Fax: (650)328-9434
E-mail: fgreene@nvcap.com
Website: http://www.nvcap.com

Norwest Equity Partners (Palo Alto)
245 Lytton Ave., Ste. 250
Palo Alto, CA 94301-1426
(650)321-8000
Fax: (650)321-8010
Website: http://www.norwestvp.com

Oak Investment Partners
525 University Ave., Ste. 1300
Palo Alto, CA 94301
(650)614-3700
Fax: (650)328-6345
Website: http://www.oakinv.com

**Patricof & Co. Ventures, Inc. (Palo
Alto)**
2100 Geng Rd., Ste. 150
Palo Alto, CA 94303
(650)494-9944
Fax: (650)494-6751
Website: http://www.patricof.com

RWI Group
835 Page Mill Rd.
Palo Alto, CA 94304
(650)251-1800
Fax: (650)213-8660
Website: http://www.rwigroup.com

Summit Partners (Palo Alto)
499 Hamilton Ave., Ste. 200
Palo Alto, CA 94301
(650)321-1166
Fax: (650)321-1188
Website: http://www.summit
partners.com

Sutter Hill Ventures
755 Page Mill Rd., Ste. A-200
Palo Alto, CA 94304
(650)493-5600
Fax: (650)858-1854
E-mail: shv@shv.com

Vanguard Venture Partners
525 University Ave., Ste. 600
Palo Alto, CA 94301
(650)321-2900
Fax: (650)321-2902
Website: http://www.vanguard
ventures.com

Venture Growth Associates
2479 East Bayshore St., Ste. 710
Palo Alto, CA 94303

(650)855-9100
Fax: (650)855-9104

Worldview Technology Partners
435 Tasso St., Ste. 120
Palo Alto, CA 94301
(650)322-3800
Fax: (650)322-3880
Website: http://www.worldview.com

Draper, Fisher, Jurvetson / Draper Associates
400 Seaport Ct., Ste.250
Redwood City, CA 94063
(415)599-9000
Fax: (415)599-9726
Website: http://www.dfj.com

Gabriel Venture Partners
350 Marine Pkwy., Ste. 200
Redwood Shores, CA 94065
(650)551-5000
Fax: (650)551-5001
Website: http://www.gabrielvp.com

Hallador Venture Partners, L.L.C.
740 University Ave., Ste. 110
Sacramento, CA 95825-6710
(916)920-0191
Fax: (916)920-5188
E-mail: chris@hallador.com

Emerald Venture Group
12396 World Trade Dr., Ste. 116
San Diego, CA 92128
(858)451-1001
Fax: (858)451-1003
Website: http://www.emerald
venture.com

Forward Ventures
9255 Towne Centre Dr.
San Diego, CA 92121
(858)677-6077
Fax: (858)452-8799
E-mail: info@forwardventure.com
Website: http://www.forward
venture.com

Idanta Partners Ltd.
4660 La Jolla Village Dr., Ste. 850
San Diego, CA 92122
(619)452-9690
Fax: (619)452-2013
Website: http://www.idanta.com

Kingsbury Associates
3655 Nobel Dr., Ste. 490
San Diego, CA 92122
(858)677-0600
Fax: (858)677-0800

Kyocera International Inc.
Corporate Development
8611 Balboa Ave.
San Diego, CA 92123
(858)576-2600
Fax: (858)492-1456

Sorrento Associates, Inc.
4370 LaJolla Village Dr., Ste. 1040
San Diego, CA 92122
(619)452-3100
Fax: (619)452-7607
Website: http://www.sorrento
ventures.com

Western States Investment Group
9191 Towne Ctr. Dr., Ste. 310
San Diego, CA 92122
(619)678-0800
Fax: (619)678-0900

Aberdare Ventures
One Embarcadero Center, Ste. 4000
San Francisco, CA 94111
(415)392-7442
Fax: (415)392-4264
Website: http://www.aberdare.com

Acacia Venture Partners
101 California St., Ste. 3160
San Francisco, CA 94111
(415)433-4200
Fax: (415)433-4250
Website: http://www.acaciavp.com

Access Venture Partners
319 Laidley St.
San Francisco, CA 94131
(415)586-0132
Fax: (415)392-6310
Website: http://www.access
venturepartners.com

Alta Partners
One Embarcadero Center, Ste. 4050
San Francisco, CA 94111
(415)362-4022
Fax: (415)362-6178
E-mail: alta@altapartners.com
Website: http://www.altapartners.com

Bangert Dawes Reade Davis & Thom
220 Montgomery St., Ste. 424
San Francisco, CA 94104
(415)954-9900
Fax: (415)954-9901
E-mail: bdrdt@pacbell.net

Berkeley International Capital Corp.
650 California St., Ste. 2800
San Francisco, CA 94108-2609

(415)249-0450
Fax: (415)392-3929
Website: http://www.berkeleyvc.com

Blueprint Ventures LLC
456 Montgomery St., 22nd Fl.
San Francisco, CA 94104
(415)901-4000
Fax: (415)901-4035
Website: http://www.blue
printventures.com

Blumberg Capital Ventures
580 Howard St., Ste. 401
San Francisco, CA 94105
(415)905-5007
Fax: (415)357-5027
Website: http://www.blumberg-
capital.com

Burr, Egan, Deleage, and Co. (San Francisco)
1 Embarcadero Center, Ste. 4050
San Francisco, CA 94111
(415)362-4022
Fax: (415)362-6178

Burrill & Company
120 Montgomery St., Ste. 1370
San Francisco, CA 94104
(415)743-3160
Fax: (415)743-3161
Website: http://www.burrillandco.com

CMEA Ventures
235 Montgomery St., Ste. 920
San Francisco, CA 94401
(415)352-1520
Fax: (415)352-1524
Website: http://www.cmeaventures.com

Crocker Capital
1 Post St., Ste. 2500
San Francisco, CA 94101
(415)956-5250
Fax: (415)959-5710

Dominion Ventures, Inc.
44 Montgomery St., Ste. 4200
San Francisco, CA 94104
(415)362-4890
Fax: (415)394-9245

Dorset Capital
Pier 1
Bay 2
San Francisco, CA 94111
(415)398-7101
Fax: (415)398-7141
Website: http://www.dorsetcapital.com

Gatx Capital
Four Embarcadero Center, Ste. 2200
San Francisco, CA 94904
(415)955-3200
Fax: (415)955-3449

IMinds
135 Main St., Ste. 1350
San Francisco, CA 94105
(415)547-0000
Fax: (415)227-0300
Website: http://www.iminds.com

LF International Inc.
360 Post St., Ste. 705
San Francisco, CA 94108
(415)399-0110
Fax: (415)399-9222
Website: http://www.lfvc.com

Newbury Ventures
535 Pacific Ave., 2nd Fl.
San Francisco, CA 94133
(415)296-7408
Fax: (415)296-7416
Website: http://www.newburyven.com

Quest Ventures (San Francisco)
333 Bush St., Ste. 1750
San Francisco, CA 94104
(415)782-1414
Fax: (415)782-1415

Robertson-Stephens Co.
555 California St., Ste. 2600
San Francisco, CA 94104
(415)781-9700
Fax: (415)781-2556
Website: http://www.omegaad
ventures.com

Rosewood Capital, L.P.
One Maritime Plaza, Ste. 1330
San Francisco, CA 94111-3503
(415)362-5526
Fax: (415)362-1192
Website: http://www.rosewoodvc.com

Ticonderoga Capital Inc.
555 California St., No. 4950
San Francisco, CA 94104
(415)296-7900
Fax: (415)296-8956

21st Century Internet Venture Partners
Two South Park
2nd Floor
San Francisco, CA 94107
(415)512-1221
Fax: (415)512-2650
Website: http://www.21vc.com

VK Ventures
600 California St., Ste.1700
San Francisco, CA 94111
(415)391-5600
Fax: (415)397-2744

Walden Group of Venture Capital Funds
750 Battery St., Seventh Floor
San Francisco, CA 94111
(415)391-7225
Fax: (415)391-7262

Acer Technology Ventures
2641 Orchard Pkwy.
San Jose, CA 95134
(408)433-4945
Fax: (408)433-5230

Authosis
226 Airport Pkwy., Ste. 405
San Jose, CA 95110
(650)814-3603
Website: http://www.authosis.com

Western Technology Investment
2010 N. First St., Ste. 310
San Jose, CA 95131
(408)436-8577
Fax: (408)436-8625
E-mail: mktg@westerntech.com

Drysdale Enterprises
177 Bovet Rd., Ste. 600
San Mateo, CA 94402
(650)341-6336
Fax: (650)341-1329
E-mail: drysdale@aol.com

Greylock
2929 Campus Dr., Ste. 400
San Mateo, CA 94401
(650)493-5525
Fax: (650)493-5575
Website: http://www.greylock.com

Technology Funding
2000 Alameda de las Pulgas, Ste. 250
San Mateo, CA 94403
(415)345-2200
Fax: (415)345-1797

2M Invest Inc.
1875 S. Grant St.
Suite 750
San Mateo, CA 94402
(650)655-3765
Fax: (650)372-9107
E-mail: 2minfo@2minvest.com
Website: http://www.2minvest.com

Phoenix Growth Capital Corp.
2401 Kerner Blvd.
San Rafael, CA 94901
(415)485-4569
Fax: (415)485-4663

NextGen Partners LLC
1705 East Valley Rd.
Santa Barbara, CA 93108
(805)969-8540
Fax: (805)969-8542
Website: http://www.nextgen
partners.com

Denali Venture Capital
1925 Woodland Ave.
Santa Clara, CA 95050
(408)690-4838
Fax: (408)247-6979
E-mail: wael@denaliventurecapital.com
Website: http://www.denali
venturecapital.com

Dotcom Ventures LP
3945 Freedom Circle, Ste. 740
Santa Clara, CA 95045
(408)919-9855
Fax: (408)919-9857
Website: http://www.dotcom
venturesatl.com

Silicon Valley Bank
3003 Tasman
Santa Clara, CA 95054
(408)654-7400
Fax: (408)727-8728

Al Shugart International
920 41st Ave.
Santa Cruz, CA 95062
(831)479-7852
Fax: (831)479-7852
Website: http://www.alshugart.com

Leonard Mautner Associates
1434 Sixth St.
Santa Monica, CA 90401
(213)393-9788
Fax: (310)459-9918

Palomar Ventures
100 Wilshire Blvd., Ste. 450
Santa Monica, CA 90401
(310)260-6050
Fax: (310)656-4150
Website: http://www.palomar
ventures.com

Medicus Venture Partners
12930 Saratoga Ave., Ste. D8
Saratoga, CA 95070

(408)447-8600
Fax: (408)447-8599
Website: http://www.medicusvc.com

Redleaf Venture Management
14395 Saratoga Ave., Ste. 130
Saratoga, CA 95070
(408)868-0800
Fax: (408)868-0810
E-mail: nancy@redleaf.com
Website: http://www.redleaf.com

Artemis Ventures
207 Second St., Ste. E
3rd Fl.
Sausalito, CA 94965
(415)289-2500
Fax: (415)289-1789
Website: http://www.artemisventures.com

Deucalion Venture Partners
19501 Brooklime
Sonoma, CA 95476
(707)938-4974
Fax: (707)938-8921

Windward Ventures
PO Box 7688
Thousand Oaks, CA 91359-7688
(805)497-3332
Fax: (805)497-9331

National Investment Management, Inc.
2601 Airport Dr., Ste.210
Torrance, CA 90505
(310)784-7600
Fax: (310)784-7605

Southern California Ventures
406 Amapola Ave. Ste. 125
Torrance, CA 90501
(310)787-4381
Fax: (310)787-4382

Sandton Financial Group
21550 Oxnard St., Ste. 300
Woodland Hills, CA 91367
(818)702-9283

Woodside Fund
850 Woodside Dr.
Woodside, CA 94062
(650)368-5545
Fax: (650)368-2416
Website: http://www.woodsidefund.com

Colorado

Colorado Venture Management
Ste. 300
Boulder, CO 80301

(303)440-4055
Fax: (303)440-4636

Dean & Associates
4362 Apple Way
Boulder, CO 80301
Fax: (303)473-9900

Roser Ventures LLC
1105 Spruce St.
Boulder, CO 80302
(303)443-6436
Fax: (303)443-1885
Website: http://www.roserventures.com

Sequel Venture Partners
4430 Arapahoe Ave., Ste. 220
Boulder, CO 80303
(303)546-0400
Fax: (303)546-9728
E-mail: tom@sequelvc.com
Website: http://www.sequelvc.com

New Venture Resources
445C E. Cheyenne Mtn. Blvd.
Colorado Springs, CO 80906-4570
(719)598-9272
Fax: (719)598-9272

The Centennial Funds
1428 15th St.
Denver, CO 80202-1318
(303)405-7500
Fax: (303)405-7575
Website: http://www.centennial.com

Rocky Mountain Capital Partners
1125 17th St., Ste. 2260
Denver, CO 80202
(303)291-5200
Fax: (303)291-5327

Sandlot Capital LLC
600 South Cherry St., Ste. 525
Denver, CO 80246
(303)893-3400
Fax: (303)893-3403
Website: http://www.sandlotcapital.com

Wolf Ventures
50 South Steele St., Ste. 777
Denver, CO 80209
(303)321-4800
Fax: (303)321-4848
E-mail: businessplan@wolf
ventures.com
Website: http://www.wolfventures.com

The Columbine Venture Funds
5460 S. Quebec St., Ste. 270
Englewood, CO 80111

(303)694-3222
Fax: (303)694-9007

Investment Securities of Colorado, Inc.
4605 Denice Dr.
Englewood, CO 80111
(303)796-9192

Kinship Partners
6300 S. Syracuse Way, Ste. 484
Englewood, CO 80111
(303)694-0268
Fax: (303)694-1707
E-mail: block@vailsys.com

Boranco Management, L.L.C.
1528 Hillside Dr.
Fort Collins, CO 80524-1969
(970)221-2297
Fax: (970)221-4787

Aweida Ventures
890 West Cherry St., Ste. 220
Louisville, CO 80027
(303)664-9520
Fax: (303)664-9530
Website: http://www.aweida.com

Access Venture Partners
8787 Turnpike Dr., Ste. 260
Westminster, CO 80030
(303)426-8899
Fax: (303)426-8828

Medmax Ventures LP
1 Northwestern Dr., Ste. 203
Bloomfield, CT 06002
(860)286-2960
Fax: (860)286-9960

James B. Kobak & Co.
Four Mansfield Place
Darien, CT 06820
(203)656-3471
Fax: (203)655-2905

Orien Ventures
1 Post Rd.
Fairfield, CT 06430
(203)259-9933
Fax: (203)259-5288

ABP Acquisition Corporation
115 Maple Ave.
Greenwich, CT 06830
(203)625-8287
Fax: (203)447-6187

Catterton Partners
9 Greenwich Office Park
Greenwich, CT 06830
(203)629-4901

Fax: (203)629-4903
Website: http://www.cpequity.com

Consumer Venture Partners
3 Pickwick Plz.
Greenwich, CT 06830
(203)629-8800
Fax: (203)629-2019

Insurance Venture Partners
31 Brookside Dr., Ste. 211
Greenwich, CT 06830
(203)861-0030
Fax: (203)861-2745

The NTC Group
Three Pickwick Plaza
Ste. 200
Greenwich, CT 06830
(203)862-2800
Fax: (203)622-6538

Regulus International Capital Co., Inc.
140 Greenwich Ave.
Greenwich, CT 06830
(203)625-9700
Fax: (203)625-9706

Axiom Venture Partners
City Place II
185 Asylum St., 17th Fl.
Hartford, CT 06103
(860)548-7799
Fax: (860)548-7797
Website: http://www.axiomventures.com

Conning Capital Partners
City Place II
185 Asylum St.
Hartford, CT 06103-4105
(860)520-1289
Fax: (860)520-1299
E-mail: pe@conning.com
Website: http://www.conning.com

First New England Capital L.P.
100 Pearl St.
Hartford, CT 06103
(860)293-3333
Fax: (860)293-3338
E-mail: info@firstnewenglandcapital.com
Website: http://www.firstnewengland
capital.com

Northeast Ventures
One State St., Ste. 1720
Hartford, CT 06103
(860)547-1414
Fax: (860)246-8755

Windward Holdings
38 Sylvan Rd.
Madison, CT 06443
(203)245-6870
Fax: (203)245-6865

Advanced Materials Partners, Inc.
45 Pine St.
PO Box 1022
New Canaan, CT 06840
(203)966-6415
Fax: (203)966-8448
E-mail: wkb@amplink.com

RFE Investment Partners
36 Grove St.
New Canaan, CT 06840
(203)966-2800
Fax: (203)966-3109
Website: http://www.rfeip.com

Connecticut Innovations, Inc.
999 West St.
Rocky Hill, CT 06067
(860)563-5851
Fax: (860)563-4877
E-mail: pamela.hartley@ctin
novations.com
Website: http://www.ctinnovations.com

Canaan Partners
105 Rowayton Ave.
Rowayton, CT 06853
(203)855-0400
Fax: (203)854-9117
Website: http://www.canaan.com

Landmark Partners, Inc.
10 Mill Pond Ln.
Simsbury, CT 06070
(860)651-9760
Fax: (860)651-8890
Website: http://
www.landmarkpartners.com

Sweeney & Company
PO Box 567
Southport, CT 06490
(203)255-0220
Fax: (203)255-0220
E-mail: sweeney@connix.com

Baxter Associates, Inc.
PO Box 1333
Stamford, CT 06904
(203)323-3143
Fax: (203)348-0622

Beacon Partners Inc.
6 Landmark Sq., 4th Fl.
Stamford, CT 06901-2792

(203)359-5776
Fax: (203)359-5876

Collinson, Howe, and Lennox, LLC
1055 Washington Blvd., 5th Fl.
Stamford, CT 06901
(203)324-7700
Fax: (203)324-3636
E-mail: info@chlmedical.com
Website: http://www.chlmedical.com

Prime Capital Management Co.
550 West Ave.
Stamford, CT 06902
(203)964-0642
Fax: (203)964-0862

Saugatuck Capital Co.
1 Canterbury Green
Stamford, CT 06901
(203)348-6669
Fax: (203)324-6995
Website: http://www.sauga
tuckcapital.com

Soundview Financial Group Inc.
22 Gatehouse Rd.
Stamford, CT 06902
(203)462-7200
Fax: (203)462-7350
Website: http://www.sndv.com

TSG Ventures, L.L.C.
177 Broad St., 12th Fl.
Stamford, CT 06901
(203)406-1500
Fax: (203)406-1590

Whitney & Company
177 Broad St.
Stamford, CT 06901
(203)973-1400
Fax: (203)973-1422
Website: http://www.jhwhitney.com

Cullinane & Donnelly Venture Partners L.P.
970 Farmington Ave.
West Hartford, CT 06107
(860)521-7811

The Crestview Investment and Financial Group
431 Post Rd. E, Ste. 1
Westport, CT 06880-4403
(203)222-0333
Fax: (203)222-0000

Marketcorp Venture Associates, L.P. (MCV)
274 Riverside Ave.
Westport, CT 06880

(203)222-3030
Fax: (203)222-3033

Oak Investment Partners (Westport)
1 Gorham Island
Westport, CT 06880
(203)226-8346
Fax: (203)227-0372
Website: http://www.oakinv.com

Oxford Bioscience Partners
315 Post Rd. W
Westport, CT 06880-5200
(203)341-3300
Fax: (203)341-3309
Website: http://www.oxbio.com

Prince Ventures (Westport)
25 Ford Rd.
Westport, CT 06880
(203)227-8332
Fax: (203)226-5302

LTI Venture Leasing Corp.
221 Danbury Rd.
Wilton, CT 06897
(203)563-1100
Fax: (203)563-1111
Website: http://www.ltileasing.com

Delaware

Blue Rock Capital
5803 Kennett Pike, Ste. A
Wilmington, DE 19807
(302)426-0981
Fax: (302)426-0982
Website: http://www.bluerockcapital.com

District of Columbia

Allied Capital Corp.
1919 Pennsylvania Ave. NW
Washington, DC 20006-3434
(202)331-2444
Fax: (202)659-2053
Website: http://www.alliedcapital.com

Atlantic Coastal Ventures, L.P.
3101 South St. NW
Washington, DC 20007
(202)293-1166
Fax: (202)293-1181
Website: http://www.atlanticcv.com

Columbia Capital Group, Inc.
1660 L St. NW, Ste. 308
Washington, DC 20036
(202)775-8815
Fax: (202)223-0544

Core Capital Partners
901 15th St., NW
9th Fl.
Washington, DC 20005
(202)589-0090
Fax: (202)589-0091
Website: http://www.core-capital.com

Next Point Partners
701 Pennsylvania Ave. NW, Ste. 900
Washington, DC 20004
(202)661-8703
Fax: (202)434-7400
E-mail: mf@nextpoint.vc
Website: http://www.nextpointvc.com

Telecommunications Development Fund
2020 K. St. NW
Ste. 375
Washington, DC 20006
(202)293-8840
Fax: (202)293-8850
Website: http://www.tdfund.com

Wachtel & Co., Inc.
1101 4th St. NW
Washington, DC 20005-5680
(202)898-1144

Winslow Partners LLC
1300 Connecticut Ave. NW
Washington, DC 20036-1703
(202)530-5000
Fax: (202)530-5010
E-mail: winslow@winslowpartners.com

Women's Growth Capital Fund
1054 31st St., NW
Ste. 110
Washington, DC 20007
(202)342-1431
Fax: (202)341-1203
Website: http://www.wgcf.com

Sigma Capital Corp.
22668 Caravelle Circle
Boca Raton, FL 33433
(561)368-9783

North American Business Development Co., L.L.C.
111 East Las Olas Blvd.
Ft. Lauderdale, FL 33301
(305)463-0681
Fax: (305)527-0904
Website: http://www.northamericanfund.com

Chartwell Capital Management Co. Inc.
1 Independent Dr., Ste. 3120

Jacksonville, FL 32202
(904)355-3519
Fax: (904)353-5833
E-mail: info@chartwellcap.com

CEO Advisors
1061 Maitland Center Commons
Ste. 209
Maitland, FL 32751
(407)660-9327
Fax: (407)660-2109

Henry & Co.
8201 Peters Rd., Ste. 1000
Plantation, FL 33324
(954)797-7400

Avery Business Development Services
2506 St. Michel Ct.
Ponte Vedra, FL 32082
(904)285-6033

New South Ventures
5053 Ocean Blvd.
Sarasota, FL 34242
(941)358-6000
Fax: (941)358-6078
Website: http://www.newsouthventures.com

Venture Capital Management Corp.
PO Box 2626
Satellite Beach, FL 32937
(407)777-1969

Florida Capital Venture Ltd.
325 Florida Bank Plaza
100 W. Kennedy Blvd.
Tampa, FL 33602
(813)229-2294
Fax: (813)229-2028

Quantum Capital Partners
339 South Plant Ave.
Tampa, FL 33606
(813)250-1999
Fax: (813)250-1998
Website: http://www.quantumcapitalpartners.com

South Atlantic Venture Fund
614 W. Bay St.
Tampa, FL 33606-2704
(813)253-2500
Fax: (813)253-2360
E-mail: venture@southatlantic.com
Website: http://www.southatlantic.com

LM Capital Corp.
120 S. Olive, Ste. 400
West Palm Beach, FL 33401

(561)833-9700
Fax: (561)655-6587
Website: http://www.lmcapital
securities.com

Georgia

Venture First Associates
4811 Thornwood Dr.
Acworth, GA 30102
(770)928-3733
Fax: (770)928-6455

Alliance Technology Ventures
8995 Westside Pkwy., Ste. 200
Alpharetta, GA 30004
(678)336-2000
Fax: (678)336-2001
E-mail: info@atv.com
Website: http://www.atv.com

Cordova Ventures
2500 North Winds Pkwy., Ste. 475
Alpharetta, GA 30004
(678)942-0300
Fax: (678)942-0301
Website: http://www.cordovaventures.
com

**Advanced Technology Development
Fund**
1000 Abernathy, Ste. 1420
Atlanta, GA 30328-5614
(404)668-2333
Fax: (404)668-2333

CGW Southeast Partners
12 Piedmont Center, Ste. 210
Atlanta, GA 30305
(404)816-3255
Fax: (404)816-3258
Website: http://www.cgwlp.com

Cyberstarts
1900 Emery St., NW
3rd Fl.
Atlanta, GA 30318
(404)267-5000
Fax: (404)267-5200
Website: http://www.cyberstarts.com

EGL Holdings, Inc.
10 Piedmont Center, Ste. 412
Atlanta, GA 30305
(404)949-8300
Fax: (404)949-8311

Equity South
1790 The Lenox Bldg.
3399 Peachtree Rd. NE
Atlanta, GA 30326

(404)237-6222
Fax: (404)261-1578

Five Paces
3400 Peachtree Rd., Ste. 200
Atlanta, GA 30326
(404)439-8300
Fax: (404)439-8301
Website: http://www.fivepaces.com

Frontline Capital, Inc.
3475 Lenox Rd., Ste. 400
Atlanta, GA 30326
(404)240-7280
Fax: (404)240-7281

Fuqua Ventures LLC
1201 W. Peachtree St. NW, Ste. 5000
Atlanta, GA 30309
(404)815-4500
Fax: (404)815-4528
Website: http://www.fuquaventures.com

Noro-Moseley Partners
4200 Northside Pkwy., Bldg. 9
Atlanta, GA 30327
(404)233-1966
Fax: (404)239-9280
Website: http://www.noro-moseley.com

Renaissance Capital Corp.
34 Peachtree St. NW, Ste. 2230
Atlanta, GA 30303
(404)658-9061
Fax: (404)658-9064

River Capital, Inc.
Two Midtown Plaza
1360 Peachtree St. NE, Ste. 1430
Atlanta, GA 30309
(404)873-2166
Fax: (404)873-2158

State Street Bank & Trust Co.
3414 Peachtree Rd. NE, Ste. 1010
Atlanta, GA 30326
(404)364-9500
Fax: (404)261-4469

UPS Strategic Enterprise Fund
55 Glenlake Pkwy. NE
Atlanta, GA 30328
(404)828-8814
Fax: (404)828-8088
E-mail: jcacyce@ups.com
Website: http://www.ups.com/sef/
sef_home

Wachovia
191 Peachtree St. NE, 26th Fl.
Atlanta, GA 30303

(404)332-1000
Fax: (404)332-1392
Website: http://www.wachovia.com/wca

Brainworks Ventures
4243 Dunwoody Club Dr.
Chamblee, GA 30341
(770)239-7447

First Growth Capital Inc.
Best Western Plaza, Ste. 105
PO Box 815
Forsyth, GA 31029
(912)781-7131

Financial Capital Resources, Inc.
21 Eastbrook Bend, Ste. 116
Peachtree City, GA 30269
(404)487-6650

Hawaii

HMS Hawaii Management Partners
Davies Pacific Center
841 Bishop St., Ste. 860
Honolulu, HI 96813
(808)545-3755
Fax: (808)531-2611

Idaho

Sun Valley Ventures
160 Second St.
Ketchum, ID 83340
(208)726-5005
Fax: (208)726-5094

Illinois

Open Prairie Ventures
115 N. Neil St., Ste. 209
Champaign, IL 61820
(217)351-7000
Fax: (217)351-7051
E-mail: inquire@openprairie.com
Website: http://www.openprairie.com

ABN AMRO Private Equity
208 S. La Salle St., 10th Fl.
Chicago, IL 60604
(312)855-7079
Fax: (312)553-6648
Website: http://www.abnequity.com

Alpha Capital Partners, Ltd.
122 S. Michigan Ave., Ste. 1700
Chicago, IL 60603
(312)322-9800
Fax: (312)322-9808
E-mail: acp@alphacapital.com

Ameritech Development Corp.
30 S. Wacker Dr., 37th Fl.
Chicago, IL 60606
(312)750-5083
Fax: (312)609-0244

Apex Investment Partners
225 W. Washington, Ste. 1450
Chicago, IL 60606
(312)857-2800
Fax: (312)857-1800
E-mail: apex@apexvc.com
Website: http://www.apexvc.com

Arch Venture Partners
8725 W. Higgins Rd., Ste. 290
Chicago, IL 60631
(773)380-6600
Fax: (773)380-6606
Website: http://www.archventure.com

The Bank Funds
208 South LaSalle St., Ste. 1680
Chicago, IL 60604
(312)855-6020
Fax: (312)855-8910

Batterson Venture Partners
303 W. Madison St., Ste. 1110
Chicago, IL 60606-3309
(312)269-0300
Fax: (312)269-0021
Website: http://www.battersonvp.com

William Blair Capital Partners, L.L.C.
222 W. Adams St., Ste. 1300
Chicago, IL 60606
(312)364-8250
Fax: (312)236-1042
E-mail: privateequity@wmblair.com
Website: http://www.wmblair.com

Bluestar Ventures
208 South LaSalle St., Ste. 1020
Chicago, IL 60604
(312)384-5000
Fax: (312)384-5005
Website: http://www.bluestarventures.com

The Capital Strategy Management Co.
233 S. Wacker Dr.
Box 06334
Chicago, IL 60606
(312)444-1170

DN Partners
77 West Wacker Dr., Ste. 4550
Chicago, IL 60601
(312)332-7960
Fax: (312)332-7979

Dresner Capital Inc.
29 South LaSalle St., Ste. 310
Chicago, IL 60603
(312)726-3600
Fax: (312)726-7448

Eblast Ventures LLC
11 South LaSalle St., 5th Fl.
Chicago, IL 60603
(312)372-2600
Fax: (312)372-5621
Website: http://www.eblastventures.com

Essex Woodlands Health Ventures, L.P.
190 S. LaSalle St., Ste. 2800
Chicago, IL 60603
(312)444-6040
Fax: (312)444-6034
Website: http://www.essexwoodlands.com

First Analysis Venture Capital
233 S. Wacker Dr., Ste. 9500
Chicago, IL 60606
(312)258-1400
Fax: (312)258-0334
Website: http://www.firstanalysis.com

Frontenac Co.
135 S. LaSalle St., Ste.3800
Chicago, IL 60603
(312)368-0044
Fax: (312)368-9520
Website: http://www.frontenac.com

GTCR Golder Rauner, LLC
6100 Sears Tower
Chicago, IL 60606
(312)382-2200
Fax: (312)382-2201
Website: http://www.gtcr.com

High Street Capital LLC
311 South Wacker Dr., Ste. 4550
Chicago, IL 60606
(312)697-4990
Fax: (312)697-4994
Website: http://www.highstr.com

IEG Venture Management, Inc.
70 West Madison
Chicago, IL 60602
(312)644-0890
Fax: (312)454-0369
Website: http://www.iegventure.com

JK&B Capital
180 North Stetson, Ste. 4500
Chicago, IL 60601
(312)946-1200
Fax: (312)946-1103

E-mail: gspencer@jkbcapital.com
Website: http://www.jkbcapital.com

Kettle Partners L.P.
350 W. Hubbard, Ste. 350
Chicago, IL 60610
(312)329-9300
Fax: (312)527-4519
Website: http://www.kettlevc.com

Lake Shore Capital Partners
20 N. Wacker Dr., Ste. 2807
Chicago, IL 60606
(312)803-3536
Fax: (312)803-3534

LaSalle Capital Group Inc.
70 W. Madison St., Ste. 5710
Chicago, IL 60602
(312)236-7041
Fax: (312)236-0720

Linc Capital, Inc.
303 E. Wacker Pkwy., Ste. 1000
Chicago, IL 60601
(312)946-2670
Fax: (312)938-4290
E-mail: bdemars@linccap.com

Madison Dearborn Partners, Inc.
3 First National Plz., Ste. 3800
Chicago, IL 60602
(312)895-1000
Fax: (312)895-1001
E-mail: invest@mdcp.com
Website: http://www.mdcp.com

Mesirow Private Equity Investments Inc.
350 N. Clark St.
Chicago, IL 60610
(312)595-6950
Fax: (312)595-6211
Website: http://www.meisrowfinancial.com

Mosaix Ventures LLC
1822 North Mohawk
Chicago, IL 60614
(312)274-0988
Fax: (312)274-0989
Website: http://www.mosaixventures.com

Nesbitt Burns
111 West Monroe St.
Chicago, IL 60603
(312)416-3855
Fax: (312)765-8000
Website: http://www.harrisbank.com

Polestar Capital, Inc.
180 N. Michigan Ave., Ste. 1905
Chicago, IL 60601
(312)984-9090
Fax: (312)984-9877
E-mail: wl@polestarvc.com
Website: http://www.polestarvc.com

Prince Ventures (Chicago)
10 S. Wacker Dr., Ste. 2575
Chicago, IL 60606-7407
(312)454-1408
Fax: (312)454-9125

Prism Capital
444 N. Michigan Ave.
Chicago, IL 60611
(312)464-7900
Fax: (312)464-7915
Website: http://www.prismfund.com

Third Coast Capital
900 N. Franklin St., Ste. 700
Chicago, IL 60610
(312)337-3303
Fax: (312)337-2567
E-mail: manic@earthlink.com
Website: http://www.third
coastcapital.com

Thoma Cressey Equity Partners
4460 Sears Tower, 92nd Fl.
233 S. Wacker Dr.
Chicago, IL 60606
(312)777-4444
Fax: (312)777-4445
Website: http://www.thomacressey.com

Tribune Ventures
435 N. Michigan Ave., Ste. 600
Chicago, IL 60611
(312)527-8797
Fax: (312)222-5993
Website: http://www.tribuneventures.com

Wind Point Partners (Chicago)
676 N. Michigan Ave., Ste. 330
Chicago, IL 60611
(312)649-4000
Website: http://www.wppartners.com

Marquette Venture Partners
520 Lake Cook Rd., Ste. 450
Deerfield, IL 60015
(847)940-1700
Fax: (847)940-1724
Website: http://www.marquette
ventures.com

Duchossois Investments Limited, LLC
845 Larch Ave.
Elmhurst, IL 60126

(630)530-6105
Fax: (630)993-8644
Website: http://www.duchtec.com

Evanston Business Investment Corp.
1840 Oak Ave.
Evanston, IL 60201
(847)866-1840
Fax: (847)866-1808
E-mail: t-parkinson@nwu.com
Website: http://www.ebic.com

Inroads Capital Partners L.P.
1603 Orrington Ave., Ste. 2050
Evanston, IL 60201-3841
(847)864-2000
Fax: (847)864-9692

The Cerulean Fund/WGC Enterprises
1701 E. Lake Ave., Ste. 170
Glenview, IL 60025
(847)657-8002
Fax: (847)657-8168

Ventana Financial Resources, Inc.
249 Market Sq.
Lake Forest, IL 60045
(847)234-3434

Beecken, Petty & Co.
901 Warrenville Rd., Ste. 205
Lisle, IL 60532
(630)435-0300
Fax: (630)435-0370
E-mail: hep@bpcompany.com
Website: http://www.bpcompany.com

Allstate Private Equity
3075 Sanders Rd., Ste. G5D
Northbrook, IL 60062-7127
(847)402-8247
Fax: (847)402-0880

KB Partners
1101 Skokie Blvd., Ste. 260
Northbrook, IL 60062-2856
(847)714-0444
Fax: (847)714-0445
E-mail: keith@kbpartners.com
Website: http://www.kbpartners.com

Transcap Associates Inc.
900 Skokie Blvd., Ste. 210
Northbrook, IL 60062
(847)753-9600
Fax: (847)753-9090

**Graystone Venture Partners, L.L.C. /
Portage Venture Partners**
One Northfield Plaza, Ste. 530
Northfield, IL 60093

(847)446-9460
Fax: (847)446-9470
Website: http://www.portage
ventures.com

Motorola Inc.
1303 E. Algonquin Rd.
Schaumburg, IL 60196-1065
(847)576-4929
Fax: (847)538-2250
Website: http://www.mot.com/mne

Indiana

Irwin Ventures LLC
500 Washington St.
Columbus, IN 47202
(812)373-1434
Fax: (812)376-1709
Website: http://www.irwinventures.com

Cambridge Venture Partners
4181 East 96th St., Ste. 200
Indianapolis, IN 46240
(317)814-6192
Fax: (317)944-9815

CID Equity Partners
One American Square, Ste. 2850
Box 82074
Indianapolis, IN 46282
(317)269-2350
Fax: (317)269-2355
Website: http://www.cidequity.com

Gazelle Techventures
6325 Digital Way, Ste. 460
Indianapolis, IN 46278
(317)275-6800
Fax: (317)275-1101
Website: http://www.gazellevc.com

Monument Advisors Inc.
Bank One Center/Circle
111 Monument Circle, Ste. 600
Indianapolis, IN 46204-5172
(317)656-5065
Fax: (317)656-5060
Website: http://www.monumentadv.com

MWV Capital Partners
201 N. Illinois St., Ste. 300
Indianapolis, IN 46204
(317)237-2323
Fax: (317)237-2325
Website: http://www.mwvcapital.com

First Source Capital Corp.
100 North Michigan St.
PO Box 1602
South Bend, IN 46601

(219)235-2180
Fax: (219)235-2227

Iowa

Allsop Venture Partners
118 Third Ave. SE, Ste. 837
Cedar Rapids, IA 52401
(319)368-6675
Fax: (319)363-9515

InvestAmerica Investment Advisors, Inc.
101 2nd St. SE, Ste. 800
Cedar Rapids, IA 52401
(319)363-8249
Fax: (319)363-9683

Pappajohn Capital Resources
2116 Financial Center
Des Moines, IA 50309
(515)244-5746
Fax: (515)244-2346
Website: http://www.pappajohn.com

Berthel Fisher & Company Planning Inc.
701 Tama St.
PO Box 609
Marion, IA 52302
(319)497-5700
Fax: (319)497-4244

Kansas

Enterprise Merchant Bank
7400 West 110th St., Ste. 560
Overland Park, KS 66210
(913)327-8500
Fax: (913)327-8505

Kansas Venture Capital, Inc. (Overland Park)
6700 Antioch Plz., Ste. 460
Overland Park, KS 66204
(913)262-7117
Fax: (913)262-3509
E-mail: jdalton@kvci.com

Child Health Investment Corp.
6803 W. 64th St., Ste. 208
Shawnee Mission, KS 66202
(913)262-1436
Fax: (913)262-1575
Website: http://www.chca.com

Kansas Technology Enterprise Corp.
214 SW 6th, 1st Fl.
Topeka, KS 66603-3719
(785)296-5272
Fax: (785)296-1160

E-mail: ktec@ktec.com
Website: http://www.ktec.com

Kentucky

Kentucky Highlands Investment Corp.
362 Old Whitley Rd.
London, KY 40741
(606)864-5175
Fax: (606)864-5194
Website: http://www.khic.org

Chrysalis Ventures, L.L.C.
1850 National City Tower
Louisville, KY 40202
(502)583-7644
Fax: (502)583-7648
E-mail: bobsany@chrysalisventures.com
Website: http://www.chrysalis
ventures.com

Humana Venture Capital
500 West Main St.
Louisville, KY 40202
(502)580-3922
Fax: (502)580-2051
E-mail: gemont@humana.com
George Emont, Director

Summit Capital Group, Inc.
6510 Glenridge Park Pl., Ste. 8
Louisville, KY 40222
(502)332-2700

Louisiana

Bank One Equity Investors, Inc.
451 Florida St.
Baton Rouge, LA 70801
(504)332-4421
Fax: (504)332-7377

Advantage Capital Partners
LLE Tower
909 Poydras St., Ste. 2230
New Orleans, LA 70112
(504)522-4850
Fax: (504)522-4950
Website: http://www.advantagecap.com

Maine

CEI Ventures / Coastal Ventures LP
2 Portland Fish Pier, Ste. 201
Portland, ME 04101
(207)772-5356
Fax: (207)772-5503
Website: http://www.ceiventures.com

Commwealth Bioventures, Inc.
4 Milk St.
Portland, ME 04101

(207)780-0904
Fax: (207)780-0913

Maryland

Annapolis Ventures LLC
151 West St., Ste. 302
Annapolis, MD 21401
(443)482-9555
Fax: (443)482-9565
Website: http://www.annapolis
ventures.com

Delmag Ventures
220 Wardour Dr.
Annapolis, MD 21401
(410)267-8196
Fax: (410)267-8017
Website: http://www.delmag
ventures.com

Abell Venture Fund
111 S. Calvert St., Ste. 2300
Baltimore, MD 21202
(410)547-1300
Fax: (410)539-6579
Website: http://www.abell.org

ABS Ventures (Baltimore)
1 South St., Ste. 2150
Baltimore, MD 21202
(410)895-3895
Fax: (410)895-3899
Website: http://www.absventures.com

Anthem Capital, L.P.
16 S. Calvert St., Ste. 800
Baltimore, MD 21202-1305
(410)625-1510
Fax: (410)625-1735
Website: http://www.anthemcapital.com

Catalyst Ventures
1119 St. Paul St.
Baltimore, MD 21202
(410)244-0123
Fax: (410)752-7721

Maryland Venture Capital Trust
217 E. Redwood St., Ste. 2200
Baltimore, MD 21202
(410)767-6361
Fax: (410)333-6931

New Enterprise Associates (Baltimore)
1119 St. Paul St.
Baltimore, MD 21202
(410)244-0115
Fax: (410)752-7721
Website: http://www.nea.com

T. Rowe Price Threshold Partnerships
100 E. Pratt St., 8th Fl.
Baltimore, MD 21202
(410)345-2000
Fax: (410)345-2800

Spring Capital Partners
16 W. Madison St.
Baltimore, MD 21201
(410)685-8000
Fax: (410)727-1436
E-mail: mailbox@springcap.com

Arete Corporation
3 Bethesda Metro Ctr., Ste. 770
Bethesda, MD 20814
(301)657-6268
Fax: (301)657-6254
Website: http://www.arete-
microgen.com

Embryon Capital
7903 Sleaford Place
Bethesda, MD 20814
(301)656-6837
Fax: (301)656-8056

Potomac Ventures
7920 Norfolk Ave., Ste. 1100
Bethesda, MD 20814
(301)215-9240
Website: http://www.potomac
ventures.com

Toucan Capital Corp.
3 Bethesda Metro Center, Ste. 700
Bethesda, MD 20814
(301)961-1970
Fax: (301)961-1969
Website: http://www.toucancapital.com

Kinetic Ventures LLC
2 Wisconsin Cir., Ste. 620
Chevy Chase, MD 20815
(301)652-8066
Fax: (301)652-8310
Website: http://www.kineticventures.com

Boulder Ventures Ltd.
4750 Owings Mills Blvd.
Owings Mills, MD 21117
(410)998-3114
Fax: (410)356-5492
Website: http://www.boulderventures.com

Grotech Capital Group
9690 Deereco Rd., Ste. 800
Timonium, MD 21093
(410)560-2000
Fax: (410)560-1910
Website: http://www.grotech.com

Massachusetts

Adams, Harkness & Hill, Inc.
60 State St.
Boston, MA 02109
(617)371-3900

Advent International
75 State St., 29th Fl.
Boston, MA 02109
(617)951-9400
Fax: (617)951-0566
Website: http://www.adventiner
national.com

American Research and Development
30 Federal St.
Boston, MA 02110-2508
(617)423-7500
Fax: (617)423-9655

Ascent Venture Partners
255 State St., 5th Fl.
Boston, MA 02109
(617)270-9400
Fax: (617)270-9401
E-mail: info@ascentvp.com
Website: http://www.ascentvp.com

Atlas Venture
222 Berkeley St.
Boston, MA 02116
(617)488-2200
Fax: (617)859-9292
Website: http://www.atlasventure.com

Axxon Capital
28 State St., 37th Fl.
Boston, MA 02109
(617)722-0980
Fax: (617)557-6014
Website: http://www.axxoncapital.com

BancBoston Capital/BancBoston Ventures
175 Federal St., 10th Fl.
Boston, MA 02110
(617)434-2509
Fax: (617)434-6175
Website: http://
www.bancbostoncapital.com

Boston Capital Ventures
Old City Hall
45 School St.
Boston, MA 02108
(617)227-6550
Fax: (617)227-3847
E-mail: info@bcv.com
Website: http://www.bcv.com

Boston Financial & Equity Corp.
20 Overland St.
PO Box 15071
Boston, MA 02215
(617)267-2900
Fax: (617)437-7601
E-mail: debbie@bfec.com

Boston Millennia Partners
30 Rowes Wharf
Boston, MA 02110
(617)428-5150
Fax: (617)428-5160
Website: http://www.millennia
partners.com

Bristol Investment Trust
842A Beacon St.
Boston, MA 02215-3199
(617)566-5212
Fax: (617)267-0932

Brook Venture Management LLC
50 Federal St., 5th Fl.
Boston, MA 02110
(617)451-8989
Fax: (617)451-2369
Website: http://www.brookventure.com

Burr, Egan, Deleage, and Co. (Boston)
200 Clarendon St., Ste. 3800
Boston, MA 02116
(617)262-7770
Fax: (617)262-9779

Cambridge/Samsung Partners
One Exeter Plaza
Ninth Fl.
Boston, MA 02116
(617)262-4440
Fax: (617)262-5562

Chestnut Street Partners, Inc.
75 State St., Ste. 2500
Boston, MA 02109
(617)345-7220
Fax: (617)345-7201
E-mail: chestnut@chestnutp.com

Claflin Capital Management, Inc.
10 Liberty Sq., Ste. 300
Boston, MA 02109
(617)426-6505
Fax: (617)482-0016
Website: http://www.claflincapital.com

Copley Venture Partners
99 Summer St., Ste. 1720
Boston, MA 02110
(617)737-1253
Fax: (617)439-0699

Corning Capital / Corning Technology Ventures
121 High Street, Ste. 400
Boston, MA 02110
(617)338-2656
Fax: (617)261-3864
Website: http://www.corningventures.com

Downer & Co.
211 Congress St.
Boston, MA 02110
(617)482-6200
Fax: (617)482-6201
E-mail: cdowner@downer.com
Website: http://www.downer.com

Fidelity Ventures
82 Devonshire St.
Boston, MA 02109
(617)563-6370
Fax: (617)476-9023
Website: http://www.fidelityventures.com

Greylock Management Corp. (Boston)
1 Federal St.
Boston, MA 02110-2065
(617)423-5525
Fax: (617)482-0059

Gryphon Ventures
222 Berkeley St., Ste.1600
Boston, MA 02116
(617)267-9191
Fax: (617)267-4293
E-mail: all@gryphoninc.com

Halpern, Denny & Co.
500 Boylston St.
Boston, MA 02116
(617)536-6602
Fax: (617)536-8535

Harbourvest Partners, LLC
1 Financial Center, 44th Fl.
Boston, MA 02111
(617)348-3707
Fax: (617)350-0305
Website: http://www.hvpllc.com

Highland Capital Partners
2 International Pl.
Boston, MA 02110
(617)981-1500
Fax: (617)531-1550
E-mail: info@hcp.com
Website: http://www.hcp.com

Lee Munder Venture Partners
John Hancock Tower T-53
200 Clarendon St.
Boston, MA 02103

(617)380-5600
Fax: (617)380-5601
Website: http://www.leemunder.com

M/C Venture Partners
75 State St., Ste. 2500
Boston, MA 02109
(617)345-7200
Fax: (617)345-7201
Website: http://www.mcventure
partners.com

Massachusetts Capital Resources Co.
420 Boylston St.
Boston, MA 02116
(617)536-3900
Fax: (617)536-7930

Massachusetts Technology Development Corp. (MTDC)
148 State St.
Boston, MA 02109
(617)723-4920
Fax: (617)723-5983
E-mail: jhodgman@mtdc.com
Website: http://www.mtdc.com

New England Partners
One Boston Place, Ste. 2100
Boston, MA 02108
(617)624-8400
Fax: (617)624-8999
Website: http://www.nepartners.com

North Hill Ventures
Ten Post Office Square
11th Fl.
Boston, MA 02109
(617)788-2112
Fax: (617)788-2152
Website: http://www.northhill
ventures.com

OneLiberty Ventures
150 Cambridge Park Dr.
Boston, MA 02140
(617)492-7280
Fax: (617)492-7290
Website: http://www.oneliberty.com

Schroder Ventures
Life Sciences
60 State St., Ste. 3650
Boston, MA 02109
(617)367-8100
Fax: (617)367-1590
Website: http://www.shroderventures.com

Shawmut Capital Partners
75 Federal St., 18th Fl.
Boston, MA 02110

(617)368-4900
Fax: (617)368-4910
Website: http://www.shawmutcapital.com

Solstice Capital LLC
15 Broad St., 3rd Fl.
Boston, MA 02109
(617)523-7733
Fax: (617)523-5827
E-mail: solticecapital@solcap.com

Spectrum Equity Investors
One International Pl., 29th Fl.
Boston, MA 02110
(617)464-4600
Fax: (617)464-4601
Website: http://www.spectrumequity.com

Spray Venture Partners
One Walnut St.
Boston, MA 02108
(617)305-4140
Fax: (617)305-4144
Website: http://www.sprayventure.com

The Still River Fund
100 Federal St., 29th Fl.
Boston, MA 02110
(617)348-2327
Fax: (617)348-2371
Website: http://www.stillriverfund.com

Summit Partners
600 Atlantic Ave., Ste. 2800
Boston, MA 02210-2227
(617)824-1000
Fax: (617)824-1159
Website: http://www.summitpartners.com

TA Associates, Inc. (Boston)
High Street Tower
125 High St., Ste. 2500
Boston, MA 02110
(617)574-6700
Fax: (617)574-6728
Website: http://www.ta.com

TVM Techno Venture Management
101 Arch St., Ste. 1950
Boston, MA 02110
(617)345-9320
Fax: (617)345-9377
E-mail: info@tvmvc.com
Website: http://www.tvmvc.com

UNC Ventures
64 Burough St.
Boston, MA 02130-4017
(617)482-7070
Fax: (617)522-2176

Venture Investment Management Company (VIMAC)
177 Milk St.
Boston, MA 02190-3410
(617)292-3300
Fax: (617)292-7979
E-mail: bzeisig@vimac.com
Website: http://www.vimac.com

MDT Advisers, Inc.
125 Cambridge Park Dr.
Cambridge, MA 02140-2314
(617)234-2200
Fax: (617)234-2210
Website: http://www.mdtai.com

TTC Ventures
One Main St., 6th Fl.
Cambridge, MA 02142
(617)528-3137
Fax: (617)577-1715
E-mail: info@ttcventures.com

Zero Stage Capital Co. Inc.
101 Main St., 17th Fl.
Cambridge, MA 02142
(617)876-5355
Fax: (617)876-1248
Website: http://www.zerostage.com

Atlantic Capital
164 Cushing Hwy.
Cohasset, MA 02025
(617)383-9449
Fax: (617)383-6040
E-mail: info@atlanticcap.com
Website: http://www.atlanticcap.com

Seacoast Capital Partners
55 Ferncroft Rd.
Danvers, MA 01923
(978)750-1300
Fax: (978)750-1301
E-mail: gdeli@seacoastcapital.com
Website: http://www.seacoast
capital.com

Sage Management Group
44 South Street
PO Box 2026
East Dennis, MA 02641
(508)385-7172
Fax: (508)385-7272
E-mail: sagemgt@capecod.net

Applied Technology
1 Cranberry Hill
Lexington, MA 02421-7397
(617)862-8622
Fax: (617)862-8367

Royalty Capital Management
5 Downing Rd.
Lexington, MA 02421-6918
(781)861-8490

Argo Global Capital
210 Broadway, Ste. 101
Lynnfield, MA 01940
(781)592-5250
Fax: (781)592-5230
Website: http://www.gsmcapital.com

Industry Ventures
6 Bayne Lane
Newburyport, MA 01950
(978)499-7606
Fax: (978)499-0686
Website: http://
www.industryventures.com

Softbank Capital Partners
10 Langley Rd., Ste. 202
Newton Center, MA 02459
(617)928-9300
Fax: (617)928-9305
E-mail: clax@bvc.com

Advanced Technology Ventures (Boston)
281 Winter St., Ste. 350
Waltham, MA 02451
(781)290-0707
Fax: (781)684-0045
E-mail: info@atvcapital.com
Website: http://www.atvcapital.com

Castile Ventures
890 Winter St., Ste. 140
Waltham, MA 02451
(781)890-0060
Fax: (781)890-0065
Website: http://www.castileventures.com

Charles River Ventures
1000 Winter St., Ste. 3300
Waltham, MA 02451
(781)487-7060
Fax: (781)487-7065
Website: http://www.crv.com

Comdisco Venture Group (Waltham)
Totton Pond Office Center
400-1 Totten Pond Rd.
Waltham, MA 02451
(617)672-0250
Fax: (617)398-8099

Marconi Ventures
890 Winter St., Ste. 310
Waltham, MA 02451
(781)839-7177

Fax: (781)522-7477
Website: http://www.marconi.com

Matrix Partners
Bay Colony Corporate Center
1000 Winter St., Ste.4500
Waltham, MA 02451
(781)890-2244
Fax: (781)890-2288
Website: http://www.matrix
partners.com

North Bridge Venture Partners
950 Winter St. Ste. 4600
Waltham, MA 02451
(781)290-0004
Fax: (781)290-0999
E-mail: eta@nbvp.com

Polaris Venture Partners
Bay Colony Corporate Ctr.
1000 Winter St., Ste. 3500
Waltham, MA 02451
(781)290-0770
Fax: (781)290-0880
E-mail: partners@polarisventures.com
Website: http://www.polar
isventures.com

Seaflower Ventures
Bay Colony Corporate Ctr.
1000 Winter St. Ste. 1000
Waltham, MA 02451
(781)466-9552
Fax: (781)466-9553
E-mail: moot@seaflower.com
Website: http://www.seaflower.com

Ampersand Ventures
55 William St., Ste. 240
Wellesley, MA 02481
(617)239-0700
Fax: (617)239-0824
E-mail: info@ampersandventures.com
Website: http://www.ampersand
ventures.com

Battery Ventures (Boston)
20 William St., Ste. 200
Wellesley, MA 02481
(781)577-1000
Fax: (781)577-1001
Website: http://www.battery.com

Commonwealth Capital Ventures, L.P.
20 William St., Ste.225
Wellesley, MA 02481
(781)237-7373
Fax: (781)235-8627
Website: http://www.ccvlp.com

Fowler, Anthony & Company
20 Walnut St.
Wellesley, MA 02481
(781)237-4201
Fax: (781)237-7718

Gemini Investors
20 William St.
Wellesley, MA 02481
(781)237-7001
Fax: (781)237-7233

Grove Street Advisors Inc.
20 William St., Ste. 230
Wellesley, MA 02481
(781)263-6100
Fax: (781)263-6101
Website: http://www.groves
treetadvisors.com

Mees Pierson Investeringsmaat B.V.
20 William St., Ste. 210
Wellesley, MA 02482
(781)239-7600
Fax: (781)239-0377

Norwest Equity Partners
40 William St., Ste. 305
Wellesley, MA 02481-3902
(781)237-5870
Fax: (781)237-6270
Website: http://www.norwestvp.com

Bessemer Venture Partners (Wellesley Hills)
83 Walnut St.
Wellesley Hills, MA 02481
(781)237-6050
Fax: (781)235-7576
E-mail: travis@bvpny.com
Website: http://www.bvp.com

Venture Capital Fund of New England
20 Walnut St., Ste. 120
Wellesley Hills, MA 02481-2175
(781)239-8262
Fax: (781)239-8263

Prism Venture Partners
100 Lowder Brook Dr., Ste. 2500
Westwood, MA 02090
(781)302-4000
Fax: (781)302-4040
E-mail: dwbaum@prismventure.com

Palmer Partners LP
200 Unicorn Park Dr.
Woburn, MA 01801
(781)933-5445
Fax: (781)933-0698

Michigan

Arbor Partners, L.L.C.
130 South First St.
Ann Arbor, MI 48104
(734)668-9000
Fax: (734)669-4195
Website: http://www.arborpartners.com

EDF Ventures
425 N. Main St.
Ann Arbor, MI 48104
(734)663-3213
Fax: (734)663-7358
E-mail: edf@edfvc.com
Website: http://www.edfvc.com

White Pines Management, L.L.C.
2401 Plymouth Rd., Ste. B
Ann Arbor, MI 48105
(734)747-9401
Fax: (734)747-9704
E-mail: ibund@whitepines.com
Website: http://www.whitepines.com

Wellmax, Inc.
3541 Bendway Blvd., Ste. 100
Bloomfield Hills, MI 48301
(248)646-3554
Fax: (248)646-6220

Venture Funding, Ltd.
Fisher Bldg.
3011 West Grand Blvd., Ste. 321
Detroit, MI 48202
(313)871-3606
Fax: (313)873-4935

Investcare Partners L.P. / GMA Capital LLC
32330 W. Twelve Mile Rd.
Farmington Hills, MI 48334
(248)489-9000
Fax: (248)489-8819
E-mail: gma@gmacapital.com
Website: http://www.gmacapital.com

Liberty Bidco Investment Corp.
30833 Northwestern Highway, Ste. 211
Farmington Hills, MI 48334
(248)626-6070
Fax: (248)626-6072

Seaflower Ventures
5170 Nicholson Rd.
PO Box 474
Fowlerville, MI 48836
(517)223-3335
Fax: (517)223-3337
E-mail: gibbons@seaflower.com
Website: http://www.seaflower.com

Ralph Wilson Equity Fund LLC
15400 E. Jefferson Ave.
Gross Pointe Park, MI 48230
(313)821-9122
Fax: (313)821-9101
Website: http://www.Ralph
WilsonEquityFund.com
J. Skip Simms, President

Minnesota

Development Corp. of Austin
1900 Eighth Ave., NW
Austin, MN 55912
(507)433-0346
Fax: (507)433-0361
E-mail: dca@smig.net
Website: http://www.spamtownusa.com

Northeast Ventures Corp.
802 Alworth Bldg.
Duluth, MN 55802
(218)722-9915
Fax: (218)722-9871

Medical Innovation Partners, Inc.
6450 City West Pkwy.
Eden Prairie, MN 55344-3245
(612)828-9616
Fax: (612)828-9596

St. Paul Venture Capital, Inc.
10400 Vicking Dr., Ste. 550
Eden Prairie, MN 55344
(612)995-7474
Fax: (612)995-7475
Website: http://www.stpaulvc.com

Cherry Tree Investments, Inc.
7601 France Ave. S, Ste. 150
Edina, MN 55435
(612)893-9012
Fax: (612)893-9036
Website: http://www.cherrytree.com

Shared Ventures, Inc.
6550 York Ave. S
Edina, MN 55435
(612)925-3411

Sherpa Partners LLC
5050 Lincoln Dr., Ste. 490
Edina, MN 55436
(952)942-1070
Fax: (952)942-1071
Website: http://www.sherpapartners.com

Affinity Capital Management
901 Marquette Ave., Ste. 1810
Minneapolis, MN 55402
(612)252-9900

Fax: (612)252-9911
Website: http://www.affinitycapital.com

Artesian Capital
1700 Foshay Tower
821 Marquette Ave.
Minneapolis, MN 55402
(612)334-5600
Fax: (612)334-5601
E-mail: artesian@artesian.com

Coral Ventures
60 S. 6th St., Ste. 3510
Minneapolis, MN 55402
(612)335-8666
Fax: (612)335-8668
Website: http://www.coralventures.com

Crescendo Venture Management, L.L.C.
800 LaSalle Ave., Ste. 2250
Minneapolis, MN 55402
(612)607-2800
Fax: (612)607-2801
Website: http://www.crescendo
ventures.com

Gideon Hixon Venture
1900 Foshay Tower
821 Marquette Ave.
Minneapolis, MN 55402
(612)904-2314
Fax: (612)204-0913

Norwest Equity Partners
3600 IDS Center
80 S. 8th St.
Minneapolis, MN 55402
(612)215-1600
Fax: (612)215-1601
Website: http://www.norwestvp.com

Oak Investment Partners (Minneapolis)
4550 Norwest Center
90 S. 7th St.
Minneapolis, MN 55402
(612)339-9322
Fax: (612)337-8017
Website: http://www.oakinv.com

Pathfinder Venture Capital Funds (Minneapolis)
7300 Metro Blvd., Ste. 585
Minneapolis, MN 55439
(612)835-1121
Fax: (612)835-8389
E-mail: jahrens620@aol.com

U.S. Bancorp Piper Jaffray Ventures, Inc.
800 Nicollet Mall, Ste. 800
Minneapolis, MN 55402

(612)303-5686
Fax: (612)303-1350
Website: http://www.paperjaffrey
ventures.com

The Food Fund, Ltd. Partnership
5720 Smatana Dr., Ste. 300
Minnetonka, MN 55343
(612)939-3950
Fax: (612)939-8106

Mayo Medical Ventures
200 First St. SW
Rochester, MN 55905
(507)266-4586
Fax: (507)284-5410
Website: http://www.mayo.edu

Missouri

Bankers Capital Corp.
3100 Gillham Rd.
Kansas City, MO 64109
(816)531-1600
Fax: (816)531-1334

Capital for Business, Inc. (Kansas City)
1000 Walnut St., 18th Fl.
Kansas City, MO 64106
(816)234-2357
Fax: (816)234-2952
Website: http://
www.capitalforbusiness.com

De Vries & Co. Inc.
800 West 47th St.
Kansas City, MO 64112
(816)756-0055
Fax: (816)756-0061

InvestAmerica Venture Group Inc. (Kansas City)
Commerce Tower
911 Main St., Ste. 2424
Kansas City, MO 64105
(816)842-0114
Fax: (816)471-7339

Kansas City Equity Partners
233 W. 47th St.
Kansas City, MO 64112
(816)960-1771
Fax: (816)960-1777
Website: http://www.kcep.com

Bome Investors, Inc.
8000 Maryland Ave., Ste. 1190
St. Louis, MO 63105
(314)721-5707
Fax: (314)721-5135

Website: http://www.gateway
ventures.com

Capital for Business, Inc. (St. Louis)
11 S. Meramac St., Ste. 1430
St. Louis, MO 63105
(314)746-7427
Fax: (314)746-8739
Website: http://www.capitalfor
business.com

Crown Capital Corp.
540 Maryville Centre Dr., Ste. 120
Saint Louis, MO 63141
(314)576-1201
Fax: (314)576-1525
Website: http://www.crown-
cap.com

Gateway Associates L.P.
8000 Maryland Ave., Ste. 1190
St. Louis, MO 63105
(314)721-5707
Fax: (314)721-5135

Harbison Corp.
8112 Maryland Ave., Ste. 250
Saint Louis, MO 63105
(314)727-8200
Fax: (314)727-0249

Heartland Capital Fund, Ltd.
PO Box 642117
Omaha, NE 68154
(402)778-5124
Fax: (402)445-2370
Website: http://www.heartland
capitalfund.com

Odin Capital Group
1625 Farnam St., Ste. 700
Omaha, NE 68102
(402)346-6200
Fax: (402)342-9311
Website: http://www.odincapital.com

Nevada

Edge Capital Investment Co. LLC
1350 E. Flamingo Rd., Ste. 3000
Las Vegas, NV 89119
(702)438-3343
E-mail: info@edgecapital.net
Website: http://www.edgecapital.net

The Benefit Capital Companies Inc.
PO Box 542
Logandale, NV 89021
(702)398-3222
Fax: (702)398-3700

Millennium Three Venture Group LLC
6880 South McCarran Blvd., Ste. A-11
Reno, NV 89509
(775)954-2020
Fax: (775)954-2023
Website: http://www.m3vg.com

New Jersey

Alan I. Goldman & Associates
497 Ridgewood Ave.
Glen Ridge, NJ 07028
(973)857-5680
Fax: (973)509-8856

CS Capital Partners LLC
328 Second St., Ste. 200
Lakewood, NJ 08701
(732)901-1111
Fax: (212)202-5071
Website: http://www.cs-capital.com

Edison Venture Fund
1009 Lenox Dr., Ste. 4
Lawrenceville, NJ 08648
(609)896-1900
Fax: (609)896-0066
E-mail: info@edisonventure.com
Website: http://www.edisonventure.com

Tappan Zee Capital Corp. (New Jersey)
201 Lower Notch Rd.
PO Box 416
Little Falls, NJ 07424
(973)256-8280
Fax: (973)256-2841

The CIT Group/Venture Capital, Inc.
650 CIT Dr.
Livingston, NJ 07039
(973)740-5429
Fax: (973)740-5555
Website: http://www.cit.com

Capital Express, L.L.C.
1100 Valleybrook Ave.
Lyndhurst, NJ 07071
(201)438-8228
Fax: (201)438-5131
E-mail: niles@capitalexpress.com
Website: http://www.capitalexpress.com

Westford Technology Ventures, L.P.
17 Academy St.
Newark, NJ 07102
(973)624-2131
Fax: (973)624-2008

Accel Partners
1 Palmer Sq.
Princeton, NJ 08542

(609)683-4500
Fax: (609)683-4880
Website: http://www.accel.com

Cardinal Partners
221 Nassau St.
Princeton, NJ 08542
(609)924-6452
Fax: (609)683-0174
Website: http://www.cardinal
healthpartners.com

Domain Associates L.L.C.
One Palmer Sq., Ste. 515
Princeton, NJ 08542
(609)683-5656
Fax: (609)683-9789
Website: http://www.domainvc.com

Johnston Associates, Inc.
181 Cherry Valley Rd.
Princeton, NJ 08540
(609)924-3131
Fax: (609)683-7524
E-mail: jaincorp@aol.com

Kemper Ventures
Princeton Forrestal Village
155 Village Blvd.
Princeton, NJ 08540
(609)936-3035
Fax: (609)936-3051

Penny Lane Parnters
One Palmer Sq., Ste. 309
Princeton, NJ 08542
(609)497-4646
Fax: (609)497-0611

Early Stage Enterprises L.P.
995 Route 518
Skillman, NJ 08558
(609)921-8896
Fax: (609)921-8703
Website: http://www.esevc.com

MBW Management Inc.
1 Springfield Ave.
Summit, NJ 07901
(908)273-4060
Fax: (908)273-4430

BCI Advisors, Inc.
Glenpointe Center W.
Teaneck, NJ 07666
(201)836-3900
Fax: (201)836-6368
E-mail: info@bciadvisors.com
Website: http://www.bci
partners.com

Demuth, Folger & Wetherill / DFW Capital Partners
Glenpointe Center E., 5th Fl.
300 Frank W. Burr Blvd.
Teaneck, NJ 07666
(201)836-2233
Fax: (201)836-5666
Website: http://www.dfwcapital.com

First Princeton Capital Corp.
189 Berdan Ave., No. 131
Wayne, NJ 07470-3233
(973)278-3233
Fax: (973)278-4290
Website: http://www.lytellcatt.net

Edelson Technology Partners
300 Tice Blvd.
Woodcliff Lake, NJ 07675
(201)930-9898
Fax: (201)930-8899
Website: http://www.edelsontech.com

New Mexico

Bruce F. Glaspell & Associates
10400 Academy Rd. NE, Ste. 313
Albuquerque, NM 87111
(505)292-4505
Fax: (505)292-4258

High Desert Ventures, Inc.
6101 Imparata St. NE, Ste. 1721
Albuquerque, NM 87111
(505)797-3330
Fax: (505)338-5147

New Business Capital Fund, Ltd.
5805 Torreon NE
Albuquerque, NM 87109
(505)822-8445

SBC Ventures
10400 Academy Rd. NE, Ste. 313
Albuquerque, NM 87111
(505)292-4505
Fax: (505)292-4528

Technology Ventures Corp.
1155 University Blvd. SE
Albuquerque, NM 87106
(505)246-2882
Fax: (505)246-2891

New York

New York State Science & Technology Foundation
Small Business Technology Investment Fund
99 Washington Ave., Ste. 1731
Albany, NY 12210

(518)473-9741
Fax: (518)473-6876

Rand Capital Corp.
2200 Rand Bldg.
Buffalo, NY 14203
(716)853-0802
Fax: (716)854-8480
Website: http://www.randcapital.com

Seed Capital Partners
620 Main St.
Buffalo, NY 14202
(716)845-7520
Fax: (716)845-7539
Website: http://www.seedcp.com

Coleman Venture Group
5909 Northern Blvd.
PO Box 224
East Norwich, NY 11732
(516)626-3642
Fax: (516)626-9722

Vega Capital Corp.
45 Knollwood Rd.
Elmsford, NY 10523
(914)345-9500
Fax: (914)345-9505

Herbert Young Securities, Inc.
98 Cuttermill Rd.
Great Neck, NY 11021
(516)487-8300
Fax: (516)487-8319

Sterling/Carl Marks Capital, Inc.
175 Great Neck Rd., Ste. 408
Great Neck, NY 11021
(516)482-7374
Fax: (516)487-0781
E-mail: stercrlmar@aol.com
Website: http://www.serling
carlmarks.com

Impex Venture Management Co.
PO Box 1570
Green Island, NY 12183
(518)271-8008
Fax: (518)271-9101

Corporate Venture Partners L.P.
200 Sunset Park
Ithaca, NY 14850
(607)257-6323
Fax: (607)257-6128

Arthur P. Gould & Co.
One Wilshire Dr.
Lake Success, NY 11020
(516)773-3000
Fax: (516)773-3289

Dauphin Capital Partners
108 Forest Ave.
Locust Valley, NY 11560
(516)759-3339
Fax: (516)759-3322
Website: http://www.dauphincapital.com

550 Digital Media Ventures
555 Madison Ave., 10th Fl.
New York, NY 10022
Website: http://www.550dmv.com

Aberlyn Capital Management Co., Inc.
500 Fifth Ave.
New York, NY 10110
(212)391-7750
Fax: (212)391-7762

Adler & Company
342 Madison Ave., Ste. 807
New York, NY 10173
(212)599-2535
Fax: (212)599-2526

Alimansky Capital Group, Inc.
605 Madison Ave., Ste. 300
New York, NY 10022-1901
(212)832-7300
Fax: (212)832-7338

Allegra Partners
515 Madison Ave., 29th Fl.
New York, NY 10022
(212)826-9080
Fax: (212)759-2561

The Argentum Group
The Chyrsler Bldg.
405 Lexington Ave.
New York, NY 10174
(212)949-6262
Fax: (212)949-8294
Website: http://www.argentum
group.com

Axavision Inc.
14 Wall St., 26th Fl.
New York, NY 10005
(212)619-4000
Fax: (212)619-7202

Bedford Capital Corp.
18 East 48th St., Ste. 1800
New York, NY 10017
(212)688-5700
Fax: (212)754-4699
E-mail: info@bedfordnyc.com
Website: http://www.bedfordnyc.com

Bloom & Co.
950 Third Ave.

New York, NY 10022
(212)838-1858
Fax: (212)838-1843

Bristol Capital Management
300 Park Ave., 17th Fl.
New York, NY 10022
(212)572-6306
Fax: (212)705-4292

**Citicorp Venture Capital Ltd.
(New York City)**
399 Park Ave., 14th Fl.
Zone 4
New York, NY 10043
(212)559-1127
Fax: (212)888-2940

CM Equity Partners
135 E. 57th St.
New York, NY 10022
(212)909-8428
Fax: (212)980-2630

Cohen & Co., L.L.C.
800 Third Ave.
New York, NY 10022
(212)317-2250
Fax: (212)317-2255
E-mail: nlcohen@aol.com

Cornerstone Equity Investors, L.L.C.
717 5th Ave., Ste. 1100
New York, NY 10022
(212)753-0901
Fax: (212)826-6798
Website: http://www.cornerstone-
equity.com

CW Group, Inc.
1041 3rd Ave., 2nd fl.
New York, NY 10021
(212)308-5266
Fax: (212)644-0354
Website: http://www.cwventures.com

DH Blair Investment Banking Corp.
44 Wall St., 2nd Fl.
New York, NY 10005
(212)495-5000
Fax: (212)269-1438

Dresdner Kleinwort Capital
75 Wall St.
New York, NY 10005
(212)429-3131
Fax: (212)429-3139
Website: http://www.dresdnerkb.com

East River Ventures, L.P.
645 Madison Ave., 22nd Fl.

New York, NY 10022
(212)644-2322
Fax: (212)644-5498

Easton Hunt Capital Partners
641 Lexington Ave., 21st Fl.
New York, NY 10017
(212)702-0950
Fax: (212)702-0952
Website: http://www.eastoncapital.com

Elk Associates Funding Corp.
747 3rd Ave., Ste. 4C
New York, NY 10017
(212)355-2449
Fax: (212)759-3338

EOS Partners, L.P.
320 Park Ave., 22nd Fl.
New York, NY 10022
(212)832-5800
Fax: (212)832-5815
E-mail: mfirst@eospartners.com
Website: http://www.eospartners.com

Euclid Partners
45 Rockefeller Plaza, Ste. 3240
New York, NY 10111
(212)218-6880
Fax: (212)218-6877
E-mail: graham@euclidpartners.com
Website: http://www.euclidpartners.com

Evergreen Capital Partners, Inc.
150 East 58th St.
New York, NY 10155
(212)813-0758
Fax: (212)813-0754

Exeter Capital L.P.
10 E. 53rd St.
New York, NY 10022
(212)872-1172
Fax: (212)872-1198
E-mail: exeter@usa.net

Financial Technology Research Corp.
518 Broadway
Penthouse
New York, NY 10012
(212)625-9100
Fax: (212)431-0300
E-mail: fintek@financier.com

4C Ventures
237 Park Ave., Ste. 801
New York, NY 10017
(212)692-3680
Fax: (212)692-3685
Website: http://www.4cventures.com

Fusient Ventures
99 Park Ave., 20th Fl.
New York, NY 10016
(212)972-8999
Fax: (212)972-9876
E-mail: info@fusient.com
Website: http://www.fusient.com

Generation Capital Partners
551 Fifth Ave., Ste. 3100
New York, NY 10176
(212)450-8507
Fax: (212)450-8550
Website: http://www.genpartners.com

Golub Associates, Inc.
555 Madison Ave.
New York, NY 10022
(212)750-6060
Fax: (212)750-5505

Hambro America Biosciences Inc.
650 Madison Ave., 21st Floor
New York, NY 10022
(212)223-7400
Fax: (212)223-0305

Hanover Capital Corp.
505 Park Ave., 15th Fl.
New York, NY 10022
(212)755-1222
Fax: (212)935-1787

Harvest Partners, Inc.
280 Park Ave, 33rd Fl.
New York, NY 10017
(212)559-6300
Fax: (212)812-0100
Website: http://www.harvpart.com

Holding Capital Group, Inc.
10 E. 53rd St., 30th Fl.
New York, NY 10022
(212)486-6670
Fax: (212)486-0843

Hudson Venture Partners
660 Madison Ave., 14th Fl.
New York, NY 10021-8405
(212)644-9797
Fax: (212)644-7430
Website: http://www.hudsonptr.com

IBJS Capital Corp.
1 State St., 9th Fl.
New York, NY 10004
(212)858-2018
Fax: (212)858-2768

InterEquity Capital Partners, L.P.
220 5th Ave.
New York, NY 10001

(212)779-2022
Fax: (212)779-2103
Website: http://www.interequity-capital.com

The Jordan Edmiston Group Inc.
150 East 52nd St., 18th Fl.
New York, NY 10022
(212)754-0710
Fax: (212)754-0337

Josephberg, Grosz and Co., Inc.
633 3rd Ave., 13th Fl.
New York, NY 10017
(212)974-9926
Fax: (212)397-5832

J.P. Morgan Capital Corp.
60 Wall St.
New York, NY 10260-0060
(212)648-9000
Fax: (212)648-5002
Website: http://www.jpmorgan.com

The Lambda Funds
380 Lexington Ave., 54th Fl.
New York, NY 10168
(212)682-3454
Fax: (212)682-9231

Lepercq Capital Management Inc.
1675 Broadway
New York, NY 10019
(212)698-0795
Fax: (212)262-0155

Loeb Partners Corp.
61 Broadway, Ste. 2400
New York, NY 10006
(212)483-7000
Fax: (212)574-2001

Madison Investment Partners
660 Madison Ave.
New York, NY 10021
(212)223-2600
Fax: (212)223-8208

MC Capital Inc.
520 Madison Ave., 16th Fl.
New York, NY 10022
(212)644-0841
Fax: (212)644-2926

**McCown, De Leeuw and Co.
(New York)**
65 E. 55th St., 36th Fl.
New York, NY 10022
(212)355-5500
Fax: (212)355-6283
Website: http://www.mdcpartners.com

Morgan Stanley Venture Partners
1221 Avenue of the Americas, 33rd Fl.
New York, NY 10020
(212)762-7900
Fax: (212)762-8424
E-mail: msventures@ms.com
Website: http://www.msvp.com

Nazem and Co.
645 Madison Ave., 12th Fl.
New York, NY 10022
(212)371-7900
Fax: (212)371-2150

Needham Capital Management, L.L.C.
445 Park Ave.
New York, NY 10022
(212)371-8300
Fax: (212)705-0299
Website: http://www.needhamco.com

Norwood Venture Corp.
1430 Broadway, Ste. 1607
New York, NY 10018
(212)869-5075
Fax: (212)869-5331
E-mail: nvc@mail.idt.net
Website: http://www.norven.com

Noveltek Venture Corp.
521 Fifth Ave., Ste. 1700
New York, NY 10175
(212)286-1963

Paribas Principal, Inc.
787 7th Ave.
New York, NY 10019
(212)841-2005
Fax: (212)841-3558

**Patricof & Co. Ventures, Inc.
(New York)**
445 Park Ave.
New York, NY 10022
(212)753-6300
Fax: (212)319-6155
Website: http://www.patricof.com

The Platinum Group, Inc.
350 Fifth Ave, Ste. 7113
New York, NY 10118
(212)736-4300
Fax: (212)736-6086
Website: http://www.platinumgroup.com

Pomona Capital
780 Third Ave., 28th Fl.
New York, NY 10017
(212)593-3639
Fax: (212)593-3987
Website: http://www.pomonacapital.com

Prospect Street Ventures
10 East 40th St., 44th Fl.
New York, NY 10016
(212)448-0702
Fax: (212)448-9652
E-mail: wkohler@prospectstreet.com
Website: http://www.prospectstreet.com

Regent Capital Management
505 Park Ave., Ste. 1700
New York, NY 10022
(212)735-9900
Fax: (212)735-9908

Rothschild Ventures, Inc.
1251 Avenue of the Americas, 51st Fl.
New York, NY 10020
(212)403-3500
Fax: (212)403-3652
Website: http://www.nmrothschild.com

Sandler Capital Management
767 Fifth Ave., 45th Fl.
New York, NY 10153
(212)754-8100
Fax: (212)826-0280

Siguler Guff & Company
630 Fifth Ave., 16th Fl.
New York, NY 10111
(212)332-5100
Fax: (212)332-5120

Spencer Trask Ventures Inc.
535 Madison Ave.
New York, NY 10022
(212)355-5565
Fax: (212)751-3362
Website: http://www.spencertrask.com

Sprout Group (New York City)
277 Park Ave.
New York, NY 10172
(212)892-3600
Fax: (212)892-3444
E-mail: info@sproutgroup.com
Website: http://www.sproutgroup.com

US Trust Private Equity
114 W.47th St.
New York, NY 10036
(212)852-3949
Fax: (212)852-3759
Website: http://www.ustrust.com/
privateequity

Vencon Management Inc.
301 West 53rd St., Ste. 10F
New York, NY 10019
(212)581-8787
Fax: (212)397-4126
Website: http://www.venconinc.com

Venrock Associates
30 Rockefeller Plaza, Ste. 5508
New York, NY 10112
(212)649-5600
Fax: (212)649-5788
Website: http://www.venrock.com

Venture Capital Fund of America, Inc.
509 Madison Ave., Ste. 812
New York, NY 10022
(212)838-5577
Fax: (212)838-7614
E-mail: mail@vcfa.com
Website: http://www.vcfa.com

Venture Opportunities Corp.
150 E. 58th St.
New York, NY 10155
(212)832-3737
Fax: (212)980-6603

Warburg Pincus Ventures, Inc.
466 Lexington Ave., 11th Fl.
New York, NY 10017
(212)878-9309
Fax: (212)878-9200
Website: http://www.warburgpincus.com

Wasserstein, Perella & Co. Inc.
31 W. 52nd St., 27th Fl.
New York, NY 10019
(212)702-5691
Fax: (212)969-7879

Welsh, Carson, Anderson, & Stowe
320 Park Ave., Ste. 2500
New York, NY 10022-6815
(212)893-9500
Fax: (212)893-9575

Whitney and Co. (New York)
630 Fifth Ave. Ste. 3225
New York, NY 10111
(212)332-2400
Fax: (212)332-2422
Website: http://www.jhwitney.com

Winthrop Ventures
74 Trinity Place, Ste. 600
New York, NY 10006
(212)422-0100

The Pittsford Group
8 Lodge Pole Rd.
Pittsford, NY 14534
(716)223-3523

Genesee Funding
70 Linden Oaks, 3rd Fl.
Rochester, NY 14625
(716)383-5550
Fax: (716)383-5305

Gabelli Multimedia Partners
One Corporate Center
Rye, NY 10580
(914)921-5395
Fax: (914)921-5031

Stamford Financial
108 Main St.
Stamford, NY 12167
(607)652-3311
Fax: (607)652-6301
Website: http://www.stamford
financial.com

Northwood Ventures LLC
485 Underhill Blvd., Ste. 205
Syosset, NY 11791
(516)364-5544
Fax: (516)364-0879
E-mail: northwood@northwood.com
Website: http://www.north
woodventures.com

Exponential Business Development Co.
216 Walton St.
Syracuse, NY 13202-1227
(315)474-4500
Fax: (315)474-4682
E-mail: dirksonn@aol.com
Website: http://www.exponential-ny.com

Onondaga Venture Capital Fund Inc.
714 State Tower Bldg.
Syracuse, NY 13202
(315)478-0157
Fax: (315)478-0158

Bessemer Venture Partners (Westbury)
1400 Old Country Rd., Ste. 109
Westbury, NY 11590
(516)997-2300
Fax: (516)997-2371
E-mail: bob@bvpny.com
Website: http://www.bvp.com

Ovation Capital Partners
120 Bloomingdale Rd., 4th Fl.
White Plains, NY 10605
(914)258-0011
Fax: (914)684-0848
Website: http://www.ovation
capital.com

North Carolina

Carolinas Capital Investment Corp.
1408 Biltmore Dr.
Charlotte, NC 28207
(704)375-3888
Fax: (704)375-6226

First Union Capital Partners
1st Union Center, 12th Fl.
301 S. College St.
Charlotte, NC 28288-0732
(704)383-0000
Fax: (704)374-6711
Website: http://www.fucp.com

Frontier Capital LLC
525 North Tryon St., Ste. 1700
Charlotte, NC 28202
(704)414-2880
Fax: (704)414-2881
Website: http://www.frontierfunds.com

Kitty Hawk Capital
2700 Coltsgate Rd., Ste. 202
Charlotte, NC 28211
(704)362-3909
Fax: (704)362-2774
Website: http://www.kittyhawk
capital.com

Piedmont Venture Partners
One Morrocroft Centre
6805 Morisson Blvd., Ste. 380
Charlotte, NC 28211
(704)731-5200
Fax: (704)365-9733
Website: http://www.piedmontvp.com

Ruddick Investment Co.
1800 Two First Union Center
Charlotte, NC 28282
(704)372-5404
Fax: (704)372-6409

The Shelton Companies Inc.
3600 One First Union Center
301 S. College St.
Charlotte, NC 28202
(704)348-2200
Fax: (704)348-2260

Wakefield Group
1110 E. Morehead St.
PO Box 36329
Charlotte, NC 28236
(704)372-0355
Fax: (704)372-8216
Website: http://www.wakefiel
dgroup.com

Aurora Funds, Inc.
2525 Meridian Pkwy., Ste. 220
Durham, NC 27713
(919)484-0400
Fax: (919)484-0444
Website: http://www.aurora
funds.com

Intersouth Partners
3211 Shannon Rd., Ste. 610
Durham, NC 27707
(919)493-6640
Fax: (919)493-6649
E-mail: info@intersouth.com
Website: http://www.intersouth.com

Geneva Merchant Banking Partners
PO Box 21962
Greensboro, NC 27420
(336)275-7002
Fax: (336)275-9155
Website: http://www.geneva
merchantbank.com

The North Carolina Enterprise Fund, L.P.
3600 Glenwood Ave., Ste. 107
Raleigh, NC 27612
(919)781-2691
Fax: (919)783-9195
Website: http://www.ncef.com

Ohio

Senmend Medical Ventures
4445 Lake Forest Dr., Ste. 600
Cincinnati, OH 45242
(513)563-3264
Fax: (513)563-3261

The Walnut Group
312 Walnut St., Ste. 1151
Cincinnati, OH 45202
(513)651-3300
Fax: (513)929-4441
Website: http://www.thewal
nutgroup.com

Brantley Venture Partners
20600 Chagrin Blvd., Ste. 1150
Cleveland, OH 44122
(216)283-4800
Fax: (216)283-5324

Clarion Capital Corp.
1801 E. 9th St., Ste. 1120
Cleveland, OH 44114
(216)687-1096
Fax: (216)694-3545

Crystal Internet Venture Fund, L.P.
1120 Chester Ave., Ste. 418
Cleveland, OH 44114
(216)263-5515
Fax: (216)263-5518
E-mail: jf@crystalventure.com
Website: http://www.crystal
venture.com

ORGANIZATIONS, AGENCIES, & CONSULTANTS

Key Equity Capital Corp.
127 Public Sq., 28th Fl.
Cleveland, OH 44114
(216)689-3000
Fax: (216)689-3204
Website: http://www.keybank.com

Morgenthaler Ventures
Terminal Tower
50 Public Square, Ste. 2700
Cleveland, OH 44113
(216)416-7500
Fax: (216)416-7501
Website: http://www.morgenthaler.com

National City Equity Partners Inc.
1965 E. 6th St.
Cleveland, OH 44114
(216)575-2491
Fax: (216)575-9965
E-mail: nccap@aol.com
Website: http://www.nccapital.com

Primus Venture Partners, Inc.
5900 LanderBrook Dr., Ste. 2000
Cleveland, OH 44124-4020
(440)684-7300
Fax: (440)684-7342
E-mail: info@primusventure.com
Website: http://www.primusventure.com

Banc One Capital Partners (Columbus)
150 East Gay St., 24th Fl.
Columbus, OH 43215
(614)217-1100
Fax: (614)217-1217

Battelle Venture Partners
505 King Ave.
Columbus, OH 43201
(614)424-7005
Fax: (614)424-4874

Ohio Partners
62 E. Board St., 3rd Fl.
Columbus, OH 43215
(614)621-1210
Fax: (614)621-1240

Capital Technology Group, L.L.C.
400 Metro Place North, Ste. 300
Dublin, OH 43017
(614)792-6066
Fax: (614)792-6036
E-mail: info@capitaltech.com
Website: http://www.capitaltech.com

Northwest Ohio Venture Fund
4159 Holland-Sylvania R., Ste. 202
Toledo, OH 43623
(419)824-8144

Fax: (419)882-2035
E-mail: bwalsh@novf.com

Oklahoma

Moore & Associates
1000 W. Wilshire Blvd., Ste. 370
Oklahoma City, OK 73116
(405)842-3660
Fax: (405)842-3763

Chisholm Private Capital Partners
100 West 5th St., Ste. 805
Tulsa, OK 74103
(918)584-0440
Fax: (918)584-0441
Website: http://www.chisholmvc.com

Davis, Tuttle Venture Partners (Tulsa)
320 S. Boston, Ste. 1000
Tulsa, OK 74103-3703
(918)584-7272
Fax: (918)582-3404
Website: http://www.davistuttle.com

RBC Ventures
2627 E. 21st St.
Tulsa, OK 74114
(918)744-5607
Fax: (918)743-8630

Oregon

Utah Ventures II LP
10700 SW Beaverton-Hillsdale Hwy.,
Ste. 548
Beaverton, OR 97005
(503)574-4125
E-mail: adishlip@uven.com
Website: http://www.uven.com

Orien Ventures
14523 SW Westlake Dr.
Lake Oswego, OR 97035
(503)699-1680
Fax: (503)699-1681

OVP Venture Partners (Lake Oswego)
340 Oswego Pointe Dr., Ste. 200
Lake Oswego, OR 97034
(503)697-8766
Fax: (503)697-8863
E-mail: info@ovp.com
Website: http://www.ovp.com

Oregon Resource and Technology Development Fund
4370 NE Halsey St., Ste. 233
Portland, OR 97213-1566
(503)282-4462
Fax: (503)282-2976

Shaw Venture Partners
400 SW 6th Ave., Ste. 1100
Portland, OR 97204-1636
(503)228-4884
Fax: (503)227-2471
Website: http://www.shawventures.com

Pennsylvania

Mid-Atlantic Venture Funds
125 Goodman Dr.
Bethlehem, PA 18015
(610)865-6550
Fax: (610)865-6427
Website: http://www.mavf.com

Newspring Ventures
100 W. Elm St., Ste. 101
Conshohocken, PA 19428
(610)567-2380
Fax: (610)567-2388
Website: http://www.news
printventures.com

Patricof & Co. Ventures, Inc.
455 S. Gulph Rd., Ste. 410
King of Prussia, PA 19406
(610)265-0286
Fax: (610)265-4959
Website: http://www.patricof.com

Loyalhanna Venture Fund
527 Cedar Way, Ste. 104
Oakmont, PA 15139
(412)820-7035
Fax: (412)820-7036

Innovest Group Inc.
2000 Market St., Ste. 1400
Philadelphia, PA 19103
(215)564-3960
Fax: (215)569-3272

Keystone Venture Capital Management Co.
1601 Market St., Ste. 2500
Philadelphia, PA 19103
(215)241-1200
Fax: (215)241-1211
Website: http://www.keystonevc.com

Liberty Venture Partners
2005 Market St., Ste. 200
Philadelphia, PA 19103
(215)282-4484
Fax: (215)282-4485
E-mail: info@libertyvp.com
Website: http://www.libertyvp.com

Penn Janney Fund, Inc.
1801 Market St., 11th Fl.
Philadelphia, PA 19103

(215)665-4447
Fax: (215)557-0820

Philadelphia Ventures, Inc.
The Bellevue
200 S. Broad St.
Philadelphia, PA 19102
(215)732-4445
Fax: (215)732-4644

Birchmere Ventures Inc.
2000 Technology Dr.
Pittsburgh, PA 15219-3109
(412)803-8000
Fax: (412)687-8139
Website: http://www.birchmerevc.com

CEO Venture Fund
2000 Technology Dr., Ste. 160
Pittsburgh, PA 15219-3109
(412)687-3451
Fax: (412)687-8139
E-mail: ceofund@aol.com
Website: http://www.ceoventure
fund.com

Innovation Works Inc.
2000 Technology Dr., Ste. 250
Pittsburgh, PA 15219
(412)681-1520
Fax: (412)681-2625
Website: http://www.innovation
works.org

Keystone Minority Capital Fund L.P.
1801 Centre Ave., Ste. 201
Williams Sq.
Pittsburgh, PA 15219
(412)338-2230
Fax: (412)338-2224

Mellon Ventures, Inc.
One Mellon Bank Ctr., Rm. 3500
Pittsburgh, PA 15258
(412)236-3594
Fax: (412)236-3593
Website: http://www.mellon
ventures.com

Pennsylvania Growth Fund
5850 Ellsworth Ave., Ste. 303
Pittsburgh, PA 15232
(412)661-1000
Fax: (412)361-0676

Point Venture Partners
The Century Bldg.
130 Seventh St., 7th Fl.
Pittsburgh, PA 15222
(412)261-1966
Fax: (412)261-1718

Cross Atlantic Capital Partners
5 Radnor Corporate Center, Ste. 555
Radnor, PA 19087
(610)995-2650
Fax: (610)971-2062
Website: http://www.xacp.com

Meridian Venture Partners (Radnor)
The Radnor Court Bldg., Ste. 140
259 Radnor-Chester Rd.
Radnor, PA 19087
(610)254-2999
Fax: (610)254-2996
E-mail: mvpart@ix.netcom.com

TDH
919 Conestoga Rd., Bldg. 1, Ste. 301
Rosemont, PA 19010
(610)526-9970
Fax: (610)526-9971

Adams Capital Management
500 Blackburn Ave.
Sewickley, PA 15143
(412)749-9454
Fax: (412)749-9459
Website: http://www.acm.com

S.R. One, Ltd.
Four Tower Bridge
200 Barr Harbor Dr., Ste. 250
W. Conshohocken, PA 19428
(610)567-1000
Fax: (610)567-1039

Greater Philadelphia Venture Capital Corp.
351 East Conestoga Rd.
Wayne, PA 19087
(610)688-6829
Fax: (610)254-8958

PA Early Stage
435 Devon Park Dr., Bldg. 500, Ste. 510
Wayne, PA 19087
(610)293-4075
Fax: (610)254-4240
Website: http://www.paearlystage.com

The Sandhurst Venture Fund, L.P.
351 E. Constoga Rd.
Wayne, PA 19087
(610)254-8900
Fax: (610)254-8958

TL Ventures
700 Bldg.
435 Devon Park Dr.
Wayne, PA 19087-1990
(610)975-3765
Fax: (610)254-4210
Website: http://www.tlventures.com

Rockhill Ventures, Inc.
100 Front St., Ste. 1350
West Conshohocken, PA 19428
(610)940-0300
Fax: (610)940-0301

Puerto Rico

Advent-Morro Equity Partners
Banco Popular Bldg.
206 Tetuan St., Ste. 903
San Juan, PR 00902
(787)725-5285
Fax: (787)721-1735

North America Investment Corp.
Mercantil Plaza, Ste. 813
PO Box 191831
San Juan, PR 00919
(787)754-6178
Fax: (787)754-6181

Rhode Island

Manchester Humphreys, Inc.
40 Westminster St., Ste. 900
Providence, RI 02903
(401)454-0400
Fax: (401)454-0403

Navis Partners
50 Kennedy Plaza, 12th Fl.
Providence, RI 02903
(401)278-6770
Fax: (401)278-6387
Website: http://www.navis
partners.com

South Carolina

Capital Insights, L.L.C.
PO Box 27162
Greenville, SC 29616 2162
(864)242-6832
Fax: (864)242-6755
E-mail: jwarner@capitalinsights.com
Website: http://www.capitalin
sights.com

Transamerica Mezzanine Financing
7 N. Laurens St., Ste. 603
Greenville, SC 29601
(864)232-6198
Fax: (864)241-4444

Tennessee

Valley Capital Corp.
Krystal Bldg.
100 W. Martin Luther King Blvd.,
Ste. 212

Chattanooga, TN 37402
(423)265-1557
Fax: (423)265-1588

Coleman Swenson Booth Inc.
237 2nd Ave. S
Franklin, TN 37064-2649
(615)791-9462
Fax: (615)791-9636
Website: http://
www.colemanswenson.com

Capital Services & Resources, Inc.
5159 Wheelis Dr., Ste. 106
Memphis, TN 38117
(901)761-2156
Fax: (907)767-0060

Paradigm Capital Partners LLC
6410 Poplar Ave., Ste. 395
Memphis, TN 38119
(901)682-6060
Fax: (901)328-3061

SSM Ventures
845 Crossover Ln., Ste. 140
Memphis, TN 38117
(901)767-1131
Fax: (901)767-1135
Website: http://www.ssm
ventures.com

Capital Across America L.P.
501 Union St., Ste. 201
Nashville, TN 37219
(615)254-1414
Fax: (615)254-1856
Website: http://
www.capitalacrossamerica.com

Equitas L.P.
2000 Glen Echo Rd., Ste. 101
PO Box 158838
Nashville, TN 37215-8838
(615)383-8673
Fax: (615)383-8693

Massey Burch Capital Corp.
One Burton Hills Blvd., Ste. 350
Nashville, TN 37215
(615)665-3221
Fax: (615)665-3240
E-mail: tcalton@masseyburch.com
Website: http://www.masseyburch.com

Nelson Capital Corp.
3401 West End Ave., Ste. 300
Nashville, TN 37203
(615)292-8787
Fax: (615)385-3150

Texas

Phillips-Smith Specialty Retail Group
5080 Spectrum Dr., Ste. 805 W
Addison, TX 75001
(972)387-0725
Fax: (972)458-2560
E-mail: pssrg@aol.com
Website: http://www.phillips-smith.com

Austin Ventures, L.P.
701 Brazos St., Ste. 1400
Austin, TX 78701
(512)485-1900
Fax: (512)476-3952
E-mail: info@ausven.com
Website: http://www.austinventures.com

The Capital Network
3925 West Braker Lane, Ste. 406
Austin, TX 78759-5321
(512)305-0826
Fax: (512)305-0836

Techxas Ventures LLC
5000 Plaza on the Lake
Austin, TX 78746
(512)343-0118
Fax: (512)343-1879
E-mail: bruce@techxas.com
Website: http://www.techxas.com

Alliance Financial of Houston
218 Heather Ln.
Conroe, TX 77385-9013
(936)447-3300
Fax: (936)447-4222

Amerimark Capital Corp.
1111 W. Mockingbird, Ste. 1111
Dallas, TX 75247
(214)638-7878
Fax: (214)638-7612
E-mail: amerimark@amcapital.com
Website: http://www.amcapital.com

AMT Venture Partners / AMT Capital Ltd.
5220 Spring Valley Rd., Ste. 600
Dallas, TX 75240
(214)905-9757
Fax: (214)905-9761
Website: http://www.amtcapital.com

Arkoma Venture Partners
5950 Berkshire Lane, Ste. 1400
Dallas, TX 75225
(214)739-3515
Fax: (214)739-3572
E-mail: joelf@arkomavp.com

Capital Southwest Corp.
12900 Preston Rd., Ste. 700
Dallas, TX 75230
(972)233-8242
Fax: (972)233-7362
Website: http://
www.capitalsouthwest.com

Dali, Hook Partners
One Lincoln Center, Ste. 1550
5400 LBJ Freeway
Dallas, TX 75240
(972)991-5457
Fax: (972)991-5458
E-mail: dhook@hookpartners.com
Website: http://www.hookpartners.com

HO2 Partners
Two Galleria Tower
13455 Noel Rd., Ste. 1670
Dallas, TX 75240
(972)702-1144
Fax: (972)702-8234
Website: http://www.ho2.com

Interwest Partners (Dallas)
2 Galleria Tower
13455 Noel Rd., Ste. 1670
Dallas, TX 75240
(972)392-7279
Fax: (972)490-6348
Website: http://www.interwest.com

Kahala Investments, Inc.
8214 Westchester Dr., Ste. 715
Dallas, TX 75225
(214)987-0077
Fax: (214)987-2332

MESBIC Ventures Holding Co.
2435 North Central Expressway, Ste. 200
Dallas, TX 75080
(972)991-1597
Fax: (972)991-4770
Website: http://www.mvhc.com

North Texas MESBIC, Inc.
9500 Forest Lane, Ste. 430
Dallas, TX 75243
(214)221-3565
Fax: (214)221-3566

Richard Jaffe & Company, Inc,
7318 Royal Cir.
Dallas, TX 75230
(214)265-9397
Fax: (214)739-1845

Sevin Rosen Management Co.
13455 Noel Rd., Ste. 1670
Dallas, TX 75240

(972)702-1100
Fax: (972)702-1103
E-mail: info@srfunds.com
Website: http://www.srfunds.com

Stratford Capital Partners, L.P.
300 Crescent Ct., Ste. 500
Dallas, TX 75201
(214)740-7377
Fax: (214)720-7393
E-mail: stratcap@hmtf.com

Sunwestern Investment Group
12221 Merit Dr., Ste. 935
Dallas, TX 75251
(972)239-5650
Fax: (972)701-0024

Wingate Partners
750 N. St. Paul St., Ste. 1200
Dallas, TX 75201
(214)720-1313
Fax: (214)871-8799

Buena Venture Associates
201 Main St., 32nd Fl.
Fort Worth, TX 76102
(817)339-7400
Fax: (817)390-8408
Website: http://www.buenaventure.com

The Catalyst Group
3 Riverway, Ste. 770
Houston, TX 77056
(713)623-8133
Fax: (713)623-0473
E-mail: herman@thecatalystgroup.net
Website: http://www.thecatalyst
group.net

Cureton & Co., Inc.
1100 Louisiana, Ste. 3250
Houston, TX 77002
(713)658-9806
Fax: (713)658-0476

Davis, Tuttle Venture Partners (Dallas)
8 Greenway Plaza, Ste. 1020
Houston, TX 77046
(713)993-0440
Fax: (713)621-2297
Website: http://www.davistuttle.com

Houston Partners
401 Louisiana, 8th Fl.
Houston, TX 77002
(713)222-8600
Fax: (713)222-8932

Southwest Venture Group
10878 Westheimer, Ste. 178

Houston, TX 77042
(713)827-8947
(713)461-1470

AM Fund
4600 Post Oak Place, Ste. 100
Houston, TX 77027
(713)627-9111
Fax: (713)627-9119

Ventex Management, Inc.
3417 Milam St.
Houston, TX 77002-9531
(713)659-7870
Fax: (713)659-7855

MBA Venture Group
1004 Olde Town Rd., Ste. 102
Irving, TX 75061
(972)986-6703

First Capital Group Management Co.
750 East Mulberry St., Ste. 305
PO Box 15616
San Antonio, TX 78212
(210)736-4233
Fax: (210)736-5449

The Southwest Venture Partnerships
16414 San Pedro, Ste. 345
San Antonio, TX 78232
(210)402-1200
Fax: (210)402-1221
E-mail: swvp@aol.com

Medtech International Inc.
1742 Carriageway
Sugarland, TX 77478
(713)980-8474
Fax: (713)980-6343

Utah

First Security Business Investment Corp.
15 East 100 South, Ste. 100
Salt Lake City, UT 84111
(801)246-5737
Fax: (801)246-5740

Utah Ventures II, L.P.
423 Wakara Way, Ste. 206
Salt Lake City, UT 84108
(801)583-5922
Fax: (801)583-4105
Website: http://www.uven.com

Wasatch Venture Corp.
1 S. Main St., Ste. 1400
Salt Lake City, UT 84133
(801)524-8939

Fax: (801)524-8941
E-mail: mail@wasatchvc.com

Vermont

North Atlantic Capital Corp.
76 Saint Paul St., Ste. 600
Burlington, VT 05401
(802)658-7820
Fax: (802)658-5757
Website: http://www.north
atlanticcapital.com

Green Mountain Advisors Inc.
PO Box 1230
Quechee, VT 05059
(802)296-7800
Fax: (802)296-6012
Website: http://www.gmtcap.com

Virginia

Oxford Financial Services Corp.
Alexandria, VA 22314
(703)519-4900
Fax: (703)519-4910
E-mail: oxford133@aol.com

Continental SBIC
4141 N. Henderson Rd.
Arlington, VA 22203
(703)527-5200
Fax: (703)527-3700

Novak Biddle Venture Partners
1750 Tysons Blvd., Ste. 1190
McLean, VA 22102
(703)847-3770
Fax: (703)847-3771
E-mail: roger@novakbiddle.com
Website: http://www.novakbiddle.com

Spacevest
11911 Freedom Dr., Ste. 500
Reston, VA 20190
(703)904-9800
Fax: (703)904-0571
E-mail: spacevest@spacevest.com
Website: http://www.spacevest.com

Virginia Capital
1801 Libbie Ave., Ste. 201
Richmond, VA 23226
(804)648-4802
Fax: (804)648-4809
E-mail: webmaster@vacapital.com
Website: http://www.vacapital.com

Calvert Social Venture Partners
402 Maple Ave. W
Vienna, VA 22180

(703)255-4930
Fax: (703)255-4931
E-mail: calven2000@aol.com

Fairfax Partners
8000 Towers Crescent Dr., Ste. 940
Vienna, VA 22182
(703)847-9486
Fax: (703)847-0911

Global Internet Ventures
8150 Leesburg Pike, Ste. 1210
Vienna, VA 22182
(703)442-3300
Fax: (703)442-3388
Website: http://www.givinc.com

Walnut Capital Corp. (Vienna)
8000 Towers Crescent Dr., Ste. 1070
Vienna, VA 22182
(703)448-3771
Fax: (703)448-7751

Washington

Encompass Ventures
777 108th Ave. NE, Ste. 2300
Bellevue, WA 98004
(425)486-3900
Fax: (425)486-3901
E-mail: info@evpartners.com
Website: http://www.encom
passventures.com

Fluke Venture Partners
11400 SE Sixth St., Ste. 230
Bellevue, WA 98004
(425)453-4590
Fax: (425)453-4675
E-mail: gabelein@flukeventures.com
Website: http://www.flukeventures.com

Pacific Northwest Partners SBIC, L.P.
15352 SE 53rd St.
Bellevue, WA 98006
(425)455-9967
Fax: (425)455-9404

Materia Venture Associates, L.P.
3435 Carillon Pointe
Kirkland, WA 98033-7354
(425)822-4100
Fax: (425)827-4086

OVP Venture Partners (Kirkland)
2420 Carillon Pt.
Kirkland, WA 98033
(425)889-9192
Fax: (425)889-0152
E-mail: info@ovp.com
Website: http://www.ovp.com

Digital Partners
999 3rd Ave., Ste. 1610
Seattle, WA 98104
(206)405-3607
Fax: (206)405-3617
Website: http://www.digitalpartners.com

Frazier & Company
601 Union St., Ste. 3300
Seattle, WA 98101
(206)621-7200
Fax: (206)621-1848
E-mail: jon@frazierco.com

Kirlan Venture Capital, Inc.
221 First Ave. W, Ste. 108
Seattle, WA 98119-4223
(206)281-8610
Fax: (206)285-3451
Website: http://www.kirlanventure.com

Phoenix Partners
1000 2nd Ave., Ste. 3600
Seattle, WA 98104
(206)624-8968
Fax: (206)624-1907

Voyager Capital
800 5th St., Ste. 4100
Seattle, WA 98103
(206)470-1180
Fax: (206)470-1185
E-mail: info@voyagercap.com
Website: http://www.voyagercap.com

Northwest Venture Associates
221 N. Wall St., Ste. 628
Spokane, WA 99201
(509)747-0728
Fax: (509)747-0758
Website: http://www.nwva.com

Wisconsin

Venture Investors Management, L.L.C.
University Research Park
505 S. Rosa Rd.
Madison, WI 53719
(608)441-2700
Fax: (608)441-2727
E-mail: roger@ventureinvestors.com
Website: http://www.venture
investers.com

Capital Investments, Inc.
1009 West Glen Oaks Lane, Ste. 103
Mequon, WI 53092
(414)241-0303
Fax: (414)241-8451
Website: http://
www.capitalinvestmentsinc.com

Future Value Venture, Inc.
2745 N. Martin Luther King
Dr., Ste. 204
Milwaukee, WI 53212-2300
(414)264-2252
Fax: (414)264-2253
E-mail: fvvventures@aol.com
William Beckett, President

Lubar and Co., Inc.
700 N. Water St., Ste. 1200
Milwaukee, WI 53202
(414)291-9000
Fax: (414)291-9061

GCI
20875 Crossroads Cir., Ste. 100
Waukesha, WI 53186
(262)798-5080
Fax: (262)798-5087

Glossary of Small Business Terms

Absolute liability
Liability that is incurred due to product defects or negligent actions. Manufacturers or retail establishments are held responsible, even though the defect or action may not have been intentional or negligent.

ACE
See Active Corps of Executives

Accident and health benefits
Benefits offered to employees and their families in order to offset the costs associated with accidental death, accidental injury, or sickness.

Account statement
A record of transactions, including payments, new debt, and deposits, incurred during a defined period of time.

Accounting system
System capturing the costs of all employees and/or machinery included in business expenses.

Accounts payable
See Trade credit

Accounts receivable
Unpaid accounts which arise from unsettled claims and transactions from the sale of a company's products or services to its customers.

Active Corps of Executives (ACE)
A group of volunteers for a management assistance program of the U.S. Small Business Administration; volunteers provide one-on-one counseling and teach workshops and seminars for small firms.

ADA
See Americans with Disabilities Act

Adaptation
The process whereby an invention is modified to meet the needs of users.

Adaptive engineering
The process whereby an invention is modified to meet the manufacturing and commercial requirements of a targeted market.

Adverse selection
The tendency for higher-risk individuals to purchase health care and more comprehensive plans, resulting in increased costs.

Advertising
A marketing tool used to capture public attention and influence purchasing decisions for a product or service. Utilizes various forms of media to generate consumer response, such as flyers, magazines, newspapers, radio, and television.

Age discrimination
The denial of the rights and privileges of employment based solely on the age of an individual.

Agency costs
Costs incurred to insure that the lender or investor maintains control over assets while allowing the borrower or entrepreneur to use them. Monitoring and information costs are the two major types of agency costs.

Agribusiness
The production and sale of commodities and products from the commercial farming industry.

America Online
An online service which is accessible by computer modem. The service features Internet access, bulletin boards, online periodicals, electronic mail, and other services for subscribers.

Americans with Disabilities Act (ADA)
Law designed to ensure equal access and opportunity to handicapped persons.

Annual report
Yearly financial report prepared by a business that adheres to the requirements set forth by the Securities and Exchange Commission (SEC).

Antitrust immunity
Exemption from prosecution under antitrust laws. In the transportation industry, firms with antitrust immunity are permitted under certain conditions to set schedules and sometimes prices for the public benefit.

Applied research
Scientific study targeted for use in a product or process.

Asians
A minority category used by the U.S. Bureau of the Census to represent a diverse group that includes Aleuts, Eskimos, American Indians, Asian Indians, Chinese, Japanese, Koreans, Vietnamese, Filipinos, Hawaiians, and other Pacific Islanders.

Assets
Anything of value owned by a company.

Audit
The verification of accounting records and business procedures conducted by an outside accounting service.

Average cost
Total production costs divided by the quantity produced.

Balance Sheet
A financial statement listing the total assets and liabilities of a company at a given time.

Bankruptcy
The condition in which a business cannot meet its debt obligations and petitions a federal district court either for reorganization of its debts (Chapter 11) or for liquidation of its assets (Chapter 7).

Basic research
Theoretical scientific exploration not targeted to application.

Basket clause
A provision specifying the amount of public pension funds that may be placed in investments not included on a state's legal list (see separate citation).

BBS
See Bulletin Board Service

BDC
See Business development corporation

Benefit
Various services, such as health care, flextime, day care, insurance, and vacation, offered to employees as part of a hiring package. Typically subsidized in whole or in part by the business.

BIDCO
See Business and industrial development company

Billing cycle
A system designed to evenly distribute customer billing throughout the month, preventing clerical backlogs.

Birth
See Business birth

Blue chip security
A low-risk, low-yield security representing an interest in a very stable company.

Blue sky laws
A general term that denotes various states' laws regulating securities.

Bond
A written instrument executed by a bidder or contractor (the principal) and a second party (the surety or sureties) to assure fulfillment of the principal's obligations to a third party (the obligee or government) identified in the bond. If the principal's obligations are not met, the bond assures payment to the extent stipulated of any loss sustained by the obligee.

Bonding requirements
Terms contained in a bond (see separate citation).

Bonus
An amount of money paid to an employee as a reward for achieving certain business goals or objectives.

Brainstorming
A group session where employees contribute their ideas for solving a problem or meeting a company objective without fear of retribution or ridicule.

Brand name
The part of a brand, trademark, or service mark that can be spoken. It can be a word, letter, or group of words or letters.

Bridge financing
A short-term loan made in expectation of intermediateterm or long-term financing. Can be used when a company plans to go public in the near future.

Broker
One who matches resources available for innovation with those who need them.

Budget
An estimate of the spending necessary to complete a project or offer a service in comparison to cash-on-hand and expected earnings for the coming year, with an emphasis on cost control.

Bulletin Board Service (BBS)
An online service enabling users to communicate with each other about specific topics.

Business and industrial development company (BIDCO)
A private, for-profit financing corporation chartered by the state to provide both equity and long-term debt capital to small business owners (see separate citations for equity and debt capital).

Business birth
The formation of a new establishment or enterprise. The appearance of a new establishment or enterprise in the Small Business Data Base (see separate citation).

Business conditions
Outside factors that can affect the financial performance of a business.

Business contractions
The number of establishments that have decreased in employment during a specified time.

Business cycle
A period of economic recession and recovery. These cycles vary in duration.

Business death
The voluntary or involuntary closure of a firm or establishment. The disappearance of an establishment or enterprise from the Small Business Data Base (see separate citation).

Business development corporation (BDC)
A business financing agency, usually composed of the financial institutions in an area or state, organized to assist in financing businesses unable to obtain assistance through normal channels; the risk is spread among various members of the business development corporation, and interest rates may vary somewhat from those charged by member institutions. A venture capital firm in which shares of ownership are publicly held and to which the Investment Act of 1940 applies.

Business dissolution
For enumeration purposes, the absence of a business that was present in the prior time period from any current record.

Business entry
See Business birth

Business ethics
Moral values and principles espoused by members of the business community as a guide to fair and honest business practices.

Business exit
See Business death

Business expansions
The number of establishments that added employees during a specified time.

Business failure
Closure of a business causing a loss to at least one creditor.

Business format franchising
The purchase of the name, trademark, and an ongoing business plan of the parent corporation or franchisor by the franchisee.

Business license
A legal authorization issued by municipal and state governments and required for business operations.

Business name
Enterprises must register their business names with local governments usually on a "doing business as" (DBA) form. (This name is sometimes referred to as a "fictional name.") The procedure is part of the business licensing process and prevents any other business from using that same name for a similar business in the same locality.

Business norms
See Financial ratios

Glossary

Business permit
See Business license

Business plan
A document that spells out a company's expected course of action for a specified period, usually including a detailed listing and analysis of risks and uncertainties. For the small business, it should examine the proposed products, the market, the industry, the management policies, the marketing policies, production needs, and financial needs. Frequently, it is used as a prospectus for potential investors and lenders.

Business proposal
See Business plan

Business service firm
An establishment primarily engaged in rendering services to other business organizations on a fee or contract basis.

Business start
For enumeration purposes, a business with a name or similar designation that did not exist in a prior time period.

Cafeteria plan
See Flexible benefit plan

Capacity
Level of a firm's, industry's, or nation's output corresponding to full practical utilization of available resources.

Capital
Assets less liabilities, representing the ownership interest in a business. A stock of accumulated goods, especially at a specified time and in contrast to income received during a specified time period. Accumulated goods devoted to production. Accumulated possessions calculated to bring income.

Capital expenditure
Expenses incurred by a business for improvements that will depreciate over time.

Capital gain
The monetary difference between the purchase price and the selling price of capital. Capital gains are taxed at a rate of 28% by the federal government.

Capital intensity
The relative importance of capital in the production process, usually expressed as the ratio of capital to labor but also sometimes as the ratio of capital to output.

Capital resource
The equipment, facilities and labor used to create products and services.

Caribbean Basin Initiative
An interdisciplinary program to support commerce among the businesses in the nations of the Caribbean Basin and the United States. Agencies involved include: the Agency for International Development, the U.S. Small Business Administration, the International Trade Administration of the U.S. Department of Commerce, and various private sector groups.

Catastrophic care
Medical and other services for acute and long-term illnesses that cost more than insurance coverage limits or that cost the amount most families may be expected to pay with their own resources.

CDC
See Certified development corporation

CD-ROM
Compact disc with read-only memory used to store large amounts of digitized data.

Certified development corporation (CDC)
A local area or statewide corporation or authority (for profit or nonprofit) that packages U.S. Small Business Administration (SBA), bank, state, and/or private money into financial assistance for existing business capital improvements. The SBA holds the second lien on its maximum share of 40 percent involvement. Each state has at least one certified development corporation. This program is called the SBA 504 Program.

Certified lenders
Banks that participate in the SBA guaranteed loan program (see separate citation). Such banks must have a good track record with the U.S. Small Business Administration (SBA) and must agree to certain conditions set forth by the agency. In return, the SBA agrees to process any guaranteed loan application within three business days.

Champion
An advocate for the development of an innovation.

Channel of distribution
The means used to transport merchandise from the manufacturer to the consumer.

Chapter 7 of the 1978 Bankruptcy Act
Provides for a court-appointed trustee who is responsible for liquidating a company's assets in order to settle outstanding debts.

Chapter 11 of the 1978 Bankruptcy Act
Allows the business owners to retain control of the company while working with their creditors to reorganize their finances and establish better business practices to prevent liquidation of assets.

Closely held corporation
A corporation in which the shares are held by a few persons, usually officers, employees, or others close to the management; these shares are rarely offered to the public.

Code of Federal Regulations
Codification of general and permanent rules of the federal government published in the Federal Register.

Code sharing
See Computer code sharing

Coinsurance
Upon meeting the deductible payment, health insurance participants may be required to make additional health care cost-sharing payments. Coinsurance is a payment of a fixed percentage of the cost of each service; copayment is usually a fixed amount to be paid with each service.

Collateral
Securities, evidence of deposit, or other property pledged by a borrower to secure repayment of a loan.

Collective ratemaking
The establishment of uniform charges for services by a group of businesses in the same industry.

Commercial insurance plan
See Underwriting

Commercial loans
Short-term renewable loans used to finance specific capital needs of a business.

Commercialization
The final stage of the innovation process, including production and distribution.

Common stock
The most frequently used instrument for purchasing ownership in private or public companies. Common stock generally carries the right to vote on certain corporate actions and may pay dividends, although it rarely does in venture investments. In liquidation, common stockholders are the last to share in the proceeds from the sale of a corporation's assets; bondholders and preferred shareholders have priority. Common stock is often used in firstround start-up financing.

Community development corporation
A corporation established to develop economic programs for a community and, in most cases, to provide financial support for such development.

Competitor
A business whose product or service is marketed for the same purpose/use and to the same consumer group as the product or service of another.

Computer code sharing
An arrangement whereby flights of a regional airline are identified by the two-letter code of a major carrier in the computer reservation system to help direct passengers to new regional carriers.

Consignment
A merchandising agreement, usually referring to secondhand shops, where the dealer pays the owner of an item a percentage of the profit when the item is sold.

Consortium
A coalition of organizations such as banks and corporations for ventures requiring large capital resources.

Consultant
An individual that is paid by a business to provide advice and expertise in a particular area.

Consumer price index
A measure of the fluctuation in prices between two points in time.

Consumer research
Research conducted by a business to obtain information about existing or potential consumer markets.

Continuation coverage
Health coverage offered for a specified period of time to employees who leave their jobs and to their widows, divorced spouses, or dependents.

Contractions
See Business contractions

Convertible preferred stock
A class of stock that pays a reasonable dividend and is convertible into common stock (see separate citation). Generally the convertible feature may only be exercised after being held for a stated period of time. This arrangement is usually considered second-round financing when a company needs equity to maintain its cash flow.

Convertible securities
A feature of certain bonds, debentures, or preferred stocks that allows them to be exchanged by the owner for another class of securities at a future date and in accordance with any other terms of the issue.

Copayment
See Coinsurance

Copyright
A legal form of protection available to creators and authors to safeguard their works from unlawful use or claim of ownership by others. Copyrights may be acquired for works of art, sculpture, music, and published or unpublished manuscripts. All copyrights should be registered at the Copyright Office of the Library of Congress.

Corporate financial ratios
The relationship between key figures found in a company's financial statement expressed as a numeric value. Used to evaluate risk and company performance. Also known as Financial averages, Operating ratios, and Business ratios.

Corporation
A legal entity, chartered by a state or the federal government, recognized as a separate entity having its own rights, privileges, and liabilities distinct from those of its members.

Cost containment
Actions taken by employers and insurers to curtail rising health care costs; for example, increasing

employee cost sharing (see separate citation), requiring second opinions, or preadmission screening.

Cost sharing
The requirement that health care consumers contribute to their own medical care costs through deductibles and coinsurance (see separate citations). Cost sharing does not include the amounts paid in premiums. It is used to control utilization of services; for example, requiring a fixed amount to be paid with each health care service.

Cottage industry
Businesses based in the home in which the family members are the labor force and family-owned equipment is used to process the goods.

Credit Rating
A letter or number calculated by an organization (such as Dun & Bradstreet) to represent the ability and disposition of a business to meet its financial obligations.

Customer service
Various techniques used to ensure the satisfaction of a customer.

Cyclical peak
The upper turning point in a business cycle.

Cyclical trough
The lower turning point in a business cycle.

DBA
See Business name

Death
See Business death

Debenture
A certificate given as acknowledgment of a debt (see separate citation) secured by the general credit of the issuing corporation. A bond, usually without security, issued by a corporation and sometimes convertible to common stock.

Debt
Something owed by one person to another. Financing in which a company receives capital that must be repaid; no ownership is transferred.

Debt capital
Business financing that normally requires periodic interest payments and repayment of the principal within a specified time.

Debt financing
See Debt capital

Debt securities
Loans such as bonds and notes that provide a specified rate of return for a specified period of time.

Deductible
A set amount that an individual must pay before any benefits are received.

Demand shock absorbers
A term used to describe the role that some small firms play by expanding their output levels to accommodate a transient surge in demand.

Demographics
Statistics on various markets, including age, income, and education, used to target specific products or services to appropriate consumer groups.

Demonstration
Showing that a product or process has been modified sufficiently to meet the needs of users.

Deregulation
The lifting of government restrictions; for example, the lifting of government restrictions on the entry of new businesses, the expansion of services, and the setting of prices in particular industries.

Desktop Publishing
Using personal computers and specialized software to produce camera-ready copy for publications.

Disaster loans
Various types of physical and economic assistance available to individuals and businesses through the U.S. Small Business Administration (SBA). This is the only SBA loan program available for residential purposes.

Discrimination
The denial of the rights and privileges of employment based on factors such as age, race, religion, or gender.

Diseconomies of scale
The condition in which the costs of production increase faster than the volume of production.

Dissolution
See Business dissolution

Distribution
Delivering a product or process to the user.

Distributor
One who delivers merchandise to the user.

Diversified company
A company whose products and services are used by several different markets.

Doing business as (DBA)
See Business name

Dow Jones
An information services company that publishes the Wall Street Journal and other sources of financial information.

Dow Jones Industrial Average
An indicator of stock market performance.

Earned income
A tax term that refers to wages and salaries earned by the recipient, as opposed to monies earned through interest and dividends.

Economic efficiency
The use of productive resources to the fullest practical extent in the provision of the set of goods and services that is most preferred by purchasers in the economy.

Economic indicators
Statistics used to express the state of the economy. These include the length of the average work week, the rate of unemployment, and stock prices.

Economically disadvantaged
See Socially and economically disadvantaged

Economies of scale
See Scale economies

EEOC
See Equal Employment Opportunity Commission

8(a) Program
A program authorized by the Small Business Act that directs federal contracts to small businesses owned and

operated by socially and economically disadvantaged individuals.

Electronic mail (e-mail)
The electronic transmission of mail via phone lines.

E-mail
See Electronic mail

Employee leasing
A contract by which employers arrange to have their workers hired by a leasing company and then leased back to them for a management fee. The leasing company typically assumes the administrative burden of payroll and provides a benefit package to the workers.

Employee tenure
The length of time an employee works for a particular employer.

Employer identification number
The business equivalent of a social security number. Assigned by the U.S. Internal Revenue Service.

Enterprise
An aggregation of all establishments owned by a parent company. An enterprise may consist of a single, independent establishment or include subsidiaries and other branches under the same ownership and control.

Enterprise zone
A designated area, usually found in inner cities and other areas with significant unemployment, where businesses receive tax credits and other incentives to entice them to establish operations there.

Entrepreneur
A person who takes the risk of organizing and operating a new business venture.

Entry
See Business entry

Equal Employment Opportunity Commission (EEOC)
A federal agency that ensures nondiscrimination in the hiring and firing practices of a business.

Equal opportunity employer
An employer who adheres to the standards set by the Equal Employment Opportunity Commission (see separate citation).

Equity
The ownership interest. Financing in which partial or total ownership of a company is surrendered in exchange for capital. An investor's financial return comes from dividend payments and from growth in the net worth of the business.

Equity capital
See Equity; Equity midrisk venture capital

Equity financing
See Equity; Equity midrisk venture capital

Equity midrisk venture capital
An unsecured investment in a company. Usually a purchase of ownership interest in a company that occurs in the later stages of a company's development.

Equity partnership
A limited partnership arrangement for providing start-up and seed capital to businesses.

Equity securities
See Equity

Equity-type
Debt financing subordinated to conventional debt.

Establishment
A single-location business unit that may be independent (a single-establishment enterprise) or owned by a parent enterprise.

Establishment and Enterprise Microdata File
See U.S. Establishment and Enterprise Microdata File

Establishment birth
See Business birth

Establishment Longitudinal Microdata File
See U.S. Establishment Longitudinal Microdata File

Ethics
See Business ethics

Evaluation
Determining the potential success of translating an invention into a product or process.

Exit
See Business exit

Experience rating
See Underwriting

Export
A product sold outside of the country.

Export liccnse
A general or specific license granted by the U.S. Department of Commerce required of anyone wishing to export goods. Some restricted articles need approval from the U.S. Departments of State, Defense, or Energy.

Failure
See Business failure

Fair share agreement
An agreement reached between a franchisor and a minority business organization to extend business ownership to minorities by either reducing the amount of capital required or by setting aside certain marketing areas for minority business owners.

Feasibility study
A study to determine the likelihood that a proposed product or development will fulfill the objectives of a particular investor.

Federal Trade Commission (FTC)
Federal agency that promotes free enterprise and competition within the U.S.

Federal Trade Mark Act of 1946
See Lanham Act

Fictional name
See Business name

Fiduciary
An individual or group that hold assets in trust for a beneficiary.

Financial analysis
The techniques used to determine money needs in a business. Techniques include ratio analysis, calculation of return on investment, guides for measuring profitability, and break-even analysis to determine ultimate success.

Financial intermediary
A financial institution that acts as the intermediary between borrowers and lenders. Banks, savings and loan associations, finance companies, and venture capital companies are major financial intermediaries in the United States.

Financial ratios
See Corporate financial ratios; Industry financial ratios

Financial statement
A written record of business finances, including balance sheets and profit and loss statements.

Financing
See First-stage financing; Second-stage financing; Thirdstage financing

First-stage financing
Financing provided to companies that have expended their initial capital, and require funds to start full-scale manufacturing and sales. Also known as First-round financing.

Fiscal year
Any twelve-month period used by businesses for accounting purposes.

504 Program
See Certified development corporation

Flexible benefit plan
A plan that offers a choice among cash and/or qualified benefits such as group term life insurance, accident and health insurance, group legal services, dependent care assistance, and vacations.

FOB
See Free on board

Format franchising
See Business format franchising; Franchising

401(k) plan
A financial plan where employees contribute a percentage of their earnings to a fund that is invested in stocks, bonds, or money markets for the purpose of saving money for retirement.

Four Ps
Marketing terms referring to Product, Price, Place, and Promotion.

Franchising
A form of licensing by which the owner-the franchisor- distributes or markets a product, method, or service through affiliated dealers called franchisees. The product, method, or service being marketed is identified by a brand name, and the franchisor

maintains control over the marketing methods employed. The franchisee is often given exclusive access to a defined geographic area.

Free on board (FOB)
A pricing term indicating that the quoted price includes the cost of loading goods into transport vessels at a specified place.

Frictional unemployment
See Unemployment

FTC
See Federal Trade Commission

Fulfillment
The systems necessary for accurate delivery of an ordered item, including subscriptions and direct marketing.

Full-time workers
Generally, those who work a regular schedule of more than 35 hours per week.

Garment registration number
A number that must appear on every garment sold in the U.S. to indicate the manufacturer of the garment, which may or may not be the same as the label under which the garment is sold. The U.S. Federal Trade Commission assigns and regulates garment registration numbers.

Gatekeeper
A key contact point for entry into a network.

GDP
See Gross domestic product

General obligation bond
A municipal bond secured by the taxing power of the municipality. The Tax Reform Act of 1986 limits the purposes for which such bonds may be issued and establishes volume limits on the extent of their issuance.

GNP
See Gross national product

Good Housekeeping Seal
Seal appearing on products that signifies the fulfillment of the standards set by the Good Housekeeping Institute to protect consumer interests.

Goods sector
All businesses producing tangible goods, including agriculture, mining, construction, and manufacturing businesses.

GPO
See Gross product originating

Gross domestic product (GDP)
The part of the nation's gross national product (see separate citation) generated by private business using resources from within the country.

Gross national product (GNP)
The most comprehensive single measure of aggregate economic output. Represents the market value of the total output of goods and services produced by a nation's economy.

Gross product originating (GPO)
A measure of business output estimated from the income or production side using employee compensation, profit income, net interest, capital consumption, and indirect business taxes.

HAL
See Handicapped assistance loan program

Handicapped assistance loan program (HAL)
Low-interest direct loan program through the U.S. Small Business Administration (SBA) for handicapped persons. The SBA requires that these persons demonstrate that their disability is such that it is impossible for them to secure employment, thus making it necessary to go into their own business to make a living.

Health maintenance organization (HMO)
Organization of physicians and other health care professionals that provides health services to subscribers and their dependents on a prepaid basis.

Health provider
An individual or institution that gives medical care. Under Medicare, an institutional provider is a hospital, skilled nursing facility, home health agency, or provider of certain physical therapy services.

Hispanic
A person of Cuban, Mexican, Puerto Rican, Latin American (Central or South American), European Spanish, or other Spanish-speaking origin or ancestry.

HMO
See Health maintenance organization

Home-based business
A business with an operating address that is also a residential address (usually the residential address of the proprietor).

Hub-and-spoke system
A system in which flights of an airline from many different cities (the spokes) converge at a single airport (the hub). After allowing passengers sufficient time to make connections, planes then depart for different cities.

Human Resources Management
A business program designed to oversee recruiting, pay, benefits, and other issues related to the company's work force, including planning to determine the optimal use of labor to increase production, thereby increasing profit.

Idea
An original concept for a new product or process.

Import
Products produced outside the country in which they are consumed.

Income
Money or its equivalent, earned or accrued, resulting from the sale of goods and services.

Income statement
A financial statement that lists the profits and losses of a company at a given time.

Incorporation
The filing of a certificate of incorporation with a state's secretary of state, thereby limiting the business owner's liability.

Incubator
A facility designed to encourage entrepreneurship and minimize obstacles to new business formation and growth, particularly for high-technology firms, by housing a number of fledgling enterprises that share an array of services, such as meeting areas, secretarial services, accounting, research library, on-site financial and management counseling, and word processing facilities.

Independent contractor
An individual considered self-employed (see separate citation) and responsible for paying Social Security taxes and income taxes on earnings.

Indirect health coverage
Health insurance obtained through another individual's health care plan; for example, a spouse's employersponsored plan.

Industrial development authority
The financial arm of a state or other political subdivision established for the purpose of financing economic development in an area, usually through loans to nonprofit organizations, which in turn provide facilities for manufacturing and other industrial operations.

Industry financial ratios
Corporate financial ratios averaged for a specified industry. These are used for comparison purposes and reveal industry trends and identify differences between the performance of a specific company and the performance of its industry. Also known as Industrial averages, Industry ratios, Financial averages, and Business or Industrial norms.

Inflation
Increases in volume of currency and credit, generally resulting in a sharp and continuing rise in price levels.

Informal capital
Financing from informal, unorganized sources; includes informal debt capital such as trade credit or loans from friends and relatives and equity capital from informal investors.

Initial public offering (IPO)
A corporation's first offering of stock to the public.

Innovation
The introduction of a new idea into the marketplace in the form of a new product or service or an improvement in organization or process.

Intellectual property
Any idea or work that can be considered proprietary in nature and is thus protected from infringement by others.

Internal capital
Debt or equity financing obtained from the owner or through retained business earnings.

Internet
A government-designed computer network that contains large amounts of information and is accessible through various vendors for a fee.

Intrapreneurship
The state of employing entrepreneurial principles to nonentrepreneurial situations.

Invention
The tangible form of a technological idea, which could include a laboratory prototype, drawings, formulas, etc.

IPO
See Initial public offering

Job description
The duties and responsibilities required in a particular position.

Job tenure
A period of time during which an individual is continuously employed in the same job.

Joint marketing agreements
Agreements between regional and major airlines, often involving the coordination of flight schedules, fares, and baggage transfer. These agreements help regional carriers operate at lower cost.

Joint venture
Venture in which two or more people combine efforts in a particular business enterprise, usually a single transaction or a limited activity, and agree to share the profits and losses jointly or in proportion to their contributions.

Keogh plan
Designed for self-employed persons and unincorporated businesses as a tax-deferred pension account.

Labor force
Civilians considered eligible for employment who are also willing and able to work.

Labor force participation rate
The civilian labor force as a percentage of the civilian population.

Labor intensity
The relative importance of labor in the production process, usually measured as the capital-labor ratio; i.e., the ratio of units of capital (typically, dollars of tangible assets) to the number of employees. The higher the capital-labor ratio exhibited by a firm or industry, the lower the capital intensity of that firm or industry is said to be.

Labor surplus area
An area in which there exists a high unemployment rate. In procurement (see separate citation), extra points are given to firms in counties that are designated a labor surplus area; this information is requested on procurement bid sheets.

Labor union
An organization of similarly-skilled workers who collectively bargain with management over the conditions of employment.

Laboratory prototype
See Prototype

LAN
See Local Area Network

Lanham Act
Refers to the Federal Trade Mark Act of 1946. Protects registered trademarks, trade names, and other service marks used in commerce.

Large business-dominated industry
Industry in which a minimum of 60 percent of employment or sales is in firms with more than 500 workers.

LBO
See Leveraged buy-out

Leader pricing
A reduction in the price of a good or service in order to generate more sales of that good or service.

Legal list
A list of securities selected by a state in which certain institutions and fiduciaries (such as pension funds, insurance companies, and banks) may invest. Securities not on the list are not eligible for investment. Legal lists typically restrict investments to high quality securities meeting certain specifications. Generally, investment is

limited to U.S. securities and investment-grade blue chip securities (see separate citation).

Leveraged buy-out (LBO)

The purchase of a business or a division of a corporation through a highly leveraged financing package.

Liability

An obligation or duty to perform a service or an act. Also defined as money owed.

License

A legal agreement granting to another the right to use a technological innovation.

Limited partnerships

See Venture capital limited partnerships

Liquidity

The ability to convert a security into cash promptly.

Loans

See Commercial loans; Disaster loans; SBA direct loans; SBA guaranteed loans; SBA special lending institution categories Local Area Network (LAN) Computer networks contained within a single building or small area; used to facilitate the sharing of information.

Local development corporation

An organization, usually made up of local citizens of a community, designed to improve the economy of the area by inducing business and industry to locate and expand there. A local development corporation establishes a capability to finance local growth.

Long-haul rates

Rates charged by a transporter in which the distance traveled is more than 800 miles.

Long-term debt

An obligation that matures in a period that exceeds five years.

Low-grade bond

A corporate bond that is rated below investment grade by the major rating agencies (Standard and Poor's, Moody's).

Macro-efficiency

Efficiency as it pertains to the operation of markets and market systems.

Managed care

A cost-effective health care program initiated by employers whereby low-cost health care is made available to the employees in return for exclusive patronage to program doctors.

Management Assistance Programs

See SBA Management Assistance Programs

Management and technical assistance

A term used by many programs to mean business (as opposed to technological) assistance.

Mandated benefits

Specific treatments, providers, or individuals required by law to be included in commercial health plans.

Market evaluation

The use of market information to determine the sales potential of a specific product or process.

Market failure

The situation in which the workings of a competitive market do not produce the best results from the point of view of the entire society.

Market information

Data of any type that can be used for market evaluation, which could include demographic data, technology forecasting, regulatory changes, etc.

Market research

A systematic collection, analysis, and reporting of data about the market and its preferences, opinions, trends, and plans; used for corporate decision-making.

Market share

In a particular market, the percentage of sales of a specific product.

Marketing

Promotion of goods or services through various media.

Master Establishment List (MEL)

A list of firms in the United States developed by the U.S. Small Business Administration; firms can be selected by industry, region, state, standard metropolitan statistical area (see separate citation), county, and zip code.

Maturity

The date upon which the principal or stated value of a bond or other indebtedness becomes due and payable.

Medicaid (Title XIX)

A federally aided, state-operated and administered program that provides medical benefits for certain low income persons in need of health and medical care who are eligible for one of the government's welfare cash payment programs, including the aged, the blind, the disabled, and members of families with dependent children where one parent is absent, incapacitated, or unemployed.

Medicare (Title XVIII)

A nationwide health insurance program for disabled and aged persons. Health insurance is available to insured persons without regard to income. Monies from payroll taxes cover hospital insurance and monies from general revenues and beneficiary premiums pay for supplementary medical insurance.

MEL

See Master Establishment List

MESBIC

See Minority enterprise small business investment corporation

MET

See Multiple employer trust

Metropolitan statistical area (MSA)

A means used by the government to define large population centers that may transverse different governmental jurisdictions. For example, the Washington, D.C. MSA includes the District of Columbia and contiguous parts of Maryland and Virginia because all of these geopolitical areas comprise one population and economic operating unit.

Mezzanine financing

See Third-stage financing

Micro-efficiency

Efficiency as it pertains to the operation of individual firms.

Microdata

Information on the characteristics of an individual business firm.

Mid-term debt

An obligation that matures within one to five years.

Midrisk venture capital

See Equity midrisk venture capital

Minimum premium plan

A combination approach to funding an insurance plan aimed primarily at premium tax savings. The employer self-funds a fixed percentage of estimated monthly claims and the insurance company insures the excess.

Minimum wage

The lowest hourly wage allowed by the federal government.

Minority Business Development Agency

Contracts with private firms throughout the nation to sponsor Minority Business Development Centers which provide minority firms with advice and technical assistance on a fee basis.

Minority Enterprise Small Business Investment Corporation (MESBIC)

A federally funded private venture capital firm licensed by the U.S. Small Business Administration to provide capital to minority-owned businesses (see separate citation).

Minority-owned business

Businesses owned by those who are socially or economically disadvantaged (see separate citation).

Mom and Pop business

A small store or enterprise having limited capital, principally employing family members.

Moonlighter

A wage-and-salary worker with a side business.

MSA

See Metropolitan statistical area

Multi-employer plan

A health plan to which more than one employer is required to contribute and that may be maintained through a collective bargaining agreement and required to meet standards prescribed by the U.S. Department of Labor.

Multi-level marketing

A system of selling in which you sign up other people to assist you and they, in turn, recruit others to help them. Some entrepreneurs have built successful companies on this concept because the main focus of their activities is their product and product sales.

Multimedia
The use of several types of media to promote a product or service. Also, refers to the use of several different types of media (sight, sound, pictures, text) in a CD-ROM (see separate citation) product.

Multiple employer trust (MET)
A self-funded benefit plan generally geared toward small employers sharing a common interest.

NAFTA
See North American Free Trade Agreement

NASDAQ
See National Association of Securities Dealers Automated Quotations

National Association of Securities Dealers Automated Quotations
Provides price quotes on over-the-counter securities as well as securities listed on the New York Stock Exchange.

National income
Aggregate earnings of labor and property arising from the production of goods and services in a nation's economy.

Net assets
See Net worth

Net income
The amount remaining from earnings and profits after all expenses and costs have been met or deducted. Also known as Net earnings.

Net profit
Money earned after production and overhead expenses (see separate citations) have been deducted.

Net worth
The difference between a company's total assets and its total liabilities.

Network
A chain of interconnected individuals or organizations sharing information and/or services.

New York Stock Exchange (NYSE)
The oldest stock exchange in the U.S. Allows for trading in stocks, bonds, warrants, options, and rights that meet listing requirements.

Niche
A career or business for which a person is well-suited. Also, a product which fulfills one need of a particular market segment, often with little or no competition.

Nodes
One workstation in a network, either local area or wide area (see separate citations).

Nonbank bank
A bank that either accepts deposits or makes loans, but not both. Used to create many new branch banks.

Noncompetitive awards
A method of contracting whereby the federal government negotiates with only one contractor to supply a product or service.

Nonmember bank
A state-regulated bank that does not belong to the federal bank system.

Nonprofit
An organization that has no shareholders, does not distribute profits, and is without federal and state tax liabilities.

Norms
See Financial ratios

North American Free Trade Agreement (NAFTA)
Passed in 1993, NAFTA eliminates trade barriers among businesses in the U.S., Canada, and Mexico.

NYSE
See New York Stock Exchange

Occupational Safety & Health Administration (OSHA)
Federal agency that regulates health and safety standards within the workplace.

Optimal firm size
The business size at which the production cost per unit of output (average cost) is, in the long run, at its minimum.

Glossary

Organizational chart
A hierarchical chart tracking the chain of command within an organization.

OSHA
See Occupational Safety & Health Administration

Overhead
Expenses, such as employee benefits and building utilities, incurred by a business that are unrelated to the actual product or service sold.

Owner's capital
Debt or equity funds provided by the owner(s) of a business; sources of owner's capital are personal savings, sales of assets, or loans from financial institutions.

P & L
See Profit and loss statement

Part-time workers
Normally, those who work less than 35 hours per week. The Tax Reform Act indicated that part-time workers who work less than 17.5 hours per week may be excluded from health plans for purposes of complying with federal nondiscrimination rules.

Part-year workers
Those who work less than 50 weeks per year.

Partnership
Two or more parties who enter into a legal relationship to conduct business for profit. Defined by the U.S. Internal Revenue Code as joint ventures, syndicates, groups, pools, and other associations of two or more persons organized for profit that are not specifically classified in the IRS code as corporations or proprietorships.

Patent
A grant made by the government assuring an inventor the sole right to make, use, and sell an invention for a period of 17 years.

PC
See Professional corporation

Peak
See Cyclical peak

Pension
A series of payments made monthly, semiannually, annually, or at other specified intervals during the lifetime of the pensioner for distribution upon retirement. The term is sometimes used to denote the portion of the retirement allowance financed by the employer's contributions.

Pension fund
A fund established to provide for the payment of pension benefits; the collective contributions made by all of the parties to the pension plan.

Performance appraisal
An established set of objective criteria, based on job description and requirements, that is used to evaluate the performance of an employee in a specific job.

Permit
See Business license

Plan
See Business plan

Pooling
An arrangement for employers to achieve efficiencies and lower health costs by joining together to purchase group health insurance or self-insurance.

PPO
See Preferred provider organization

Preferred lenders program
See SBA special lending institution categories

Preferred provider organization (PPO)
A contractual arrangement with a health care services organization that agrees to discount its health care rates in return for faster payment and/or a patient base.

Premiums
The amount of money paid to an insurer for health insurance under a policy. The premium is generally paid periodically (e.g., monthly), and often is split between the employer and the employee. Unlike deductibles and coinsurance or copayments, premiums are paid for coverage whether or not benefits are actually used.

Prime-age workers
Employees 25 to 54 years of age.

Prime contract
A contract awarded directly by the U.S. Federal Government.

Private company
See Closely held corporation

Private placement
A method of raising capital by offering for sale an investment or business to a small group of investors (generally avoiding registration with the Securities and Exchange Commission or state securities registration agencies). Also known as Private financing or Private offering.

Pro forma
The use of hypothetical figures in financial statements to represent future expenditures, debts, and other potential financial expenses.

Proactive
Taking the initiative to solve problems and anticipate future events before they happen, instead of reacting to an already existing problem or waiting for a difficult situation to occur.

Procurement
A contract from an agency of the federal government for goods or services from a small business.

Prodigy
An online service which is accessible by computer modem. The service features Internet access, bulletin boards, online periodicals, electronic mail, and other services for subscribers.

Product development
The stage of the innovation process where research is translated into a product or process through evaluation, adaptation, and demonstration.

Product franchising
An arrangement for a franchisee to use the name and to produce the product line of the franchisor or parent corporation.

Production
The manufacture of a product.

Production prototype
See Prototype

Productivity
A measurement of the number of goods produced during a specific amount of time.

Professional corporation (PC)
Organized by members of a profession such as medicine, dentistry, or law for the purpose of conducting their professional activities as a corporation. Liability of a member or shareholder is limited in the same manner as in a business corporation.

Profit and loss statement (P & L)
The summary of the incomes (total revenues) and costs of a company's operation during a specific period of time. Also known as Income and expense statement.

Proposal
See Business plan

Proprietorship
The most common legal form of business ownership; about 85 percent of all small businesses are proprietorships. The liability of the owner is unlimited in this form of ownership.

Prospective payment system
A cost-containment measure included in the Social Security Amendments of 1983 whereby Medicare payments to hospitals are based on established prices, rather than on cost reimbursement.

Prototype
A model that demonstrates the validity of the concept of an invention (laboratory prototype); a model that meets the needs of the manufacturing process and the user (production prototype).

Prudent investor rule or standard
A legal doctrine that requires fiduciaries to make investments using the prudence, diligence, and intelligence that would be used by a prudent person in making similar investments. Because fiduciaries make investments on behalf of third-party beneficiaries, the standard results in very conservative investments. Until recently, most state regulations required the fiduciary to apply this standard to each investment. Newer, more progressive regulations permit fiduciaries to apply this standard to the portfolio taken as a whole, thereby allowing a fiduciary to balance a portfolio with higher-yield, higher-risk investments. In states with more progressive regulations, practically every type of security is eligible for inclusion in the portfolio of investments made by a fiduciary, provided

that the portfolio investments, in their totality, are those of a prudent person.

Public equity markets
Organized markets for trading in equity shares such as common stocks, preferred stocks, and warrants. Includes markets for both regularly traded and nonregularly traded securities.

Public offering
General solicitation for participation in an investment opportunity. Interstate public offerings are supervised by the U.S. Securities and Exchange Commission (see separate citation).

Quality control
The process by which a product is checked and tested to ensure consistent standards of high quality.

Rate of return
The yield obtained on a security or other investment based on its purchase price or its current market price. The total rate of return is current income plus or minus capital appreciation or depreciation.

Real property
Includes the land and all that is contained on it.

Realignment
See Resource realignment

Recession
Contraction of economic activity occurring between the peak and trough (see separate citations) of a business cycle.

Regulated market
A market in which the government controls the forces of supply and demand, such as who may enter and what price may be charged.

Regulation D
A vehicle by which small businesses make small offerings and private placements of securities with limited disclosure requirements. It was designed to ease the burdens imposed on small businesses utilizing this method of capital formation.

Regulatory Flexibility Act
An act requiring federal agencies to evaluate the impact of their regulations on small businesses before

the regulations are issued and to consider less burdensome alternatives.

Research
The initial stage of the innovation process, which includes idea generation and invention.

Research and development financing
A tax-advantaged partnership set up to finance product development for start-ups as well as more mature companies.

Resource mobility
The ease with which labor and capital move from firm to firm or from industry to industry.

Resource realignment
The adjustment of productive resources to interindustry changes in demand.

Resources
The sources of support or help in the innovation process, including sources of financing, technical evaluation, market evaluation, management and business assistance, etc.

Retained business earnings
Business profits that are retained by the business rather than being distributed to the shareholders as dividends.

Revolving credit
An agreement with a lending institution for an amount of money, which cannot exceed a set maximum, over a specified period of time. Each time the borrower repays a portion of the loan, the amount of the repayment may be borrowed yet again.

Risk capital
See Venture capital

Risk management
The act of identifying potential sources of financial loss and taking action to minimize their negative impact.

Routing
The sequence of steps necessary to complete a product during production.

S corporations
See Sub chapter S corporations

SBA
See Small Business Administration

SBA direct loans
Loans made directly by the U.S. Small Business Administration (SBA); monies come from funds appropriated specifically for this purpose. In general, SBA direct loans carry interest rates slightly lower than those in the private financial markets and are available only to applicants unable to secure private financing or an SBA guaranteed loan.

SBA 504 Program
See Certified development corporation

SBA guaranteed loans
Loans made by lending institutions in which the U.S. Small Business Administration (SBA) will pay a prior agreed-upon percentage of the outstanding principal in the event the borrower of the loan defaults. The terms of the loan and the interest rate are negotiated between theborrower and the lending institution, within set parameters.

SBA loans
See Disaster loans; SBA direct loans; SBA guaranteed loans; SBA special lending institution categories

SBA Management Assistance Programs
Classes, workshops, counseling, and publications offered by the U.S. Small Business Administration.

SBA special lending institution categories
U.S. Small Business Administration (SBA) loan program in which the SBA promises certified banks a 72-hour turnaround period in giving its approval for a loan, and in which preferred lenders in a pilot program are allowed to write SBA loans without seeking prior SBA approval.

SBDB
See Small Business Data Base

SBDC
See Small business development centers

SBI
See Small business institutes program

SBIC
See Small business investment corporation

SBIR Program
See Small Business Innovation Development Act of 1982

Scale economies
The decline of the production cost per unit of output (average cost) as the volume of output increases.

Scale efficiency
The reduction in unit cost available to a firm when producing at a higher output volume.

SCORE
See Service Corps of Retired Executives

SEC
See Securities and Exchange Commission

SECA
See Self-Employment Contributions Act

Second-stage financing
Working capital for the initial expansion of a company that is producing, shipping, and has growing accounts receivable and inventories. Also known as Second-round financing.

Secondary market
A market established for the purchase and sale of outstanding securities following their initial distribution.

Secondary worker
Any worker in a family other than the person who is the primary source of income for the family.

Secondhand capital
Previously used and subsequently resold capital equipment (e.g., buildings and machinery).

Securities and Exchange Commission (SEC)
Federal agency charged with regulating the trade of securities to prevent unethical practices in the investor market.

Securitized debt
A marketing technique that converts long-term loans to marketable securities.

Seed capital
Venture financing provided in the early stages of the innovation process, usually during product development.

Self-employed person
One who works for a profit or fees in his or her own business, profession, or trade, or who operates a farm.

Self-Employment Contributions Act (SECA)
Federal law that governs the self-employment tax (see separate citation).

Self-employment income
Income covered by Social Security if a business earns a net income of at least $400.00 during the year. Taxes are paid on earnings that exceed $400.00.

Self-employment retirement plan
See Keogh plan

Self-employment tax
Required tax imposed on self-employed individuals for the provision of Social Security and Medicare. The tax must be paid quarterly with estimated income tax statements.

Self-funding
A health benefit plan in which a firm uses its own funds to pay claims, rather than transferring the financial risks of paying claims to an outside insurer in exchange for premium payments.

Service Corps of Retired Executives (SCORE)
Volunteers for the SBA Management Assistance Program who provide one-on-one counseling and teach workshops and seminars for small firms.

Service firm
See Business service firm

Service sector
Broadly defined, all U.S. industries that produce intangibles, including the five major industry divisions of transportation, communications, and utilities; wholesale trade; retail trade; finance, insurance, and real estate; and services.

Set asides
See Small business set asides

Short-haul service
A type of transportation service in which the transporter supplies service between cities where the maximum distance is no more than 200 miles.

Short-term debt
An obligation that matures in one year.

SIC codes
See Standard Industrial Classification codes

Single-establishment enterprise
See Establishment

Small business
An enterprise that is independently owned and operated, is not dominant in its field, and employs fewer than 500 people. For SBA purposes, the U.S. Small Business Administration (SBA) considers various other factors (such as gross annual sales) in determining size of a business.

Small Business Administration (SBA)
An independent federal agency that provides assistance with loans, management, and advocating interests before other federal agencies.

Small Business Data Base
A collection of microdata (see separate citation) files on individual firms developed and maintained by the U.S. Small Business Administration.

Small business development centers (SBDC)
Centers that provide support services to small businesses, such as individual counseling, SBA advice, seminars and conferences, and other learning center activities. Most services are free of charge, or available at minimal cost.

Small business development corporation
See Certified development corporation

Small business-dominated industry
Industry in which a minimum of 60 percent of employment or sales is in firms with fewer than 500 employees.

Small Business Innovation Development Act of 1982
Federal statute requiring federal agencies with large extramural research and development budgets to allocate a certain percentage of these funds to small research and development firms. The program, called the Small Business Innovation Research (SBIR) Program, is designed to stimulate technological innovation and make greater use of small businesses in meeting national innovation needs.

Small business institutes (SBI) program
Cooperative arrangements made by U.S. Small Business Administration district offices and local colleges and

universities to provide small business firms with graduate students to counsel them without charge.

Small business investment corporation (SBIC)
A privately owned company licensed and funded through the U.S. Small Business Administration and private sector sources to provide equity or debt capital to small businesses.

Small business set asides
Procurement (see separate citation) opportunities required by law to be on all contracts under $10,000 or a certain percentage of an agency's total procurement expenditure.

Smaller firms
For U.S. Department of Commerce purposes, those firms not included in the Fortune 1000.

SMSA
See Metropolitan statistical area

Socially and economically disadvantaged
Individuals who have been subjected to racial or ethnic prejudice or cultural bias without regard to their qualities as individuals, and whose abilities to compete are impaired because of diminished opportunities to obtain capital and credit.

Sole proprietorship
An unincorporated, one-owner business, farm, or professional practice.

Special lending institution categories
See SBA special lending institution categories

Standard Industrial Classification (SIC) codes
Four-digit codes established by the U.S. Federal Government to categorize businesses by type of economic activity; the first two digits correspond to major groups such as construction and manufacturing, while the last two digits correspond to subgroups such as home construction or highway construction.

Standard metropolitan statistical area (SMSA)
See Metropolitan statistical area

Start-up
A new business, at the earliest stages of development and financing.

Start-up costs
Costs incurred before a business can commence operations.

Start-up financing
Financing provided to companies that have either completed product development and initial marketing or have been in business for less than one year but have not yet sold their product commercially.

Stock
A certificate of equity ownership in a business.

Stop-loss coverage
Insurance for a self-insured plan that reimburses the company for any losses it might incur in its health claims beyond a specified amount.

Strategic planning
Projected growth and development of a business to establish a guiding direction for the future. Also used to determine which market segments to explore for optimal sales of products or services.

Structural unemployment
See Unemployment

Sub chapter S corporations
Corporations that are considered noncorporate for tax purposes but legally remain corporations.

Subcontract
A contract between a prime contractor and a subcontractor, or between subcontractors, to furnish supplies or services for performance of a prime contract (see separate citation) or a subcontract.

Surety bonds
Bonds providing reimbursement to an individual, company, or the government if a firm fails to complete a contract. The U.S. Small Business Administration guarantees surety bonds in a program much like the SBA guaranteed loan program (see separate citation).

Swing loan
See Bridge financing

Target market
The clients or customers sought for a business' product or service.

Targeted Jobs Tax Credit
Federal legislation enacted in 1978 that provides a tax credit to an employer who hires structurally unemployed individuals.

Tax number
A number assigned to a business by a state revenue department that enables the business to buy goods without paying sales tax.

Taxable bonds
An interest-bearing certificate of public or private indebtedness. Bonds are issued by public agencies to finance economic development.

Technical assistance
See Management and technical assistance

Technical evaluation
Assessment of technological feasibility.

Technology
The method in which a firm combines and utilizes labor and capital resources to produce goods or services; the application of science for commercial or industrial purposes.

Technology transfer
The movement of information about a technology or intellectual property from one party to another for use.

Tenure
See Employee tenure

Term
The length of time for which a loan is made.

Terms of a note
The conditions or limits of a note; includes the interest rate per annum, the due date, and transferability and convertibility features, if any.

Third-party administrator
An outside company responsible for handling claims and performing administrative tasks associated with health insurance plan maintenance.

Third-stage financing
Financing provided for the major expansion of a company whose sales volume is increasing and that is breaking even or profitable. These funds are used for further plant expansion, marketing, working capital,

or development of an improved product. Also known as Third-round or Mezzanine financing.

Time deposit
A bank deposit that cannot be withdrawn before a specified future time.

Time management
Skills and scheduling techniques used to maximize productivity.

Trade credit
Credit extended by suppliers of raw materials or finished products. In an accounting statement, trade credit is referred to as "accounts payable."

Trade name
The name under which a company conducts business, or by which its business, goods, or services are identified. It may or may not be registered as a trademark.

Trade periodical
A publication with a specific focus on one or more aspects of business and industry.

Trade secret
Competitive advantage gained by a business through the use of a unique manufacturing process or formula.

Trade show
An exhibition of goods or services used in a particular industry. Typically held in exhibition centers where exhibitors rent space to display their merchandise.

Trademark
A graphic symbol, device, or slogan that identifies a business. A business has property rights to its trademark from the inception of its use, but it is still prudent to register all trademarks with the Trademark Office of the U.S. Department of Commerce.

Translation
See Product development

Treasury bills
Investment tender issued by the Federal Reserve Bank in amounts of $10,000 that mature in 91 to 182 days.

Treasury bonds
Long-term notes with maturity dates of not less than seven and not more than twenty-five years.

Treasury notes
Short-term notes maturing in less than seven years.

Trend
A statistical measurement used to track changes that occur over time.

Trough
See Cyclical trough

UCC
See Uniform Commercial Code

UL
See Underwriters Laboratories

Underwriters Laboratories (UL)
One of several private firms that tests products and processes to determine their safety. Although various firms can provide this kind of testing service, many local and insurance codes specify UL certification.

Underwriting
A process by which an insurer determines whether or not and on what basis it will accept an application for insurance. In an experience-rated plan, premiums are based on a firm's or group's past claims; factors other than prior claims are used for community-rated or manually rated plans.

Unfair competition
Refers to business practices, usually unethical, such as using unlicensed products, pirating merchandise, or misleading the public through false advertising, which give the offending business an unequitable advantage over others.

Unfunded accrued liability
The excess of total liabilities, both present and prospective, over present and prospective assets.

Unemployment
The joblessness of individuals who are willing to work, who are legally and physically able to work, and who are seeking work. Unemployment may represent the temporary joblessness of a worker between jobs (frictional unemployment) or the joblessness of a worker whose skills are not suitable for jobs available in the labor market (structural unemployment).

Uniform Commercial Code (UCC)
A code of laws governing commercial transactions across the U.S., except Louisiana. Their purpose is to bring uniformity to financial transactions.

Uniform product code (UPC symbol)
A computer-readable label comprised of ten digits and stripes that encodes what a product is and how much it costs. The first five digits are assigned by the Uniform Product Code Council, and the last five digits by the individual manufacturer.

Unit cost
See Average cost

UPC symbol
See Uniform product code

U.S. Establishment and Enterprise Microdata (USEEM) File
A cross-sectional database containing information on employment, sales, and location for individual enterprises and establishments with employees that have a Dun & Bradstreet credit rating.

U.S. Establishment Longitudinal Microdata (USELM) File
A database containing longitudinally linked sample microdata on establishments drawn from the U.S. Establishment and Enterprise Microdata file (see separate citation).

U.S. Small Business Administration 504 Program
See Certified development corporation

USEEM
See U.S. Establishment and Enterprise Microdata File

USELM
See U.S. Establishment Longitudinal Microdata File

VCN
See Venture capital network

Venture capital
Money used to support new or unusual business ventures that exhibit above-average growth rates, significant potential for market expansion, and are in need of additional financing to sustain growth or further research and development; equity or equity-type financing traditionally provided at the

commercialization stage, increasingly available prior to commercialization.

Venture capital company

A company organized to provide seed capital to a business in its formation stage, or in its first or second stage of expansion. Funding is obtained through public or private pension funds, commercial banks and bank holding companies, small business investment corporations licensed by the U.S. Small Business Administration, private venture capital firms, insurance companies, investment management companies, bank trust departments, industrial companies seeking to diversify their investment, and investment bankers acting as intermediaries for other investors or directly investing on their own behalf.

Venture capital limited partnerships

Designed for business development, these partnerships are an institutional mechanism for providing capital for young, technology-oriented businesses. The investors' money is pooled and invested in money market assets until venture investments have been selected. The general partners are experienced investment managers who select and invest the equity and debt securities of firms with high growth potential and the ability to go public in the near future.

Venture capital network (VCN)

A computer database that matches investors with entrepreneurs.

WAN

See Wide Area Network

Wide Area Network (WAN)

Computer networks linking systems throughout a state or around the world in order to facilitate the sharing of information.

Withholding

Federal, state, social security, and unemployment taxes withheld by the employer from employees' wages; employers are liable for these taxes and the corporate umbrella and bankruptcy will not exonerate an employer from paying back payroll withholding. Employers should escrow these funds in a separate account and disperse them quarterly to withholding authorities.

Workers' compensation

A state-mandated form of insurance covering workers injured in job-related accidents. In some states, the state is the insurer; in other states, insurance must be acquired from commercial insurance firms. Insurance rates are based on a number of factors, including salaries, firm history, and risk of occupation.

Working capital

Refers to a firm's short-term investment of current assets, including cash, short-term securities, accounts receivable, and inventories.

Yield

The rate of income returned on an investment, expressed as a percentage. Income yield is obtained by dividing the current dollar income by the current market price of the security. Net yield or yield to maturity is the current income yield minus any premium above par or plus any discount from par in purchase price, with the adjustment spread over the period from the date of purchase to the date of maturity.

Index

Listings in this index are arranged alphabetically by business plan type, then alphabetically by business plan name. Users are provided with the volume number in which the plan appears.

Academic Testing Improvement Service
Academic Assistance, 14

Accounting Service
Marcus Accounting LLC, 7

Accounting Systems Consultants
Accounting Management Systems, 1

Adventure Travel Lodging Company
Cobra Travel Adventure Group, 11

Advertising Agency
BlueIsland.com, 8

Advertising Brokerage Firm
Cover Art Advertising, 13

Aerospace Supplier
Flatland Manufacturing, Inc., 1

Aftermarket Internet Applications
AutoAftermarket.com, 8

Aftermarket Skate Store
Pegasus Sports International, 8

Air Brushing Services
Workz of Art, 15

Airlines
Puddle Jumpers Airlines, Inc., 6
SkyTrails Airlines, Ltd., 9

Ambulance Service
CareOne Ambulance Service, 20

Apartment Complex
Olde Towne Apartments, 20

Apparel Manufacturer
TTK Outdoor Apparel Company, 17

Architecture Firm
Smith Architecture Firm, Inc., 17

Art Easel Manufacturer
Art Easels and Supplies, Inc., 15

Art Gallery
Cooke Gallery, 14

Art Glass Studio
Phyllis Farmington Art Glass, 6

Assisted Living Facility
Home Again Assisted Living, 19

Audio Production Service
Jack Cornwall Productions, 4

Auto Accessories and Detailing
Auto Accessories Unlimited, 3
J.E.M. Ventures, Inc., 3

Auto Detailing
Johnson's Mobile Detail, 19

Automated Teller Machines (ATMs)
Quick Cash Services, 16

Automobile Advertising
Carvertising, 18

Automobile Assembly
Dream Cars, 2

Automotive Dealer
Pompei-Schmidt Auto Dealers Inc., 4
Pallisimo Motors, 19

Automotive Repair Service
Collision Experts Inc., 10
LR Automotive, 4 and 19

Auto Sales Company
Mountain View Lease, LLC, 7

AV Equipment Rental Business
Galaxy Equipment Works Inc., 21

Bagel Shop
USA Bagels, 5

Barbecue Sauce Manufacturer
Flamethrower Barbecue Sauce, 13

Barbershop
D'Angelo's Choice Cut Barbershop Inc., 20

Beauty Salon
Salon Flora, 12

Bed & Breakfast
Aphrodite's Dream Bed & Breakfast, 6
Home Again Bed & Breakfast, 17
Red Barron Bed & Breakfast, 1
Rocheport Bed and Breakfast, 16
Victoria Bed & Breakfast, 4

Beekeeping Business
B. Strand's Bees, 16

Bicycle Shop
Wheelies, 15

Bioterrorism Prevention Organization
Bioterrorism & Infections Prevention Organization, 10

Biscotti Bakery
Italian Eatery, The, 1

Bistro and Wine Bar
Wine Bistro, The, 10

Bookkeeping Practice
Kohn Bookkeeping Practice, 17

Bookstore
Betty's Books, 18

Bottled Water Manufacturer
Sparkling Horizon Bottled Water, 4

Bowling Alley
Family Bowl, The, 7
Strikers Lanes, 19

Bread Bakery
Breadcrafter, 5

Brewpub
Hopstreet Brewery, 11

Bridal Salon
Megan's Bridal Boutique, 6

Business Consulting
Blake & Associates, 1, 21
Koshu, 1

Business Development Firm
NKR Consulting, Inc., 9

Cafe and Gas Station
Troon Cafe and Gas Station, 14

Campground
California RV & Campgrounds, 12

Campus Apartment Complex
Fourwinds Apartments, 13

Car Service
The Personal Touch Car Service, 18

Car Wash
ABC, Inc., 7
Dirt Buster, The, 1
J&A Ventures, Inc., 5
Platinum Carwash, 12

Car Wash and Car Detailing Business
Wash and Go, 16

Caribbean Café
Calypso Café, 6

Carpet Cleaning Service
Carpet Chem Corporation, 3

Caviar Company
Caviar Delights, 9

Charity Youth Hockey Tournament
Lucky Pucks, 8

Chemical Manufacturer
Chemalyze, Inc., 8

Child Transportation Service
Kid Cart, 4

Children's Bookstore
Under the Shade Tree, 17

Children's Catering Business
Katering2Kidz Inc., 18

Childrens' Indoor Recreation Center
Interactive Garden, 13

Chiropractic Office
Cole's Care Chiropractic, 6

Christmas Ornament Company
Scriptures for You, Inc., 6

Cigar Company
Smokescreen Cigars, 11

Cigar Shop
Holy Smokes, 5

Climbing Outfitter
Rockhound Outfitters, 5

Coatings Inspection Company
Professional Coatings Services, Inc. 10

Coffee Bean Plant/Exporter
Silvera & Sons Ltda., 7

Coffee House
Coffee Circus, 4

Coffee Roaster
Venezia Coffee Roasters, 4

Combination Coffeehouse/Play Spot
JavaJumpz LLC, 18

Comedy Club
The Comedy Corner, 15

Commodities Trading Firm
Admirian Commodities, 19

Computer Matchmaking Service
Matchmate, Inc., 3

Computer Reseller
Computech Management, 5
Ellipse Technologies, Inc., 5

Computer Training Service Business
Enhanced Occupations Center, 9

Concert Promotions Company
Good Vibrations, Inc., 9

Concrete Coating Company
Techno–Coatings USA, 12

Condiment Manufacturer
Salvador Sauces, Inc., 6

Construction Development & Real Estate Firm
Black Pearl Development and Real Estate LLC, 11

Construction and Home Rehabilitation Company
Pedro's Construction, 11

Convenience Store & Bait Shop
The Dock Store, 8

Cookie Shop
Grandma Miller's Cookies and Muffins, 6

Corner Store
Martin General Store, 13

Counseling Center
Juniper Counseling Center, 9

Counseling Practice
Roper Counseling Services Inc., 16

Courier Service
Corporate Courier, 14

Crane Service
Chesterfield Crane Service, 1

Creative Agency
Oceania Creative Print & Interactive, 8

Currency Trading
Fundex Currency Trading Co. Inc., 17

Custodial Cleaning Company
Spic and Span, 12

Custom Carpentry Shop
Choice Cut Carpentry Inc., 16

Custom Denim Retailer
Patch Denim Company, 18

Dance and Skate Outfitter
Arabesque Dance & Skate Shop, 3

Day Camp Organizer
Camp in the Park, 16

Daycare Facility
Childhood Dreams Inc., 12
Rachel's Clubhouse, 11
Ziggle Zag Zip Daycare/Childcare, 12

Daycare/Preschool
Little Lambs Daycare and Preschool, 18

Day Spa
Temple Creek Day Spa, 21

Dentist
Fremont Dental Office, 12
Stanley M. Kramer, DDS, LLC, 8

Desktop Publishing Company
Power Desk Top Publishing, Inc., 7

Detective Agency
Barr Detective Agency, 5

Dial-It Service
Callmaster, Inc., 3

Diaper Delivery
Diapers 'n More, 1 and 19

Digital Presentations
Martin Productions, 19

Diner
Shoestrings, 16

Direct Mail Outlet
Post Direct, 4

Discount Internet Securities Broker
E-Best-Trade.com, 8

Display Technology Company
TouchTop Technologies, Inc., 7

DJ Service
MID-MO MUSIC, 21

Dog Training Business
A-1 Dog Training & Behavior LLC, 17

Dollar Store
Dollar Daze, 9

Domestic Services Provider
Helping Hands Personal Services LLC, 16

Dry Cleaner
A.Z. Ventures/Expert Cleaning, 3

DVD Kiosk Rental Business
Rent DVDs Now, 15

E–Commerce Website Producer
Internet Capabilities, 12

Editorial Services & Consulting
Hilton & Associates, 1

Elder Care
Summer Gardens Residential Care Facility for the Ambulatory Elderly, 1 and 20

Electronic Document Security Company
GoldTrustMark.com, 9

Emu Ranch
Southwestern Emu Ranch, 4

Energy Consultant
Jacobs Consulting, 15

Energy Efficiency Auditing Firm
Energy Physicians, 16

Energy Solutions Company
Abaka Energy Solutions, 8

Engineering Management Consultant
Herman Livingston Consultants, 4

Entertainment Production, Distribution, and Performance Company
Mentonic Hero Inc., 12

Environmentally–Friendly Greenhouse
Green Greenhouse, 15

Environmentally–Minded Residential Construction Company
Green Earth Construction, 13

Equipment Rental
Rich Rentals, 1

Ethanol Fuel Production
Ontario Ethanol Supply, 14

Ethnic Food Supplier
World Cuisine, 13

Event Photography Service
brightroom, Inc., 10

Event Planning Company
Occasions, The Event Planning Specialists, 7

Family Entertainment Center
FunXplosion LLC, 18

Fantasy Book & Memorabilia Store
Wizard and Warlock Books, 14

Farm
Gilmore Farms, 19

Fast Food
Pasta Express, 3
Pasta Now!, 3

Fertilizer & Commodity Chemicals Company
Agronix Organics, Inc., 10

Financial Services Company
Diamond Strategic Services, 7
Prisma Microfinance, Inc., 9

Fire Equipment Retailer
Gallagher's Fire Service, 5

Fitness Center
Woodland Gym Ltd., 13

Food and Beverage Vending Company
Paco Bello Vending, 14

Food, Diet, & Nutrition Company
Think Thin Weight Loss Corporation, 10

Food Processor
Rio Grande, 3

Food Truck
Eddie's Edibles Mobile Food, 21

Framing/Antiques Store
Flora's Frames & Antiques, 1

Franchise Postal Service
Express Postal Center, 5

Freelance Editor
Scrivener, The, 2
Word for Word, 2

Freight Expediting
Gazelle Expediting Inc., 5

Furniture Resale Shop
Furniture Finds, 15

Furniture Restoration Company
Furniture Restoration Business, 15

Furniture Store
Collins Furniture, 19

Gas Station
Rapid Roger's Gas Station, 19

General Contracting Company
Smith Contracting Company, 7

General Staffing Company
GENRX LLC, 12

Gift Shop
The Busy Bee, 16

Gift Store
Crystal Creek Gifts, 5
Little Treasures Gift Shop, 13

Giftware Company
Jenni Frey Gifts, 11

Go–Cart Designer and Supplier
Speedy Go–Cart, 12

Go Kart Track
Supersonic Racing, 21

Gold Mining
Davis Gold Mining, 21

Golf Driving Range
Mountain Cedar Golf Club, 9

Golf Grip Manufacturer
ProGrip, 10

Gourmet Foods Company
Good Earth Foods Company, 8

Graffiti Removal Service
Graffiti, Inc., 3

Grant Writer
Whitfield Resources LLC, 18

Green/Sustainability Consulting Firm
Ward & O'Neil LLC, 18

Greenhouse and Flower Shop
Little Greenie Shop, 14

Grocery Store
Viking Grocery Stores, 9

Hair Salon
Epiphany Salon, 6

Handmade Greeting Card Company
Heartsongs, 11

Handyman Service
"I'm the Man!" Handyman Services, 11

Health Advocacy Business
Medical Navigation Services Inc., 17

Healthcare Marketing Agency
Johnson & Brooks LLC, 15

Healthcare Software Company
QuikMed Info., 7

Healthcare Translation & Interpretation Business
Cross–Cultural Communications Inc., 17

Health Insurance Company
Southeast Healthplans, Inc., 6

Holistic Health Center
Holistic Choices, LLC, 10

Home Décor Products Manufacturer
Burton Decor, Inc., 10

Home Furnishing Manufacturer
Castellini Manufacturing, 14

Home Inspection Company
Home Inspectors Are We, 12

Home Organization Service
Break Free Organizing, 16

Home Renovation Contractor
Stephens Contracting, 13

Home Repair and Improvement Contractor
HandyGals Inc., 17

Homeless Shelter
Sister Joan of Arc Center, 11

Hotel Resort
Seven Elms Resort, 7

House Cleaning
Mid-Missouri Maid Service, 16

Housing Rehabilitation Company
Madison Builders, LLC, 10

Human Resources Consultant
Anders Johnson LLC, 20

Ice Cream Parlor
SonnyScoops, 16

Ice Cream Shop
Fran's Ice, 3 and 19

Import Boutique
Bellisimo Imports, Inc., 1

Import/Export Store
Central Import/Export, 9

Indoor Playground
Kid's World, 3

Information Technology Personnel Agency
Rekve IT Staffing, 12

Inn/Resort
Lighthouse Inn, The, 1

Interior Decorator
Lindsay Smith Interiors LLC, 19

Interior Design Company
Gable & Nash LLC, 19
Make It Your Own Space Inc., 11

Interior Painting Service
Eyecatching Interiors LLC, 11

Interior Renovation Company
Addams Interiors, 14

Internet & Network Security Solution Provider
Safety Net Canada, Inc., 10

Internet Bid Clearinghouse
Opexnet, LLC, 5

Internet Cafe
Wired Bean, 5

Internet Communications Service Provider
Appian Way Communications Network, Ltd., 9

Internet Consultant
Allen Consulting, 3
Worldwide Internet Marketing Services, 3

Internet Loyalty Program
Tunes4You, 11

Internet Marketplace
ABC Internet Marketplace, Inc., 8

Internet Services Portal Site
Net Solutions, 11

Internet Software Company
Poggle, Inc., 9

Internet Travel Agency Business
Memory Lane Cruises, 9

Investor Trading Software Company
Investor Trends, Inc., 6

Jewelry Designer
Oswipi Custom Costume Jewelry Designs, 18

Junk Removal Business
Harry's Haul-Away Service Inc., 21

Kennel
Best Friend Kennel, 2

Ladder Company
Jacks' Ladder Inc., 1

Landscaping Service
G & D Landscaping, 20
Helping Hand, Inc., 13

Laundry Mat
Duds and Suds Laundry Mat, 19

Leasing Company
Leasing Group, 8

Leather Accessory Manufacturer
Safari Leatherworks, 13

Limited Liability Company
Northern Investments, LLC, 7

Litigation Services Company
Acme Litigation Company, 10

Low–Cost Home Decorating Service
Your Home Stylists, 15

Magazine Publisher
GRAPEVINE, 1

Mailing List Service
Forest Mail Service, 3

Management Consulting Service
Salmon & Salmon, 3

Manufacturing Business
Fiber Optic Automation, Inc., 3

Marble Quarry
Vomarth Marble Quarry, 9

Marina
The Bayshore Marina, 19

Marketing Communications Firm
Cornelius Marketing, 4

Marketing Consultancy
Meridian Consulting, 5
Simmons Marketing Associates, 3
TargetPoint Consulting LLC, 20

Massage Therapists
MASSAGEWORKS, 11

Maternity Aid
Nest in Comfort, 2

Meal Facilitation and Preparation Company
Kitchen Helper, LLC, 13

Media Conversion Company
The Memory Keeper, 18

Media Duplication & Transferring Business
DupliPro Inc., 21

Media Producer
Dynamic Video, 2
Dynamic Video (Revised), 2
Shalimar Films, Inc., 2

Medical Billing Company
Physicians 1st Billing and Claims, 7

Medical Equipment Producer
Mediquip, Inc., 6
Premium Therapy, LLC, 10

Men's Clothing Retailer
Van Schaack, 4

Mentally Disabled Care Facility
Welcome Home Organization, 11

Metal Shop
Krosnow Metal Works, 5

Microbrewery
Harbor Brewing Company, 2
Juniper Brewing Company, 2
Smith Microbrewery, Inc., 17

Mobile App Development Business
AppStax LLC, 21

Mobile Pizza Kitchen Business
Pizza2go–go Inc., 19

Mobile Studio
CRS Mobile Studio, 2

Mobile Veterinary Practice
PetWheelz Inc., 17

Montessori School
Edison Park Montessori, 20

Mortgage Company
National Mortgage, Inc., 7
Stiles Mortgage Banking Firm, Inc., 17

Motorcycle Dealership and Racetrack
Zoom Motors, 11

Multilevel Marketing
RFM Enterprises, 3

Mural Company
Smith Ray Design, 10

Music Lessons Business
MelodyWorx Inc., 21

Music Store
The Fret Board, 15

Natural Gas Home Filling Station Provider
Green Fuel Stations, 15

Nature Photography Business
Shutterbugs Inc., 16

Network Game Centers
PowerPlay Gaming, LLC, 10

Newsletter
Network Journal, 2
Network Journal (Revised), 2

Nightclub
Wild Oasis, 7

Non-Medical Assistance
Helping Hands Companion Service, 20

Nonprofit Youth Outreach Ministry
Life Works Cincinnati, 9

Novelty Shop
Great Pretender, The, 5

Nursery
Wonderland Nursery, 7

Office Furniture
Powerline of Northern Minnesota, 5

Oil and Gas Manufacturing and Services Co.
Russel Oil and Gas Valves Co. Inc., 17

Online Consulting
Borderline Transmissions, Inc., 1

Online Customer Service Support
live e-care, Inc., 10

Online Government Contract Service
U.S.Consulting - GOV.COM, 4

Online Hospitality Service
Tinner Corp., 4

Online Job Service
CareerConnections.com, 8

Online Merchant
E-Return Solutions, 8

Online Mortgage Company
Valuable Mortgage, 11

Online Outdoor Company
Outdoorsman.com, 8

Online Party–Planning Company
Theme Party in a Box, 16

Online Payment Services
Exactor Technologies, LLC, 12

Online Publishing System
Moonbeam Publishing, 9

Index

Online Woodworking Manufacturing & Retailing
U–nique Woodworking, 12

Organic Cleaning Supplies
Green Home Care Solutions, 16

Organic Food Store
Earth's Bounty Organic Foods, 20

Organic Grower and Supplier
Great Lakes Organics, 14

Organic Lawn Care Services
Evergreen Organic Lawn Care Services, 17

Outdoor Adventure Travel Company
RAD-Venture, 4

Paint Distributor
Eartham Distributors, 4

Paintball Sport Company
Paintball Sport Palace, 6

Painting Company
Ko-Bas Painting Company, 10

Parts Manufacturer
Zemens Metal Corporation, 5

Party Planning
Perfect Party, 18

Party Supply Store
Celebrations, 5

Pasta Franchise
Pasta Express, 5

Personal Organizing Consultant
All In Place Inc., 21

Pet Sitting Service
Pet Care People, 14
Pet Watchers Inc., 20

Pet Waste Removal Business
The Scoop, 20

Pharmaceutical Company
Pain Away, Inc., 3

Photo Framing
Talking Photo Technology, 2

Photography Studio
Midwest Studios, 15

Physical Therapy Practice
Healing Hands Physical Therapy Inc., 16

Pipeline Fracture Testing Service
ADSL Pipeline Services Inc., 17

Pizza & Pasta Restaurant
Geno's Pizza & Pasta Restaurant, 18

Pizzeria
Coastal Pizza, 11
Pizza to Go, Inc., 6

Plant Nursery
Village Garden Center, 21

Plastic Drum Company
River City Drum, Inc., 7

Plumbing Service
Jax Plumbing, 3
Matt's Plumbing and Air Conditioning, 12

Plus–Sized Children's Clothing Store
Jennifer's Clothing Corner, 15

Powder Coating Manufacturer
Brudder Coating Systems Inc., 4
Innovative Over Coast, 4

Printing Company
Big Picture Press Inc., 21
Master Printer and Partners Printing, 1
Printer Perfect, 1

Private Investigator
FBEyes, 11
Ferguson Investigation LLC, 18

Private Label Food Manufacturer
Clarence Pratt Enterprises, Inc., 6

Producer and Supplier of Plants and Flowers
Bountyfull Farms, 13

Professional Organizing Consultant
Marilyn Ruby Inc., 21

Public Relations Firm
SHP & Associates Business Communications, 2

Publisher
Group Publishing, The, 6
Infoguide Inc., 1

Racing Parts Store
Southeast Racing Parts, 8

Real Estate Brokerage
Thomasson Real Estate, 15

Real Estate Company
MSN Real Estate, 7

Real Estate Investment Company
Wolfe Partners, 6

Real Estate Renovation Company
ABC Corp., 6

Real Estate Renovation and Resale
HouseFlipperz, 15

Record Company
Reed Entertainment Corp., 4

Record Store
Hidden Treasure Records L.C., 6

Refrigerant Recovery
Road Runner Refrigerant Recovery System, 3

Rental Defibrillator Service
Heartsong Defibrillator, LLC, 15

Resale Clothing Store
New to You Resale Clothing Store, 18

Residential and Commercial Painting Service
Color My World, Inc., 14

Restaurant
American Diner, 1
Butcher Hollow Bar BQ, 7
Cafe Fresco, 13
Kelly House Inn, 5
Peach Blossom Diner, 1
Rock Island Tavern, 5
Tokyo Sun, 13
Whistle Shop, The, 4

Restaurant (Nonprofit)
McMurphy's Grill, 1
Murphy's Grill, 2
Murphy's Grill (Revised), 2

Restaurant Franchise
Reuben's Deli, 2

Restaurant/Bar
Plugged Nickel, The, 2
Watering Hole, The, 2

Restaurant/Microbrewery
Homesteaders' Pub & Grub, 5

Retail & Commercial Design Firm
Future Designs, 4

Retail Art Furnishings Business
Wood Designs Gallery, 6

Retail Business Incubator
Acme Incubators, 9

Retail Clothing
Boston Rags Clothing Store, 9
Clothes as Art Inc., 1 and 20

Retail Florist
Designs by Linda, 1

Retail Tobacco/Magazines
Standard Tobacco & News, 1

Rock Climber's Store & Cafe
The Boulder Stop, 8

Roller Rink
Dancing Wheels Roller Rink, 19
Santiago Roller Rink, 7

Routing/Navigation Software Company
PATH Systems, Inc., 10

Rubber Adhesive Manufacturer
Shake Proof, 4

Safety Consulting Firm
Peters, Marsh & McLellan LLC, 17

Salad Packaging
Lyons & Coyne, Inc., 1

Sandwich Shop
Romastrano Incorporated, 3

Science Information Website Company
e-Science Technologies, Inc., 9

Screen Print Drying Company
DLP, Inc., 7

Search Service
Searchers, The, 2

Self–Defense/Anti–Bullying Training Company
Safe Zone Personal Defense LLC, 18

Self Service Laundry Business
Wash 'N Go, 17

Senior Care Facility
Hearts and Hopes Senior Home, 12

Sharpening Service
The Razor's Edge LLC, 21

Shave Ice Business
Ice Dreams, 6

Shoe Store
Thomasson Shoes, 14

Ski Resort
Mounjoy, LLC, 8

Skin Cream Formulator
LaBelle Industries, Inc., 9

Smoothie and Juice Shop
Suzie's Smoothies, 14

Soap Making Business
Felson's Homemade Soaps Inc., 21

Software Developer
Data Technologies Corporation, 1

Software Engineering & Management Company
Swiss Issue WebTools, 7

Solar Energy Farm
Ward Solar Energy Farm, Inc., 17

Special Needs Clothing Store
You Can Do It!, 7

Specialty Bakery
Creative Cupcakes, 20
Kate's Cupcakery, 21

Sports Bar
Stone Oak Sports Bar & Grille, 12
Take Five Sports Bar & Grill, 6

Sports Collectibles
Diamond Collection, Inc., 2

Sports Tournament Organizer
Scramble Sports Tournament Series, 12

Stable
Miller Stables, 16

Stained Glass Business
Rose's Colored Glass, 19

Steak House
1845 Steakhouse, 20

Structural Engineering Consulting Firm
StructureAll Ltd., 8

Structural Genomics Software Provider
Pharmatech Genomics, 10

Student Services Consulting Firm
Grad Student Exchange Consultants International, 8

Tattoo & Body Piercing
Chapel Hill Tattoo, 14

Taxi Service
Lakeview Taxi, 5

Tea Shop
Cuppa!, 18

Teacher Continuing Education
The Institute for the Advancement of Teacher Education (IATE), 20

Technology Solutions Provider
Exceed Expectations, 13

Teen Night Club
Ventures, 8

Television Childproofer
Television for Kids, 2

Toiletry Company
Verde, 1

Toy Company
Toys for a New Generation Inc., 1

Trademarked Resort Wear Distributor
Muskrat Bluffs Apparel, 13

Transcription Business
Speedy Transcription Services LLC, 21

Travel Agency
International Business Tours, 4

Travel Information Service
Traveling U.S. Inc., 4

Tutoring Service
Ellen's English Tutoring Service, 18
Stuart Tutoring, 20

Used Car Business
Budget Cars, 6

Used Clothing, Furniture, and Antique Store
Rebecca's Shoppe, 14

Used Furniture Business
Furniture xCHANGE, 20

Used Records & Collectibles Business
Rudy's Record Shop, 21

Utilities Reclamation Services
Hydro Power Lines Reclamation Services Inc., 17

Vegetarian Fast Food Restaurant
Benny & Dell's, 18

Veterinary Practice
Four Legged Friends Clinic, 13

Video Production & Distribution Company
Kitamon Productions, 9

Video Service
Express Video Service, 3

Virtual Assistance
AdminiStar Services, 20

Virtual Reality
Building Aids Inc., 1
CineMedia Studios, Inc., 1

Virtual Shopping
Click 'n Shop Inc., 2

Waste Management
Waste Removal Serivces, Inc., 21

Water Purification System Distributor
Fresh Faucet Distribution, 14

Website Designer
Portal Code, Inc., 14
Web Wizards, 19

Wedding Planning Service
Together Forever Wedding Planners, 20

Windmill Distributor
Pierson Windmills, 15

Wine Merchant and Storage Facility
Wine Seller Cellar, 13

Wine Storage
Wine Portfolio Inc., 16

Wireless Internet Service
Superior XL Internet, 7

Wireless Systems Integrator
SpongeShark, LLC, 9

Wooden Furniture Manufacturer and Supplier
Nashville Furniture, 14

Yoga Studio
Namaste Family Yoga Studio, 15